The History of Furniture

The History of
FURNITURE

Introduction by
SIR FRANCIS WATSON

WILLIAM MORROW & COMPANY, INC.
New York 1976

Frontispiece: Room by William Morris dated 1866
(Victoria & Albert Museum, London)

Endpapers: Illustration of furniture manufacture from
Diderot's Encyclopédie *(1751)*

EDITORIAL CONSULTANT Jonathan Bourne
EDITOR Anne Charlish
PICTURE EDITOR Faith Perkins

First published in Great Britain
Copyright © 1976 by Orbis Publishing Limited, London
Printed in Italy by IGDA, Novara
Library of Congress Catalog Card Number 76–7256
ISBN 0–688–03083–1

CONTENTS

FOREWORD

by Sir John Pope-Hennessy
Director, The British Museum

This book describes the way in which people in the past have lived. It deals not with social attitudes, but with the appurtenances of living through which social attitudes are commonly expressed. If you are furnishing a house today, you can adopt one of two points of view. You can say to yourself that tables and chairs and cupboards are articles of convenience and nothing more, and that their appearance is of no consequence provided the tables are solidly constructed, the chairs can be sat on without discomfort, and the cupboards are sufficiently commodious to take the things you wish to keep in them. Alternatively, you may recognize that a great part of your future life will be lived in close association with the furniture you buy, and that its purpose is not simply functional; that it can, through its design and workmanship contribute a dimension of enjoyment to your daily life and enhance your peace of mind. If you take the first of these two views, this book is not for you. You will regard the furniture it illustrates, whether it was made in Egypt or in France in the late eighteenth century, as an example of conspicuous waste. But if you take the second view, you will welcome the book enthusiastically, because it shows how, over the centuries, prevalent style concepts have influenced the scenography of living, and how artists have been encouraged by perspicacious patrons to develop the prosaic trade of cabinet-making into an art form in its own right.

In museums pieces of furniture are generally shown in isolation. But this was not the way in which most of them were planned. As we know from frescoes of Renaissance rooms by Ghirlandajo, or paintings of Dutch seventeenth-century rooms by Terborch and Vermeer and French eighteenth-century rooms by De Troy, or from real rooms by Kent

Left: Mme de Sérilly's boudoir, 1778–9 (Jones Collection, Victoria & Albert Museum, London)

at Houghton and Adam at Osterley in which the original furnishings have been preserved, they were components or properties in a stage set occupied by people fairly like ourselves. This book forms a corrective to the museum view, in that it reinstates much of the furniture in the context for which it was intended, and in which, at least in the imagination, it must be seen. But though the setting not unnaturally reflected the architectural forms and ornament and therefore more generally the thinking of the age in which it was produced, the purpose for which each piece of furniture was made deviates only marginally from purposes we recognize today. Through it we can gain some impression of how people in the past went about the domestic tasks and social duties we still perform.

Until comparatively recently a line used to be drawn between the fine arts—painting, sculpture and architecture—and the decorative arts, headed by furniture. Research into the fine arts was pursued with sophistication and intelligence, while study of the decorative arts remained cruder and more approximate. In recent years this situation has undergone a change. The study of French furniture in the eighteenth century has become a complex academic discipline, and the documentary background of English furniture has also been very thoroughly investigated. As a result makers of furniture have come to be looked on as what, in the fine arts, are called artistic personalities. They are no longer names which are attached generically to certain types of furniture; they are artist-craftsmen whose style and evolution and aesthetic preferences are reconstructible. This advance is evident throughout the present book. On the one hand, it can be commended to any reader who is responsive to the quality, indeed to the imaginative fantasy of many of the works with which it deals. On the other, it offers proof of the significant advance that has been made in rewriting the history of furniture.

INTRODUCTION

by Sir Francis Watson

In 1801, the French diarist P-L Roederer wrote of a wealthy man who, having been to a firm of interior decorators, was congratulated on possessing the most complete collection of furniture in the fashionable neo-classical taste that had yet been formed. But the fortunate owner of this unique assemblage of furniture replied, 'I am not interested in this furniture at all. It is heavy, hard, ugly and uncomfortable. To be able to lie or sit in comfort, that is all I ask of my bed and my armchair.' To the consternation of his listener, he continued, 'They aim at representing the room of Themistocles or Cimon for me, whereas my purpose is that they should furnish my own room. . . . God preserve us nowadays from the temptation of letting oneself drop into an armchair; one would run the risk of breaking oneself to pieces.' This would seem a very simple and obvious view, but the speaker was clearly not representing the conventional taste of his time.

The Napoleonic era was not a period in which comfort was looked for from furniture. The omnipresent soldiers, tightly buttoned into uniforms stiff with gold braid, their legs restricted by skin-tight breeches of buckskin and high leather boots, actually needed the stiff forms of Empire furniture to provide adequate support for their bodies. To fling themselves into a well-upholstered sofa or armchair would have been neither dignified

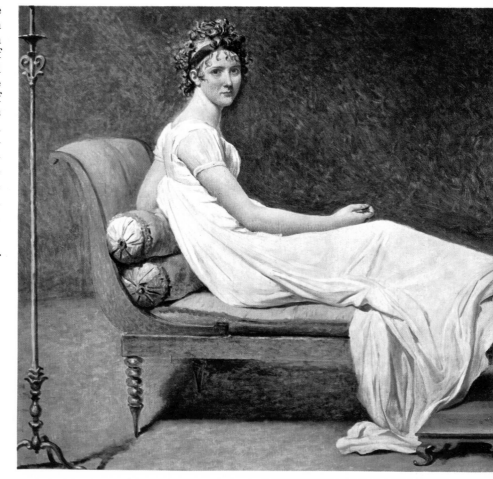

nor physically possible. The ladies of the period, too, in their high-waisted classical dresses, had no wish at all to relax into chairs and sofas. They were more concerned that they should be able to recline or sit in the elegant poses inspired by scenes depicted in Greek vase paintings.

Thus the form of the furniture reflects the demands of society at any given moment. To a considerable degree it is dictated by the social customs of the time, but furniture also has its own internal demands. It might be suggested that the distinguishing features of all good furniture are solidity, utility and decorativeness, but these three qualities do not necessarily appear at the same time in any one piece. At different periods one quality has predominated or even excluded the others altogether.

It may seem surprising today that comfort has only been required of furniture intermittently and has only become a necessity relatively recently. Decoration and display have always played a far more important role than comfort in the history of furniture. Ostentation was expressed through furniture as early as ancient Egypt—when chairs, for example, were symbols of honour found only in noble households. A similar attitude was very marked during the Baroque period in the seventeenth and eighteenth centuries, and was particularly clearly reflected in the etiquette which gave rise to so much squabbling at the court of Louis XIV where chairs were reserved for the use of the King and a few Princes of the Blood alone. At court, only duchesses were allowed to seat themselves in the presence of the sovereign, and even they were only allowed a stool. The rest of the company stood. The hierarchical role of the throne itself is a clear example of this approach to furniture.

Pure utility or functionalism as it was preached at the Bauhaus in the 1920s has remained an undercurrent of furniture design ever since, but it is a rarity in the history of furniture. Even in the Middle Ages when portability and utility were dictated by the itinerant nature of everyday life, the simplest pieces were usually given some embellishment. Where there was no carving, metal hinges and strengthening bands were usually given simple decorative shapes. The proliferation of gilt-bronze mounts, which is such a feature of French eighteenth-century furniture, originated merely from the need to protect the more vulnerable parts of a wooden construction such as the corners.

Nevertheless, even in the elegant and highly sophisticated society of eighteenth-century Paris, pure utility sometimes obtruded in strange ways. The forecorners of most Louis Seize chairs are square and quite sharply shaped. But examination of those made for

the use of the French Crown in the decade preceding the French Revolution in 1789 will reveal that a large number, generally those made for the card-rooms of the various royal palaces, are rounded. The reason is distinctly curious. The King was short-sighted and clumsy, and as he blundered about he frequently knocked his shins against the sharp corners of the chairs in his path. His officials therefore instructed the royal chair-makers to round the corners of the seats of the chairs.

Strength is of course a permanent requirement of all furniture. A chair which collapses under the weight of the human body is clearly of little use, however decorative it may be. But strength has sometimes had to be supplied at the expense of other qualities. Mediaeval benches and chairs were always solid and comfortable, but they tended to lack decorative qualities. Certain forms of contemporary chair have no form or strength at all until shaped by the human body. Intermediate between these two extremes come the sophisticated constructional methods which enabled the stretcher linking the legs of seventeenth- and early eighteenth-century chairs to be dispensed with. But such technical advances were often abandoned in the nineteenth century in the interest of economy, and many small chairs and tables made for the middle classes of the Victorian period are neither strong nor stable.

These points illuminate not merely the history of furniture but history itself. The two disciplines are complementary. It is this which makes the studies with which this book is concerned so important. Unhappily, the serious study of the history of furniture is a comparatively recent phenomenon which only appeared late in the nineteenth century. It therefore lags behind social history as a scholarly discipline.

It is no chance matter that the serious study of furniture should have begun in France. A wealth of information about historic furniture is available there which is entirely lacking in other countries. In England, for example, evidence has to be quarried from the account-books of individual country-houses or through records of transactions in the numerous offices where they have been deposited. Over the past three or four decades, scholars—including a number of the contributors to this volume—have been able to use such documents to illuminate our picture of the past considerably. But the information available varies from country to country, and much of what is known is dispersed in learned periodicals and obscure books in half a dozen languages. It is the merit of this book that it gathers together so much of this information and makes it a coherent story, full of interest to the historian of furniture, the social historian and the general reader alike.

Below: Mme Récamier by J-L David, 1800 (Louvre, Paris)

THE ARCHAEOLOGICAL RECORD
Ancient and mediaeval furniture

Left: The Golden Throne of Tutankhamun, one of the many extraordinary treasures discovered by Howard Carter in 1922, is lavishly decorated with gold-foil. The figures depicted on the back of the throne are composed of faience, lapis and precious stones. The king is shown sitting in silver garments on an upholstered chair with a high scrolled back and lion's paw feet; above him is the sun motif associated with his divinity. (Cairo Museum)

Until comparatively recently, elaborate furniture was available only to the households of royalty and their wealthiest subjects. A peasant or town-dweller might construct a crude stool or bench but would sleep on the floor and fashion only the meanest of household objects. It is natural, therefore, that the earliest surviving pieces of furniture should concern us with the ruling classes and their way of life.

Egypt

The idea of sheer comfort is relatively modern; furniture of the early civilizations through to the mediaeval period fulfilled two basic roles, ostentation or utility. The treasures of King Tutankhamun, now in the Cairo Museum, sumptuously decorated though they are, have no pretension to the comfort we expect of furniture today. The interiors of Egyptian palaces and Roman villas were decorated with elaborate murals and their furniture studded with precious materials, but their vast spaces would have seemed stark compared with the collected clutter of a modern house. The furniture of any civilization must reflect its pattern of daily life as well as being regarded as an art form in itself. Relatively few pieces of early furniture have survived intact, and a great deal of our knowledge therefore has to be culled from other contemporary sources such as wall- and vase-painting, manuscript illumination and sculpture. The picture is far from complete and one must be wary of drawing facile conclusions.

In Ancient Egypt it is only from the time of the New Kingdom (about 1567 to 1320 BC) that furniture survives in any quantity although it is clear that furniture was well known as far back as the third millennium BC. This knowledge has been made possible by the custom of burying treasures with their owner — the most famous example being the tomb of Tutankhamun (c.1361–1352 BC) discovered in 1922. Tutankhamun lived in the former palace of Amenophis III on the west bank of the Nile while his administration was based in Memphis. He is known to have made lavish gifts to the treasuries of the temple of Amun. His tomb and its treasures survive almost intact because the dry climate of the Valley of the Kings preserved the wood and the Egyptians were careful to obscure the tomb from looters. An indication of the quantity of gold used for royal possessions can be gauged from the fact that Tutankhamun's gold inner coffin weighed more than one ton.

Not only was treasure buried, but furniture was often made expressly as equipment for the afterlife. The principal woods used by Egyptian craftsmen were the local acacia, sycamore, cedar imported from Syria and Lebanon, and ebony. They were also skilful in the art of veneering and intricate inlay in lapis lazuli, ivory, glass and faience (decorated earthenware).

Seat furniture is the dominating and most interesting form in this period and had a lasting importance for later civilizations. The chair has frequently been recognized as a symbol of honour and in Egypt it was only used in noble households. Chairs had legs carved as bull's hooves or lion's paws or were left unadorned with square, slightly curving and usually sloping backs and with seats of plaited rushwork or leather. Occasionally the seat was quite near the ground and the occupant would have squatted rather than have adopted the normal sitting position. The armchair was less common and was used for

important ceremonial occasions. The best known examples are the gold-covered thrones of Queen Hetapheres and Tutankhamun himself. The influential folding-stool appears to have been introduced during the Middle Kingdom with two frames turning on metal bolts forming an X-shape and usually terminating in duck's heads. A very similar folding-stool dating from about 1200 BC was found in Jutland which raises the interesting possibility of intercourse between Egypt and northern Europe. The most common seat, however, was the easily movable painted rectangular stool with strutted supports and a top of leather or wood, often curved. The peasant classes would have used small rush-seat stools.

A great deal is known about the layout of the interior of a typical, affluent Egyptian town-house from the excavations at El-Amarna. The central hall was the main living area with portable furniture arranged as the occasion demanded while the walls were brightly painted. Other excavations and tomb finds reveal that most non-royal furniture consisted of simple but solidly constructed stools and chests. The latter, of varying shapes, are often quite ornate with painted geometric and floral patterns.

Tables were purely functional but in general use; they were easily portable and may have

served as trays. Otherwise three-legged *jardinières* — ornamental display stands — and occasional tables fulfilled the carrying function. As with painted stools the strutted-support construction was favoured. Possessions were stored in chests or baskets; there were over 30 chests in the tomb of Tutankhamun. As well as larger decorative linen-chests which came in all shapes and sizes, several miniature jewellery and toilet caskets survive which were made of ivory and ebony and these often had drawers. Beds were a luxury afforded only by the very rich; early examples sloped downwards towards the footboard. Tutankhamun's beds were very high off the ground and would have needed a mounting-block. Linen was used sparingly in such a hot climate and curious crescent-shaped headrests acted as pillows. It may be presumed that cushions were used on seats and beds.

Mesopotamia

Contemporary with the civilization of Ancient Egypt was that of Mesopotamia. The difference in the climate and construction of their tombs has meant that only a few ornamental fragments have survived although there are a large number of representations of furniture on sculpture and seals. The Sumerian civilization was centred on Ur, Nippur and Lagash. Important excavations at Ur earlier this century included the discovery of the 'Royal Tombs' dating from about 2600 BC where the jewel-like 'Standard of Ur' was found. Antedating these tombs are a great number of cylindrical stone seals whose depictions of furniture made of reed and wood show stools and sideboards of lattice construction, the earliest of which probably dates back to the fourth millennium BC, before the first dynasty of Egypt. The emergence of the folding-stool in about 2300 BC also occurred probably earlier than in Egypt. Slightly later, chairs and thrones with curving scrolled backs and bull's legs appear.

During the course of the Assyrian and Babylonian eras (c.1350–539 BC) types of furniture appeared with a new emphasis on the use of precious materials such as ivory, ebony and gold. Particularly notable are the impressive sculptured reliefs in the palaces of such kings as Ashurbanipal at Nineveh in the ninth century BC, Sargon II (721–705) at Khorsabad and Sennacherib (704–681) at Nimrud. These reliefs commemorating new territorial conquests show a variety of heavily ornamented thrones, couches and tables often being carried by slaves.

Greece

The emergence of the Greek civilization is one of the most remarkable phenomena of the pre-Christian era, particularly in the field of the decorative arts. As in earlier civilizations

Left: Ebony and ivory gaming-board found in Tutankhamun's tomb. It stands on four paw feet on an unusual sledge base. (Cairo Museum)

Above: A limestone relief taken from the palace of Nineveh, showing Ashurbanipal, King of Assyria in the seventh century BC. All the furniture is shown with intricately carved legs and stretchers. (Courtesy of the Trustees of the British Museum, London)

Right: This Greek vase painting shows the gods feasting. The couches with their small painted volutes and rectangular legs are covered with mattresses. The three-legged side-table on the right would have been pushed under the couches after the meal. (Museo Nazionale, Naples)

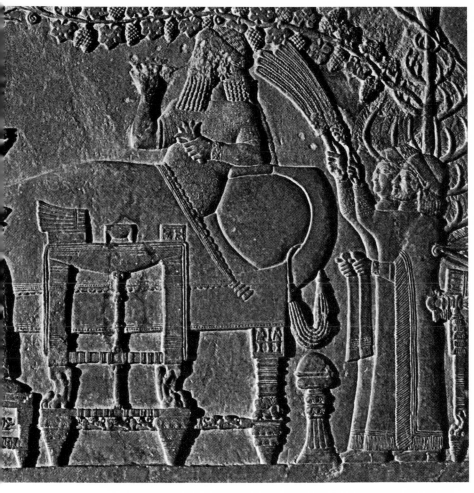

very few pieces of furniture survive, but we may rely on 'second-hand' representations on vase-paintings, coins, reliefs and terracotta models. Depictions on funerary stelae are the most useful as they give an idea of the third dimension on a large scale that the necessarily flat treatment of vase decoration cannot. There are also many evocations in heroic literature of the splendour of the Greek interior.

In vase-painting the gods, dead heroes and important mortals sat on thrones *(thronoi)* although the difference between a throne and a chair is often indistinguishable. Early or Archaic examples have animal feet, swan-head finials on low backs with carved side aprons. In the fifth century BC a new type emerged with either turned or rectangular legs, the latter with incised patterns topped by rosettes and volutes, and aprons with carved or painted mythological scenes. Then the throne with a solid back and sides appeared, usually in marble, and was especially popular in the Hellenistic and Roman periods. This was chiefly for ceremonial or theatrical use.

The Greeks' most startling creation ranking high in the history of early furniture design was the *klismos*, a beautifully simple chair much favoured by classical artists. The peak of its popularity was in the latter half of the fifth century BC. It is typified by the elegant splayed legs, with an enclosing backrest and a lack of surface decoration as seen in the

Hegeso stele example. There are many variations in its design and dimensions; from the fourth century the proportions became heavier and more exaggerated with a resulting loss in much of its earlier beauty. The klismos was clearly a most refined and original article whose elegant curves lead one to suppose that the technique of steam-bending was understood from an early stage. The seat was usually plaited and a cushion or piece of leather placed on top.

The easily portable backless and armless rectangular stool with turned legs, known as the *diphros*, was the usual form of seat for deities and mortals alike, as in the Parthenon frieze, and in basic form originates from Egypt and Assyria. The ubiquitous folding-stool or *diphros okladias* is usually shown carried by slaves for their masters' convenience. These were often highly decorated with either fixed or collapsible legs. They fall into two types, one with plain, straight legs, the other with inwardly curving legs and animal feet. Footstools usually accompanied seat furniture as the natural accessories to couches, thrones and chairs.

Banquets of the gods are among the more popular scenes on vase-paintings and in these the couch *(kline)* and table *(trapeza)* play an important part. The couch fulfilled a dual role, being used both for sleeping and eating; as a bed it loses the Egyptian slope and

14

footboard and gains a pillowrest of more natural form. Couches with animal legs deriving from the Egyptian model are found mainly in the sixth century BC. Examples with turned legs appear from the Archaic period, and some bronze-mounted ones have survived. Scrolled headboards or pillow-rests dating from the fourth century BC are of great importance for Roman developments. There are also couches with rectangular legs with carved and incised decoration similar to that on thrones. Some of these were evidently long enough for two people. Banqueting scenes show couches placed end to end against a wall with side-tables for carrying food and wine which were pushed under the couches afterwards. The less wealthy appear to have sat on diphroi at a large table — it was a mark of distinction to recline at a meal rather than sit. Side-tables were rectangular with three legs in the Egyptian manner, with feet that were often fluted and tapered towards lion's paws. The four-legged table was much less common and there are rare representations of small pedestal tables. From the fourth century BC the round-topped tripod-table with animal and foliate designs became increasingly popular and served as the prototype for Roman usage. One found in Luxor is now in the Brussels Museum. The linen-chest *(kibotos)*, again following the Egyptian pattern, is often found in paintings of ladies' boudoirs. From the Greek word *kiste,* generally meaning casket, are derived the Latin *cista* and the English *chest.*

Etruscan furniture from the seventh to the third centuries BC mainly comes from graves, but the evidence is rather fragmentary. Most forms seem to correspond to those of contemporary Greece and these provided another source for Rome to copy. Coloured terracotta models show typical Greek couches.

Rome

Developments in Greece during the later Classical and Hellenistic periods, tending towards luxury as well as practicality, are the stepping-off point for a study of the furniture of Ancient Rome. The spread of the Roman way of life throughout the Empire from Africa in the South to Britain in the North is seen in the remarkable uniformity of furniture styles. The wall-paintings at Pompeii together with many finds from villas and palaces, the use of bronze and marble as basic materials and the evidence of contemporary literature provide us with a variety of information not surviving from earlier civilizations. Roman furniture forms were surprisingly restricted in number, however; the idea of the ostentatious interior was more important than that of comfort or convenience — and it was Roman ornament that was re-employed in later centuries rather than structural designs.

Tacitus considered the dining-room and baths as the hallmarks of civility and the social centre of Roman life. Family meals were often taken in the enclosed courtyard *(atrium)* with the paterfamilias alone reclining on a couch, his wife on a chair beside him and the children on stools by the table, with a separate table for the slaves. Citron and maple were particularly prized materials for which high sums were paid by leading personalities. The Romans were also fond of elaborate veneers and inlay in wood, ivory and precious metals.

As in Greece the couch *(lectus)* was an important and desirable article of which several survive. Of special note are the large number of bronze and ivory ornaments for foot and headboards *(fulcra)* of exquisite workmanship. The most common variety was the long couch with turned legs, which was popular in the late Republican and early Imperial periods. Bronze examples from Pompeii show a multitude of turnings of no structural importance; bone and ivory were used as main supports. The height of the couch varied according to its purpose; in the dining-room couches were arranged in threes at right-angles to one another. The highly decorated couch must have been the most expensive item of furniture in the villa.

The throne *(solium)* is found in representations of deities and their followers, close to

15

bronze or marble round-topped tripod-table of which several were found at Pompeii. The pedestal table with a central marble support and bronze mounts were also used. Often tables for specific use in the dining-room had semi-circular tops to fit the couch base. Large rectangular marble tables with two carved slab supports were mainly used outdoors and these designs were re-used in the Renaissance.

Byzantium and the Middle Ages

The decline in living standards following the collapse of the Roman Empire had an immediate and lasting effect on the function and importance of furniture in Western European society, while the foundation of

Above: This painting from the Codex Amiatinus (AD 689–716) depicts the prophet Ezra writing. He is seated on a low bench with painted edges; his feet rest on a simple stool with a pegged stretcher. The panelled cupboard has two doors—rare at this time. (Laurentian Library, Florence)

Above right: The 'Throne of Dagobert', probably ninth century, is an outstanding example of early mediaeval bronze-casting from the Court School of Charlemagne. (Bibliothèque Nationale, Paris)

the Greek pattern but with a greater elaboration of turned members and a general increase in proportions. Thrones with solid sides became popular for ceremonial occasions with high, rounded backs and stepped sides (hardly suitable as armrests) and two solid end-supports carved with palmettes, scrolls and winged lions. The high-backed, all-enclosing wicker chair found favour with ladies at their toilet. The klismos assumed heavy, unbalanced proportions with thick legs and wide, curving backrests and was favoured in representations of female deities. The stool, especially the folding variety, was the most common seat form, attaining special significance as the *sella curulis* used by senators and magistrates.

As in the modern idiom the Romans used tables as permanent stands for displaying possessions, and of particular note was the

Constantinople and the Empire in the East assured the continuation of the classical tradition. At the same time the spread of Christianity, and in particular its off-shoot, monasticism, provided the basis for the pursuit of learning and the development of the arts. It was the achievement of the Frankish dynasty under Charlemagne to emerge as the dominant force and partially re-kindle the flames of Ancient Rome with a Christian spirit, setting a seal on the course of early mediaeval history in the West. Internal squabbles, however, and Viking raids from outside the Empire, made for a constantly changing map of Europe.

It is this background of territorial uncertainty from which the fabric of mediaeval society evolved—a society consisting of a small ruling class with a vast majority of serfs and peasants, the former geared for war and always on the move, the latter bound to the land eking out a bare subsistence. Through necessity, therefore, articles of furniture were scanty and essentially portable; of course virtually nothing has survived. The wealth of the king was either transported along with his retinue or stored for safe keeping in monasteries.

Many fine works of art remain from the early mediaeval period to testify to the high standard of craftsmanship and quality of materials used. It is from such objects as jewel-caskets, reliquaries and other sacred receptacles that we may assume that elaborate pieces of furniture existed. Manuscript illumination and occasionally monumental sculpture give us an insight into the world of the royal and monastic scriptoria. Characteristic artistic styles developed throughout Europe, notably under the patronage of the Holy Roman Emperor.

There are representations of kings seated on the most elaborate architecturally-contrived thrones with painted canopies and cushions. Whether these were the artists' fanciful creations or not is open to question. It is clear, however, that only royal personages could expect to be associated with furniture of any size or quality. Such is the bronze 'Throne of Dagobert' which probably dates from the early ninth century and has tenuous connections with King Dagobert (AD 622–638), the supposed founder of the Abbey of Saint Denis. The folding legs with their lion's heads and paws are typical of late antique work; it is possible that it does date from the seventh century, but is more likely to be a good example of the resuscitation of classical motifs after the time of Charlemagne.

The folding-stool is certainly the most illustrated piece of furniture in the early Middle Ages, examples being found on ivory panels, in manuscript borders and on cathedral façade sculpture. It usually had a regal connection or at least indicated the secular or religious significance of the sitter depicted. Its social importance of course dates back to Ancient Egypt. There is a richly decorated example from Styria, now in Vienna, dating from about 1200.

That a high standard of craftsmanship was maintained in Byzantium at the same time is indicated in the series of ivory panels attached to the throne of Archbishop Maximianus of Ravenna (AD 545–556) in which one sees the ultimate flowering of the Hellenistic style. Byzantine manuscripts of saints and scholars show that the lectern was a favoured article, often with a cabinet beneath for storing books. And the mosaics of the churches of Ravenna reveal a taste for elaborate hangings and interior decoration in the Eastern Empire not seen elsewhere till the fourteenth century.

There is no doubt that living conditions at this time were squalid and uncomfortable. Life was centred on the great hall which was used for meals, entertainment, the administration of justice and all daily business. It was sparsely furnished with trestles, benches and stools strewn with mattresses or pillows, with only the one chair or folding-stool for the king or lord. The walls might be hung with tapestries; in the epic poem, *Beowulf*, there is mention of hangings inwoven with gold used for ceremonial occasions. And the Bayeux

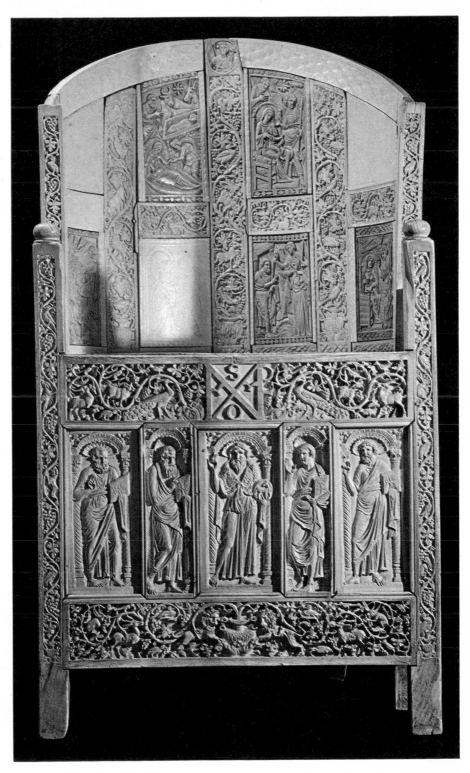

Below: The ivory throne of Maximianus, early sixth century AD. The ivory panels attached to the wooden core show the final stages of the Hellenistic style in Byzantium. The five figures in the front panels represent John the Baptist and the four Evangelists. (Museo Nazionale, Ravenna)

tapestry as well as providing evidence of royal furniture gives one an idea of the quality attained in eleventh-century textiles with its variety of colours and animated depiction of the Norman Conquest of Britain.

The essence of mediaeval furniture was its portability to suit the itinerant nature of everyday life. Although sacred caskets and reliquaries do not fall under the general category of furniture, they do have a family connection with travelling-chests which could have been carried under the arm or on horseback. These were either simple wooden boxes or more often were made of leather bound with iron. Such items as trestles, benches and large

chests would have remained in the hall or monastery. Treasure chests and less decorative or valuable pieces would have accompanied the retinue. Not unnaturally most of the surviving examples of the ubiquitous chest, at any rate until the later fourteenth century, have a history of Church ownership as they have tended to remain *in situ*. Decoration on such chests frequently relies on architectural motifs such as arcades, columns and decorative mouldings, notable examples of which are the chests or *standards* from Valère in Switzerland with their cloister-like arcades and geometric patterns.

Among the more important types of 'static'

18

that the artisan, as opposed to the carpenter, would have come. It was only after the organization of the craftsmen's guilds in the thirteenth century that the cabinet-maker's art was separately identified.

After about 1250 it becomes easier to date existing pieces of furniture with a degree of certainty as the Gothic style gained a firm and lasting grip on the applied arts throughout Europe. It was an exuberant style with great decorative potential that went hand in hand with the new age of chivalry and heraldry, the rise of the merchant classes, the emergence of the city-state and secular artistic patronage rivalling that of the Church.

Later mediaeval furniture and interior decoration reflects a new distribution of wealth. A glance at the sumptuously painted *Très Riches Heures du Duc de Berry* gives a vivid impression of the richness and colour of court life with its fairy-tale architecture and wealth of hangings and textiles complementing articles of furniture. In England Edward III created the office of King's Tapestry-Maker and such fourteenth-century work was renowned throughout Europe as *opus anglicanum*. From the late thirteenth century onward we find wills and inventories

Above: A mid-fifteenth century master-carver's workshop. The bench-front has linenfold panels. (Ecole des Beaux Arts, Paris)

Above right: The Blessed Agnes attending a sick man by Nicholas Puchner. The simple bed is constructed of planks within a double frame formed of solid beams. (National Gallery, Prague)

furniture are also those ceremonial chairs and thrones, both secular and ecclesiastical, such as Charlemagne's throne at Aachen, the episcopal thrones at Bari and Canossa, Saint Augustine's chair at Canterbury and the sanctuary chairs at Beverley and Hexham, all made of stone or marble and of varying degrees of sophistication.

The ordered and relatively sedentary life of the monastery and cathedral no doubt required certain specific types of furniture such as lecterns, choir stalls and of course altars of which there are some beautifully sculpted survivors, notably that of Avenas in Burgundy. And it was largely from ecclesiastical *ateliers*

that specifically mention furniture in lists of chattels; the lack of earlier documentation has led to the conclusion that furniture was hitherto held in low esteem, although representations of elaborate royal furniture would seem to negate this notion. The earlier dominance of the great hall as the social centre gradually gave way to the smaller chamber with the result that functional furniture with a degree of comfort became necessary. In Italy, however, the Gothic style did not find favour and furniture there was painted, rather than carved, with scenes of

city life and relatively few architectural motifs.

The beginnings of the Gothic style can be traced well back into early twelfth-century architectural developments in France, the various stylistic and constructional elements fusing in the 1140s in such buildings as the abbey of St Denis and the cathedrals of Sens and Noyon. It is this fresh array of detail that became the basis of mediaeval furniture decoration, the most widely used motifs being the pointed arch, multi-foil shapes and tracery patterns. These details did not appear in

Below: Detail from a fifteenth-century History of Alexander the Great, showing a banquet. The elegant stepped dresser in the centre displays faience vessels and plate and has an overhead canopy with a lozenge frieze surmounted by pinnacles and leaves. (Petit Palais, Paris)

21

pieces of furniture immediately, however, as the Romanesque tradition was still very strong in the non-architectural field in the twelfth and thirteenth centuries. The architectural origins of later medieval furniture design were often openly displayed in their construction; for example, many chests have buttress-shaped corner- and side-strengthening members. Master craftsmen were able to translate what they saw in stone into the medium of wood. Indeed, there is every reason to suppose that the carver working on a stone altar-screen or sculptured façade would also execute furnishings such as choir stalls and episcopal thrones. Certainly during the fourteenth century an interest in delicate Gothic forms led to a much more economical use of materials and constructional methods, with less reliance on the simple slab or plank of wood. This was also achieved by the breaking-up of the surface by the use of pierced forms and elegant overall patterns.

The chest was still the most widespread article of domestic furniture in the later Middle Ages. Thirteenth-century examples from France reveal a taste for attached iron

Right: The Birth of the
Virgin by the Master of the
Life of the Virgin. The
raised bed has a full tester.
Behind it is a painted panel
with flowers and scrolls.
The bedside linen-chest
has ogee-arched feet and
typical late Gothic panel
ornament. (Alte Pinakothek,
Munich)

scroll-work and also raised feet with chip-carved geometric and foliate ornament. From the early fourteenth century architecturally-contrived chests appear with blind arcading, crockets, ogival tracery patterns and pinnacles of the type found on the 'flamboyant' façades of French cathedrals such as Strasbourg and Rouen, and Perpendicular elevations in England like the nave of Canterbury. Another tradition was the representation of jousting scenes, the lives of the saints and animal life. In Spain profuse and complex Moorish ornament was combined with Gothic to produce an encrusted wedding-cake effect. One of the finest vehicles in furniture for elaborate tracery was the ceremonial throne, two notable examples being the coronation chair in Westminster Abbey completed for Edward I in 1300–1, and the splendid silver-gilt throne of King Martin of Aragon, now in Barcelona, dating from the second half of the fourteenth century.

As the guilds recognized the trade of the cabinet-maker so a fresh variety of woods were employed. Oak and beech were the principal materials in northern Europe while walnut, cypress and fruitwoods found favour in the Mediterranean lands.

Linen-fold panelling is of fifteenth-century Flemish origin and became popular in northern Europe not only in the decoration of furniture but also for the wainscoting of chambers in whose corners a bed with a canopied tester might be fitted. The origins of specialized writing-desks as boxes with sloping, hinged lids date to earlier centuries and vary in size from those held in the laps of the figures of Aristotle and Pythagoras from the mid-twelfth century Portail Royal at Chartres to substantial fifteenth-century examples which would have been placed on a table. Trestle tables remained the main dining-room furnishing and there are Flemish paintings showing occasional tables of various shapes. Cupboards, sideboards and presses dating from the fifteenth century for storing and displaying plate, clothes and books have a wealth of delicate ornament, often in bands because of their size. There are earlier examples with a specific function such as the sacristy cupboard in Halberstadt Cathedral dating from perhaps the twelfth century.

The impact of the Italian Renaissance was relatively slow to affect furniture north of the Alps, notably in England where the tradition of Gothic was deeply entrenched and thrived for the next four centuries. Indeed in the nineteenth century the decorative impact of the 'Early English' style was the basis for the school of design of Gothic ornament fostered by A W N Pugin and his circle which so dominated Victorian taste.

THE CLASSICAL REVIVAL
Europe's Renaissance

In the mid-thirteenth century when Villard d'Honnecourt was sketching details of buildings — towers, flying buttresses, choir stalls and windows — into his now famous album he thought of no other style than Gothic. It was the style which fashioned the great cathedrals, created to soar upwards in linear and vaulted complexity. They proclaimed throughout Europe the church, powerful and triumphant, and provided a vivid and visually exciting experience to those who moved forward through long nervous lengths of grey stone, and coloured imagery in leaded glass. At Amiens, Strasbourg, Milan, and other cathedrals, the choirs were filled with filigree wooden stalls and bedecked organ cases, with polychromatic saints in stiff array in the scented gloom. Joiners and carvers, not yet tightly bound to guild tradition, found their most sympathetic, yet demanding, patrons among the Prince Bishops.

The feelings of greatest moment and enquiry seem to have arisen in the city of Florence, and within the circle of its most talented architect Filippo Brunelleschi (1377–1446). He was to surmount the Gothic cathedral with a great dome which eschewed the normal use of timber centering for its construction. In its majestic proportion it was a fitting statement of what the age was to be about. He initiated the mathematical formulae governing perspective which his friend the young painter Masaccio used to powerful effect in the late 1420s. Groups of engravers in Germany and France later scribed its intricacies for editions of architectural and decorative prints which were to interest furniture-makers, goldsmiths and sculptors throughout Europe.

In the experiments which artists carried out the rigours of International Gothic were finally abandoned. For too long this style had dictated that what the court painter to the Dukes of Burgundy did would look similar to work produced for imperious masters in Florence or Mantua. In the Netherlands in 1434 Jan van Eyck painted the Italian merchant Giovanni Arnolfini and his wife. They were depicted standing before the bed, chair, and mirror of a real and recognizable room rather than in a stylized sacred setting. But in achieving freedom from tyranny of style, artists and craftsmen became subordinate to the particular school of painting or craftsmanship in their town or region.

The status of the house was also changing. The hall, with its large carved wooden screen, became the entrance to the great English house rather than the hub of its existence. The dining-room and parlour were created with a corresponding demand for furniture. Money once spent on fortification of an Italian town-palace could be spared for gilded beds, inlaid tables, chairs with reclining backs, and pedimented cupboards with reclining figures.

25

There were also the variations created by the use of different woods. In the north oak was easily available and it could be chiselled with precision to form panels in high relief: in the south it was necessary to work in soft woods such as pine and larch and this gave a flatter quality to all that was decorated. The techniques of inlay and marquetry developed as the trade guilds trained and supervised the system of apprenticeship. They produced the men to create the cabinets of wonders, encrusted with precious stones, and the men who created the simple 'best bed' described in many a yeoman's inventory. The grammar of ornament which the Renaissance had spread substituted classicism for Gothic detail. The men who created furniture were, within a hundred years or so of Michelangelo's birth, to be looked on as artists themselves and furniture itself at last shook off its mediaeval origins.

Italy

In 1386 on the orders of Gian Galeazzo Visconti the Gothic cathedral at Milan was begun. Across the succeeding years and as late as the sixteenth century French, German, and Italian master-masons directed its erection—a wonder of white marble gables, pinnacles, belfries, rose-windows and statues. But it was almost alone in Italy in its portrayal of the pointed style of Gothic architecture. Gothic stone tracery, thin and strong in its arch formation, allowed for large areas of glass to be disposed within a frame. To Italians intent on restricting bright hot sunlight entering their buildings this was a disadvantage. Instead they painted in fresco the coloured pictures which enlivened the wall spaces between any small windows. As a

Left: With its lion paw feet and painted panels, this Florentine cassone or marriage-chest of about 1492 is an outstanding example of the gilder's and painter's art. The narrative panels are painted in tempera on gesso. The Bible, Italian literature and classical mythology provided the most frequently used sources of inspiration for such panels. Many cassoni were executed in famous workshops such as those led by Uccello and Ghirlandajo. (Courtauld Institute of Fine Art, London)

result Italian schemes of decoration and furniture owed little to Gothic.

It made its brief appearance most effectively as the International style and is seen in the structure of the great wooden altarpieces of the early fifteenth century. Two examples in the Uffizi Gallery in Florence are typically grand and flamboyant. Lorenzo Monaco's *Coronation of the Virgin* (signed and dated 1413) shows how persistent the archaic styles were, even as the Renaissance was about to dawn. The polyptych has pinnacles, pilasters and is set as usual on a pierced and painted platform known as a *predella*. Ten years later Gentile de Fabriano painted his *Adoration of the Magi* for a powerful patron, Palla Strozzi. The altarpiece is triple arched with superb decorated finials and elaborately pierced columns, thickly encrusted with gold leaf. As International Gothic came to its end it produced these richest and most splendid creations, with Lorenzo Monaco's influence on this style being of paramount importance.

There are few ways of ascertaining what furniture was in certain rooms at various periods other than to examine a wide range of paintings which show interiors. It is necessary to take into account that they sometimes depict an ideal world, or one distorted by symbolic and allegorical allusions. Allowing for this and for a certain time-lapse, the furniture bears some relationship to what was familiar to the artist and his contemporaries.

In 1491 Domenico Ghirlandajo completed a wall-painting of the *Birth of the Virgin* in the church of Sta Maria Novella, Florence. It is concerned with the birth of the Virgin Mary and several relatives of her mother St Anne coming to visit her to offer greetings and congratulations. The room has a classical frieze of riotous *putti* (or cherub-like infants), an elegant staircase at the left, correctly drawn in perspective, and four richly decorated, Ionic capped, square columns. The wainscoting is decorated in intarsia — a form of decorated wood inlay — and St Anne is

27

seated on a version of a *cassapanca* — a chest to which there is a back and the seat of which opens to reveal a storage space. Vittore Carpaccio's *Dream of St Ursula* in the Accademia, Venice, of some four years later shows a very sparsely furnished room. With its double-arched window, the room is dominated by a bed on a decorated plinth, with slender turned posts, a Gothic chair with pointed back and scrolled arms, the ubiquitous splayed stool, a small square table covered with a fringed cloth and a small cupboard. The rare appearance of Gothic, and the Renaissance interest in perspective, is exemplified in Perugino's *The Virgin appearing to St Bernard* of about 1490 (now in the Alte Pinakothek, Munich). Six figures are ranged in two groups of three, with St Bernard seated on a simple square bench at a small desk with a plain lectern on top and a diamond lozenge motif on its sides. Triple arches frame the simple landscape. It indicates in stark symmetry the marked paucity of furniture even when the architectural setting itself is magnificent and imposing.

If by contrast with Gothic detail one explores the grand sweep of only one Renaissance house — the Palazzo Farnese in Rome — differences are apparent. It housed the rich collections of antiques and works of art gathered by the Farnese family. There were grand salons decorated in paint and gold by the Carracci studio, but little furniture — the great table of inlaid marble (now in the Metropolitan Museum, New York) stood in the *sala degli imperatori*, named after the twelve busts of Roman emperors which were

ranged along its walls. The second-floor rooms were filled with tapestries, services of plate, and rock crystal, and the libraries of the Farnese and Orsini families.

Much early Italian furniture was itself painted rather than carved and its highest expression was in the wedding-chests or *cassoni*, created particularly in Florence. Continuity and rank were cemented in the marriage alliances between great families, who attached considerable importance to the grandeur of the marriage ceremony as a result. To produce the chests in sufficient number was reason enough to avoid any unusual techniques – the Florentines in any case well understood painting on prepared wood panels, or decorating in a stucco relief which was composed of sand, marble dust and gypsum. The long panels of the cassone were admirably suited to spatial and perspective compositions in miniature and famous artists became adept in their decoration.

The sixteenth-century Italian architect and painter Giorgio Vasari explained to his readers that earlier artists had felt no concern at employing themselves in the painting of furniture. They had still to acquire a unique and decisive status and were versatile enough to vary their accomplishments. The great Florentine artists — Botticelli, Uccello, the sculptor Donatello and Pollaiuolo — all worked on cassoni in the first half of the fifteenth century.

This was the period when important families dominated Italian life and vied with each other for power, possessions, and the right to bestow patronage or misery. The riches of the

Below: This fifteenth-century Florentine cassone has a simple, rough construction with three painted panels. Compared with the grand examples produced in the best workshops, it is obviously an inferior piece, but it shows the sort of cassone that the more modest families might wish to possess. (Palazzo Davanzati, Florence)

Above: In St Augustine in his Study by Vittore Carpaccio, the flamboyant chair and scrolled lectern on the left owe much to the combined skills of carver, embroiderer and leather-worker. With swooping scrolls and splayed legs they are tasselled and studded, set on their own covered kneeling platform and are en suite with the furniture in the room. The Saint sits working at an elegant thin table, again with a covered and studded top. (San Giorgio Maggiore, Venice)

Medici, the Sforza and the Gonzaga raised art to an intense level. Lodovico Gonzaga, Duke of Mantua (1414–78) had a wide-ranging ability which encompassed that of action and scholarship. He persuaded Mantegna to become his court-painter, he employed Alberti as his architect, and collected the writings of Dante, Petrarch, Boccaccio and the earlier classical authors. The cassoni painters found it expedient to paint scenes from such authors —the *Decameron* was popular. Their virile depiction enhanced an object which had been created in strict accordance with classical rules of proportion. The knights and ladies of an age of chivalry which are found on a cassone of the late fourteenth century, now in the Victoria & Albert Museum, London, were in keeping with the ideas which emanated from Mantua with the residence, in the time of Lodovico's father, of the great humanist Vittorino da Feltre.

The subjects depicted on cassoni were wide-ranging. While the spirit of rivalry between neighbouring states often erupted into violent war, the cassoni rarely portrayed this. There are some tournament scenes, with prancing horses and tilted lances, and also classical subjects with a violent theme, for example Cephalus hurling his spear and killing his wife, or the equally tragic death of Actaeon torn to pieces by his own hounds. Much more acceptable were the paintings, sometimes erotic, based on the many love-poems by Ovid, even if they were denounced by Savonarola, whose own love-suit in the 1470s of a member of the Strozzi family was treated with a disdain sufficient to cause him to enter the church.

What is slightly more puzzling are the large panels in cassone style which are obviously too large to be so used. When Schubring issued his two-volume work on the marriage-chests in 1923 he indicated that the panels were fixed to the walls of rooms above the painted wainscoting. With parts of the whole wall to work on it was possible for an artist to imitate his peers who had covered all before them with a painterly virtuosity. The cassoni became a small part of a greater whole, but remained important statements about Italian life and manners. As the Renaissance gained momentum they were created as classical monuments in sarcophagus form, carved in high relief in walnut. They displayed classical motifs of urns, griffins, leaves and flowers, or were decorated with an intarsia of exotic woods.

At the beginning of the sixteenth century in Italy—a period when Bramante, Michelangelo, Leonardo da Vinci, Raphael and Titian were at work—the role of the artist underwent a change. No longer was he a craftsman content to paint a chest but a person capable of keen enquiry and observation of anatomy, natural laws and mathematics. The courts were seeking prestige one above the other, and were wise in their investments, often to the exclusion of aesthetic considerations in what they bought. Michelangelo had begun his long acquaintance with the Sistine Chapel works, the tomb of Julius II and St Peter's. Giulio Romano was to spend the 1520s erecting the Palazzo del Te at Mantua for the Gonzagas, and Alessandro Farnese (later Pope Paul III) strained his vast fortune for 40 years with the erection from 1514 of the Palazzo Farnese. These buildings created luxurious settings for paintings by the Carracci and others, which in riots of exuberant colour portrayed the mythological amours of unconsidered hordes of gods and goddesses.

One of the noblest acts of creation was the decision by Pope Leo X—a Medici—to continue the work on St Peter's and the Vatican under the supervision of Raphael. Raphael worked from about 1515, with his assistants, Giulio Romano, Giovanni da Udine and his associate Baldassare Peruzzi at the Villa Madama for the Pope's cousin, Cardinal Giulio de' Medici. It was work in stucco and paint which was to have an important influence on the decoration of Fontainebleau for the French king, François I. Vasari in his near-contemporary *Lives of the Artists* says that Pope Leo was well pleased with Raphael's work in the *stanze* of the Vatican 'and to make the panelling worthy of the paintings he sent to Monte Oliverto di Chiusuri in the Siena district for Fra Giovanni da Verona, who in those days was a great master of perspective-views in wood inlay. Fra Giovanni executed not only the surrounding panelling but also some very fine doors and chairs, with perspective studies, which won him generous praise and rewards from the Pope.'

The expenditure of vast sums on such decorative richness seems, however, to have prevented too much expenditure on furniture. Carpets and luxuriant cut velvets, and tables holding bronzes, and vessels of gold and silver were there in profusion. The *studiolo* of Francesco I de' Medici, a room designed in the 1570s by Vasari, has walls and ceiling covered with paintings, and has bronze statuettes in niches. Of furniture it only had enough to form a proportioned central feature. No great sixteenth-century bed survives in Rome or

Venice, although they appear in paintings, with Corinthian capitals to the posts and a classical frieze to the canopy. Furniture that was rough and practical could be rendered fit to set on the marble patterned floor of the *piano-nobile* (the main floor) simply by covering it with a Turkish carpet or a damask cloth. Even Raphael's famous painting of Pope Leo X, painted in 1518, shows the Holy Father seated in a red tasselled and upholstered armchair at a table covered with a scarlet cloth.

We have mentioned intarsia decoration on cassoni, and there is also a splendid room,

Above: This sixteenth-century Florentine credenza is more than usually architectural, with the grotesque masks and caryatid figures contained within a frieze supported by three pilasters. (Villa Medici, Florence)

Left: An elaborate bed, made in about 1500. It has wonderful, almost Baroque posts with incised swirled carving, urn finials and carved supports to the stretcher. (Palazzo Davanzati, Florence)

Right: The Sala della Biblioteca of the Castel Sant'Angelo, Rome. This ancient library is decorated with remarkable stuccoes and frescoes by Perin del Vaga and Baccio da Montelupo. The tables are low, with shaped end supports. After the middle of the sixteenth century, walnut was most commonly used for such tables affording the woodcarver excellent opportunities. (Castel Sant'Angelo, Rome)

the Studiolo of Federigo de Montefeltro in the Ducal Palace at Urbino, of about 1470, with superb intarsia decoration by an unknown artist. As an art it attracted its own groups of craftsmen. One of the best known was Fra Giovanni da Verona, whom we have noted working for Pope Leo X under Raphael's supervision. He also decorated choir stalls and library cupboards with double-panelled doors. The cupboards were decorated with urns, arches and *trompe l'oeil* depictions of enigmatic open cupboards. The side panels of foliate decoration and a classical ornament in the frieze completed an object at once practical and imposing. Walnut was used frequently for the manufacture of cassoni and for sideboards, *credenza*, which replaced the simple tables covered with rich cloths. They were at once architectural in form, but were plain by comparison with the tables and caskets created in a moment of high Mannerist eccentricity.

The greatest of the palaces in Rome needed objects which would not be completely subordinated by rich decoration. The Farnese table of 1570 with its carved marble supports

and inlaid marble top was possibly designed for the Palazzo Farnese by the architect Vignola. Carved wood tables of the period also have boldly sculptured supports which show the fantasies of Mannerism. It is a style which defies quick analysis, but in essence was the result of an excessive addiction to a distinctive style which had evolved in courtly circles. Painted and sculptured figures were produced in a manner which betokened a poise and refinement capable of resolving all difficulties, but which was grounded deep in the philosophy of the age, particularly neo-Platonism. Some of the figures on Michelangelo's Sistine Chapel ceiling, or *The Dying Slave* (1513), have the new abstraction about them. His marble sculptures affected the work of silversmiths and furniture-makers in awakening them to adornment with figures. Cellini, too, had employed the Mannerist style in his *Perseus with the Head of Medusa* (1545) in Florence, and when the Farnese casket (now in the Museo di Capodimonte, Naples) was created a few years later in rich

silver gilt it bore small figures in caryatid form as on the marble and bronze base of the Cellini *Perseus*.

While exact references are not possible, it is nevertheless sensible to bear in mind that the decorative arts followed the social scene. The moderates in the church had fought to see that at the 1563 Council of Trent the visual arts were defended from the extremists. The resulting pursuit of simplicity, clarity and avoidance of the nude figure were contrary to the spirit of Mannerism, and they diverted attention from the essays in flamboyance, into which category fell the lavish creations in *pietra dura* — hard-stone. In 1580 Francesco I de' Medici summoned craftsmen from Milan to set up a hard-stone workshop — the *Opificio delle Pietre Dure* in Florence. The aim was to have within his patronage a means of adding works to his own extensive collections, and to have an easy facility for providing gifts to those whose support and friendship he earnestly desired. When John Evelyn visited the Opificio in 1644 he saw: 'divers incomparable

Above: The Sala dei Pappagalli provides an elaborate setting for a fine bed with finials to its posts, a carved headboard, draperies and valances. A leather upholstered elbow chair with brass studs stands against the wall. (Palazzo Davanzati, Florence)

Above right: Contained in four panels below a Roman lettered frieze, this late sixteenth-century grand chest exemplifies Renaissance furniture at its best and most formal. (Palazzo Davanzati, Florence)

32

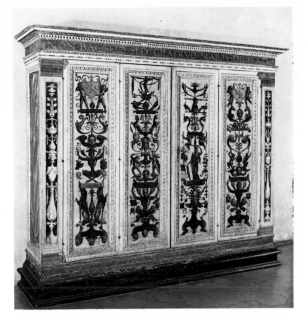

scene in Europe. But the estates were built on the many smaller houses and the devoted work of humbler men and women. They used simple rush-seated ladderback chairs, benches and stools which were made across the centuries with little variation. In the larger towns the shopkeepers were numerous and powerful, and, by forming their own guilds, they guarded jealously their customs and enhanced their own status. This produced the demand for a more sophisticated form of furniture in which the ladderback chair was upholstered, the bellows covered with crimson velvet and carved in relief, and the pinewood mirrors gilded. There was also a church which each guild patronized, with a steady demand for seats, small altars and chapel furniture. Plague and fever might frequently visit the houses of the poor but religion was a purging grace which gave secular strength, and hopes of a status with possessions to match.

Below: Grand cabinet with architectural compartments containing bronze statuettes. The panels of pietra dura, made fashionable in Florence from the end of the sixteenth century, are of fruit and flowers, with incrustations of lapis lazuli. The base has eight legs in four conjoined pairs, and the cabinet has a galleried top. (Museo Stibbert, Florence)

tables of Pietra Commessa, which is a marble ground inlaid with several sorts of marbles and stones of divers colours, in the shapes of flowers, trees, beasts, birds and Landskips like the natural.' With commendable perception, a splendid table made in about 1640 had been put in the Tribune of the Uffizi to catch the eye of visitors on the Grand Tour, such as Evelyn, who journeyed to Italy from all over Europe. It was perhaps similar to the one, still in the Opificio museum, designed by Jacopo Ligozzi and Bernardino Poccetti for Ferdinando de' Medici in 1633–49. The top is composed of a mosaic of semi-precious stones —jaspers, agates, lapis lazuli—set into a ground of black marble with a dexterity that defies comprehension.

In the presence of studied opulence in furniture it is easy to find further examples. The gems in the Medici collection were priceless and the Grand Duke of Tuscany was said to have lavished a fortune on a table and a desk, both richly set with precious stones. Caskets housed precious relics and in themselves were small expressions of wealth and the acquisitive urge. They were fashioned with ebony and ivory inlays, contrasting dark and light woods and overlaid with silver, silver gilt and precious and semi-precious stones. A Milanese cabinet of drawers in the Wallace Collection, London, of the late sixteenth century, is of pine, veneered with ebony. The walnut drawers are faced with ebony which frames embossed steel plaques damascened in gold with mythological subjects of Orpheus, Venus, Cupid and Mars. Furniture such as this had reached a position where it was venerated as much as the relic caskets and tapestries of a mediaeval court.

Mediaeval and Renaissance Italy has long been known for the contributions its great families made to the political and financial

France

The brilliantly coloured world exemplified in the International Gothic style was not only portrayed by Italian artists of the fourteenth century but was precisely drawn by German and Flemish engravers. In the early years of the fifteenth century, the Franco-Flemish style of the lavish courts of the Dukes of Burgundy and the Dukes of Berry was most influential. The courts encouraged important contributions to the arts of miniature painting and illumination including the famous *Books of Hours* created for Jean, Duc de Berry, in the 1420s by Pol, Hennequin and Herman de Limbourg. Work inspired by the Flemish style also made its appearance in Angers and Provence, areas which were under the rule of René of Anjou, King of Sicily, an ardent patron of Flemish artists. Philippe le Bon, Duke of Burgundy, also owned paintings by the van Eycks — Jan van Eyck was his court painter in about 1425 — and Roger van der Weyden.

It was a period in France for flamboyant furniture designed for display, both within its complex ornamentation and for the showing of gold and silver plate. The *buffet* or sideboard during the Gothic years resembled architecture in miniature — rich tracery ornament above, cusping and linen-fold panelling below, with a locking compartment for valuable plate and upper and lower shelves for display of various pieces. The observance of architectural forms was the result of the furniture-makers copying work by regional schools of stonemasons, and being inspired by the great Gothic structures, such as Milan Cathedral, being built at about this time.

As early as the thirteenth century the wooden chest had shown this preoccupation with architecture and carving in high relief. A chest of this date in the Musée de Cluny, Paris, shows a relief carving of 12 knights in armour, and other examples have elaborate banding in metal. They depicted status and this was taken to extreme lengths in the frequent possession, by personages such as Margaret of Flanders, of two cradles — one for the child, one for ceremonial parade. Such cradles frequently had what became a common element in display furniture — the canopy. This was equated with rank and high office and was frequently depicted in paintings and engravings — surmounting the throne of a heavenly or temporal ruler. They were also used as temporary erections of timber and fabric for important state occasions, and in varying forms were adapted as testers for beds, and over buffets — the *dressouer de parement* which appears in fifteenth-century inventories.

At the meeting-point of European influences, French furniture soon came under the subtle, influential spread of classicism. The process

was helped to a high point of achievement by the advance into Italy in 1494 of Charles VIII of France, intent on conquering Naples and recovering Angevin possessions elsewhere in northern Italy. Italian ideas began to interest seriously those young, ardent intellectuals who saw, beyond the sword-point, a world which had known, which had almost created, symmetry and order in architecture and decoration.

Charles VIII had been born in the Château of Amboise — he also died there — and was intent, even prior to his Italian campaign, on improving it. From Italy he brought back the Modenese sculptor, Guido Mazzoni, masons proficient in the 'antique style', decorators and garden architects. While hardly anything survives of their work their presence was an important means of diffusing Renaissance ornamentation throughout France. Abbot Antoine Bohier returned to Fécamp with Italian sculptures and later craftsmen to work on his church. The carved stone screens, made in about 1518, show in their pierced scrolling

and acanthus-type relief foliage the pre-occupation with a new ornamental form. The work is paralleled at many other French churches and in the decoration of tombs. It was pursued with royal obsession — imperious and demanding — by François I at Blois, Chambord and Fontainebleau. He succeeded Louis XII in 1515, and commissioned the Italian sculptors Antonio and Giovanni Giusti to provide, over the next 16 years, the splendid arched tomb at St Denis for his predecessor. All traces of Gothic were now banished, and courtly life at Amboise took on the mantle of the Italian Renaissance, with Leonardo da Vinci spending the last years of his life there. But François was concerned that the residence of the kings should be centred at Fontainebleau, and that power should be moved nearer to Paris rather than being wielded from the Loire valley.

The ideal was, however, somewhat removed from its realization. François I was defeated by the Holy Roman Emperor, Charles V, at Pavia in 1525 and imprisoned in Spain. After his return from Madrid and his reconciliation with the Emperor, François identified himself with the Catholic faith and the Papal alliance, with the active support of his sister, Marguerite de Navarre. He also set about making Paris his centre and in an elaborate building programme at several châteaux entrenched the Italian style — notably at the Château de Madrid, begun in 1528, and in a second phase of activity at Fontainebleau and Villers-Cotterêts. We only know what 'Madrid' looked like from the engravings of du Cerceau, whose depiction of a mantelpiece at the château shows it adorned with classical figures flanking armorials — motifs which lent themselves to Mannerist interpretation. This work was complex and flamboyant, and in contrast, the work of 1528 to 1540 at Fontainebleau may be seen to portray classical simplicity. It was almost entirely realized in the interior decoration by two major Italian artists, Francesco Primaticcio and Giovanni Battista Rosso. Primaticcio had trained and worked under the supervision of Raphael's pupil, Giulio Romano, and Rosso had worked in Florence and Rome.

It is the Galerie François I, Rosso's main creation, which survives—most of the stucco-work by Primaticcio having disappeared. If, however, one looks at the splendid mantelpiece in the Chambre de la Reine by Primaticcio, on its two Corinthian columns, and with sphinx-like and caryatid figures, it is easy to see how such motifs in all their promise of movement and elegant stance affected the furniture-makers. Rosso's Galerie has been much altered but as a room it is divided along its vertical surfaces almost equally by panelling (carved by an Italian, Scibec de Carpi), and in the upper part by painting and stucco figures. The intertwined strapwork, cut into elaborate stucco-shapes and based on Italian engravings, was an important decorative theme which spread throughout Europe.

The influence of the Fontainebleau decoration was well set out by the engravers and there is a remarkable series of dressers which follows drawings by Hugues Sambin and Androuet Du Cerceau. That in New York (in the Frick Collection) has caryatid figures at each corner and flanking the centre upper section, and has flamboyant scrolls terminating in lion's feet. An example in the Philadelphia Museum of Art has the figure of Minerva on the upper door, and five caryatid figures on the upper and lower stages. In France, a cabinet of about 1600 (Conservation des Musées, Tours) from the Château of Azay-le-Ferron is similar to an example now in the Wallace Collection, London. Both have an elaborate broken pediment with reclining figures, flanking a smaller, pedimented arch. All four doors are richly carved in relief and disposed within architectural columns or pilasters. This formality may have owed, in its title-page rigidity, just a little to Sebastiano Serlio, who had come from Italy in the 1540s to the court of François I's successor, Henri II. He was put in charge of works at Fontainebleau but his international reputation was to be secured by his important treatise on architecture which was widely disseminated and translated throughout Europe.

It is never wise in the documentation of French furniture of the Renaissance period to pay too much attention to regional variations. Many of them were led by the influence of the main centres and by Du Cerceau's engravings. Jean Goujon was partly responsible for the distinctive style of Normandy and Hugues Sambin of Dijon was known as the creator of the flamboyant and splendidly-fashioned furniture and carving for the allies of the Dukes of Burgundy. But these exceptional cases of regional originality led the field and were many years ahead of the anonymous host.

In 1539 there was published in Lyon a small

Left: A royal bedroom in the Château de Blois, France, one of a suite designed for François I between 1515 and 1524. The king developed a passion for building and decorating at a time when Italian influence was predominant. The bed has tapered, fluted posts of walnut and the mattress is set on a wooden platform. The tester is arranged so that the embroidered hangings can be fastened to its inner side and also suspended at the head of the bed. In this way, and almost for the first time, the bed could be totally enclosed overnight. (Château de Blois)

37

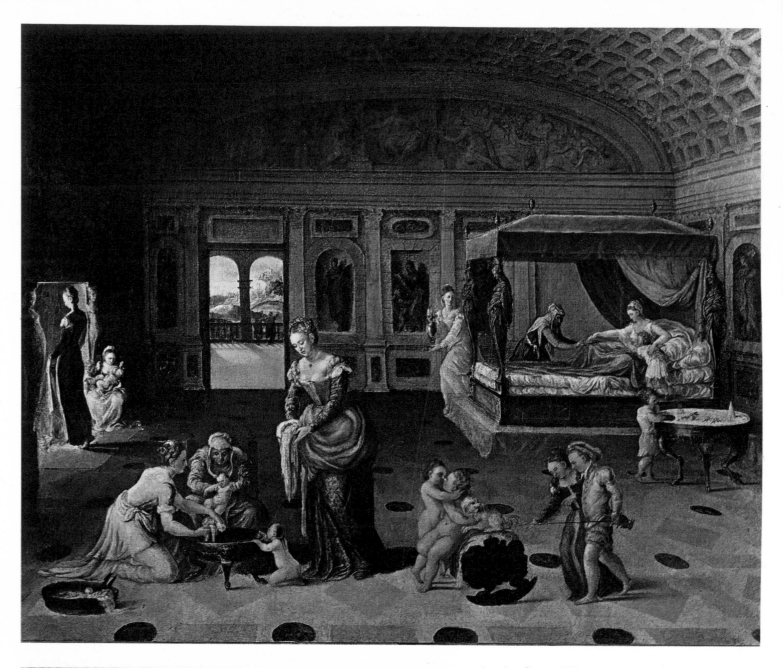

book by Gilles Corrozet, *Les Blasons Domestiques*. It set out a description of the furnishing of a gentleman's house, although it would be wrong to regard the observations on furnishing as typical of what was available. Corrozet thought that the *salon* should contain a bed, a buffet, a table and a chest as well as a great chair and several stools — there should be a concern for domestic comfort, rather than austere architectural forms. In particular the gradual disappearance of the chest — long a symbol of authority and importance — took place, to be replaced by the wardrobe, or *armoire*, which was sometimes incorporated into the panelling of the room in the way that corner-beds had been in earlier times. It was the older buffet in a new guise. Rooms were also changing their style and size, as they were required for dining and entertaining by smaller groups. This allowed the use of a smaller table than the long imposing ones made for refectory and great hall use, and it gradually took up its position at the centre of the room.. Each person also had his own stool, with a chair provided for the head of the family. An inventory of the Hôtel de Montmorency, home of Anne de Montmorency, taken in 1556 lists 'four dozen escabelles serving for all the house—eight demi-tables serving both for the said chamber of the king and for elsewhere'. The age of completely portable furniture, moved from room to room as needed, had come. The 'escabelle' was a low short bench, and had also appeared in the 1514 inventory of the possessions of Cesare Borgia, the warlike son of Pope Alexander VI, who had married a Frenchwoman.

The latter half of the sixteenth century in France was a period torn by religious wars—a bitter struggle between Catholics and Calvinists. The houses of Lorraine and Bourbon ranged in opposite camps and the violence registered itself in the arts of the period. The attitudes at the court of Henri III, however, continued to embrace cultural activity and in furniture appeared as an advanced form of Mannerism. The engravings of the elder du Cerceau and Hugues Sambin, the sculptures of Germain Pilon which reflected the earlier example of Cellini, and the paintings of Antoine Caron, Jean Cousin the Younger and the portrait-painters made important contributions. It might be said that furniture, useful, sophisticated and on occasion elevated to a high art, merely shook off the trappings of Gothic for the thin precise cloak of classical ornament. That would deny, however, the achievement of those, Sambin among them—his Maison Milsand at Dijon of about 1561 shows him as an accomplished architect—who created furniture in a conscious architectural form with its own decorative repertoire.

When Henri IV entered Paris as king in 1594 it was as head of a France worn out by civil war and strife with the Spaniards, and also uneasy under heavy taxation. Within four years he had secured relief from the invaders and his Edict of Nantes established a religious toleration that was to last to the late years of the seventeenth century. From 1598 there was the chance to give time to reviving trade and industry, and to the reconstruction of Paris by many ambitious town-planning projects. The crafts were given their own impetus by the setting-up in 1608 of workshops in the Louvre, with royal patronage and protection for artisans. The architect Salomon de Brosse, steeped in classicism, needed them for the decoration of châteaux and royal palaces. Progress halted and was then uncertain in the troubled period when the King was assassinated in 1610.

Henri had devoted considerable time and money to his residences, patronizing, in effect, the Second School of Fontainebleau. When he was killed the future Louis XIII was a minor and power passed for a short time to Marie de' Medici, an Italian with a taste for Flemish art and the skills of Rubens. Great mansions such as the Hôtel Chalois-Luxembourg and the Hôtel de Sully were erected for rich financiers and ministers—Sully was in the service of Henri IV. With precise inner courts and beamed ceilings (known as *plafonds à la française*) they reflected the architectural achievements of a new age which needed rich trappings to fill them. The state apartments of the long gallery or *galerie des fêtes* dazzled the eye, with mirrors, paint, stucco, gilding and silk fabrics. None more so than at Richelieu where the King's minister, Cardinal Richelieu, gathered around him treasures of furniture, painting and sculpture, which rivalled those of his royal master.

Under Richelieu, and more particularly his successor, Cardinal Mazarin, the middle classes increased their financial power and influence. This in turn filtered down to craftsmen in the form of commissions for paintings, furniture and works of art. Many

French artists went to Italy — Mazarin was Italian — and the taste of the Queen, Anne of Austria — Spanish by birth — was also affected by Mazarin's ideas and by the work of his compatriots. Marquetry inlay of tortoiseshell and pewter was to be highly developed. It reached a supreme point under Louis XIV by the work of the eminent André-Charles Boulle (1642–1732). The art of veneering in ebony was to be found in the work of Jean Mace who had been recalled from the Netherlands by Marie de' Medici. There was also a keen demand for furniture with legs and stretchers turned on the lathe in various complex forms. Upholstery was becoming more popular and was fringed and brass-nailed into subjection. When an inventory was drawn up for Mazarin in 1653 he had, in a bedroom, no fewer than 14 chairs of various kinds, of which the two armchairs were entirely covered with velvet nailed to the wooden frames. The rest of the bedroom was equally impressive, with bed-curtains and draperies for the bases and posts of the bed. Elsewhere in the house were 22 cabinets of ebony or tortoiseshell which had been made in Italy, the Low Countries or Germany. There were also Venetian mirrors and tables with

pietre dure inlays which stood beneath painted ceilings with Renaissance motifs.

France had lived through a long period of austerity and the underprivileged sections of the nobility and bourgeoisie endeavoured to right their position in a series of bitter struggles. The opposition group known as the Fronde, however, collapsed in confusion in 1653. With the power of the nobility thus eroded Louis XIV could divert them with the grandest of schemes — the settling of the court at Versailles. The King was 23 at Mazarin's death in 1661, and was ready to introduce all France to the rise of classicism in a series of great galleries and *salons*. They survive as witness to the fact that he achieved his aim in a style of complete grandeur.

Germany and Scandinavia

By the thirteenth century the Gothic style was dominant throughout Europe and had penetrated as far to the north and south as Norway and Portugal. It had spread rapidly and had also put its linear and patterned mark on metalwork and furniture. As very little German mediaeval furniture has survived even from the fourteenth century, it is difficult

Above: Detail from The Peasant Wedding by Peter Breughel the elder (c. 1525–69). This simple composition depicts a way of life in sixteenth-century Flanders unaffected by Italian ideas and status. The long refectory tables of joined planks of oak are flanked by long benches with splayed turned legs fitted into the upper seat. Such furniture was the creation of a joiner with a basic skill rather than a sophisticated repertoire of knowledge of ornament and design. (Kunsthistorisches Museum, Vienna)

to establish how rooms were furnished. It may be assumed that the poor used expediency and no small amount of ingenuity to provide simple necessities — tables, benches and stools — which always have a certain dateless anonymity and span the years. They are found in the Flemish paintings of country scenes by Peter Breughel the elder — his *Peasant Wedding* (in the Kunsthistorisches Museum, Vienna) shows a typical bench and stool with splayed legs, strong, unpretentious, and in consequence disregarded.

In 1969 Max Piendl discovered a careful inventory dated 1376 in the archives at Ratisbon listing the property of Erhard der Rainer who lived in Lower Bavaria. He owned three benches and four trestle-tables, all with cushions; a round table and a bench; eight chests of maple, spruce, pine and limewood; eleven cupboards together with two store cupboards, one of which was of oak. There were also nine small letter-boxes, three of maple. We may assume that Rainer had beds but the inventory page is missing — he had mattresses and bed-linen enough for all the servants as well as the family. Very little of his furniture was of oak, which was not often

used in southern Germany. Carved limewood and light-coloured maple of good grain served instead. With bright fabrics and a brocaded cloth threaded with gold for the table, the furniture in Rainer's house represented a good standard of living, and a sharp contrast to the peasant style.

By 1400 changes were taking place in Germany as a result of political, religious and economic expansion. The countries which now form Scandinavia, for example, relied on their trade connections with the ports of Hamburg and Bremen. There was a chance for itinerant craftsmen to succeed. Vert Stoss who lived for most of the latter half of the fourteenth century at Nuremberg was commissioned to provide a great carved altar in 1477 for the Polish city of Cracow. In triptych form it depicts the death of the Virgin Mary, surrounded by the twelve apostles. The two wings carry six representations of important moments in the life of the Virgin — carved with great virtuosity. It was this precise German skill which led to an even more important event than any altar by Vert Stoss — the invention in the mid-fifteenth century of printing. It was then possible with

Gutenberg's work with movable letters to combine them with impressions from woodblocks, and later copper plates, to issue patterns and pattern-books. Artists learned of each other's ideas — furniture-makers could copy from the work of the Masters HS and HG, Peter Flötner and others.

Recent research by Simon Jervis has done much to clarify the importance of printed furniture designs prior to 1650. They are essential documents for the understanding of the development of furniture in an obscure period, although many of the designs were also destined to be used by a wider range of craftsmen such as goldsmiths and embroiderers. Those that portrayed perspective were of more use to the furniture-maker and the inlayer. He could of course widen his practical experience, as Vert Stoss had done, by travel. It has been shown that of some 400 foreign craftsmen who had come to London between 1511 and 1621, several were from Germany — 12 from Cologne. There were also other artists, such as Dürer, heir to the great Gothic artistic traditions, who journeyed abroad — in his case to northern Italy and later to Venice — thus coming into contact with Renaissance philosophy and art. The

German engravers soon turned to classical ornament and the supremacy of Gothic declined in favour of the Italian examples. Peter Flötner of Nuremberg may have made two journeys to Italy in the 1520s and he became one of the principal exponents of the Renaissance style in Germany. His design for a wooden door of about 1540 is a flamboyant affair with richly decorated pilasters, a tympanum of swirling foliation, and urns and cherubs over all — fit for a Medici palace. His beds are equally grand, four-posted in the Corinthian style.

Presses and cupboards of various specialized kinds survive from the fifteenth century in some profusion. In southern Germany there was a two-tiered cupboard used in church sacristies as a secure place to keep plate and precious books. In the north the *Schenkschieve* was a four-doored cupboard, but was used in sideboard fashion to store plate and documents and, in versatile form, to serve drinks to guests. Made in maple, pine, larch and limewood, they have foliated friezes in strong vertical and horizontal bands and are sometimes covered with coloured leather.

There were of course variants of the two-tier cupboard evolved in south-west Germany,

Above: This painting by Bartholomew Bassen is an attempt to carry the Renaissance beyond the Alps — there are vistas through the architectural screens on the right and a wonderful fireplace with an elaborate overmantel. The two-stage dresser on the left is Gothic in origin, but the coffered ceiling and the caryatid figures flanking the intricate door indicate the pervading influence of Italianate decoration. (Hessisches Landesmuseum, Darmstadt)

Bavaria and Austria. The Austrian cupboards have ornament in low relief, and shallow carving is also found on Bavarian examples — lines of flowers in precise *paterae* formation. The cupboard was universally useful and had its counterpart in the horizontal, long chest which was used for storing linen and, on occasion, food. It was usually raised on a Gothic pierced plinth with two carrying handles, a hinged lid, and often a brightly coloured interior of green, red, or blue. Salzburg was an important centre for their manufacture, with panels of rich elaborate tracery being executed in limewood and inlaid with oak and maple. The origins of the decoration may be traced to northern Italy up to the southern edge of the Alps — a natural transfer-point for decorative detail.

Solid tables in limewood, pine and maple disposed together in the same piece are common — the *Wangentisch* of about 1500. The legs are splayed at an angle with a low surrounding stretcher which gives great stability. A rarer type *(Schragentisch)* had cylindrical legs, turned or carved, placed diagonally. Four of the tables listed in Rainer's house in Bavaria were of this type.

Beds of the Gothic period are unusually rare apart from their depiction in engraved form. The mediaeval bed was usually a part of a small separate room, built into the wainscoting. Another kind has a tester or canopy which hangs from a tall backboard and is architectural in form, in that the tester has timber 'vaulting' in architectural style. The use of different woods affected the decorative treatment. The north German use of oak allowed for deep carving with expert use of the chisel. The south German blend of various soft woods, often in the same object, dictated a low relief, two-dimensional carving. Its flatness demanded accentuation by the use of colour and the selection of woods with attractive grain.

The highest forms of German furniture in respect of style and skill were undoubtedly the elaborate writing-desks or cabinets and the works in chiselled steel, produced at Nuremberg and Augsburg. German cabinets were exported in considerable numbers in the late sixteenth and early seventeenth centuries. The trade was monopolistic and affected the Spanish furniture market in particular, to such an extent that Philip III in retaliatory spirit banned further imports of Nuremberg cabinets into Spain and Portugal. In form the cabinet developed from the *vargueño,* which has a fall-front serving as a writing area, to one with hinged central doors. These enclosed from immediate view a variety of smaller drawers which could be utilized for the safe keeping and distribution of all those items beloved of collectors — coins, medals, jewels, miniatures. Wood was used but the precious and semi-precious stones and filigree metal played no small part, the latter being an especial feature of Augsburg cabinets.

One of the most famous of the Augsburg cabinets, the *Kunstschrank*, was given a variant name, the *Wrangelschrank*, because Count Wrangel, commander of the Swedish forces in the Thirty Years War, took it as booty. It was made at Augsburg in 1566 and differs a little from the usual pattern in that its length is covered by two hinged doors. They open to reveal small drawers ornamented in boxwood flanked by coupled alabaster columns. They pale into a partial insignificance against the main doors which are decorated with intarsia of scenes of Hieronymus Bosch complexity showing animals and ruins.

In 1567 Lorenz Stoer issued his *Geometria et Perspectiva* at Augsburg — a book of designs for inlay on furniture reflecting his interest in the ruins of antiquity. Hieronymus Cock issued his *Preacipua Romanae Antiquitatis Ruinarum Monimenta* at Antwerp in 1551 which included many views of ruins. The same

Below: Detail of a splendid German cabinet made in Augsburg in about 1566, which epitomizes the effect of the Renaissance. Corinthian alabaster columns, gilding, inlays, pierced hinges and lock plate are all included, but it is the inlaid woods which amaze the eye with their intricate patterns. This cabinet is called Wrangelschrank, a variant of the usual name Kunstschrank, after Count Wrangel, Commander of the Swedish forces in the Thirty Years War. (Landesmuseum für Kunst und Kulturgeschichte, Munster)

Above: Presentation of the Pommerscher Kunstschrank. The cabinet in the painting was ordered in Augsburg in 1610 by Duke Philipp II von Pommera. It was finished by 1616 and presented to him in the following year. Regrettably, it was destroyed during the Second World War. (Staatliche Museen, Berlin)

preoccupation is found in France at this time in a suite of prints by Leonard Thiry published by Du Cerceau in 1550.

These cabinets came to a triumphal conclusion with a splendid series initiated by Philip Hainhofer, a diplomat-collector and owner of a successful art-export business who had been born at Augsburg in 1578. The *Pommersche Kunstschrank*, ordered in 1610 by Duke Philipp II von Pommera, was destroyed in the Second World War in Berlin. The *Florentiner Kunstschrank* was acquired in 1628 by Leopold, the Grand Duke of Austria, as a gift to the Grand Duke of Tuscany, and is now in the Palazzo Pitti in Florence. The *Kunstschrank* of Gustavus Adolphus was first in Hainhofer's own collection and was then acquired by the City of Augsburg as a gift to Gustavus Adolphus of Sweden in 1632 —it is now in Uppsala University. They were bright stars of achievement in an already dazzling firmament of accomplishment.

Both Augsburg and Nuremberg were renowned centres for the production of intricate gold and silver work in a high Mannerist style, and of complex clocks. In addition they gave attention to elaborate furniture in chiselled steel and some of the most splendid pieces were those given by the City itself as presents to other ruling bodies or influential individuals. In 1574 Thomas Rucker was commissioned to make a chair to present to the Emperor Rudolf II. After a hundred years in Prague it passed into Sweden and finally England, where it has remained. It has an elaborate four-tier top rail which illustrates the Babylonian, Persian, Greek and Roman

monarchies. The centre roundel depicts Nebuchadnezzar's dream.

Most German chairs were of course much less elaborate than these flamboyant pieces. The bench, popular in Gothic times, continued in use superseded by more convenient chairs with slightly raked backs, no armrests, and on occasion upholstered in the Italian manner. There was also a chair in common use of a decorated X-formation with a leather back and seat. It was a popular style, found in many countries throughout the Gothic and Renaissance period, but did not always fold as its earlier prototype, the folding-stool, did.

The start of the Thirty Years War in 1618, however, brought to a quick end the German supremacy in the creation of prestige furniture. A religious war, it was fought with great bitterness and had strong political and feudal overtones added to the struggle. Military violence was rife, and it embroiled most of the European monarchies before it came to an uneasy halt in 1648.

The main architectural styles current in Renaissance Europe did not penetrate the northern Scandinavian countries to any considerable degree. The main inspiration in Swedish architecture and decoration of the sixteenth century came from the Low Countries as the castles of Gripsholm, Uppsala and Kalmar show. It was a scene dominated by foreigners — German portrait painters worked in Denmark, and the court painter of the 1560s, Melchior Lorichs, had trained in Italy and was Mannerist in style. The decorative arts followed suit in their allegiance to Flanders, but were given some direct impetus by the great royal building patrons, Frederick II and Christian IV in Denmark and Eric XIV and John III in Sweden. But again it was Dutch, French and German architects who restored and extended old castles and built new ones and gave them furniture that came from workshops beyond the Alps. Even in Norway, which understood the uses of timber and had fashioned it in exemplary manner, the old Stave churches were not provided with furniture of quality or style.

We have also seen that the trophies of war carried back into Sweden were the great cabinets made at Augsburg. They spawned no copies and gave no inspiration to craftsmen mesmerized by intricacies they did not understand. The engravings of Hans Vredeman de Vries were, however, very influential in Sweden, as in Germany, England and the Netherlands, in showing what could be done.

The Low Countries

In 1508 the Flemish painter, Jan Gossaert, called Mabuse, left for Italy and on his return to Flanders introduced classical ideas of figure studies, poses and perspective into his painting. He was aided in the transfer of

Renaissance ideas on these subjects by the work of the designer Hans Vredeman de Vries (1527–1604), who had moved through Germany and the Low Countries living at various towns such as Antwerp and Hamburg. He was a prolific producer of series of prints which blended together his studies of Renaissance ornament, architecture, and gardens. They were published in numerous editions and had a considerable influence on architecture and decoration throughout northern Europe. In particular his *Differents pourtraicts de menuiserie* of about 1588 has designs for several sorts of furniture which joiners could show to undecided customers. It was a pattern-book of a most beguiling kind, ranging from stools, tables and buffets, to very elaborate beds, some with sphinx-like figures supporting fluted posts and canopies. His son Paul, born in Antwerp in 1567 — in a city which had become the principal centre of a Flemish school of painters won over to Italianate ideas — also produced designs suitable for use by furniture-makers. There is a mid-sixteenth century stone table at Lacock Abbey, Wiltshire, which bears a strong resemblance to one of his designs.

The work of the two de Vries, father and son, was widespread, and they poured forth engravings which joined those of many who were similarly talented. Two such were Cornelis Bos and, especially, Cornelis Floris. They published designs which incorporated the new type of interlacing strapwork which the Italians had taken into France when working for François I at Fontainebleau in the 1520s.

The important architectural treatise of Sebastiano Serlio, which spread knowledge of the orders of architecture throughout Renaissance Europe, was also given a Flemish translation in 1539. Serlio's engravings were those which in title-page formality could be enlarged into the three-dimensional form of furniture. They were also typical of those engravings which by their wide adoption rid the Low Countries and many other places of the last vestiges of Gothic furniture. The cupboard, always important in the Gothic period, took on several roles — of chest, of proud flamboyant statement, and of storage. Intricate carved figures adorned the door-panels and the best examples have caryatids which support, or appear to support, the richly decorated friezes. They were cabinets which followed the success of the trade-guilds in defining the respective roles of cabinet-maker and carver. The cabinet-maker made the carcase and the carver overlaid it with pierced ornament and showed his particular

Above: Frans Franken II's painting, The Living Room in the house of Peter Paul Rubens. While the chairs are shown as simple turned or pegged frames enhanced by leather backs and seats, the cupboard, with its canted pilasters and built-up stand at the back, is more Renaissance in feeling than the furniture of any Protestant country at this time. (Nationalmuseum, Stockholm)

Right: Fifteenth-century cabinet from Flanders. The mask faces, caryatid figures and Corinthian-capped pilasters show how architectural style affected furniture. The cabinet stands on a decorated plinth with ball feet at the front and plain ones at the rear so that it could be set against the wall. (Rijksmuseum, Amsterdam)

47

talent in the creation of the caryatid and other figures.

Like Augsburg in Germany, Antwerp became an important centre for production of fine cabinets. They were not in metal however, but were veneered and painted. They had the usual complicated, profuse and richly adorned sets of drawers in which gold coins, jewels, shells and other curiosities could be stored, or almost lost in interlocking labyrinths of secret drawers at the back of seemingly solid wood façades. Ebony was a wood which was extensively used for veneering these small drawers, and ebony cabinets were exported throughout Europe. Many of them were also painted with mythological scenes, or beloved stories from the Old and New Testaments. The most characteristic have tortoiseshell mounted against a reddish foil. This throws the tortoiseshell into sharp contrast, rendered even more striking by the black ebony veneers. The original stands have often been altered or replaced but usually consisted of eight tapered columns surmounting ball feet and a solid lower platform.

Ebony was also occasionally used for chairs, but walnut was more usual by the early seventeenth century. Some were upholstered or covered in leather, velvet or various cloths kept in position by large brass nails. An examination of Dutch portraits and genre paintings will show many detailed views of chairs, chests, screens and interior views. The sitters in Rembrandt portraits, for example, are frequently depicted on a form of folding-chair. The bed was also important and appears in many paintings, sometimes built into the corner of the room depicted. They are of a more human scale than any of those in the engravings of the de Vries and look as though they might have afforded a comfortable rest undisturbed by any architectural extravagances. They would appear soon enough at the introduction of the Baroque style into a Flanders which, as the centre of the Counter-Reformation, used all the devices of Catholic propaganda against the strongly entrenched Protestant reformists. Henri Pirenne has written that 'the entire society was worked on, and so to speak moulded, by religion'. The Jesuit movement introduced generations to Greek and Roman cultures and numbered amongst its ranks scholars, philosophers, painters, architects, and not least Peter Paul Rubens. With his vibrant sensibility and considerable skills Rubens was an able leader and exponent of all that was best in early seventeenth-century Flemish art. His great panels for the gallery of the Luxembourg palace in Paris, painted from 1622 to 1625, deal with the history of Marie de' Medici. They tell of reality and of myth and, above all, of a patronage to which all

artists from lowly carpenter to skilled carver
were indebted.

Spain and Portugal

The strongly Catholic country of Spain took
the classical rigours of the Renaissance in a
severe, reformist spirit. In its architecture it
prepared itself by ridding itself of Gothic and
in its material progress it could look to the
first 50 years of the sixteenth century as
witnessing the defeat of the Moors, the
discovery of America and the conquest of
Mexico and Peru. These were events which
were to excite the volatile temperament of its
people to abandon intellectual austerity and
lead them towards the heady exuberance of
Baroque. Spain concentrated its architectural
effort in the building of the palace and
monastery of the Escorial—at once a con-
tradiction in its geometry and austerity to the
richness which followed. It also had a long
period of regal stability in the reigns of
Charles V (1516–66) and Philip II (1566–98).
This encouraged every kind of creative
achievement, and in furniture the extensive
use of walnut, chestnut, poplar, pine and
orangewood gave exotic variants to what was
common elsewhere in Europe. The Americas
also had silver—particularly in Peru—and
this was imported and used in its normal role
and as a decorative addition to furniture.

In the Museo de Artes Decorativas in
Madrid it is possible to see a wide range of
furniture which displays the main woods,
fabrics and decorative motifs. Tables and
chairs were frequently hung with soft leather
or fringed brocade studded with large brass
nails. The chairs, called *sillónes de fraileros*,

are the most typical of Spanish seat furniture,
and were sometimes hinged to allow for folding
and easy transportation. Most tables were
covered with fringed 'table-cloths' and at a
later stage were given filigree iron stretchers
and ornate slender legs. Fabric also covered
the four posts of the bed, the ornament being
confined to the carved headboard.

The principal and richest piece of Spanish
furniture, however, was the cabinet with a
fall-front mounted on a stand. The vargueño,
as it has been called since the nineteenth
century, was usually placed on a stand (*pie
de puente*) and was frequently decorated in
the rich Plateresque style which resembled
the grotesque ornament found on silver work.
A superb vargueño in the Victoria and Albert
Museum, London, is in the usual walnut with
marquetry side panels, and the fall-front has
carved boxwood reliefs mounted on a velvet
ground, flanked by carved portrait heads.
Other versions have *trompe l'oeil* landscapes,
and some emulate the German Augsburg
silver cabinets by having gilt-bronze plaques
mounted in ebony.

In 1580 Philip II claimed the throne of
Portugal and united the two Iberian kingdoms.
During the seventeenth century its joiners,
carpenters and turners created a national
style of furniture-making which was outstanding in Europe for its use of extravagantly
turned rosewood, imported from the
Portuguese colony of Brazil. This was overlaid
with pierced ornaments in gilt-brass. The
great Benedictine and Cistercian abbeys in
northern Portugal had long needed choir
stalls, lecterns and monumental pieces of
church furniture and many of these were

garnished with gilt-brass. Both Spain and Portugal were obsessed with the search for precious metals in the New World, and these, together with brass, were then set over the walnut and local chestnut. During the second half of the sixteenth century Europe had been flooded with gold from the Americas. By the early seventeenth century this was no longer arriving and the colonial power of Portugal declined in the 1640s. Its furniture had long been influenced by trading contacts with the Orient and items appeared with lacquer and inlaid panels of ivory. Trade laid the basis, therefore, for the superb Baroque achievements in gilded and exotic woods which rivalled the finest in Europe.

England

By the time England's major writer and poet Geoffrey Chaucer died in 1400 the country had started the establishment of independence from French thought and contemporary European literature. The French had been setting the pace, too, in architecture with supreme achievements in the Gothic style, and Henry III's Westminster Abbey reflected this mood. But a growing disinterest in French ways led to the establishment of the Perpendicular style, a cheaper form of linear decoration in cut stone which appealed to generations who had been impoverished by war, the decline of agriculture and the ravages of the Black Death. Timber had always been abundant in England and the knowledge of working it had led to the creation of many fine roofs of hammer-beam type and also to the formation of strong guilds of joiners and of carpenters.

The hall of the great house was the hub of

Above: English armchair of about 1600, made of oak inlaid with various woods. The cresting and the brackets are carved with foliage. The legs and arm supports are fluted, the arms themselves being carved from a single piece of wood. (Victoria & Albert Museum, London)

Left: This early sixteenth-century English coffer has unusual horizontal linenfold panels, and is an example of the type of furniture made for small manor-houses or churches. (Courtesy of Leonard Lassalle, Tunbridge Wells)

50

*Above: English table
and chairs, made in about
1580, known as the
'Bromley by Bow' group, an
allusion to the old Palace
of Bromley by Bow in
London. The bulbous legs
of the table reflect Flemish
and German influences
introduced by itinerant
craftsmen and through
published designs. The
joined stools are made of
oak—stools with plain
wooden tops continued to be
made well into the
seventeenth century.
(Victoria & Albert
Museum, London)*

the family's existence and was impressive in its splendour. Hangings were rich and plentiful with the frequent use of covers and cushions made in dyed wool. There were heavy travelling chests—some in iron or iron-bound wood. Benches, boards on trestles, a dresser for the display of plate and great chairs at the high table were surrounded by ornate and abundant tapestries, illuminated books and manuscripts on lecterns, and musical instruments such as small organs and virginals. The religious devotion of the time found its expression not only in the building of many private chapels and parish churches but in their decoration. Apart from the splendid roofs — particularly to be found in the counties of Norfolk and Suffolk — choir stalls and rood-screens were lavishly embellished. The northern schools of woodcarvers who created the choir stalls at Lincoln, Ripon, Beverley and Chester were pre-eminent and their skill was also extended to the misericord seats with carvings of animals, foliage and domestic scenes of amusing reality.

The evident skill depicted in the carving of the misericords was not confined to church furniture. In the earlier house a sombre interior had been disguised by tapestry. The rising middle class now felt a desire for greater comfort and saw no reason why they should not pursue it. They wanted more furniture, better in construction by being framed and panelled rather than of simple design. At the beginning of Henry VII's reign the simple chests and walls were decorated with panelling of varying widths, pattern and Renaissance detail — particularly the Romayne style, where carved heads were surrounded by a classical wreath. When King's College Chapel at Cambridge was ready to be equipped in the early sixteenth century, the organ-screen (built in about 1532) was carved in full-blooded Renaissance style. It was a transitional point between mediaeval and modern. The hall of the house was still impressive but changes in hospitality, the use of servants and estate management meant that it declined in use. Other rooms became

more frequent and were defined by particular uses such as eating, relaxing and sleeping.

The most skilled furniture craftsman of this period of the early sixteenth century was the cofferer. The travelling coffer, usually of oak covered in leather, and tooled and gilt like an elaborate book-binding, was an important object for storage of papers, valuables and clothes. The early examples in iron had elaborate locking systems with inner and outer locks — a good example of 1427 is preserved at the Guildhall in London — and displayed an accomplished technique in their creation. There was still, however, a sharp demarcation between the oak furniture produced for church and small manor-house and the grander objects for the larger house in exotic woods such as ebony, holly and box.

The grand conception of Nonsuch Palace was planned in 1538 for Henry VIII by Nicholas Bellin of Modena, who acted as adviser to the chief officers of the King's Works. Bellin provided the link by which the Renaissance style, in all its jumble of Italian and French pattern, transferred to England. No effort was spared to make Nonsuch grand and enduring, though sadly it was pulled

down in the seventeenth century. A series of chests exists, heavily inlaid with designs representing formal architectural views — the so-called 'Nonsuch chests'. Recent research suggests, however, that this association was a nineteenth-century fantasy created because of a superficial resemblance of the marquetry panels to Henry VIII's palace. For the most part they represent contemporary buildings in the 'antique' style and were created by continental furniture craftsmen working in London in the late sixteenth century.

From this time the big houses of Elizabethan and Jacobean venturers incorporated not only Renaissance ideas of symmetry but also — as at Hatfield, Charlton and Bramshill — the well-proportioned loggias that suggested the white stucco and rich grotesque painting and furnishings of villas under a hot Italian sun. Furniture also started to incorporate within its repertory of decoration the interlaced strapwork that Rosso Fiorentino took as an idea from Italy to incorporate in his Gallery at Fontainebleau in 1535. Before long the Fleming, Cornelis Floris, was filling the pages of his pattern-books with it, and the Elizabethans prepared to abandon themselves

Above: The High Great Chamber of Hardwick Hall, Derbyshire. This house was built in 1597 for Elizabeth, Countess of Shrewsbury, 'Bess of Hardwick', to the designs of Robert Smythson. It typifies the emergence of the Renaissance in England. The marble chimney-piece is probably the work of Thomas Accres, a marble carver who also worked at Wollaton and the first Chatsworth. The details in the house are based on architectural pattern-books by Sebastiano Serlio and also reflect Flemish sources. (National Trust, Hardwick Hall, Derbyshire)

to a riot of robust and vulgar styles. Before the Reformation in 1534, however, England had been able to boast few 'gorgeous, sumpteous, superfluous buildings' despite all the opportunities which the decoration and furnishing of such houses gave to artists intent on furthering their skills.

One of the best documented of the late Elizabethan houses is Hardwick Hall, Derbyshire, the creation of the much-married Elizabeth, Countess of Shrewsbury — 'Bess of Hardwick' — and her architect, Robert Smythson. The death of her husband in 1590 made Bess very rich and she started at once to build a new and grander house than the one a few hundred yards distant on which she had been lavishing her attention. Hardwick was built over seven years, Bess moving into it in October 1597, and the famous inventory of its contents, dated 1601, was published by The Furniture History Society in 1971. It shows the humble alongside the grander pieces such as the famous table, still in the High Great Chamber. This was made in 1568 upon the marriage of Bess's son, Henry Cavendish, with her step-daughter Grace Talbot. Her coat of arms impaled by Henry's appears amid strapwork ornament upon the walnut top which is also richly veneered with a profusion of coloured woods depicting musical instruments — viols, lutes, rebecs, flutes and sackbuts — an open music book, flowers, playing cards and a romantic legend.

The use of marble on furniture, while so well understood in Italy, was rare in England. Another inventory — that of 1590 of the possessions of John, Lord Lumley — shows, however, in rare illustrations in the inventory itself such a marble-topped table on six bulbous legs. None of these inventory pieces is known to survive but the tables are shown in the company of marble cisterns, fountains and lavabos, decorated with the Lumley arms and owing much in form to the drawings of Du Cerceau. Richly upholstered chairs were just as fashionable and the Lumley inventory shows that in the three residences listed there were '76 chares of clothe of gold, velvet and sylke'. The Great Chamber at Lumley Castle also contained two draw-leaf tables — a type which could be extended by leaves beneath the main top and which seems to have come into use in the 1550s.

These late Elizabethan inventories also contain references to the court cupboard, an open structure of three tiers which resembled those in France and the Low Countries. It was used for the display of plate and pewter and at a later stage, when enclosed, for the storage of these items and of food. Beds followed the Renaissance pattern of a richly carved tester being supported on a carved and inlaid headboard, frequently depicting bas-relief portraits. The posts, which first came into use about 1500, were usually turned or made up, in more elaborate examples, of combinations of joinery and ornament — carved lion supports and strapwork and arabesque scrolls in box and holly. There is a superb example of about 1605 at Berkeley Castle, Gloucestershire, which has small figures in the framing of the bedposts.

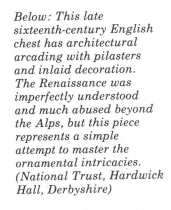

Below: This late sixteenth-century English chest has architectural arcading with pilasters and inlaid decoration. The Renaissance was imperfectly understood and much abused beyond the Alps, but this piece represents a simple attempt to master the ornamental intricacies. (National Trust, Hardwick Hall, Derbyshire)

The growth of trade which came about due to the efforts of the late Elizabethan merchant venturers encouraged an interest in the decoration of other countries and provided the means to indulge in copies. It also allowed for the occasional extravagance which can be found in the silver furniture at the great house at Knole, Kent, built for the Earl of Dorset about 1607. It was a period which recognized quality and even more acutely its absence. There was also an increasing use of walnut in less grand pieces than the silver pieces at Knole.

The early seventeenth century in England was characterized, however, by the influence of classical architecture. This was encouraged due to the travels of England's first strictly classical architect Inigo Jones, made in the entourage of Thomas Howard, second Earl of Arundel. The Earl became one of the greatest of English art collectors, was a leading figure in court circles and was intent on gathering works of art abroad. It gave Jones the opportunity to study Italian art and architecture for a second time — he had paid a previous visit to Italy in the last year of the sixteenth century. His return to England on both occasions gave encouragement to those intent on shaking off the rigours then imposed on interior design and furnishings. In 1615–16 Jones was appointed Surveyor of the King's Works, with all that meant in the supervision of work in the royal palaces. In the 10 years that followed his appointment he worked on

some 16 tasks for the King and Queen and other patrons of high rank. His approach was precise and moderate but the furniture in the interiors he created was, nevertheless, very elaborate.

The travels Jones and his contemporaries made accustomed English eyes to foreign decorative trends. Upholstery for the backs and seats of chairs came into widespread use in a growing search and demand for more comfort. At the same time there was much that was humble and practical. The university archives at Oxford contain hundreds of inventories of the 'goods and chattels' of 706

Top left: One of the 'Nonsuch' chests made in England about 1600. The front is divided into panels which are crudely inlaid. (National Trust, Montacute House, Somerset)

Above left: Early seventeenth-century English cupboard in carved and inlaid oak. (Temple Newsam House, Leeds)

university members from 1568 to 1699. Those for the early seventeenth century show the ways in which various rooms were furnished. The main wood in use was oak, with occasional exceptions referring to walnut, elm, deal, cedar and the sweet chestnut which John Evelyn noted in his *Silva* was, next to oak, one of the woods 'most sought after by the Carpenter and Joyner'. There were many varieties of table, but most chairs were versions of extended stools with plenty of materials available, by the start of the Civil War, for their upholstery. Various leathers, Turkey work, baize and other fabrics and rushes for wicker chairs have been listed. Couches, settles, close stools, beds, desks, chests and chests of drawers, cupboards and presses, boxes, screens, bookcases and candlestands are among the many items which furnished Oxford colleges. The greater items in gilt gesso were made in later years and belonged to those houses which Ben Jonson categorized in his poem *To Penshurst* — 'proud ambitious heaps and nothing else . . . '. The trauma of the Civil War and the death of Inigo Jones in 1652 sealed off the influences of the early years from those which followed the King's Restoration in 1660.

FORMAL SPLENDOUR
The Baroque age

Furniture is one of our most tangible links with the past, presenting us with direct visual evidence of a whole way of life centuries remote. Yet it can easily mislead. Without knowing from a whole range of other sources, from paintings and drawings, from contemporary literature and manuscripts, just how this furniture was placed and used, we could form the impression that these distant ancestors lived roughly in the same way as we do, that their tables, chairs and beds served just the same simple purpose as ours. Nothing could in fact be further from the truth, particularly with furniture of the Baroque period.

The Counter-Reformation, begun by the rigorous reforms of the Council of Trent in 1563, is always held to have precipitated the Baroque style, and there is no doubt that the arts were constantly employed to fulfil its primarily religious and political aims. Bernini's famous *St Teresa in Ecstasy* at Santa Maria della Vittoria in Rome, or Rubens' *Assumption of James I* on the ceiling of the Banqueting House, Whitehall, are unashamed propaganda, for Church and State respectively. Some of the most elaborate pieces of seventeenth-century furniture were made with the same obvious intention, like Prince Eugene's state bed at the Monastery of St Florian, borne by chained Turks to represent his relief of Vienna. The great beds with their gilded balustrades, the canopies of state, the tiered buffets with their dazzling displays of plate, even the more utilitarian pieces, like the endless chairs and stools in regimented rows along the walls, served equally for propaganda, though in a less direct way. They were the necessary equipment for the ritual of a prince's life, the stage props (appropriately, since their design was so often derived from the theatre) for the daily performance of kingship.

The divine right of kings, that favourite theory of the Counter-Reformation, produced in seventeenth-century Europe one of the most rigidly structured, hieratic societies ever to exist. Louis XIV's self-identification with the sun-god Apollo brought the theory to its most advanced, quasi-religious stage. His *levée*, his audience, his meals (taken invariably in the public gaze), his various entertainments, and finally his *coucher*, became the secular offices of the day, at which the courtiers of Versailles officiated—in the same way as priests observed the daily offices of Terce and Nones, Mattins and Vespers.

The extremes of formality to which this led, not only in France but in every country open to French and Italian influences, reaching a climax in the small German courts of the early eighteenth century, must be clearly understood to realize how Baroque furniture came to be made. A state bed like those

illustrated in the engravings of Daniel Marot is explicable only as a ceremonial object, an incredibly expensive but rarely used status symbol. The prince in his own palace, or the distinguished visitor to another's house, would be escorted by a large number of attendants and with great solemnity to his bedchamber, would be disrobed and put to bed. After the departure of the crowd, he would almost invariably retire to a smaller, warmer and far more comfortable dressing-room immediately behind the bedchamber. The balustrade served an even more ceremonial and less utilitarian role, separating those functionaries honoured enough to play an active part in the proceedings from those of lesser rank who merely observed from outside the bed alcove. The Duke of Portland as English ambassador to Louis XIV in 1698 was given the taper-stick to hold at one of the king's *couchers*, and this was considered a great honour since usually only Princes of the Blood were allowed inside the balustrade.

The Canopy of State, though comparatively few examples survive, was another key feature of the Baroque interior. The most likely explanation of its development is that it stems from the mediaeval practice of lords receiving requests, administering justice, and later even eating, from an armchair or throne on a raised dais with a canopy above. In time the chair and canopy became in their own right symbols of state, to which obeisance had to be made whether they were occupied or not. Strict rules existed for the proportions of canopies proper to each rank: the backcloth of a king's canopy for instance reached the ground, while a duke's would be shorter and an earl's still less. Strict rules also existed for the use of quite ordinary chairs and stools. In general, armchairs (which seem to have derived from the traditional X-frame chairs of state, and placed under canopies from the sixteenth to the mid-seventeenth century) were reserved for sovereigns only at court, and nobles in their own houses; chairs with backs could be used only by the most privileged (usually members of the royal family); and at Versailles it was a much coveted honour to be able to use either the stool called the *tabouret*, or the *pliant*, an X-frame folding stool. Most people had to remain standing.

The placing of furniture in rooms was invariably formal, and usually followed the same pattern, adopted all over Europe. Chairs were placed very close to each other in straight lines along inside walls, while against the pier between the windows stood an almost inevitable set of matching furniture: a pier-glass with a table under it, flanked by a pair of candlestands or *guéridons*. Over and over again this arrangement can be found, executed

in different techniques: from ebony Goanese sets of the 1650s, to Dutch and English floral marquetry of the 1680s, to Boulle and silver sets of the next decade and to gilt gesso versions of the early eighteenth century. Such was the rigidity of Baroque furniture arrangement that Louis XIV is said to have sharply rebuked one of his mistresses who had brought out a chair and left it in the middle of the room, thereby destroying its architecture. The almost complete absence of furniture in the centre of a Baroque interior is perhaps slightly misleading, for at any time chairs could be brought out from the wall by footmen and card-tables or eating-tables set up. These were, however, only temporary arrangements and the architectural character of the *chambre de parade* was at all other times preserved.

The use of allegory, that favourite Baroque device, became more and more standardized in the decoration of different rooms: staircases would be painted with Assemblies of the Gods, so that receptions of ambassadors or concourses of courtiers should be appropriately mirrored by the divinities above; antechambers used for dining now might have Ganymede or Bacchus to inspire the company below to food and drink; bedchambers told the story of Psyche; and long galleries the Labours of Hercules. Furniture, made always for a particular place in a particular room,

Above: A great lady at her toilette, from an anonymous picture by a late seventeenth-century French artist. This crudely painted but charming evocation of contemporary life shows the typical arrangement of a Baroque state bedchamber: the bed itself stands in an alcove, with tall chairs, usually called backstools, ranged in straight lines against the walls on either side. (Musée des Beaux Arts, Rheims)

was of course influenced by this iconographical plan. Tables used in eating-rooms began to be decorated with vine leaves, and chairs in bedrooms to be carved with cupids holding bows and arrows.

The sequence of rooms also followed a strict pattern in practically every Baroque house, from stuccoed palaces in Sicily to granite castles in Scotland. The progression from great staircase to guard, presence, withdrawing and bedchambers, with closets and 'cabinet' rooms beyond, became almost universal, even if certain rooms assumed greater importance in some countries than in others. At Versailles, for example, the sequence began from either side of the building converging on the King's bedchamber in the centre, while in Germany a gigantic staircase (or *Treppenhaus*) with an equally vast hall of assembly usually occupied the centre leading to suites of apartments either side.

In general, while the size of the rooms diminished during this progression, the decoration and the furniture became richer. Eventually those fortunate enough to have a private interview with the great person might be ushered through the state bedchamber to a room no more than nine or ten feet square, either hung with the most expensive Genoa velvet and with the choicest small pictures from the collection, or, as in Queen Mary's Water Gallery at Hampton Court, crammed with porcelain crowded onto the walls on tiny brackets — or laden with glass as at Frederik IV's castle of Rosenborg in Denmark. 'Cabinet' rooms like these, partly developed from the idea of the Renaissance princes' 'Wunderkabinetts', were also devised to give some privacy, impossible in the vast halls and galleries at the centre of the palace, permanently thronged with suitors. The clear distinction between state-rooms, used solely for great occasions and for public display, and private apartments, used for everyday living, began to develop gradually during the Baroque period, though it did not reach its fullest expression until houses like Holkham and Kedleston, later in the eighteenth century, were built with entirely separate family wings. The Baroque 'cabinet' room or closet pointed the way to this solution however, and with its upholstered furniture pioneered a wholly new attempt at comfort, with 'sleeping chayres' (as they are described in English inventories) whose backs could be adjusted by means of ratchets, daybeds, wing chairs and 'squabs' — low, caned stools with small frames and enormous cushions. All these were of course supplied by upholsterers who, towards the end of the seventeenth century, began to supplant the carvers, up to that time easily the most important Baroque furniture-makers.

60

*Left: The ante-chamber to
the Queen's Bedchamber
at Ham House, Surrey,
furnished by the Duchess
of Lauderdale in the 1670s.
It exemplifies the passion
for lacquer, part of the taste
for the exotic which was so
typical of the Baroque era.
The artificially grained
wainscoting, the damask
and velvet wall-hangings,
and the placing of the
furniture around the walls
are all as they would
have been originally.
(National Trust, Ham
House, Surrey)*

More important than this change, however, is the emergence during the Baroque period of a new phenomenon, that of the universal designer. The seeds of this idea, as with so many other components of the style, are to be found in early seventeenth-century Rome, with the total unity of Bernini's, Borromini's or da Cortona's church interiors. The extension of this practice to secular interiors quickly followed and spread north. As might be expected it received its strongest expression at Versailles where Charles Le Brun and Jean Bérain between them controlled absolutely, thanks to the ruthless order of Colbert's system, the appearance of every room. Their dictatorship in matters of design was helped by the strict guild system operating in France, which meant that an important piece of furniture might have to pass through the hands of five or six master-craftsmen working in different workshops at different techniques. Obviously the co-ordination of a *dessinateur* was essential to ensure harmony and unity in the final result.

In the hands of Bérain's most famous pupil, Daniel Marot, this treatment of whole rooms as a unity spread to Holland and England. The Adam brothers are often credited with being the first to design complete interiors 'in key', from plasterwork ceilings to carpets to sofas and tables and even door-knobs; in reality Marot was doing exactly the same 70 or 80 years earlier. His engraved designs cover every aspect of the decorative arts — patterns for silks, sedan chairs, clocks, beds, chairs,

garden urns, painted ceilings — and his series of views of rooms show the care with which even the smallest piece of furniture had been designed and placed to achieve an effect of unity.

Unlike the spread of Renaissance ornament through Europe, which was a relatively uncomplicated northward movement, the Baroque is difficult to trace geographically. To follow its course country by country, as in the following pages, can therefore be misleading. While Italy, for instance, can be said to be the cradle of the Baroque, one of its most distinctive forms of furniture, the massive pietra-dura cabinet, was almost certainly derived from furniture made in Antwerp, Augsburg and Nuremberg. In other countries, such as Portugal and Holland, furniture design and technique was at least as much influenced by their contacts with the East, as with other parts of Europe. The discovery of new techniques in themselves gave certain places a virtual monopoly of certain pieces: the perfection of veneering made the Low Countries the home of floral marquetry from the early seventeenth century, while England after the Restoration was similarly the primary source of clocks. The Baroque was in fact a truly international style, not only because of the increase of imports and exports (velvet from Genoa, leather from Spain, marble from Livorno) but because the improvement of communications also brought increased mobility. In the past famous foreign artists had been summoned to distant courts — Torrigiani by Henry VII, Leonardo by François I — but from the middle of the seventeenth century more obscure sculptors, plasterers or furniture-makers began to move of their own accord to wherever the greatest demand for their services appeared to be. Louis XIV's expulsion of the Huguenots certainly played a large part in the diffusion of French Baroque forms to the rest of Europe, but it is interesting that a number of the best craftsmen who left France in the 1690s were in fact Catholics, forced to find employment elsewhere after the closure of the Gobelin factory and retrenchment at Versailles to pay for Louis' wars.

The inter-marrying of so many furniture-making, designing, carving or painting families also began to set up such a complicated international web of relationships that it is hard to disentangle influences and movements generally. It is typical for instance that the Flemish-born Pierre Golle, perhaps the most famous *marqueteur* in Paris before Boulle, should at the time of his death have owed money for glue and nails to a London cabinet-maker, John Johnson. Golle's brother Cornelius was another furniture-maker, practising in England, and both were brothers-in-law of Daniel Marot, William III's architect

63

in The Hague. In turn Marot's own family included two engravers, four furniture-makers, five painters and a goldsmith, divided almost equally between France and Holland. Relationships such as these are typical, and should be a warning against seeing Baroque furniture simply in terms of national characteristics, distinct as these may seem initially.

Political and economic touchstones are rather safer. The Baroque has already been described as the style of absolutism, and in general the more despotic the system, the grander and more elaborate its setting. Florence under the later Medici and Venice under its oligarchy (a republic but scarcely a democracy), France under Louis XIV and the German courts after his death, reactionary and traditionalist, are the true homes of the Baroque. In England it was a court style abruptly halted after William III's failure to control Parliament and the advent of a limited monarchy in 1714. In the Low Countries, comparison between Rubens' house in Antwerp with its exuberant twisted columns and rich furniture, and the Town Hall in Amsterdam, altogether more restrained and classical, a monument to civic pride, leaves no doubt as to the political connotations of the style. It was no accident that the financial collapse in France after Louis XIV's death, and the more relaxed social atmosphere of the Régence, should have brought about the birth of a new and less rigid style, the Rococo.

Italy

Like so many useful words which have come to sum up a whole ideal, whether political or artistic, the Italian *barocco* began life as a term of abuse. Originally used by those still steeped in the order and balance of the early Renaissance to describe the tortured and grotesque, almost surrealist, exaggeration of Giulio Romano and his followers, we now think of the Baroque more as a synthesis of those two opposing attitudes — as seen in the work of Bernini and Cortona. Movement is still the key to their work (and even more to the work of Borromini), but it is balanced in the play of forces, in projection and recession, whether applied to a whole façade or to a mere confessional. The excitement is there, but it never oversteps the bounds of authority.

As an authoritarian, propagandist style the Baroque is often held to have been born at the Council of Trent in 1563. But although the new militant atmosphere of the Counter-Reformation undoubtedly affected painting and sculpture in the following generation, it was not until the early seventeenth century that this impetus began to reach the decorative arts. As always it was a case of supply and demand. Rome, which had remained weak and underpopulated ever since its sack by the French in 1520, was now once more the seat

of a powerful Papacy, entering perhaps the period of its greatest prosperity. Vast town-planning schemes and the rebuilding of innumerable *palazzi* resulted in a ferment of creative activity.

Utilitarian furniture for the private apartments of these great houses continued to be made extremely simply by carpenters or joiners and little effort was made, unlike in England and France later in the century, to make these pieces of any artistic value. For the state apartments, however, and in particular for the gallery which was where the best pictures were hung and where the artistic ambitions of the great Roman families were primarily displayed, huge console tables or cabinets were made by leading sculptors, fresh from carving statues for churches or fountains. A legacy of the Renaissance still

Above: The nuptial chamber in Villa La Rocca, Soragna, in northern Italy, decorated in about 1690. The ceremonial character of a Baroque state bedchamber is clear from this dazzling gilded room which is more like the chancel and high altar of a cathedral than a domestic interior. (Villa La Rocca, Soragna)

64

very much alive in seventeenth-century Rome was the idea of the artist as an all-round craftsman, to whom painting a Crucifixion, carving a *Pietà*, designing a church or making a piece of furniture ought to come equally easily.

This influence of sculpture on Roman Baroque furniture was to be of paramount importance for the spread of the style all over Italy, and later in the century to the rest of Europe. Perhaps the best known piece of furniture ever made, Bernini's great Throne of St Peter, a giant's chair borne aloft on a swirl of clouds at the east end of the Apostle's own basilica, became a model for the huge gilded Baroque thrones which stood in the Audience Chambers of Roman princely families like the Pamphili or the Borghese. The console tables with thick tops of jasper

imported from Sicily, or of marble from elsewhere in Italy, were often supported by near life-size figures, like the famous Turkish captives at the Palazzo Colonna. A splendid pair of tables at the Palazzo Spada, made for Cardinal Bernadino Spada's new wing designed by Borromini in the 1640s, each have two great eagles supporting the slab on their heads and outstretched wings. Perhaps the ultimate in this totally representational approach to furniture was the state bed designed by Bernini's pupil J P Schor for the lying-in of the Princess Colonna in 1663. In the form of a huge shell, it was borne across windswept waves by four seahorses, while, above, a dozen or more putti held back gold brocade curtains.

In general, beds in Rome, and elsewhere in Italy, were not made with canopies until the late seventeenth century; their decoration

was then confined to heavily carved posts at the four corners. If console tables with their thickly gilt sphinxes, tritons, putti or mermaids were the most ambitious pieces, a certain number of cabinets were also made. But these mostly date from after 1650 and were inspired by Florentine or northern precedents. One particularly fine example with ivory reliefs after famous paintings, designed by the architect Carlo Fontana and made between 1678 and 1680 by the brothers Domenico and Francesco Stainhart, is at the Palazzo Colonna.

In Venice, as much as in Rome, state-room furniture was almost entirely the province of the sculptor, and if anything the division was wider between simple functional pieces which filled the family apartments at the top of every palazzo, and the massive ornament-loaded furniture intended for the vast rooms of the *piano-nobile* looking over the Grand Canal. Longhi's genre scenes of Venetian life never show one of those armchairs carved all over with wriggling putti, or those overloaded tables, only the plainest leather-seated back-stools and ungilded cabinets in the family apartments. Evidently, sumptuous furniture was not only made by sculptors but regarded in the same light as sculpture: strictly to look at, and not to use.

Undoubtedly the greatest Venetian furniture-maker of the seventeenth century was Andrea Brustolon. Born in Belluno in 1662 and employed first of all on carving crucifixes for local churches, he went to Venice and became at the age of 15 an assistant to the Genoese sculptor Filippo Parodi then working on the tomb of a Venetian patriarch, Francesco Morosini, for the church of San Nicolo da Tolentino. Contemporary documents tell us that Brustolon planned a visit to Rome, but not whether he actually went. His naturalistic and allegorical approach to furniture, however, may well be derived from Roman practice. Brustolon's fame rests on only one securely documented suite of furniture, the amazing chairs, side-table and candlestands made for Pietro Venier and now at the Ca' Rezzonico in Venice. On the basis of this, however, he has been credited with several other sets in the same style, amongst them one for the Correr family (now also in the Ca' Rezzonico) and one for the famous villa of the Pisani at Stra (now in the Quirinale Palace, Rome). The Correr chairs are if possible even less functional than the Venier suite. Their attenuated figures borne on a tidal wave of acanthus leaves must be some of the most beautiful and uncomfortable armrests ever devised. In 1699 Brustolon returned to his

Above: The Brustolon Room in the Palazzo Rezzonico, Venice, contains a famous suite of furniture made for a Venetian patrician, Pietro Venier, by Andrea Brustolon (1662–1732), the greatest Venetian sculptor-cum-cabinet-maker of the late seventeenth century. The vase stand on the left, made to hold three huge Oriental porcelain jars, incorporates the figures of Hercules, Cerberus, the Hydra and Classical river gods carved in boxwood. The guéridons are in the shape of negro captives with boxwood chains around their necks. (Ca' Rezzonico, Venice)

Right: A prie-dieu, veneered in ebony with pietra-dura mosaics and lapis lazuli columns. This piece, finished in 1687, is the work of the Grand Ducal workshops in Florence under the direction of Leonardo van der Vinne. The use of semi-precious hardstones is typically Florentine, though the openwork decoration round the central monogram of Christ is more unusual and demonstrates the northern influences of van der Vinne. (Palazzo Pitti, Florence)

here may even explain how candlestands came to be called 'guéridons', a word derived from a famous Moorish galley slave.

Above all, however, Venice was known for its glass. Since the late Middle Ages, the islands of Murano and Torcello in the Venetian lagoon had become centres of a glass-making industry unrivalled in Europe until Colbert's establishment of a factory in Paris in 1665, and the growth of England's Lambeth and Vauxhall works after 1700. Besides the large plates which were so much in demand, the Venetians developed for their own use elaborate glass sconces (wall lights) shaped like Baroque cartouches, and the enormous chandeliers still so much a feature of Venetian palaces, glowing with multi-coloured flowers and white opaque glass branches.

In many ways the development of Baroque furniture in Genoa followed a parallel path to Venice despite their distance from each other in geographical terms and their frequent conflict of mercantile interests. The system of oligarchic government in both meant that a certain number of immensely powerful families, some old, some *nouveau riche*, but all determined to outdo their rivals in ostentation and prestige, created a tremendous demand in architecture and the arts. In Genoa one particular street, the Strada Nuova (now Via Garibaldi) became, like the Grand Canal, lined with palaces jostling against each other

Below right: The Doge's throne, made in Venice about 1725, probably by Antonio Corradini. Corradini's work forms something of a bridge between the Baroque and the Rococo styles. The putti and mermaids riding horses are in the old allegorical tradition (referring to Venice's naval traditions), but the C- and S-scrolls which give movement to the whole composition point to a lighter and freer style in the years ahead. (Ca' Rezzonico, Venice)

native Belluno where he died in 1732, and where many of his furniture designs in this same extravagant style can still be found in the Museo Civico.

Brustolon's immediate successor as the leading furniture-maker in Venice seems to have been another sculptor, Antonio Corradini. The peculiarly Venetian use of natural woods in strong, contrasting colours was abandoned by him in favour of the more usual Baroque method of gilding, quicker and easier for the carver since it enabled soft woods like pear and lime to be used. A splendid throne by Corradini in the Ca' Rezzonico shows in its bold curves and scrolls how wood could be made to look as tractable and plastic as plaster. Another kind of furniture for which Venice became famous in the late seventeenth and early eighteenth centuries was lacquer, the technique of japanning having been learnt early on through Venice's trading contacts with the East. Green and gold lacquer, like the splendid set of furniture at the Palazzo Querini-Stampalia, became something of a speciality and continued to be made right through the Rococo period. Ebony blacka-moor candlestands were again a typically Venetian form, much sought after by foreign travellers and the epitome of the Venetians' love of carnival and fancy dress. Their origins

67

on both sides. Their forbidding exteriors, immortalized by Rubens' celebrated engravings, concealed an explosion of gilding, mirrors and rich textiles within. Again like Venice, the initial impetus came from Rome: Filippo Parodi (1630–1702), perhaps the best-known Genoese carver of the late seventeenth century, worked in Bernini's studio from 1655 to 1661 and the three-dimensional nature of his furniture, and that of his son Domenico, is explained by the fact that both were primarily sculptors in marble. Domenico Parodi (1668–1740) was the maker of a combined pier-glass and table, now in the Palazzo Rosso, Genoa, which has claims to be one of the most megalomaniac pieces of furniture ever made. But another sculptor, Anton Maria Maragliano, was equally adept at monumental work of the same kind.

Genoa's major contribution to the Baroque interior was, however, the development of the richest furnishing materials to be obtained anywhere in Europe. Rich cut velvets in reds, greens and yellows, damasks woven for the first time in several colours, and silks either from Genoa itself or from Livorno, were exported to countries as far away as Scotland and Sweden. The availability of these materials with their huge bold patterns, for wall-hangings, for upholstering chairs and beds, for curtains or costume had an incalculable effect on all these branches of design from about 1680 onwards.

Turin in the seventeenth century had little separate identity from Genoa in the decorative arts. Still something of a backwater, its leading lights, like the Swiss-born Daniele Seiter, who is supposed to have designed much of the furniture in the Palazzo Reale as well as painting its ceilings, relied very much on Brustolon and Parodi models for the carved figures enmeshed in acanthus which support their tables. If there is a difference, it is a slightly tighter architectural control of the whole composition, perhaps influenced by French furniture of the same period. It was not until the arrival of Filippo Juvarra from Rome in 1715 that Turin became an important artistic centre in its own right. For the palace of Stupinigi built to his designs by Vittorio Amadeo II and begun in 1729, Juvarra realized many of the Baroque furniture designs he had incorporated in his earlier stage sets: pier-tables on piles of military trophies, enormous clocks flanked by sphinxes with butterflies' wings, or tripod stands culminating in three rams' masks—the last uncannily prophesying one of Adam's favourite ideas. The Roman inspiration for these pieces is clear but Juvarra brought to them a far more architectural discipline and concern for proportion than had hitherto been the case in furniture designed and made by sculptors. Juvarra's unmistakable architectural vocabu-

Left: A combined pier-glass and table by the Genoese sculptor, Filippo Parodi (1630–1702). Parodi's six year apprenticeship in Bernini's studio in Rome explains his three-dimensional approach to furniture. This extraordinary piece has claims to one of the most megalomanic pieces of furniture ever made. About 19 feet (6 metres) high, the glass emerges out of a vast triple shell and appears to be held aloft by a squadron of flying putti. (Museo di Palazzo Rosso, Genoa)

Right: The Elector Palatine's Cabinet, executed in the Grand Ducal workshops at Florence between 1707 and 1709, and sent as a gift to the Electress from her father, Cosimo III of Tuscany. The cabinet, in ebony with pietra-dura inlay and gilt-bronze mounts, was designed by Foggini, at that time head of the Uffizi workshops, and he was also personally responsible for the figures, including that of the Elector in the central niche. This piece has been rightly acclaimed as marking the peak of Florentine cabinet-makers' craftsmanship. (Palazzo Pitti, Florence)

lary, his canted corners with convex or concave curves and his partiality for ovals and ellipses, had a profound effect on Turinese furniture of the early eighteenth century. The tradition was continued in the outstanding marquetry furniture of Pietro Piffetti, despite the latter's fluent use of Rococo ornament to clothe what remained essentially Baroque forms.

Florence lies somewhat outside the mainstream of Italian Baroque furniture in the seventeenth century, largely because of its peculiarly different system of despotic government under the later Medici. The Grand Ducal workshops, first organized by Cosimo I in the galleries of the Uffizi early in the century, became the centre for the manufacture of *pietra dura* (literally 'hard-stone') inlay, an immensely time-consuming technique of marquetry using different coloured pieces of highly polished marble. The organization of the workshops is of the greatest interest, first because it shows how the most splendid pieces produced were the result of a co-operative effort by a whole range of different craftsmen, all paid by the Duke, and second because it was to be the model for the Gobelins as conceived by Louis XIV and realized by Colbert. At the head was always a renowned artist, architect or sculptor, upon whose initial sketches, and at whose orders, almost every work of art or piece of furniture was produced. Initially this director of the *Galleria* was Buontalenti, and after him respectively P M Baldi, G M Marini and G B Foggini. Under the director came the *capomaestri* or heads of workshops, paid a fixed annual income, and under them the *cottimanti* or junior craftsmen, paid by the week: cabinet-makers, pietra-dura carvers (later removed to their own organization, the Opificio delle Pietre Dure, which still exists), as well as goldsmiths, casters, carvers and weavers.

The *stippone*, or great cabinet, which became the most characteristic product of the Florentine workshops, seems to have had a German derivation. Several Augsburg cabinets given to Cosimo I in the early years of the seventeenth century seem to have been imitated by the craftsmen in the Grand Ducal workshops, and under Ferdinand II, who reigned from 1621 to 1670, the characteristic combination of ebony, pietra dura and gilt bronze came to be developed. Ferdinand's own cabinet, which now stands in the Tribuna of the Uffizi, and a prie-dieu made for him now in the Museo degli Argenti, became the prototypes for pieces made well into the eighteenth century, so strong were the conservative traditions of the workshops.

An attachment to earlier models also explains how the *sgabelloni* and wooden stands for busts or vases originally designed by Buontalenti continued to be made up to the end of the seventeenth century. Some new types were evolved it is true, and the influence of Rome here was by no means negligible. Both Marini and Foggini came under the spell of Bernini: Foggini's showcase for the amber collection of Cosimo III recalls J P Schor's Colonna bed, while some side-tables supported by harpies and sirens, designed by Marini rather earlier, borrow an undoubtedly Roman theme, even if they are treated with a typically Florentine restraint and sense of architecture.

Pietra dura, although it remained the most famous, was by no means the only technique at which the Grand Duke's craftsmen excelled. Silver, and also steel, furniture was produced by the Galleria in some quantity. In about 1667 the arrival of an extremely accomplished Flemish or Dutch cabinet-maker, Leonardo van der Vinne, introduced the art of floral marquetry. Van der Vinne became in 1677 head cabinet-maker in the Ducal workshops, at a higher salary even than successful contemporary painters like Livio Melhus. A superb cabinet at the Pitti made by him about this date rests on a stand with ten blackamoor supports, and has four tables *en suite*, all inlaid with flowers in ivory as well as different woods.

The great strength of the Florentines was their lack of distinction between the major and the minor arts. G B Foggini as well as making designs for furniture personally executed silver statuettes and gilt-bronze ornaments for some pieces. Nor did the Grand Duke Ferdinando think it beneath his dignity to have Filippo Sangher, a lathe-turner and ivory worker by profession, as his 'uomo di fiducia', or right-hand man: both the Duke and his brother Gian Gastone practised ivory-turning themselves on occasion as a branch of science. Perhaps the peak of Florentine furniture-making was reached with the marvellous Elector Palatine's Cabinet, designed by Foggini, and made between 1707 and 1709, uniting all the skills then available in the Ducal workshops. Luckily for Florence it was later brought back to the city by the Elector's childless widow, along with an equally splendid prie-dieu made for her the previous year, 1706.

After this date, the quality of Florentine furniture design became somewhat stultified. Even the supremely inventive Foggini, designing a large table in 1716, could return for his model to a table-top (still in the Galleria Palatina) designed by Jacopo Ligozzi as early as 1649. The only breath of fresh air came from outside the Grand Ducal workshops, in the development of *scagliola*, the technique of painting on fine wet plaster, which was polished when dry. Enrico Hugford, a monk of English origin, is credited with the invention of this technique in Florence early in the eighteenth century, and another early practitioner was Piero Antonino Paolini, born in Lucca, the maker of a marvellous table dated 1732, now in the Museo degli Argenti. But scagliola only reached perfection later in the century, for instance in the superb work of Lamberto Gori; its flexibility and pastel colouring made it an ideal vehicle for Rococo ornament.

It is clear that the Baroque style lasted so long in Florence only because it was kept alive by the family piety of the last Medici and their reactionary policies. The religious mania of Cosimo III and his lugubrious daughter Anna Maria Luisa, the Electress Palatine, also played its part in seeing that sombre ebony and pietra dura continued to be made to the end of their lives — in marked contrast to what Louis XIV wished for in his last years '. . . de la jeunesse et de la gaité partout'.

France

The strong ties between France and the Protestant Netherlands, cemented by the struggle against Spain, and the equally strong ties between France and Florence, forged by two formidable Queens, Catherine and Marie de' Medici, were to have important results for the whole development of French furniture and decoration. During the gradual

recovery from the civil wars of the late sixteenth century, the nobility began to rebuild their houses in Paris, encouraged by Henri IV's example in embellishing the Louvre. The increased demand for furniture and works of art was met by a steady influx of foreign craftsmen, who settled generally in the area of the Faubourg Saint-Antoine. Here the strong mediaeval guild of joiners and furniture-makers could not enforce their monopoly as the land belonged to the nuns of Saint-Antoine and was therefore technically outside the bounds of the city. At first the majority of the immigrants were Flemish or Dutch, bringing with them new techniques of

veneering and marquetry, but Germans and Italians also followed in the period after the accession of Henri IV, when France at last entered a period of security and prosperity.

From the first, leading furniture-makers benefited by the protection and encouragement of the King. In direct imitation of Cosimo I's Galleria in the Uffizi, Henri IV and Louis XIII housed craftsmen in workshops under the Grande Galerie of the Louvre, which linked the old palace with the Tuileries — amongst them Michel Campe, Pierre Boulle (father of the famous André-Charles), Jean Mace and Laurent Stabre. The period during and just after Mazarin's ascendancy was dominated by two great furniture-makers, one Flemish in origin, Pierre Golle (or Gole), the other Italian, Domenico Cucci. Golle's early furniture made in France consisted almost entirely of great cabinets, probably based on Augsburg and Antwerp models. These began as ebony pieces, usually with exquisitely carved scenes on the doors or the fronts of drawers giving an effect of polished black ivory. After about 1660, however, they became more and more richly inlaid with other materials, different coloured marbles, lapis and tortoiseshell. A technique in which Golle specialized still later was brass inlaid with pewter, which gave an effect of solid gold and silver furniture, and in which his work prefigures and often equals the finest pieces by Boulle. Golle is also important for being one of the first to introduce the Baroque fashion for allegorical furniture to France: a Cabinet of the Liberal Arts, and a Cabinet of the Four Quarters of the World, both made by him for Cardinal Mazarin were the predecessors of Cucci's celebrated pair of cabinets representing Apollo and Diana, made for Louis XIV, or his even more famous 'War' and 'Peace' cabinets, showing the King as Mars and Marie Thérèse as Pallas Athene.

Cucci, born at Todi, though he probably worked in Florence in his youth, was summoned to France about the time of Mazarin's death in 1661, and was naturalized three years later, remaining a master-craftsman at the Gobelin factory until his death in about 1704. Cucci's cabinets are described in the early bills of the Garde-Meuble as being 'à la manière de Florence', many of them inlaid with 'commessi' (or incrustations) of semi-precious stones on a black marble background. The greatest innovation of his work was that it ignored the boundaries between the different crafts, combining always the most varied materials and techniques possible. Cucci is himself recorded as a sculptor, casting statuettes in silver or bronze for his own cabinets, as a marquetry-worker, laying a floor to a complicated design by Le Brun at Saint-Germain, as a *bronzeur*, making a casket for the King's jewels at the Tuileries, even as a musical instrument maker, supplying an organ-case, harpsichord and spinet for Louis XIV. Besides this, he had a team of mosaicists and lapidaries working under him, not to mention skilled gilders like La Baronnière. Cucci's master-pieces, such as the cabinets representing the Temples of Glory and Virtue made for the Galerie d'Apollon at the Louvre, must have been some of the most astonishing pieces of furniture ever made, a summation of Baroque craftsmanship. It is tragic to relate that so few of them still exist. A large number were in 1748 given by Louis XV to the Jardin Royal to be dismembered and their different stones kept as geological specimens, others were dispersed in a sale at the Louvre in 1751, and many more were destroyed in the Revolution. Almost the only evidence for what Cucci's furniture must have been like is provided by a pair of 'grandissimes cabinets' (as he himself would have described them) which miraculously survived the Revolution and are now in the collection of the Duke of Northumberland at Alnwick Castle.

Both Cucci and Golle were twin pillars of the Gobelins, the workshops founded in 1622 (in the former *hôtel* of the brothers Gobelin on the outskirts of Paris) in order to furnish the royal palaces. The 'Manufacture Royale

des Meubles de la Couronne', as it became in 1667, also had the wider aims of improving the standards of native craftsmanship in France, and stopping the demand for imports of luxury goods from abroad. Part of the great minister Colbert's far-reaching reforms, its foundation coincided with his strict regulations for the running of the Garde-Meuble, including the numbering of every piece of furniture, the taking of regular inventories and the indexing of accounts; this was swiftly followed by the establishment of carpet and tapestry manufactories at Aubusson and Beauvais, regular production of silk at Lyons and other textiles at Abbéville, Sedan and Carcassonne, of lace and embroidery at Alençon, Chantilly and Le Havre, and, above all, of large glass and mirror plates at the Royal factory of Saint-Gobain founded in 1665 under the direction of Noyen and Perotti (an immigrant from Altare). Saint-Gobain was soon producing larger sheets than those made in Venice, and the Galerie des Glaces at Versailles, made in 1678, is evidence both of its success and of a new aspect of Baroque taste, to reach a climax in the *Spiegelkabinets* of the German princely courts.

The hierarchical structure of the Gobelins was closely based on the Florentine Grand Ducal workshops, with the painter Charles

Above: The Grande Galerie at Versailles from an engraving by Sebastien Le Clerc. This shows the gallery in about 1685 with tables, tubs for orange-trees and chandeliers all made of silver, to the designs of Charles Le Brun. (Wallace Collection, London)

Right: One of a pair of cabinets made by Domenico Cucci in 1683, for the service of Louis XIV at Versailles, and perhaps the most splendid examples of the furniture made at the Gobelins to have survived. With their panels of pietra dura and central reliefs of inlaid stones, these pieces show how Cucci brought to France the techniques of the Florentine Grand Ducal workshops. (Collection of the Duke of Northumberland)

Le Brun as Director for the whole of the 20 years it operated at full strength. Craftsmen skilled enough to win a place in it were granted important privileges, such as immunity from the restrictions of the various guilds and free education for their children, as well as being highly paid. The list of its productions in this period makes extraordinary reading: brocades painted by Bonnemer, gigantic ormolu clocks, or whole balustrades, by Caffieri, and in particular the magnificent pieces of silver and gold furniture made by Du Tel, Loir and De Villers. Six silver guéridons, for instance, designed by Le Brun supported by sphinxes on great triangular bases, standing six feet high, *en suite* with three silver console tables and pier-glasses, give one some idea of the extraordinary splendour of Louis XIV's taste. The King personally supervised much of this work, insisting on seeing wax models for all the more important pieces.

Le Brun, the influential engraver Jean Lepautre, and Jean Bérain, who as director of the Menus-Plaisirs was second only to Le Brun in importance as an overall designer, used Baroque motifs within a more academic and classical framework than their Italian contemporaries. Their favourite forms of ornament — the arabesque and the lambrequin in particular — were derived from Raphael and the Renaissance, rather than from da Cortona and Bernini. In furniture, a similar, very much more static and balanced approach is noticeable in French as opposed to Italian pieces of the same date. Just as in Le Brun's frescoes, the heavily ornate borders of pierglasses, consoles and cabinets are all-important, continuing and counteracting the movement of the figures within them. With André-Charles Boulle, the first native French cabinet-maker to achieve the importance of a Cucci or a Golle, the desire for symmetry reached almost tyrannical proportions. Boulle's pieces seem mostly to have been executed in the technique to which he gave his name, an intricate design of tortoiseshell and brass inlaid in ebony, and were often rendered in pairs of panels called *première-partie* and *contre-partie,* that is to say with the same design appearing on two matching pieces of furniture, once in brass on tortoiseshell and once (reversed) in tortoiseshell on brass.

Boulle's innovation lay not so much in his technique (Golle had after all been working in this vein much earlier), as in his development of new forms of furniture, widely spread through his engravings, published under the title *Nouveaux Desseins de Meubles.* Bureaux and commodes were the characteristic new forms, pioneered both by Boulle and by Aubertin Gaudron. In Italy such pieces would have been considered too utilitarian ever to

have been given a place in state apartments; but in the hands of Boulle (and Gaudron, who supplied two bureaux at Versailles for Madame de Maintenon) they became indispensable furnishings for the Cabinet. The commode likewise, rather like the bureau but with fewer (usually three) drawers extending the whole width of the piece, and often with a marble top, became an essential architectural feature of the state bedchamber, based in Boulle's case on classical and Italian Renaissance sarcophagi.

Mention of Gaudron raises the question of furniture-makers outside the Royal protection of the Gobelins or the Louvre workshops, and living usually in the Faubourg Saint-Antoine. Pieces made before the craftsman's stamp or

Below: Cabinet on stand, by tradition the gift of Louis XIV to Charles II. An outstanding example of the craftsmanship practised at the Gobelins, a piece such as this would probably have been made by a whole team of craftsmen working to an overall design, possibly by Le Brun himself. (Collection of the Duke of Buccleuch)

*Right: Armoire, of ebony
with tortoiseshell and brass
inlay, made about 1690,
possibly by André-Charles
Boulle himself to the
designs of Bérain. This is
one of the finest existing
early pieces using the
Boulle technique, and the
crossed L cypher
indicates that it was made
for the Royal service, even
if not for Louis XIV's
personal use. (Jones
Collection, Victoria &
Albert Museum, London)*

Left: One of a pair of commodes by André-Charles Boulle, which are the only securely documented pieces of furniture by Boulle. They were made in 1708–9 for Louis XIV's bedchamber at the Trianon. The commode, which became the commonest form of carcase furniture in France later in the eighteenth century, acquired its specific character about this time largely due to the work of Boulle and Aubertin Gaudron. This particular example shows in its overall shape the influence of Roman sarcophagi. (Versailles)

estampille became compulsory under Louis XV are virtually impossible to attribute to particular Parisian makers. It can be said, however, that the distinction first drawn at this time, between *ébénistes,* or cabinet-makers, on the one hand, and *menuisiers,* generally chair-makers or joiners, on the other, was a sign of increasing sophistication. The Parisian ébénistes really came into their own with the gradual cutting down of the Gobelins after 1686, at the beginning of the War of the League of Augsburg. Between 1689 and 1693 when the Royal workshops were virtually closed down, an estimated 20 tons of silver furniture was sent to be melted down. While this was undoubtedly a body blow to French prestige and to the country's hitherto undoubted leadership of northern Europe in artistic matters, it brought about changes in style and technique which paved the way for the Rococo. As precious and semi-precious materials were no longer easily available an effect of richness had to be obtained simply by the use of contrasting woods, or by un-adorned woodcarving. Aubertin Gaudron, who had begun as an independent ébéniste making more or less utilitarian pieces, produced for instance an armoire for the Antechamber at Marly in 1688, rivalling Boulle in the complexity of its design, but carried out entirely in wood-marquetry — of a type which greatly influenced Huguenot *émigrés*, and in particular the famous dynasty of furniture-makers called Hache, of Grenoble. The early eighteenth-century furniture designs of Robert de Cotte and Claude Audran III also show a new feeling for elegance. Their gilt tables, relying on only one material and one colour to make their effect, demanded a simpler, more linear treatment.

A parallel development was the growing importance of upholsterers, like Bon, Delobel and Losné who, while their state beds do not on the whole seem to have approached the extravagance reached in Holland and England under William of Orange, nevertheless

introduced the taste for brightly coloured
furnishing textiles and in particular for more
comfortable seat furniture. In part this also
reflected a change in social convention. At
the time of Louis XIV's death, 1,325 *tabourets*
and *pliants* were recorded at Versailles, and
these had been reserved only for high-ranking
courtiers, others having to stand. The relaxation of these standards brought a demand
for upholstered armchairs and day-beds which
were invariably supplied by upholsterers
rather than chair-makers. In time many of
these upholsterers too became *marchands-
merciers*, or middlemen, somewhere between
interior decorators and dealers in furniture,
taking a commission on the work of the
ébénistes they ordered or sold.

But the most important change was in the
atmosphere at Versailles itself, still the
artistic centre of France. It was with the
growing informality of Louis XIV's last years,
due largely to the youthfulness and vivacity
of the Duchess of Burgundy, that delicate

colours began to take the place of pompous
ornament, and flowers, trellis-work,
arabesques and smiling masks to replace the
heavy overblown allegories of the previous
generation.

The Low Countries

At the opening of the seventeenth century
Antwerp reached the peak of a period of
extraordinary prosperity. Her international
trading empire had not only given her greater
material wealth than perhaps any other
European city of the time, it had also given
her artists and craftsmen the stimulus of
constant contact with foreign designs,
materials and techniques. While tapestries,
leather wall-hangings and gold and silver
work continued to be the most famous
Flemish products, sent all over the continent,
potters and furniture-makers alike started
to imitate for the first time the goods brought
back in increasing quantities from the East.
New methods of veneering learnt from these

77

pieces facilitated very much more elaborate and representational marquetry than had been possible before, and also inspired the first tentative efforts to make lacquer furniture in the West. Italy too was a major source of inspiration. Rubens' total of seven years spent there, and Jacques Francart's Italophile engravings were to have enormous influence respectively in Antwerp and Brussels, where the splendour of the Archduke Albert's court was legendary. Rubens is known to have had woodcarvers, as well as painters and sculptors in marble, among his apprentices, and a testimonial written by him on behalf of one of these, Louis Faydherbe, still survives.

Views of interiors, like that of Rubens' own drawing-room by Cornelis de Vos painted in about 1622, show the extent of Antwerp's opulence at this time: huge brass chandeliers and andirons, green and gold stamped leather on the walls, chairs with cushions embroidered with flowers, mirrors and porcelain must have given visiting English or Scandinavian merchants the impression of an Aladdin's cave. While techniques (like veneering, gilding or silvering, and japanning) and materials (such as tortoiseshell, ivory and marbles) improved so rapidly, traditional sixteenth-century and late mediaeval types of furniture died hard. The two-stage court cupboard or 'buffet à deux corps' was still far the most common piece of furniture, though enlivened with auricular motifs or architectural decoration taken from pattern books. As late as 1694 the Antwerp Guild still insisted that presentation pieces, carved by apprentices as a qualification for becoming master-craftsmen, should be made in this antiquated form.

In part this conservatism can be explained by social practice: just as in the early sixteenth century, the exact status of a merchant was still determined by the quantity and quality of his plate, displayed on the buffet in his parlour, or stacked on tables in four or five tiers for special occasions. The other essential piece in any Dutch or Flemish household was the huge family cupboard so familiar from the pictures of Vermeer and de Hooch, where all the fine linen and other valuables were kept locked away — opened only by the key that hung from the waist of the 'huisvreouw'. These two, lumpy and unwieldy pieces, first of all received pattern-book decoration in the shape of arched panels, heavy cornices or twisted columns, and then later in the century became more Baroque with canted corners, shaped tops like the crestings of cabinets, and often three long drawers replacing the bottom cupboard. Cabinets, on carved stands, filled with a mass of tiny drawers for collections of coins or jewels, were popular from the late sixteenth century onwards, perhaps influenced originally by Augsburg models.

The closing of the Scheldt in 1609, as part of the truce between Spain and the Dutch, although it did not at once kill Antwerp, broke the almost total dominance it had previously enjoyed. Artistically as well as politically, Amsterdam began to develop its own identity, and after 1648 with the beginning of the work on Jacob van Campen's new Town Hall can be said to have seized the initiative. Dutch, as opposed to Flemish, Baroque was at first more sober and more classical, in keeping with its Protestant background and the comparative austerity of the Stadtholders'

court. The chief sculptor employed on the Town Hall was Artus Quellin whose father had been a sculptor in Antwerp and who had received his training there and in Rome. Quellin's garlands of fruit, flowers and seashells, strictly symmetrical and used with architectural effect, became a standard type of ornament for Dutch furniture up to about 1685. Mannerist ornament was by no means dead however. Crispin van den Passe's influential *Boutique Menuiserie*, published in Amsterdam in 1642, the first manual specifically dealing with furniture design since the engravings of De Vries 75 years earlier, still has motifs close to strapwork and extravagances worthy of Dietterlin; though it also shows simpler chairs, with straight backs, double stretchers and arms carved with dolphins, far more typical of the direction Dutch furniture was taking. The auricular style, that Mannerist (and highly mannered) form of ornament so called because its sinuous curving forms were supposed to resemble those of the human ear, had a final brief fling in Amsterdam in the work of John Lutma — though gradually it developed into the shallow scrolls seen on the front stretchers and backs of so many English and Dutch chairs of the 1660s and 1670s, described in early inventories as 'horsebone' decoration.

Marquetry, once again based on techniques developed in Antwerp, was the field in which Dutch cabinet-makers of the mid-seventeenth century excelled. Different woods, some imported from the East, some stained green, or purple, some spectacularly grained, were used, occasionally with the addition of ivory. Dirk van Rijswijk, working in Amsterdam, perfected a technique of inlaying mother-of-pearl in floral patterns on black marble, but others like Philip van Santwijk, at The Hague, concentrated on complicated geometrical patterns or still-life designs in more conventional woods of contrasting colour. The influence of contemporary Dutch flower-painting is clearer in the work of perhaps the finest Amsterdam cabinet-maker of his time, Jan van Mekeren. His cabinet doors inlaid with bouquets of flowers, spilling out of enormous vases, even on occasion show the butterflies, insects and drops of water on leaves beloved of artists like Rachel Ruysch and Jan van Huysum.

The Baroque arrangement of state apartments was slow to catch on in Holland, and it was indeed only with William of Orange's careful attempts to gain absolute rule, aided by powerful families like the Bentincks, Wassenaars and Pallandts, that French practice finally prevailed in the period after 1685. Until then the merchant-nobility, who almost invariably lived in town-houses (in marked contrast with the English system of country-seats) continued the demand for old-established national forms of furniture. Three or four amazingly elaborate dolls' houses of the 1670s and 1680s still miraculously survive to show how typically Dutch features of a previous generation, such as table-carpets, enormous branched chandeliers, chimney boards painted with still-lives or *trompes l'oeil*, or whole tiled walls, survived into the Baroque period. One particularly long-lived feature was the 'lit en housse', the type of bed common in Flanders and Holland since the late Middle Ages, with a simple square-domed tester suspended from the ceiling, and curtains at the corners pulled up and down by cords and pulleys. Seen in all the paintings of Ter Borch and van Steen, they achieved slightly later a more Baroque air by their upholstery of rich velvets with tassels and fringes, and by the addition of four large painted or gilded knobs, known as 'pommes' on top of their testers.

The Dutch merchant class also led the rest of Europe in their taste for oriental porcelain and furniture. Encouraged by the great

Left: Dutch lacquer cabinet, with door panels and drawers decorated with flower paintings, and the original carved and gilt stand. The Dutch love of flowers extended to furniture as much as to painting, and this type of decoration soon became as popular as the oriental scenes on earlier lacquer pieces. The stand is exceptionally richly carved with figures emerging from a background of thick acanthus foliage in the style of Quellin and Grinling Gibbons.

successes of the Dutch East India Company, oriental customs as well as goods became all the rage. By the middle of the seventeenth century the tea-party had become firmly established as a social convention, and all the equipment necessary for it—the tea-table, either a tambour or a tripod stand (preferably lacquer but otherwise painted in imitation), the little cabinet filled with caddies, the larger cupboard to keep the precious porcelain cups and rows of small pots—were eagerly sought from Amsterdam cabinet-makers as well as from the Company's own headquarters.

After about 1685, Holland came for the first time under the dominant influence of France in the decorative arts. That this was so was largely the achievement of one man, Daniel

Marot, son of a famous French engraver, Jean Marot, nephew of the cabinet-makers, Pierre and Adrian Golle, and the chief pupil of Bérain. As a Protestant, Marot was forced to leave France at the Revocation of the Edict of Nantes, and entering the service of William of Orange soon became his *chef de dessein*, acting in the same capacity as his master had for Louis XIV. Marot's furniture designs in general remained close to Bérain's but he developed the French Baroque style in two particular ways. Undoubtedly the major effect of his style on furniture was to emphasize the new dominance of the upholsterer, whose state beds and wall-hangings of extraordinary complexity, *en suite* with the covers of daybeds, chairs and stools, matched the increasing elaboration of costume at this period, the high lace headdresses (or *fantanges*) and the endless pleats and frills of bodices and skirts. Marot's other important innovation was the porcelain cabinet, a little room with thousands of cups, saucers, pots, or *blanc de chine* figures crammed onto brackets climbing the entire height of each wall, and on carved and gilt *étagères* in each corner. This new development in the Dutch craze for porcelain probably owed much to the personal taste of Mary II, who also ordered a series of superb Delft tiles to be made by the potter Adrianus Koeckz (to Marot's designs) for her dairy at Hampton Court. Marot's adaptation of French Baroque design to these new, and typically Dutch, requirements was to have a profound effect on the furnishing of German palaces in the following decades.

The editions of Daniel Marot's collected engravings published in Amsterdam in 1702 and 1712 rapidly spread his very individual style far beyond the immediate circle of his patrons. Their very universality must have made them essential equipment for every craftsman's workshop, and their effect on traditional forms of Dutch furniture was exceptionally long-lived. The large, usually green-painted, bench (or 'bank'), which was a standard piece of furniture in every Dutch hall, was soon covered with a profusion of carving — bulbous urns with stiff garlands and heavy symmetrical scrolls — in Marot's vocabulary; while long-case clocks (their mechanisms either from England or from Friesland, now fast becoming a clock-making centre) were given enormous, often top-heavy, marquetry or lacquer cases surmounted by gilded figures of Father Time or Mercury, flanked by trumpeting angels. A measure both of the power of Daniel Marot's influence, and also of the conservatism of the Dutch in the eighteenth century, is the fact that the cabriole leg, generally adopted in England by about 1710, hardly made an appearance in the Low Countries before the late 1730s.

England

Furniture-makers in England before the Civil War rather naturally lagged behind their counterparts in the richer, more cosmopolitan Low Countries and France. The more ambitious pieces, court-cupboards and chests, were usually inspired by Mannerist engraved ornament like the designs of Jean du Cerceau, Wendel Dietterlin or Martin de Vos. The equipment of court ceremonial was even more old-fashioned: the remarkable series of X-frame state chairs and stools at Knole, almost certainly made for James I and Anne of Denmark, or a chair and footstool made for Bishop Juxon of London about 1635 (now in the Victoria & Albert Museum) are, despite their superb upholstery, almost identical to

the chairs of state seen in the backgrounds of portraits by Eworth, and even Holbein, a century earlier. Inigo Jones' introduction of Italian taste to the court of Charles I seems to have had just as limited an effect on the furniture of the period as his brand of Palladian architecture had on contemporary English houses.

The experiences of so many Royalists, forced to travel abroad in the years before the Restoration, were of tremendous importance for the development of the decorative arts in England in the second half of the seventeenth century. The ebony cabinets inlaid with specimen marbles bought by John Evelyn in Florence are good examples of the more exotic taste acquired by educated Englishmen. Thomas Povey, another of these early

Above: A state bedchamber, from an engraving in Daniel Marot's Nouveau Livre d'Appartements, 1702. This shows one of the incredibly elaborate beds which, under Marot's influence, became popular in both Holland and England during the reign of William and Mary; it is of the so-called 'angel' tester type, dispensing altogether with end-posts. (Victoria & Albert Museum, London)

cognoscenti and a friend of Pepys, bought an Indian tambour table, flanked by two Venetian candlestands in the shape of crouching blackamoors, for his parlour in London in the early 1670s, pieces which still look exotic today in the house built by his nephew, William Blathwayt, at Dyrham. Equally bizarre and fascinating to English eyes must have been the sets of carved ebony furniture from Goa, imported from the Indies after Charles II's marriage to Catharine of Braganza and its accompanying trade agreements between England and Portugal. Decorative pieces like these, but particularly lacquer from the East, were what English furniture-makers began to emulate after the Restoration.

The dominant influence in this period, up to about 1685, was Holland, whose East India Company was still the chief source of oriental imports for the whole of Europe. Oriental lacquer cabinets when they could be secured (usually at high prices) were given extremely elaborate stands and crestings by English makers after Dutch patterns. These, carved with swirling acanthus and gilt or silver gilt, set off the dark lacquer, and together with the porcelain grouped in masses above and below the cabinet created a sumptuous effect which was thought appropriate for objects of such comparative rarity. In time the cabinets themselves were imitated in England, and Stalker and Parker's *Treatise of Japanning* of 1688, the first English furniture-maker's pattern book, shows how popular lacquer had become by that date. Technically, English panels, made up into screens, chests, bureau-bookcases, mirrors, tables or pier-glasses, were initially crude. A naïve attempt at Chinese or Japanese landscapes often resulted in very English-looking ducks or swans, pursued by dragons with a marked resemblance to King Charles spaniels. Even where oriental lacquer or coromandel screens were cut up to make other kinds of furniture, no care was taken to ensure that the different scenes matched up, or even appeared the right way up. By the last years of the seventeenth and the early eighteenth centuries however, makers like Gerrit Jensen achieved extremely high standards—despite the fact that true shellac as used in the manufacture of oriental lacquer was still unobtainable in the West.

Until about 1685 most seat furniture was still produced by the joiner, although turned walnut rather than oak was now generally used for the legs, stretchers and arms. A more or less standard form of chair with caned back and seat, once more based on Dutch precedents, was developed, though makers like Thomas Roberts (who appears constantly in the Royal Wardrobe accounts) could vary the form by introducing elaborately carved aprons with 'horsebone' decoration, cupids

or garlands. These and the slightly later backstools, which had square upholstered backs, were ideal for the usual Baroque arrangement of chairs lined up against the walls, where their tall, narrow proportions gave them the appropriate look of guards on parade.

Another primarily Dutch influence was that of Grinling Gibbons, whose style of naturalistic carving, learnt from the Quellins and other carvers at work on the new Amsterdam Town Hall in the 1650s, inspired a whole generation of native English carvers. With England's economic recovery after the Civil War, the successful conclusion of the Dutch wars, and in particular with the Great Fire of 1666 which at one stroke necessitated the building and furnishing of thousands of

Above: Bow Window Room at Blenheim Palace, Oxfordshire. This room was designed by Sir John Vanbrugh as one of the family apartments for the First Duke of Marlborough. The capitals of the Corinthian columns are carved by Grinling Gibbons, whose work elsewhere at Blenheim is in stone and marble. (Blenheim Palace, Oxfordshire)

new houses and churches, London had suddenly become the centre of a thriving community of native craftsmen. It was to Gibbons' and the other Dutch immigrants' vocabulary of ripe fruit and flowers in full bloom, of dead game or fish, and plump cherubs chasing each other through luxuriant swirls of acanthus, that these craftsmen turned for inspiration. Mirror frames, the aprons of tables and the front stretchers of chairs all received this lavish Netherlandish Baroque treatment. Almost invariably these were executed in walnut, which had by now totally superseded oak as the staple furniture-making material being far easier to carve yet quite as strong as oak, and with attractive grain patterns and variations in colour that also made it ideal for marquetry.

One other important development under the last two Stuart kings was the great advance in the making of clocks and barometers, a field in which England's superiority was to last for well over a hundred years. Thanks largely to the scientific discoveries of Thomas Tompion, backed by founder members of the Royal Society like Wren and Hooke, English bracket and long-case clocks were soon *de rigueur* all over Europe. It still comes as a surprise to find the work of makers like Tompion and Quare in Venetian palaces, in Peter the Great's collection at the Hermitage in Leningrad, or in the opulent monasteries

Left: Headboard of a crimson demask state bed supplied by the Huguenot upholsterer, Francis Lapiere, to the First Duke of Devonshire in 1692. Lapiere's amazingly ornate beds are extremely close to the designs of Daniel Marot. A comparatively large number of similar beds survive to show that, in one respect at least, England rivalled the rest of Europe in Baroque fantasy. (National Trust, Hardwick Hall, Derbyshire)

Above: Daybed, from a set of furniture made in 1695 for the First Duke of Leeds. The suite is upholstered in Genoa velvet, trimmed with a tasselled fringe. The table in the background is, by contrast, Palladian in style, dating from about 1725, and demonstrating William Kent's style of furniture design. (Temple Newsam House, Leeds)

Right: English cabinet of inlaid walnut, probably dating from about 1700. The piece was made to celebrate the marriage of a Yorkshire couple whose entwined monograms can be seen on the doors. The sprays of berries tied with ribbons on the drawers are both charming and unusual, and show how quickly the marquetry techniques of immigrants like Gerrit Jensen travelled to the provinces. (Victoria & Albert Museum, London)

of Coimbra and Oporto. Apart from the undoubted mechanical excellence of these clocks their cases became more and more elaborate, japanned in green or scarlet with silver figures, inlaid with floral marquetry or in geometrical patterns with 'oysters' of olivewood, mulberry, or stained burr-maple, and often with elaborate pierced crestings.

Walnut and japanned furniture of this sort continued to be made well into the eighteenth century, but the accession of William and Mary in 1689 undoubtedly brought new fashions and new influences to bear on English furniture-makers. Surprisingly, considering William's nationality and his life-long struggle against Louis XIV, the keynote of this period was French. Since the Revocation of the Edict of Nantes in 1685, Huguenot craftsmen, often trained in the Gobelin workshops, had poured into both England and Holland. One of the most influential of the *émigrés* was Daniel Marot, who, as has already been seen, became a kind of overall director of design to William III in Holland. Summoned to England by Queen Mary in 1694, Marot made at least three visits in the next ten years, and the close similarities between his engraved designs (published in a collected edition in 1702) and so many pieces of furniture produced in England during that decade show that he was at the centre of a circle of Anglo-French and Anglo-Dutch cabinet-makers, upholsterers, carvers and gilders.

Undoubtedly the most important of the cabinet-makers was Gerrit Jensen, a Fleming by birth, and easily the most proficient

exponent of English marquetry in the manner of Boulle. As well as being from 1689 the principal supplier to the Royal Wardrobe of writing-desks, pier-glasses, stands and card-tables, his name also figures constantly in bills and receipts for other great private patrons. Jensen's work can be of 'seaweed' marquetry, in different woods of contrasting colours, of walnut inlaid with pewter, or of the usual 'Boulle' technique of brass on tortoiseshell. His designs for table-tops and the wide surrounds of cushion mirrors are sometimes close to the engraved ornament of Bérain, though they seldom include the latter's figurative content — monkeys, sphinxes and characters from the Commedia dell' Arte — relying more on involved geometrical patterns (almost filigree) to make their effect. In this he may have been influenced by contemporary metalwork pattern books such as Simon Gribelin's, primarily intended for the decoration of silver snuff-boxes. In the general design of his furniture, Jensen appears to have been strongly influenced by Daniel Marot; his tables and candlestands with caryatid supports, and his simple rectangular-shaped commodes of three drawers can be seen constantly in Marot's engravings. It is hard to believe that his masterpiece, the great writing-desk made for Queen Mary in 1693 and now at Kensington Palace, was not actually designed by the master, so novel is its form. Besides using Marot as her *dessinateur-en-chef,* Mary also patronized his cousin, the cabinet-maker Cornelius Golle (younger brother of the famous Parisian maker, Pierre Golle) who in 1692 made for her a table 'of dolphin fashion'.

In one respect England during this period surpassed all her European rivals in Baroque fantasy. While the normal mid-seventeenth century four-post state bedstead, with straight valances and with no carved or moulded decoration, continued to be used in France, in England Huguenot upholsterers like Francis Lapiere, Jean Casbert and Jean Poitevin, following the designs of (if not actually in contact with) Daniel Marot, developed an almost unbelievably ornate form of bed. Testers, backboards and bases were carved and pierced, and damask, trimmed with galloon and fringe, then applied to them; valances became gathered in impossible festoons, tied with silk cords and embellished with huge tassels; some, called angel beds or *lits à la duchesse*, dispensed with end-posts and had their testers suspended from the ceiling. Perhaps the most splendid example of all is the bed made for the Earl of Melville about 1690, now in London's Victoria & Albert Museum, but there are others which compare with the most extravagant of Marot's engravings, at Clandon, Warwick, Belvoir, Dyrham, Lyme and Knole. Beds such as these

were intended to provide a climax to the Baroque progression of state apartments and it was for this reason that they became far and away the most important and expensive pieces of furniture in English houses. Invariably the upholsterer would also supply with them a set of seat furniture *en suite* to stand around the walls, probably consisting of two armchairs, six single chairs and two stools or 'squab frames' (low, caned frames on which were placed two large squashy cushions).

Another skill at which Huguenot craftsmen in England excelled was gilding. Men like René and Peter Cousin who undertook all the gilding work for Verrio's ceilings at Burghley, Paul Pettit, and the Pelletier family brought new techniques of water-gilding and burnishing over to England. Where the stands of early Restoration cabinets had been oil-gilt, leaving a thick coat which tended to obscure the crispness of the carving and give a somewhat dull matt finish, towards the end of the century the frames carved for Monnoyer flower-pieces, or for 'landskip glasses' placed over chimneys, glittered with a paler-coloured, but brighter gold leaf. Highlights were achieved in water-gilding by polishing the raised part of the decoration to an almost metallic sheen, leaving the background undisturbed. But even greater contrasts became possible with the introduction of gilt gesso, for which René Pelletier has been given the credit. This technique allowed for decoration to be stamped onto large gilded surfaces: coats of arms or monograms, arabesques after Bérain or purely geometrical patterns. Completely matt surfaces for backgrounds could also be obtained by stamping the gesso all over, while still wet, with a small round punch.

The climax of this technique can be seen in the work of John Gumley and James Moore, whose gilt gesso furniture was to replace almost entirely the marquetry furniture of Jensen and Golle in the second decade of the eighteenth century. This change of taste in the decorative arts reflects an even more momentous change in architecture: the rejection by Lord Burlington and Kent of the French Baroque in favour of Italian classicism. But whereas houses like Tottenham Park, Wanstead and Holkham returned to the Palladian villa ideal, their contents continued to be unequivocally Baroque. Kent and Flitcroft were faced with something of a quandary, for the original furniture of Palladio's villas was not only sparse but also unacceptably simple for their Augustan interiors. When they did return to Italian models therefore, it was largely to Roman or Venetian Baroque precedents. The splendid gilt chest made for Sir James Bateman (probably by Gumley and Moore), now in the Victoria & Albert Museum, may be the nearest

an English cabinet-maker has ever come to the idea of an Italian *cassone*, but it is more reminiscent of a Bernini sarcophagus than of a simple walnut chest of Palladio's own day. Similarly the settees designed by Kent for the Double Cube Room at Wilton, where surrounded by the work of his beloved Inigo Jones he might have been expected to be at his most classical, rather recall the designs of Juvarra with their winged sphinxes and bottom-heavy proportions. Nor, with his paucity of Italian material to draw on, did Kent disdain to borrow from Daniel Marot. The candlestands, of which he was so fond, in the shape of caryatids on tapering pedestals (either cherubs or females with baskets on their heads), have almost exact parallels in Marot's engravings, despite the fact that he proudly called them 'terms' after the Italian *terme*.

In general, furniture of the Palladian period in England did, however, become gradually more architectural and less sculptural. The advent of mahogany may have been one reason, for its dark and beautifully grained surface demanded less ornamentation; the increasing availability of rich upholstery materials, cut velvets from Genoa, Chinese silks and 'bizarre' Spitalfields patterns was another, for these spoke for themselves and did not need immensely elaborate mouldings to set them off. Perhaps the last truly Baroque pieces of English furniture are the vast pier-glasses, made by the new glass manufactories first at Lambeth and then at Vauxhall. But it was the very heaviness and the ponderous

architecture of later Kentian mirrors with their pediments and egg-and-dart surrounds that eventually brought about the Rococo reaction. A world of frivolity, fantasy and lightness seemed to open up with the engravings of Gravelot and the furniture designs of Thomas Johnson.

Germany

Split into hundreds of small principalities, Catholic, Lutheran and Calvinist, constantly at loggerheads with one another, Germany cannot any more than Italy be said to have adopted a national Baroque style along the lines of Colbert's France. Each little state, open to different petty despots (enlightened or not), developed artistically along different lines. In general, however, it can be said that the full Baroque style came later to Germany than to most other European countries, that it achieved its most extravagant expression there, and that it was abandoned far less quickly, thanks largely to the innate conservatism of the German princes.

The great early centre of furniture-making was of course Augsburg, from whence magnificent cabinets and 'Prunkschreins' were exported all over Europe. The gold- and silversmiths, jewellers and sculptors who combined to produce these confections had a seminal influence on the development of Baroque furniture throughout Europe, first because they introduced the fashion for furniture made of precious metals, and second because they involved highly skilled craftsmen of every guild on the manufacture of pieces

ion in the Low Countries. The importance of Augsburg lay therefore in technique rather than design. The silver throne made by Abraham Drentwett for Queen Christina of Sweden in 1650, still in Stockholm, prefigured the silver furniture made a generation later for Louis XIV, while the sophisticated tools developed by Augsburg craftsmen, finer saws than had hitherto been made, or planes capable of producing wave-mouldings, were to have a profound effect on the development of Baroque furniture far beyond the Rhine.

The initial impulse towards sculptural furniture of flowing lines came, as might be

that would previously have been left to a single joiner or carver. On the other hand the forms (and often the decoration too) of Augsburg furniture before 1650 can hardly be called Baroque. The architecture of Ulrich Baumgartner's great cabinets, for instance, is more a development of the Renaissance altarpiece than a new departure in Baroque furniture. A marvellous octagonal table-top now at Dresden, inlaid with silver by another Augsburg craftsman, Theodosius Hasel, in 1636, also shows a devotion to flat Mannerist ornament that continued both at Augsburg and Nuremberg long after it had gone out of fash-

expected, from Italy, and though after about 1690 French, and then English and Dutch, influences were also brought to bear on German furniture-makers, certain states, particularly in the south, remained loyal to bold Italianate forms. Several pietra-dura craftsmen had crossed the Alps by the 1650s, settling in Bohemia, Moravia and Würzburg. Salzburg and Vienna, where the Hapsburg court provided great demand, also received their complement of immigrant craftsmen, as did Bavaria where the Nymphenburg palace was begun in 1663 under the direction of the Italian architect, Barelli, later succeeded by

Viscardi. Two principalities in particular came under Florentine influence in the early eighteenth century through their rulers' connections by marriage with the Medici: the Palatinate, whose Electress Anna Maria Luisa was a sister of Gian Gastone, the last Grand Duke of Tuscany, and Baden-Baden, whose Margravine, Sibylla Augusta, was his sister-in-law. In both cases the Florentine techniques of pietra dura and scagliola were imitated by native German craftsmen, and at the Schloss Favorite at Baden there was a complete Florentine room with decorative panels inlaid in mother-of-pearl, agate, onyx

Far left: Interior with Musicians, by J H Schönfeldt. The gallery depicted here, with pictures hung in three or four tiers up to the ceiling, was a common feature of the palaces of German princelings in the mid-seventeenth century. Apart from the giant cabinet on the end wall, and the two large clocks on tables either side of the room, the furniture is comparatively sparse and formally arranged. The closeness with which the armchairs have been placed in serried ranks is a particularly Baroque feature. (Gemäldegalerie, Dresden)

Left: The family dining-room, Schloss Favorite, is particulary interesting for its evidence of direct Italian influence on the German Baroque. The walls here are of scagliola with painted decoration and the chairs with their tapering cartouche backs are also Italianate in form. (Schloss-Favorite, Baden-Baden)

and marble, and with imported Italian furniture. Just as Italianate in feeling was the famous bed at the monastery of St Florian, near Linz, made about the same time for Prince Eugene, by the Austrian carver Leonhard Sattler. With its chained Turkish captives groaning under the weight of the heavy frame, and with an ornate sculptural foot and headboard rather than a tester and posts, this owes more to Roman and Venetian models than to contemporary German fashion. One other Italian practice to have a long-lasting effect in Austria and Bavaria was the vogue for elaborate stucco covering the walls and ceilings of rooms. No less than 600 plasterers were, for instance, employed at one time at Wessobrunn. The furniture for these unsurpassed interiors, such as survive at Pommersfelden or the Residenz at Würzburg, was necessarily sparse, and also tended to be plain, perhaps purposely, so as not to rival the extraordinary movement and excitement all around.

In the new wave of prosperity that followed Prince Eugene's defeat of the Turks in 1683, however, new French influences can be detected in German furniture. The man more responsible for this than any other was the Elector Max II Emanuel of Bavaria, whose

exile first in Holland and then in France, between 1704 and 1707, and whose first-hand experience of Versailles, were to be crucial. The Elector not only brought French and Dutch artists and craftsmen back with him, but he also took Germans with him to France to be trained. The most influential of these was initially Josef Effner, who became a pupil of Boffrand, and who was able to put his French ideas into practice at Nymphenburg and Schleissheim after 1716. But even more important in the long run was to be one of Effner's draughtsmen, a Walloon who began as the Elector's personal dwarf before becoming a pupil of Blondel the younger — François Cuvilliés.

The most obvious result of French influence was the popularity of Boulle furniture. In response to Bavarian and other demands, Augsburg craftsmen like Johann George Escher soon mastered the technique and, indeed, in pieces like the fantastic red tortoiseshell cabinet in the Residenz at Munich made by Escher and Wolfauer for Max Emanuel's predecessor, the Elector Ferdinand Maria, in the 1680s, equalled the work of French contemporaries. Far the most famous exponent of this style however, was Johann Daniel Sommer, who trained in Paris before settling

Above: A pier-table and matching candlestands inlaid in the Boulle style with silver and tortoiseshell. This was made at Augsburg, between 1714 and 1716, by the silversmith Jeremias Jakob Aberell, probably in conjunction with the cabinet-maker, Heinrich Eichler. They demonstrate the strong French influence on German furniture in the early eighteenth century, which was especially encouraged by the Francophile Electors of Bavaria.

92

Below: Lacquer cabinet on a stand, with decoration by Gerhard Dagly, made in Berlin about 1690 for Friedrich Wilhelm, the Great Elector of Brandenburg. Dagly specialized in imitation lacquer on a white ground, possibly influenced by oriental porcelain. His pieces were renowned all over Europe, and his scenes are in general prettier than those on Chinese lacquer. (Schloss Charlottenburg, Berlin)

in the small town of Künzelsau in south Germany. Sommer's best pieces, such as a cabinet at Charlottenburg dated 1684, as well as being technically superb show a markedly individual style of design with freer arabesques and a less architectural framework than Gaudron or Boulle himself would have used. Two other notable German makers specializing in Boulle furniture in the early eighteenth century were Anton Lüchtenstein of Düsseldorf and Ferdinand Pflitzner, whose various Boulle cabinets and pier-glasses at Pommersfelden date from about 1720.

English and Dutch influences, especially in northern Germany, became more apparent after 1700, particularly in two fields, floral marquetry and lacquer. Unlike England itself where there was a break in the tradition of floral marquetry, in Germany the fashion continued throughout the eighteenth century, becoming more and more naturalistic with scenes and landscapes rendered in different woods, until with the work of Oeben and Roentgen it had a profound effect in turn on French furniture under Louis XVI. The outstanding lacquer worker of his time, not only in Germany but in Europe, was Gerhard Dagly, appointed in 1687 'Kammerkünstler' (or 'Directeur des Ornements') to Friedrich Wilhelm, the 'Great Elector' of Brandenburg,

and to his son, who in 1700 became King of Prussia. Dagly, who came from Spa, a small town just south of the German border long renowned for its production of japanned objects, appears only to have decorated furniture made by others, but his work, much of which still survives at Charlottenburg, is of extraordinary beauty, largely because of the white background (possibly intended to look like porcelain) which he regularly gave his 'oriental' scenes. His renown at the time can be judged from the fact that the Electress of Hanover, sending an English japanned clock-case to her Prussian son-in-law, should have remarked apologetically, 'Dagly makes much better ones'. Dagly's brother, Jacques, eventually went to live in Paris where he became a partner with Claude Audran and Pierre de Neufmaison in a venture to promote a new technique of lacquering, for which they sought a patent — another interesting sidelight on how France, having influenced, in turn learnt from German cabinet-makers. Dagly's most famous pupil, Martin Schnell, went to Dresden where he worked for Augustus the Strong.

Between about 1720 and 1750, when the freer, easier lines of the Rococo were already emerging in France and England, the Baroque style reached perhaps its European summit in the extravagance of German designers and furniture-makers. Two authors of pattern books published in Augsburg and Nuremberg between 1711 and 1724, Paul Decker and J J Schübler, must take much of the credit for this. Between them they elaborated the already fantastic engraved designs of Daniel Marot and made popular a style of almost unbelievable richness and complication. Schübler's *penchant* for mechanical devices (shown for instance in a design for a table incorporating a dumb-waiter and a fountain) illustrates a particular obsession of German cabinet-makers, again to reach fruition much later in the work of Oeben. Even more than this however, the Germans brought to their interpretation of the Baroque a taste for the bizarre and the exotic. One has only to think of Augustus the Strong's state bedchamber at Schloss Maitzburg near Dresden with wall- and bed-hangings made from the brightly coloured feathers of birds imported from Mexico, of the Porcelain Room at Charlottenburg (designed by Eosander von Goethe in 1710), its pale green walls barely visible under a mass of pink porcelain perched on carved gilt brackets and ledges stretching from floor to ceiling, or of Pflitzner's 'Spiegelkabinett' at Pommersfelden reflecting in a thousand tiny mirrors the very unecclesiastical behaviour of Archbishop von Schönborn, to realize that the late nineteenth-century castles of Ludwig the Mad were not the isolated whims of a lunatic, but the expression of a long-established German taste.

Scandinavia

It is questionable how far Danish and Swedish furniture of the late seventeenth and early eighteenth centuries can properly be called Baroque. As with the countries of the Iberian peninsula very few houses, apart from the royal palaces and the castles of occasional exceptionally powerful nobles, had any furniture with pretensions to artistic merit. Purely functional joiner's chairs and tables were otherwise the rule. Most of the more ambitious pieces in the royal collections came anyway from abroad: Frederick IV of Denmark's visit to Italy in 1709 for instance brought to Rosenborg not only a Florentine pietra-dura table designed by Foggini but also a whole room of Venetian glass, to add to the Augsburg silver furniture acquired by his predecessors. When an important item was commissioned from a native craftsman, it tended to be extremely old-fashioned in form, such as the anointment throne of narwhal tooth made by a carver called Bendix Grodtschilling for the coronation of Christian V in 1681, which actually appears to have a Romanesque derivation, with its arcaded base and back.

In general, however, it can be said that the traditional political alliances of the two countries reveal the dominant artistic influences on them. In the case of Denmark, friendship with England brought typically Restoration and William and Mary forms of chairs, after a time lag of some 20 or 30 years. A fine set of chairs, again at Rosenborg, documented as the work of Johan Weys in 1718, with ebonized 'horsebone' crestings to their backs, heavy front stretchers and curving arms and scroll legs, would not look out of place at Ham or Knole in England. On the other hand in the case of Sweden, used by Louis XIV and his successors as a 'buffer' to keep Russia out of Europe, one does not have to look far for French influence. The correspondence of the architect Nicodemus Tessin reveals the extraordinarily close cultural contacts between the two countries in the late seventeenth century. A great deal of French furniture was imported direct, such as the marvellous state bed given to an ambassador, Count Rielke, by Louis XIV, or the Parisian armchairs of the 1680s which can still be seen at the castle of Skokloster. Little is known of native Swedish craftsmen of this date, though they were evidently greatly influenced by these French models. One cabinet-maker whose name is known, and whose work seems to have been far superior in quality to most of his contemporaries', was Burchardt Precht, a carver of German origin working in Stockholm in the 1690s — the maker of an extremely accomplished pair of gilt guéridons in the form of angels with outspread wings, now in the Nordiska Museet. Precht, like Boulle, had a number of sons who continued to make furniture during the eighteenth century in the 'Tessin style' so successfully adopted by their father.

Spain and Portugal

The Pyrenees represented in the seventeenth century a far more formidable cultural barrier than the Alps. Spain and Portugal had until then drawn much of their artistic inspiration not from Europe at all, but from the Moors. Both were slow to adopt the forms and the decorative vocabulary of Baroque furniture normal elsewhere on the Continent, and indeed only began to do so after about 1680. In Spain the most common types of furniture continued to be movable, in marked contrast with the huge architectural pieces produced in Italy and France. *Varguenos*, square or rectangular chests with a fall-front concealing a mass of small drawers, were the staple product of Spanish cabinet-makers, usually with ornate iron handles at each side, with which they could be placed on simple, often folding, stands. The *papeleira*, another type of chest opening at the top and intended for the storage of papers, the trestle table with wrought-iron braces in the form of lyre or yoke-shaped scrolls, and the folding X-frame

chair or *sillón de cadera*, went on being made in the traditional forms throughout this century, testifying to the still nomadic existence of the Spanish nobility. The decoration of these pieces was also conservative, the Mudéjar, or Moorish style, lingered in the south, where furniture continued to be made with intricate geometrical patterns inlaid in ivory, metal and olive or cedarwood — the technique known in the Italian Renaissance as 'alla certosina' or 'damaschina', after its supposed origins in Damascus. Representational art, forbidden by Mohammedan law, became more popular in the north with the advent of the Churrigueresque style, named after the leading architect of the day, when areas of dense ornament, usually of figure-filled arcades, contrasted with totally plain, flat surroundings, on the fronts of cabinets as much as on the façades of churches. One important technical development was in bob-

Above: The saloon at Skokloster, Sweden, built in the late seventeenth century by a Swedish general, Count Wrangel. The Swedish debt to French Baroque design is demonstrated by the grisaille paintings on the ceiling, executed in 1674, which are based on engravings by Le Pautre; the carving of the chimney-piece and overmantel are also inspired by French pattern books, and the superb gilt armchairs were imported from Paris. (Skokloster Palace, Sweden)

bin and spiral turning. Beds in particular, never as in the rest of Europe heavily curtained or with a tester (presumably because of the heat), relied for their effect on heavily carved backboards of pyramidal shape, carved as tiers of arcades with turned columns or spindles. Gilding, and also European Baroque forms like twisted columns, began to be used on later seventeenth-century vargueños, as on some unusually ornate examples in the Museo de Artes Decorativas at Madrid.

Seat furniture too, finally began to achieve a more European look through the use of turning. The X-frame chair developed first into the *sillón frailero*, a sturdy four-square armchair with straight back and arms and thick front stretcher, usually with very wide seats and backs of stamped leather, a type familiar from the portraits of Velásquez. While the simple overall shape of these chairs was largely maintained, spirally-turned legs and stretchers brought them gradually more into line with Louis XIII seat furniture, albeit long after the fashion had passed in France itself. The accession of a French king, Philip V, in 1700 brought more up-to-date Parisian fashions to furniture-makers round Madrid, but at the cost of that originality (in materials, techniques and design) which had hitherto been the hall-mark of Spanish furniture.

Portuguese furniture-makers were similarly at their most original between 1640 and 1700, after which date the fashions of London rather than Paris began to be imitated. The woods used by them were for a start strikingly different from the rest of Europe: chestnut had been and remained the most popular native wood, but Brazilian rosewood (*jacarandá* or *pau preto*), imported from her great colonial empire was increasingly used in Portugal, the first American tropical wood to be employed extensively by European cabinet-makers, at least a hundred years before the advent of mahogany in England.

Cupboards and vast chests of drawers in the sacristies of the great monastic churches were, to begin with, the only highly decorated pieces of furniture, often suggesting Spanish influence in their geometrical inlay. Two of the finest of all, at the abbey of Alcobaza (where the sacristy was described in the late eighteenth century by William Beckford as a room 'gorgeous and glistening, worthy of Versailles itself') are dated 1664 and seem to imitate in carved wood the geometric Moorish tiles of the period. The technique of parallel grooving, known as 'wave' or 'flame' pattern in northern Europe, became a favourite device in Portugal, where it was known as *tremido*. Sometimes, as on a wardrobe in the palace of the Dukes of Braganza at Guimaraës, the whole piece of furniture would be submerged in these heavy, but rippling, mouldings. Turning, too, was taken to new Baroque

heights in Portugal, where the profusion of easily worked imported rosewood enabled furniture-makers to indulge in virtuoso displays of discs, balls, reels and spiralling forms, giving a unique expression of rapid movement and revolving and exploding forms to large tables and cabinets, particularly in the region around Evora. Japanning also became popular, perhaps partly due to the influence of Stalker and Parker's treatise on the subject published in England in 1688.

In seat furniture, too, the early influence was Spanish, and leather, often stamped with coats of arms or floral designs and held in place by elaborate patterns of brass studs, remained the standard covering for seats and backs well into the eighteenth century. In about the 1680s, however, a new type of chair frame was evolved, the *cadeira de sola*, with turned (but not usually spiral) legs and arms,

Below: Ivory cabinet, the drawers inlaid with gold, silver and pearls, probably made in Portuguese Goa about 1670. Ultimately derived in form from the Augsburg cabinets popular all over Europe in the Baroque period, it is typical of much colonial furniture in its extraordinary mixture of precious materials with Buddhist and European decorative motifs.

a typically Baroque front stretcher of scrolls and a high, shaped back. In time these backs also acquired carved shells and garlands in the style of Daniel Marot, and also the so-called *pé de pincel* or 'paintbrush' foot, which was to be copied in England.

The cross-fertilization of ideas between England and Portugal is complicated. In the Restoration period, after Catherine of Braganza's marriage to Charles II, the turned ebony furniture imported by Portugal from her Indian colony, Goa, was much sought after in England, but, after the Queen's return to her native country in 1693 and the Methuen Treaty of 1703, Portugal owed much more to England. Regular cargoes from London to Lisbon and Oporto included, for instance, the scarlet and gold lacquer chairs of Giles Grendey, while native craftsmen emulated the Queen Anne style in their chairs with cabriole legs, splat backs, pad, slipper and claw-and-ball feet, the only difference being a more exaggerated curve of the back, and deeper aprons on both the chairs and tables.

Colonial Furniture

Indo-Portuguese furniture, made not only in Goa but in other trading posts along the west coast of India, and also the products of Portugal's South American colonies, deserve to be mentioned briefly as by-products of the Baroque. Although the forms they took were largely European, the materials and decorative patterns used were startlingly different. Teak, inlaid with ivory, ebony, bone and sometimes Brazilian woods in a mesh of small circles is sometimes reminiscent of the *certosina* inlay of the north Italian Renaissance, though it in fact derives from Mogul art. The caryatid figures supporting cabinets or chairs look from a distance like conventional Venetian negroes, but turn out at close range to be uncouth savages staring vacantly out of ivory eyes. Perhaps most beautiful of all was the furniture made in Goa entirely veneered in ivory, and decorated with incised lines in black. Pieces of this kind were coveted by European collectors throughout the eighteenth and well into the nineteenth century, despite the very rough finishing and naïve decoration they were so often given.

Furniture in seventeenth-century colonial America shows a familiar pattern of fashion following trade routes. Whereas in New York and New Jersey, the standard form continued to be the great Dutch cupboard, or 'kas', the New England seaports, Boston and Newport, produced joined pieces, such as chests of drawers and tallboys, of obviously English derivation. The Southern colonies had at this stage the closest links of all with England, and the ships which regularly brought tobacco and rice to London or Bristol returned with imported English furniture, thus delaying the establishment of an independent furniture-making tradition.

The time lag between English and American fashion is startlingly evident in the joined furniture of Massachusetts and Connecticut, which continued to be made until the 1700's on essentially Jacobean lines: court-cupboards, usually decorated with bobbin turning, or panelled chests, rarely ornamented and then only with stylized sunflower or geometrical motifs carved in shallow relief. It was only very gradually after that date that the more Baroque furniture of the William and Mary period in England came to be imitated. Sophisticated marquetry techniques even then did not catch on, and 'seaweed' patterns of the Gerrit Jensen type were usually imitated in painted decoration on a flat un-veneered surface. Japanning was practised in Boston, though again this amounted more to *trompe l'oeil* painting than to genuine lacquer. It also continued for a good 30 years after the fashion had died in England. Unmistakably 'Queen Anne' furniture, displaying not a hint of the

Right: Highboy by John Pimm, made in Boston, Massachusetts about 1745. Although by English standards a very old-fashioned piece, its lacquer decoration, with a background painted to look like tortoiseshell, is still of exceptional quality. (Henry Francis Du Pont Museum, Wintherthur)

Below: Early eighteenth-century revolving chair from Andra State, India, entirely veneered in ivory with incised black decoration. Like the furniture produced in Portuguese Goa, mainly for export to the home country, this shows how European forms were married to older, native techniques. (Victoria & Albert Museum, London)

Rococo, like the famous Loring family chest by a Boston maker, John Pimm, was being made as late as the 1750s. High chests of drawers on stands (or 'highboys' as they were often called) became a favourite form in America and, far more than seat furniture, achieved a style quite distinct from their English models, lighter in proportion and with broken scroll pediments and finials giving them a livelier silhouette. The concave shell ornament in the centre of the apron, a feature possibly invented by the prolific maker, Job Townsend, of Newport, Rhode Island, is another distinctively American detail.

Chairs varied greatly from area to area, within different colonies, though most were closely based on English examples. Large upholstered wing armchairs from New Hampshire, ladderbacks from the Delaware river basin, and chairs with vase-shaped splat backs, a particular speciality of a maker called John Gaines from Portsmouth, New Hampshire, could easily be mistaken for provincial English furniture of a generation earlier. One new form developed in Connecticut, which seems to have had no true European counterpart, was the 'butterfly' table, so called because of the exotic curved shapes of the supports to its hinged flaps. Set against the inward slant of its legs, these gave a sense of Baroque movement to what was essentially a simple joiner's piece. As might be expected, more variety in the woods used was also a hall-mark of American colonial furniture: as well as walnut and mahogany, both adopted very early on, maple, fruitwood and gumwoods, and rarities such as 'butternut' (or white walnut) were available, and gave an interesting range of colours and finishes to pieces that might otherwise have seemed stereotyped.

After its settlement in 1682, Philadelphia swiftly became the cabinet-making centre of America, just as it became the second most important town in the English-speaking world. The earliest signed piece of Philadelphia furniture known to exist — a fall-front walnut secretaire at Williamsburg by Edward Evans, dated 1707 — would have done credit to a London firm like Coxed & Woster. In keeping with its grand Palladian buildings, more architectural forms of furniture began to be developed in Philadelphia in the 1720s and 1730s, usually based on English pattern books. The cabinet for an air pump, presented to the Library Company of Philadelphia by Governor John Penn in 1739, made by John Harrison, sums up this rather ponderous but impressive style with its huge fluted pilasters, Doric frieze and broken pediment. But if Philadelphia saw the last gasp of the international Baroque style in these cabinet-makers' work, it was also, as the centre of American fashion by 1760, to pioneer the late arrival of the Rococo.

THE LINE OF BEAUTY
The Rococo style

'Rococo' is applied to the style prevalent in the middle of the eighteenth century. It was first used as a term of abuse, by students of the painter J-L David in Paris. 'Pompadour, rococo' stood for everything that muscular neo-classicists disliked about the Louis Quinze period. The style was luxurious, aristocratic, sensuous, and, what was worse, frivolous. Above all, for the first time since the Renaissance, the designers had presumed to ignore the example of classical antiquity.

Today classicism is not the exclusive rule, and the Rococo period is rightly seen as one of the high points in European furniture. The style, originating in Paris, swept across Europe in a mood of relaxation. It was well suited to its period, which for the most part was a peaceful one. When, during the 1750s and 1760s, the neo-classical reaction set in, the Rococo style died quickest in England and France. In more conservative countries it lingered on, almost to the time of the French Revolution.

Rococo was an international style. At the courts of Europe, from Madrid to St Petersburg, rulers and princes decorated their palaces in the lively, glittering manner that was the eighteenth century's response to the Baroque splendours of Versailles. However, the original intention had not been to provide a setting for ceremony. Rococo grew up in Paris with the desire for an intimate, agreeable way of living. This led to the use of bright, cheerful colours, and to the invention of many new forms of furniture, most of which are still in use today. At the same time, the skills of the craftsmen improved, resulting in furniture of lighter construction and greater elegance.

Rococo was a style of interior decoration, and the part played by the architect-designer was of extreme importance. Carved pieces were made to fit in with the panelling, and never look quite the same when moved away from their original setting. The range of decorative detail was largely formulated by the designers. C- or S-scrolls developed from Baroque strapwork and arabesques. Acanthus foliage originated in the ancient scrolled *rinceau*, but took on an organic form as though freely growing. Other natural forms were used, such as palms, rushes and roses. The most characteristic motif was the *rocaille* (shell- or rock-work), which was crimped and indented, and bordered on one side by a curved moulding. Only highly skilled craftsmen could properly convey the Rococo sense of vitality and movement, and it is not surprising that in Germany and Italy many of the carvers were sculptors by training.

The Catholic courts and aristocrats of southern Europe were hedonist in their outlook, and their palaces were decorated and furnished with luxury. But the eighteenth

century was also a successful time for the bourgeoisie. Particularly in the Protestant north of Europe and in America, the merchants and traders, bureaucrats and city officials were becoming increasingly prosperous. They preferred practical and convenient furniture to an opulent display. Thus, two styles existed simultaneously. The division can be seen most clearly in Germany, where bourgeois furniture continued and developed within the established formulae, while princes and potentates followed or attempted to surpass the fashions of Paris.

France

On the death of Louis XIV in 1715 the tyranny of Versailles came to an end, and the aristocracy thankfully returned to Paris to pursue their own lives without risk of royal displeasure. French Rococo has often been associated with the extravagant behaviour of her society. Yet for all its privilege, arrogance and corruption, this society was one of extreme sophistication. Paris was the centre and model of European culture, and all other countries imitated her fashions in some degree. Though not exactly private, life in Paris became informal and intimate. Poise, wit, the art of conversation and the desire to please were cultivated to a level unknown elsewhere. Social life was largely dominated by women. The men were invariably agreeable to ladies,

and the ladies to each other. All this contributed to the *douceur de vivre* of the *ancien régime*, and to such manners the refined, jewel-like furniture seems a natural accompaniment.

The three styles or periods are Régence (till about 1730), Louis Quinze (from about 1730 to 1760), and transitional. Together, the dates cover most of Louis XV's reign, but the styles overlap to a surprising extent, and furniture can seldom be accurately dated without documentary evidence. Moreover, by the time of the King's death in 1774, the neo-classical style was firmly established.

Régence is named after the duc d'Orléans, regent to the infant Louis XV. From 1716, d'Orléans redecorated the Palais Royal with G-M Oppenordt (the son of a Dutch cabinetmaker) as his architect-designer. Although many elements of Rococo can be detected before 1716—as, for example, in the delicate scrolls and arabesques of Bérain, or the grotesques and fantasy figures of Watteau—it was at the Palais Royal and other Parisian houses that the style lost the restraints of classicism. Oppenordt and others designed furniture such as side-tables, sofas and chairs. These carved pieces were probably made by the same craftsmen who worked on the panelling of the rooms for which they were intended. The designs can be florid and heavily loaded with detail.

Above: This room in the Château de Champs was panelled in the early eighteenth century, but when Madame de Pompadour acquired the Château in 1757, she employed the painter Cristophe Huet to paint it in the chinoiserie style. The fantasy landscapes and figures have little to do with true Chinese painting, but are derived from the exotic decorative style of Watteau. They are not unlike the chinoiserie tapestries designed by the painter Boucher and made at the Beauvais factory. The furniture here is in the Régence style, rather heavier than that of the following Louis Quinze period. The seat furniture is covered with Beauvais tapestry of exotic landscapes with birds and animals.

About 1718, the armrests of chairs were set back a little to allow room for panniered skirts, and the backs of chairs were lowered lest they interfere with the elaborate coiffures of the time. As for veneered furniture, a cheerful tone had been set when Boulle used kingwood about 1711, rather than the sombre ebony, tortoiseshell and brass. The typical Régence commode, known as *à tombeau*, is a solid piece with three drawers and short feet. It seems to have been made as late as the 1740s. The ormolu mounts slowly took on a Rococo vigour as acanthus and scrolls became lively, and stern classical masks gave way to more graceful forms. The influence of Watteau can be seen in the affected twisting of ormolu heads placed at the corners of tables and commodes.

During the Louis Quinze period, increased lightness of form and decoration resulted in a simplification of outline and detail. Many new types of furniture appeared, and there were fresh techniques in cabinet-making. The best known of the designers were Pineau and Meissonnier. Nicholas Pineau (1684–1754) returned from Russia in 1727. Besides designs for panelled rooms, there survive a number of his drawings for chairs. He carried the unclassical manner of Oppenordt a stage further, introducing asymmetrical scrollwork and rocaille. This, however, was more evident in the work of J-A Meissonnier (1695–1750),

originally a goldsmith in Turin, whose metalwork includes the famous and immensely influential candlesticks which were engraved in 1728. Meissonnier designed rooms and furniture, using shell- and rock-work combined with forms such as carved rocks, water and foliage. This lively asymmetrical style was known as the *goût pittoresque*. All the decoration of a room, with its gilded carving and brightly coloured upholstery, was to be reflected back and forth 'as by magic' in the great looking-glasses let into the panelling. The Rococo of Meissonnier was influential abroad, but in France it was short-lived as Parisians soon turned to a more restrained style.

The typical Louis Quinze commode was of bombé shape, with two drawers, its graceful outlines melting together in continuous curves. The mosaic-like parquetry of kingwood, purplewood or rosewood was carefully matched and gave subtle reflections with changing lights. By 1740 there was a revival of marquetry, with delicate flower stems and scrolled borders, inlaid in contrasting woods. These developed into the lavish marquetry of the 1750s, where realistic bunches of flowers were inlaid in numerous different woods, stained, etched and scorched to give detail and chiaroscuro. They could be in bright colours, but much of this work has now faded.

Right: Made in about 1730 by Charles Cressent, this magnificent commode is in the late Régence style. Cressent, one of the finest cabinet-makers of Paris, had originally been trained as a sculptor, and this accounts for the high quality of the ormolu figures. The ormolu work is set off by the sparkling background of kingwood parquetry. (National Trust, Waddesdon Manor, Buckinghamshire)

Right: The Louis Quinze type of chair frame was formed of a series of curves, giving an appearance of ease and comfort. This example by Cresson, with a flat back, is of the type known as à la reine because, it is said, it was favoured by Queen Marie Leczynska. It is painted ivory and tourquoise, and still has its original needlework cover worked with a gay Rococo fantasy. (Musée des Arts Décoratifs, Paris)

Below right: This exquisite French bureau was made for Madame de Pompadour by C Wolff in about 1755. The elaborate marquetry, with a bunch of flowers tied with a ribbon, is in the pictorial style which seems to have developed during the 1750s.

Lacquer was also used. It was carefully removed from oriental screens and cabinets, and skilfully laid down on curved surfaces of commodes and writing-tables. Japanese lacquer was superior to Chinese, but Chinese red-ground lacquer gave an exceedingly rich effect. Lacquer inspired the painted decoration known as *vernis* which was carried out best by the Martin brothers. Vernis was applied in semi-transparent layers, sometimes as many as 20 or 30, each being smoothed down before the next application, and the final decoration was of flowers or pastoral scenes. The colours matched similar work on the room panelling. Porcelain was used on furniture by 1750. A porcelain tray might be fitted as the top of a small coffee- or work-table, or decorative plaques set on the sides of a commode or writing-table. Vanrisamburgh was one of the first cabinet-makers to use this material.

Louis Quinze ormolu was superb in quality. The function of ormolu was to protect vulnerable corners, or to hold veneer in place. After a period of high elaboration during the thirties and forties, it became more logical and was

Above: The King's Private Study at Versailles. The famous bureau du roi, begun by J-F Oeben in 1760 and completed nine years later by Riesener, displays the emerging transitional style.

Right: A superb example of the small tables that were a necessary part of the intimate style of life in Rococo Paris. This one by Vanrisamburgh can be dated to 1760 by its top of Sèvres porcelain. The table is designed for serving coffee or chocolate, and the ormolu mounts include two carrying handles. The veneer is of tulipwood, with borders of purplewood.

chiefly confined to the edges of a piece, or used to outline panels of marquetry, porcelain or lacquer. Some cabinet-makers designed their own ormolu mounts, but clearly this was not often the case as the same pattern can appear on the work of different craftsmen. The best ormolu was of cast and chased bronze, gilded by the expensive mercury process, but for cheaper work the bronze might be merely polished and varnished.

The delicacy of chairs was enhanced by the fine quality of their upholstery in silk brocades, pastel-coloured damasks and velvets, and, later, printed cottons. Tapestry was sometimes used as a chair covering, but not to the extent as is popularly supposed, and it suggests a formality that is alien to the gay Louis Quinze spirit. Needlework was more usual, and gave a lighter effect.

The transitional style is hard to date accurately, and runs into the neo-classical or Louis Seize period. The neo-classical revival had, in fact, begun in Paris during the 1750s when Rococo was at its height. Oeben's famous *bureau du roi* at Versailles, begun in 1760 and

105

completed nine years later by Riesener, is a hybrid piece. The curves of the bodywork are straighter, while the lower part remains true Rococo. At the same time, classical or architectural details were beginning to appear in the ormolu work. The transitional period delighted in marquetry, but turned to classical landscapes or perspectives, urns and other utensils. Cube parquetry is a feature of the transitional period.

The forms or types of furniture became very numerous after the 1730s, and are best referred to by their French names, partly because these are in use by writers and auction houses today, and partly because there is often no proper English equivalent. Even in the eighteenth century, some of the names were already in dispute, and since then many more have been invented. Guild regulations divided the furniture craft between *menuiserie* (joinery and chair-making) and *ébénisterie* (cabinet-work and veneering), and by legislation of 1744 and 1751 makers were obliged to sign their works with an approved stamp. The considerable number of pieces that are unsigned were, presumably, made either by those who were protected by royal patronage, or who lived in areas outside the jurisdiction of the city. From 1745 to 1749, ormolu and all metalwork containing copper had to be stamped with a small mark of a crowned 'C', but this proved impossible to enforce, and the order was repealed.

Above: Known as a voyeuse, this chair, a variant of the bergère or enclosed armchair, has a flat back, surmounted by a rail for a person to lean on from behind, in order to join in conversation or watch a card game. This one was made in about 1760 by J-B Tilliard. (Musée des Arts Décoratifs, Paris)

Right: A commode with two cupboard doors rather than two drawers was known as a commode à vantaux, and was imitated in England, around 1770, by Chippendale and other London makers. This elegant example by Pierre Migeon is veneered with tulipwood, with contrasting scrolls of purplewood. (Musée des Arts Décoratifs, Paris)

The *corporation des menuisiers-ébénistes* included not only the two principal crafts but all related trades. Strict regulations ordered that the menuisier could only make the frame of the chair, which then had to go to the carver, the gilder or painter, and the upholsterer. Similarly, by law the ébéniste could only make the case and marquetry of a commode or other piece. Ormolu was a different trade, and so was painting and lacquer work. Tiresome as the guild regulations may seem, they produced specialists in all the crafts whose skills have probably never been equalled. Among the enormous number of furniture-makers, perhaps the most famous are Charles Cressent, who worked for d'Orléans; Jean-François Oeben, a German by birth, who was in Paris by 1749 and is associated with a number of new forms and marquetry styles; and Bernard Vanrisamburgh.

The sinuous forms of menuiserie are typified by the superb chairs that envelop the sitter in curves well adapted to the shape of the body. Stretchers connecting the legs of the chair could be dispensed with by about 1725. 'Architectural' chairs, made to stand against the panelling, were of the type known as *à la reine* with flat backs. Smaller movable chairs 'for convenience' included the *fauteuil en cabriolet* with a curved back, and the chair without arms *(siège)*. Louis Quinze chairs were imitated in all European countries.

Other forms of chair had special purposes. The *bergère* was the most comfortable: this had an upholstered back which sometimes had wings at each side, and arms reaching the seat which was fitted with a thick down cushion. The *voyeuse* had a padded rail across the back so that a second party could lean over it to watch a card game. The desk chair *(fauteuil de bureau)* was normally caned and cushioned, and the seat lozenge-shaped, coming forward to a central leg. This was more comfortable for those seated for long periods at a desk. The two forms of stool, the *tabouret* and the folding *pliant* were still made, but now seemed rather formal in this period of relaxed manners.

The different forms of sofa included the *canapé*, made to match the 'architectural chairs', and less formal types: the *marquise*, made for two sitters only; the *ottomane*, with curved ends; and the *veilleuse*, often made in pairs, with one high and one low end for lying upon at full length. The *chaise longue* was rather wide, with a raised end, upholstered or caned, and the *duchesse* was narrower, with one high and one low end.

There were two principal types of bed. The *lit à la française* generally had a headboard

Above: This small type of chaise longue, known as a veilleuse, made for a lady's boudoir, epitomizes the relaxed luxury of Parisian private life. The veilleuse, made for reclining, was a sofa with one high and one low end. This example is unusual in its curved ends. The thick down cushion makes it extremely comfortable, while the frame is delicately carved with flowerheads in the style typical of the Louis Quinze chairmakers. It is signed by J-B Tilliard, a famous menuisier who made chairs for the King, and dates from the 1750s. (Victoria & Albert Museum, London)

Right: An historic painting, entitled Tea in the English Style with the Princesse de Condé in the Salon of the Four Mirrors at the Temple, Paris, by Michel Olivier (1712–1784), which shows Mozart aged eight during his first visit to Paris in 1766. He is playing on a plain walnut harpsichord before a party at the Princesse de Condé's apartment. The decoration of the rooms is rather plain and old-fashioned, but typical features of the French interior are the enormous looking-glasses set in the panelling, the candle brackets, the portraits framed over the doors and the French draw-curtains. The furniture includes tea-tables and painted chairs covered with needlework. Serving and dining-tables were generally of plain deal, to be covered with damask cloths, and were brought in for occasions such as these. (Louvre, Paris)

108

Above: the bureau plat, made throughout the eighteenth century, was a writing-table of a strong and masculine character. This example, made by Charles Cressent in the late 1720s, still retains the rectangular top and sturdy legs of the Louis Quatorze period, which after 1730 developed into more supple curves. The grain of the kingwood and tulipwood veneer runs in different directions, giving subtle reflections of the light. The vivacity and freedom of the scrolling leaves, and the slightly affected female busts at the corners show the informality of the later Régence style. (Louvre, Paris)

Right: An exceptionally fine example of the drop-front secretaire (sécretaire à abattant) by J-F Dubut, which became increasingly popular in Paris after 1750. Just four feet (over one metre) high, it is designed for a lady's use. The floral marquetry at the sides is inlaid on a tulipwood and purplewood ground. The Chinese lacquer panels, taken off imported screens, is skilfully laid down on the curved surfaces, and the bold ormolu mounts emphasize the luxurious quality of the piece. (Metropolitan Museum of Art, New York)

and a footboard as well as four posts and a canopy. If the canopy was suspended from the ceiling, the bed was *à la duchesse*. But beds without canopies were also made to fit into alcoves, which were then curtained all round. The second type of bed was the *lit à la polonaise*. Here the small, oval canopy covered only about a third of the bed surface, and was supported by curved iron rods that were concealed by the curtains.

Side-tables were very elegant. In spite of their apparent delicacy, they were strong enough to support their marble tops without shaking. The console table was attached to the wall and had only two legs that curved inwards towards the feet, and were often joined by a richly carved 'nut'. Side-tables, like most 'architectural furniture', were made to match the panelling both in carving and decoration. Other forms of furniture were made by menuisiers, especially wardrobes. But the best writing-tables, dressing-tables, and buffets belonged to the cabinet-maker's art, and when they were joiners' pieces they tended to look provincial.

The art of ébénisterie lay principally in setting veneer or marquetry onto curved surfaces. All the Rococo details which in menuiserie were carved in solid wood were here applied in ormolu. The commode was always a luxurious piece, and is one of the most typical forms of the period. The top was invariably of coloured marble, generally quarried in the south of France. By 1750, small commodes were popular. The rather rare *commode en console* stood on two legs only, with its back fixed to the wall. A *commode à vantaux* had two doors in front, enclosing shelves or drawers. Buffets, or low wardrobes, were rather similar but slightly taller, and had the cumbersome name of *meuble à hauteur d'appui*, or *meuble d'appui*. Pairs of small commodes with shaped fronts (*encoignures*) were made to fit into corners, and matched other cabinet-work in the room. They often

had shelves above for porcelain, but these have only rarely survived, and their existing marble tops are generally replacements.

The *bureau-plat* or flat writing-table was a large functional piece that always remained popular. The rectangular top became serpentine, recessed at the centre of each side. Smaller *bureaux-plats* were made from about 1740, sometimes with extension slides at either end. The *bureau Mazarin* or kneehole writing-table survived only in the provinces. Meanwhile, fresh forms were developed. The English bureau, with a sloping front that could be locked up, is a rare instance of the French borrowing a foreign form, and was known as a *bureau en pente* or *bureau de dame*. It evolved by about 1760 into the cylinder writing-table. The upright secretaire (*secrétaire à abattant* or *en armoire*) made its appearance before 1750 and became very popular later in the century.

The fashionable way of life called for numerous kinds of small tables in the ladies' private apartments. They were called *tables ambulantes*, and often included differently fitted drawers, so that a single table could be used for needlework, writing, reading, taking private meals, or dressing. The *table à écrire* was a miniature bureau-plat, with a front or

side drawer fitted for pens, ink and paper. One type of table, perhaps invented by Oeben, had a top made to slide back to reveal a drawer fitted with a looking-glass, reading-stand or compartments. The French aristocracy were compulsive gamblers and ordered a large number of games tables. Madame de Pompadour had six of these in her salon at Meudon.

Dressing-room furniture tended to be more functional, but could be equally decorative. The *coiffeuse* had a central hinged mirror, flanked by two flaps underneath which were compartments for scent bottles. Bedside-tables contained small cupboards with marble shelves to hold a chamber pot, and occasionally a drawer below containing the *chaise percée*. Candlestands with tray tops, known as *guéridons*, tended to be rather wide and low, and were also useful as coffee- or worktables.

French provincial furniture was of two kinds. Important towns like Dijon, Lyons and Bordeaux had their own guilds and craftsmen who more or less followed Paris fashions to supply their merchants and officials. Such work is sometimes signed. A provincial origin of a commode may be indicated by its carcase being of pine rather than of oak, or by its general lack of finesse. True regional styles, however, are of greater interest and can have undoubted charm. Such country furniture features in paintings by Chardin and Greuze. It was made for country aristocrats and the bourgeoisie as well as for the better-off peasants. Provincial Rococo can be handsome and distinctive, but is hard to date. The style reached Brittany and Gascony later, and it survived in many districts into and beyond the nineteenth century.

Over the whole country, the basic forms did not vary much. In contrast with the increasing sophistication of Paris, provincial furniture kept alive many outmoded pieces: kneehole writing-desks, buffets, dough bins and food cupboards. Ladderback chairs with rush seats, and simple tables with curved legs seem almost timeless in their style. The show-pieces were cupboards, often in two parts, and the panelling, with chanelled and scrolled mouldings, and carved flowers either in high or low relief, can be very fine. The woods used varied slightly with the resources of each district. The best and most expensive were oak and walnut, with boxwood for turned chair legs. Other native woods such as cherry, chestnut, elm, beech, ash and poplar were less expensive.

Each region had its own traditions. Flemish influence can be seen in the north-east, while the furniture of Picardy tends to have little carving. In Normandy, fine cupboards were made in great quantity, and are hard to distinguish from those of Paris. In Brittany, where a middle class hardly existed, there was

a marked reluctance to accept Rococo decoration, and many pieces were ornamented with geometrical rather than scrolling or naturalistic patterns. A feature of Breton interiors is the use of dressers with open shelves to hold pottery. In order to exclude draughts, Breton beds were enclosed by panelling so as almost to become closets. Gascony was also conservative and kept to Louis Treize styles for a long while. In the south-east, the country styles of Burgundy were more sophisticated and bourgeois in character, while in Provence they became almost luxurious. Provençal cupboards are often swelled or even bombé, and the influence of Piedmont is obvious in the shapes of chests of drawers and their richly carved decoration.

The French provincial style extended to the Canadian colonies, centred at Quebec. Furniture was well proportioned, but sparing in its carved decoration, and the wood generally used was pine. Finer work with carving, and the use of walnut, cherry and maple, was reserved for church furnishings.

Above: Chardin's painting, Saying Grace, of about 1740 shows a simple interior typical of the French lower bourgeoisie. Of the provincial forms shown here, the high-back chairs derive from Louis Quatorze types, while the rush-seat chair and the buffet are forms which were still being made in the twentieth century. (Louvre, Paris)

111

Liège was the centre of a wealthy bishopric situated between Flanders and Germany. Although part of the Holy Roman Empire, its furniture is not typical of the German style. Some of the forms and all the decoration came from France, but the result is too fine to be classed as French provincial. The industries of Liège had been stimulated by the wars of Louis XIV, and the Walloon population included many brilliant craftsmen. The houses built by the 1730s include the Château de Seraing for the Prince-Bishop, and the Hôtel d'Ansembourg for the banker Michel Willems. The craft guilds flourished, but very little furniture is actually signed.

The principal wood was oak, carefully chosen for its fine quality, close grain, and consistent, delicate sheen. Some pieces were partly gilded and painted, but bronze and ormolu were sparingly used. The most typical pieces are the great oak cupboards and buffets in one or two parts, tall clocks, commodes with four equal drawers and short feet, writing-tables, bureaux, and glazed cabinets and bookshelves. The delicate carving, always carried out in solid wood, resembles that on French wall panelling. Furniture outlines were simple, and the effect, unlike that of

Dutch or German furniture, was never bulky or ungainly. Chairs were either in the French style and caned, or in the Germanic-Dutch tradition with back splats and loose seats. These were often of walnut, ash or elm. For simple furniture, pine and beech were also used.

Italy

Italy took up the Rococo spirit comparatively early, for a definite relaxation of style can be detected around 1700. Many features of the mature Rococo, as for instance those in Meissonnier's engravings of the thirties, originated in Italy — whether in the sixteenth-century grottoes decorated with rocks and shells, in the architecture of Borromini, or in late seventeenth-century carving, where scrolling strapwork has a surprising freedom and movement. Some late seventeenth-century sculptors, notably Filippo Parodi in Genoa, had already abandoned the seriousness of the Baroque for grace and gaiety. In the early eighteenth century, the Venetian painters like Ricci, Pellegrini and Guardi established the bright, fanciful fresco style that culminated in the work of Tiepolo. Many of these artists travelled all over Europe, and their painted

Right: This superb pedestal clock is one of the few pieces of Liège furniture that is both signed and dated. It was made in 1743 by Louis Lejeune, who was one of the most brilliant interpreters of Rococo furniture in Liège. The asymmetry of the delicate carving, all carried out in solid oak, reflects the Rococo style, and is strongly reminiscent of French boiseries or wall panelling. This form of long-case clock, developed in the Netherlands, was not favoured in Paris. (Musée de Mariemont)

ceilings and walls brought Italian light and air to northern palaces.

Thus, there is no clear division in Italy between Baroque and Rococo. The furniture is often hard to date, and in the absence of documented works, Italian furniture must be judged chiefly by its style. The general picture is one of regional characteristics modified by the various influences coming from France, Germany, and, occasionally, England, while Spanish influence can be seen in the south and Sicily.

Eighteenth-century Italy consisted of a number of separate states. In the kingdoms of Piedmont and Naples, palaces were built to rival the splendour of Versailles. In the Papal States, noble families contrived to redecorate their palaces with ceremonial splendour, even though many of their fortunes were now diminishing. Genoa and Venice were republics where there was a great demand for furniture from the nobility and successful merchants, and on the whole it is these two districts that have left us with the most distinctive variations of the Rococo style. In spite of so many regional differences, certain features developed over most of the peninsula, and make it possible to speak of 'Italian Rococo'.

Certain traditions of craftsmanship were continued. The most important was the skill of Italy's carvers. This was put to its greatest use in the churches, as in the gilded organ-cases, altar furnishings and sumptuous confessionals. The line dividing carvers and sculptors can be very thin, and Venetian and Genoese side-tables often abound with putti and nymphs or with groups of Chinese figures. At first, tables were heavily loaded with carving. Later they became extremely delicate, often appearing too fragile to support their marble tops. Luxurious mirror frames were made to hang over them, as were characteristic small looking-glasses with cartouche frames —wider at the top than at the bottom. Not much use was made of ormolu, Rococo borders and crestings on cupboards and commodes being ordinarily of carved and gilded wood.

Another traditional Italian material was marble. White or grey marble from Carrara was inexhaustible; Sicilian marble, streaked with salmon and green, was quarried principally for Naples. The famous coloured marbles, however, were taken from the ruins of classical buildings, and they too seemed to be in endless supply. *Verde antico*, yellow Siena, *cipollino,* porphyry, Egyptian alabaster and many others were all worked into table-tops. The Italian carved side-tables that are often seen in English country-houses may well have been bought for the sake of their marble tops.

Marquetry, or *intarsia*, had first been

developed in fifteenth-century Italy. Though it was now executed more extensively in France and Germany, Milanese marquetry was very delicate, showing panels of *galant* or *Commedia dell' Arte* figures in shaped Rococo borders. Natural woods rather than stained ones were used, often with ivory for the flesh parts.

Although the shaped or bombé commode originated in France, the Italian versions are instantly recognizable, whether in the exaggerated Venetian or the simpler Genoese forms. Their bodies tend to be large, the legs to be extremely thin. Chests of drawers were sometimes veneered, but by the 1750s they were often japanned or painted with flowers against white or pale grounds. The outward appearance has great charm, and conceals the case work where, by French or English standards, the joinery can be shockingly bad. In painted furniture, japan *(lacca)* at first imitated Chinese lacquer, but this gave way to a more European style decorated with flowers on a light ground. Venetian lacca was rather thickly applied, but elsewhere, as in Genoa and the South, for instance, it could be so thin as almost to show the wood underneath. This tends to add to its charm. A less expensive kind of decoration was used, especially in the Venice district, known as *lacca povera*, in which small coloured engravings of pastoral or stage scenes, or topographical views were cut out and stuck on to the furniture, the remainder being painted and gilded, and the whole varnished over.

Some types of furniture are particularly Italian in form. Prie-dieus were made in great numbers, and the more elaborate were fitted into chapels and oratories while simpler pieces were used in bedrooms. The *trespolo*, much favoured in Venice, was a light, simple stand for a candle or dressing-glass. As regards seat furniture, the Italian chair of the Louis Quinze type generally has rather wide mouldings with concave chanellings, and the upholstered back and seat may be removable. Generally, the Italian version of the French chair lacks its comfort; the lines tend to be upright and its appearance hard. A north Italian form of the sofa is that known as *a ventaglio* or 'fan-shaped', in which the arms incline outwards at an angle of 45 degrees.

German influence was strongest in Lombardy and Venice, but it can be found as far south as Naples. The elaborate bureau-cabinet, known as a *trumeau,* with an elaborately shaped lower part and an arched and crested upper part, shows how northern forms that were never popular in France were common in Italy. Sometimes these bureaux are plain and rectangular, following English types. English influence is also found in chairs of the Queen Anne pattern.

Furniture for private rooms could be quite simple, and was either painted or made of walnut or cherry. The different forms were not nearly so numerous as in France, and they consisted chiefly of chairs, tables, chests of drawers large and small, and cupboards, often made in two parts. In general, physical comfort was not well catered for.

As for the different states, the various

Right: The Games Room at Stupinigi near Turin. Stupinigi was a royal hunting-lodge in the country, and, compared with the palaces in the city, the rooms have a light and airy character. The brightly coloured wall decorations are based on Chinese wallpapers, but are carried out in an almost primitive style, and are full of humour.

Below left: This mid-eighteenth century commode is typical of the Venetian style. The curves are so exaggerated that there is little resemblance to French commodes. The lively flower sprays are beautifully painted on a yellow ground, and set within carved and gilded Rococo borders. Commodes were often made in sets of three, with one large and two narrow ones, and armchairs were decorated to match. (Ca' Rezzonico, Venice)

Right: The Chinese Room in the Palace at Turin was designed by Filippo Juvarra, the architect to the King of Piedmont, and carried out from 1735 to 1738. The state rooms in the Turin palaces have a formal character very different from the intimacy of contemporary French interiors. Chinese lacquer was removed from imported screens, and set in Rococo borders of carved and gilded wood. The furniture was made for the room about 1740, and is based on French models. There are ten folding stools, two sofas and four side-tables. (Palazzo Reale, Turin)

regional styles can often, though not always, be recognized. The northern states were more active in making fine furniture than those of the centre and south. Lombardy, with Milan as the centre, was subject to Austria from 1717, and here German influence seems to have been strongest. Milanese furniture tends to be severe in outline and precise in workmanship. The typical piece was the bureau, or bureau-cabinet, generally veneered with figured walnut, or inlaid with marquetry scenes in discreetly contrasting woods. Milan, however, could match the height of Rococo opulence, as can be seen in the gallery of the Palazzo Clerici, designed during the 1740s, with its mirrored walls, gilded tables and sofas matching the panelling, and a superb ceiling painted by Tiepolo.

Piedmont was an independent kingdom of increasing power and influence. The Duke Vittorio Amadeo II assumed the title of King in 1713, and embarked on an ambitious programme of building churches and palaces with Filippo Juvarra as his architect. The poet Thomas Gray described the Royal Palace of Turin as 'the very quintessence of gilding and looking glass, inlaid floors, carved panels,

and painting wherever they could stick a brush'. The Castello di Stupinigi, built from 1739 just outside Turin, has an even more grandiose interior with a great deal of chinoiserie decoration. Juvarra's panelling was richer than anything in Paris, and the gilded carving is equally inventive in chairs and side-tables, though not, curiously enough, in commodes. Juvarra seems to have designed much of the furniture himself, and used the best craftsmen he could find. Luigi Prinotto made splendid marquetry furniture during the 1720s, but was overshadowed by Pietro Piffetti, who was brought from Rome. Piffetti's furniture is among the most highly ornamented in Europe, with astonishing marquetry worked in all manner of rare woods, ivory, mother-of-pearl and silver. Some of it incorporated sculptured ormolu mounts made by Ladatte from Paris, while on other pieces the sculptured ornaments are of gilded wood. Apart from the great cabinets, tables and prie-dieus that are to be seen in the palace, Piffetti made simpler pieces, such as a card-table with *trompe l'oeil* inlay simulating playing cards. A feature of the Piedmontese bureau or cabinet in two parts is that the upper part is often raised up to stand on separate feet.

Furniture from republican Genoa was considerably simpler than that from the court of Turin, and its decoration was seldom excessive. Bombé chests of drawers tended to be large but well balanced, and were often painted with flowers in a pattern covering the whole front. The painting can be so thin as almost to show the wood underneath. Bureau-cabinets were always popular. Kingwood was used for veneer, and the characteristic Genoese parquetry has 'oyster' pieces of kingwood or olivewood combined in pairs to make a heart-shaped pattern. Genoese seat furniture was restrained, and close to French models. Ornamental side-tables were finely carved, and the sculptural tradition of Parodi continued with his son Domenico and other notable sculptors in wood.

The style of Venice is the most easily recognizable in Italy. The gilded tables, chairs and thrones made by the sculptor Antonio Corradini for the Ca' Rezzonico are really Baroque pieces designed in a playful mood, made to impress rather than to be used. More typical are the mid-century commodes, often made in sets, with exaggerated bombé shapes and carved, gilded borders. Chairs would still be large, with high backs when made for galleries or salons, or small and comfortable for private rooms; they were often made of walnut with open backs and seat-rails carved with interlaced mouldings. The general effect of these pieces is one of continual movement, as though reflected across rippling water, or in a distorting mirror. The Venetians loved colour, whether in damasks and silks,

or in their brilliant lacca. Venetian looking-glasses, large and small, were often engraved with Commedia dell' Arte figures in patterned borders. Glass made at Murano was exported all over Europe.

In central Italy, great silk and textile works continued to flourish at Lucca, and Lucchese beds were designed principally to show off their hangings. Florentine Rococo tends to be rather florid and formal, but is hard to assess properly because the Medici patronage ceased altogether with the death of Giovanni Gastone in 1737, and much court furniture was sent to Vienna or sold. The Florentine production of *pietre dure* for table-tops and cabinet panels continued, though the designs were not so splendid as formerly. As this was so expensive, the cheaper technique of *scagliola*, which was decorated with sprays of flowers and classical landscape scenes, continued in the hands of Lamberto Gori, the pupil of Father Hugford. Such table-tops were often bought by English tourists, but they are easily damaged and not many survive today. In Rome, the nobility liked formal magnificence in their state-rooms. The best known of the Roman galleries is in

the Palazzo Doria Pamphili, redesigned after 1734, with its gilded tables and chairs covered in Genoese velvet that can seldom if ever have been used. Other families who had their palaces redecorated included the Barberini, Borghese and Chigi.

Southern Italy became independent of Hapsburg rule in 1734. The Bourbon king, Charles III, set up tapestry, porcelain and bronze works at Naples, all of which contributed to the decoration of his palaces in Naples and at Caserta. Neapolitan furniture, however, tends to be heavy in style, and northern Italians think ill of its proportions. The parquetry, in walnut, kingwood or other closely matching materials, is often centred by a flowerhead or eight-pointed star, within rope-twist or chequered borders. Sicilian furniture is full of gaiety, making use of silvering rather than gilding, and of flowers painted against light blue grounds. Much of it has a pleasant naïvety resulting from folk traditions or Spanish influence. Raised details on chests of drawers and other pieces were often applied in composition (*pastiglia*).

Spain and Portugal

The demand for furniture by the hereditary nobility of Spain was not great. English travellers in the 1670s noticed the contrast between the vast size of their palaces and their scanty old-fashioned furnishings. At the same time, silk and velvet hangings were rich, and the eighteenth century produced a number of carved and gilded looking-glasses with tables to stand underneath. The carving on Spanish woodwork, though in the Rococo style, lacked the vitality of the French and Italian spirit. The Spanish were a conservative race, and even the tools used by the craftsmen were old-fashioned. Oak and walnut were becoming expensive, and painted furniture of soft wood was a cheaper substitute.

The old types of chair persisted, and they were often covered with tooled leather held in place by brass nailing. On the whole, the English forms were interpreted better than the French, and much English furniture was imported through Galicia or from Menorca. A different form of chair developed, with rush seating, turned uprights and carved ladder-back rails. These might appear somewhat rustic, but they were placed in noblemen's houses, and were often painted and gilded.

King Charles III, however, was a Bourbon descended from Louis XIV, and he had already been king of Naples for 25 years. He established royal furniture workshops on the lines of the Gobelins in Paris, and moved the Naples porcelain factory to El Buen Retiro. The furnishing of the palace in Madrid was directed by the Neapolitan Matteo Gasparini. The throne-room has vast looking-glasses and side-tables attributed to Ventura Rodriguez,

Above: A late Rococo ensemble (of about 1760) in the Veronese Room at the Palazzo Reale, Genoa. Rooms were then generally decorated in pale colours, the better to set off the extremely fine carving of the panelling. Genoese carvers were very skilled, and the looking-glass frame and the gilded table are of exceptional delicacy. The ormolu candle brackets are probably French.

Left: This cabinet, made in about 1732, for the Queen's Closet, shows the extreme elaboration of the work carried out for the King of Piedmont by Pietro Piffetti. The marquetry is in ebony, fig, acacia and boxwood, with ivory and mother-of-pearl. (Palazzo Reale, Turin)

and a large carved and gilded throne. Many of the chairs designed by Gasparini were not carved, but veneered with kingwood or marquetry.

In general, the furniture of Portugal was more distinguished than that of Spain. Portugal became prosperous under King John V in the first half of the eighteenth century, and the disaster of the Lisbon earthquake in 1755 must at least have stimulated the demand for furniture as the city was rebuilt. The Portuguese style shows unmistakable English influences, and there were, in fact, many resident English families conducting the wine trade who imported English furniture. Chairs show both early Georgian and 'Chippendale' characteristics, and were finely made with crisp, lively sprays of acanthus carving on the backs and cabriole legs. Portuguese tables, bureaux and commodes were made in practical, well-balanced shapes, and their joinery was good. Much of this furniture was made in a variety of rosewood imported from the Brazilian colonies.

Germany

German furniture presents a very diverse picture, which is almost as baffling as the country's political condition. In the eighteenth century, Germany consisted of over 600 different states, loosely bound together as the Holy Roman Empire. Neglecting the tiny dominions of the knights, they group roughly into temporal principalities, ecclesiastical principalities, and free cities. If, broadly

speaking, Rococo furniture can be divided between localized bourgeois styles and the international court style originating in Paris, this division is nowhere better seen than in Germany. The city merchants of the north were predominantly Protestant, and their furniture generally continued in the traditions already established by their guilds. At the courts, on the other hand, each prince, whether powerful or poor, endeavoured to rival the grandeur of Versailles and to surpass his neighbour. Palaces were built as emblems of state, and German Rococo decoration symbolizes grandeur and influence rather than informality. The southern courts were mostly Catholic, and at times interior decoration seems to have been limited neither by financial considerations nor by the nature of the materials used. The extreme of the European Rococo style came with the Bavarian churches, where the Catholic religion itself turned into a fantasy of extraordinary proportions.

The princes enjoyed chinoiserie, and Chinese rooms were constructed to display lacquered walls and collections of oriental porcelain. Chinese pleasure-houses in the parks, such as the Tea House at Potsdam, Schloss Pillnitz near Dresden, and the Pagodaburg at Nymphenburg, were for courtly diversions. Their furniture, including chairs, tea-tables and stands to display porcelain, might be either gilded, or japanned in the Chinese manner. Among the decorative arts, porcelain seems to express the epitome of

Left: Known today as the Gasparini Room, this was originally the Dressing Room of King Charles III. When Charles became King of Spain in 1759, he completed the interior of the Palace in Madrid regardless of expense, bringing painters (including Tiepolo and Mengs) and craftsmen from Italy. Mathias Gasparini was Neapolitan, and designed this room and the seat furniture. The elaborate stucco ceiling is complemented by the inlaid floor and embroidered silk wall-hangings. The chairs have something in common with German work, not only in their bulbous shapes, but in the unusual way the frames are veneered rather than carved. (Palacio Real, Madrid)

Right: One of the most famous of the Rococo commodes that were made for the Elector of Bavaria. It was made by Johann Adam Pichler in 1761, possibly to designs by Cuvilliés, and continues the delicate, pleasing style that he had established at the Munich Court 30 years before. The details show subtle refinements of the French Rococo style, and are of carved and gilded wood. In Paris they would have been of ormolu. (Residenzmuseum, Munich)

119

the German Rococo spirit, and by the end of this period many courts had established their own factories in rivalry to that at Meissen in Saxony. Exquisite porcelain figures were arranged in specially designed rooms with brackets built into the panelling. Their grace and sparkle, and the gilded furniture was reflected by the mirrored walls to make a glittering effect that could hardly be matched elsewhere in Europe.

At the beginning of the century, court architecture and decoration had been predominantly Italian, but from 1720, native designers were sent to study in Paris. Early Rococo furniture, therefore, was based on the *goût pittoresque* of Blondel, Pineau and Meissonnier, but in the important states regional variations quickly developed under the influence of court artists, sculptors and craftsmen. Among the great centres were Munich, Würzburg, Bayreuth and Bamberg, while further north, Saxony and, later, Prussia were very active. The Hapsburg court at Vienna, however, was an exception. It relied chiefly on Italian or French furniture and craftsmen. When a national Austrian style emerged after 1750, it was a predominantly middle-class one.

The most delicate of German Rococo developed in Bavaria, where the Elector Max Emanuel had his Residenz or city palace in Munich, and his Schloss Nymphenburg just outside the city. The character of Bavarian Rococo was established early by the architect Joseph Effner and the designer Cuvilliés, whose traditions were continued later by the carvers J A Pilcher and J M Schmidt. François Cuvilliés, Flemish by birth, began his royal service as the court dwarf, but his talents were recognized by the Elector, who sent him to study under Blondel in Paris from 1720 to 1724. His most famous interiors are those of the Reichenzimmer in Munich, and the Amalienburg pavilion at Nymphenburg. Cuvilliés was the most advanced of the German Rococo designers, and delighted in the French style while relaxing its disciplines. Cuvilliés' designs were reproduced in engraving, and had a great influence in France and England as well as in Germany.

Of the southern courts, one of the wealthiest was that of the Prince-Bishop Lothar Franz von Schönborn at Würzburg. His Residenz was begun in 1719 by the architect Balthasar Neumann, and during the 1750s Tiepolo went there to paint the magnificent ceilings. Much of the furniture was designed by the court sculptor Franz Anton von Schlott, and was made by a number of outstanding craftsmen. The carved furniture of Würzburg includes some of the most richly ornamented in Germany. Ansbach and Bayreuth, though Protestant courts, also have splendid interiors in their palaces, while at Bamberg the carved

furniture shows the influence of the sculptor Ferdinand Dietz.

German cabinet work, with elaborate veneers of walnut and mahogany, could be very fine, particularly at Würzburg and Bamberg. Bureaux and cabinets from Bamberg were made in surprising shapes, which could be either reticent and suave, or rather bulky and obtrusive. At Bayreuth, the Spindler brothers created a masterpiece in the marquetry room at the Schloss Fantasie (now removed to Munich), where the walls are inlaid with landscapes and classical ruins,

Below: This Prussian corner cupboard, probably made by Johann August Nahl in 1750, is veneered with cedar, and the gilded ornaments are of carved wood and ormolu. (Schloss Charlottenburg, Berlin)

and chests of drawers were made to match. During the 1750s there was a revival of landscapes and perspectives worked in marquetry, recalling the old fashion of the Renaissance. Worked as panels in the decoration of cupboards and bureaux, they looked more than ever like stage settings, peopled by actors with faces and hands picked out in ivory. Further north, marquetry designs tended to be stiff and old-fashioned, often keeping to the late Baroque formula of scrolling arabesques, and incorporating brass in the outmoded French style of Boulle.

Saxony kept closer to traditional forms than the southern courts. Typical of Dresden furniture are the bureau-cabinets and cupboards, made in two parts and fitted with mirrored doors above. Underneath their judicious Rococo decoration, they are basically solid pieces with well-defined outlines, and their restraint is said to show English influence. Japanning in the oriental style was practised by Martin Schnell from 1710, and was continued by other makers after his death in 1749. Seat furniture for the Elector's court tended to be heavily carved, as though to continue the ponderous magnificence of the Zwinger Palace, begun in 1713. Saxony suffered during the Seven Years War (1756–63), and orders for court furniture were greatly reduced.

Rococo came late to Prussia, for King Frederick William had little time or taste for the arts. Frederick the Great, who succeeded him in 1740, immediately embarked on a great building programme, which began with a new wing containing the Golden Gallery at Charlottenburg, Berlin and the Stadtschloss, or town palace, in Potsdam (now demolished). In 1745 he began his famous summer retreat, Sanssouci at Potsdam. Until 1746 his architect was Georg von Knobelsdorff, who established the rather aggressive character of 'Friderican Rococo'. When, 20 years later, the vast new palace at Potsdam was built to celebrate Frederick's victories, so conservative were the artistic tastes of the King that the style of interior decoration had hardly advanced at all.

Of Knobelsdorff's craftsmen, the carver Johann August Nahl was pre-eminent. He carried out stuccowork and panelling, and designed chairs and side-tables with bold projecting curves and florid carved details. In 1746, Knobelsdorff was succeeded by the Hoppenhaupt brothers, whose chairs, tables, commodes and looking-glasses, though bulbous and angular in design, are always

Above left: This chair was made for Frederick the Great in about 1765, probably to the designs of J C Hoppenhaupt. It is of walnut and upholstered with pale blue and silver damask. (Schloss Charlottenburg, Berlin)

Above right: Sanssouci was completed in 1747 as the summer retreat of Frederick the Great of Prussia. The Concert Room shows Knobelsdorff's decorative style at its best. (Sanssouci, Potsdam)

121

well balanced. A softer note was provided by the cabinet-work of Melchior Kambli, who arrived as a sculptor in 1746, and the Spindler brothers who came from Bayreuth in 1764. Kambli designed magnificent ormolu mounts for his commodes, which were often veneered with cedar or tortoiseshell. The cabinet-work of the Spindlers is among the highest achievements of German Rococo. The richly designed marquetry was carried out in coloured woods, with mother-of-pearl, silver and ivory.

The free cities of the north had maintained their independence through the now defunct Hanseatic League. Mainz, on the Rhine, was a free city, but it also had a Catholic episcopal court, and court influences can be detected in its marquetry and carved ornament. The Mainz craftsmen were famous for their veneered cupboards and cabinets, which were inventive in design and superb in their workmanship. Frankfurt, though not far from Mainz, was Protestant and notably conservative in spirit. The typical Frankfurt cupboard was solid and simple in shape, and it was only during the 1750s that it developed bombé or more fanciful outlines.

Throughout the north of Germany, furniture supplied to the middle classes of the cities was for use rather than for show, and cupboards, cabinets and tables tended to remain within the traditional Baroque formulae. Large surfaces lent themselves to veneers of native woods, principally walnut, oak, elm and ash, which were laid in panels of geometrical and scrolled parquetry within broad borders. The wardrobes, now commonly made in two parts, show a certain Dutch or English influence. The bureau-cabinet, also made in two parts, was another Anglo-Dutch form which became very popular throughout Germany. North Italian bureaux were clearly made in imitation of these. The curved surfaces of the lower part of a bureau were very varied in their bombé and swollen shapes. In the north, these were sometimes grossly exaggerated, and remarkable pieces were made in Schleswig-Holstein and even in Denmark. Chairs generally followed the Dutch or English style, with hooped backs and splats, often with caned seats. After the 1750s a simplified form of the English 'Chippendale' chair was made. Hanover, allied to the English crown, was probably the principal source of English influence.

One craftsman, Abraham Roentgen, deserves a special mention as he combined several national styles and achieved an international reputation. After working in England for eight years, and also in Holland, in about 1750 he opened his workshop at Neuwied on the Rhine. Sometimes he made use of English furniture forms, and he excelled at marquetry and mechanical fittings. He is also known to have made chairs

Left: This bureau-cabinet, perhaps made by Johann Raab in about 1765, shows how Rococo decoration could be applied to the rather bulky case furniture that was made in Franconia and the cities of North Germany. The walnut veneer combines diamond parquetry with interlaced scrolls.

Right: This painting, The Family of Count Vries, by J V Tischbein, shows ordinary furniture in use, and the style of the hoop-back chairs and the tea-table is clearly based on the Anglo-Dutch tradition. (Kunstmuseum der Stadt, Düsseldorf)

Below: The card-table was made in about 1755 by Abraham Roentgen. It is of cherrywood, and the top has brass inlay in the German manner. The top leaf opens to form a card-table with counter-wells, and with the second leaf open it becomes a writing-table. (Victoria & Albert Museum, London)

based on the Louis Quinze style, not carved but veneered and inlaid. This technique derived from Holland, and was widely practised during the revival of Rococo in the nineteenth century. From 1761, Roentgen was assisted by his son David, whose work was to become even more important.

Poland and Russia

Rococo in eastern Europe was not in the main of German origin, even though Poland was ruled until 1764 by the Electors of Saxony, who brought their own architects and craftsmen. The carvers, joiners and turners on Polish estates were highly skilled, but the traditional Baroque forms were only slowly displaced. Polish culture had strong links with Paris, and French furniture was imported by wealthy aristocrats. Some of Meissonnier's most elaborate designs of the 1730s, which we know of only through his engravings, were for the rooms and furniture of Polish diplomats.

In Russia, too, furniture was imported, chiefly from Paris. But the skill of Russian carvers was very great, and they had no difficulty in executing the Rococo designs. Russian Rococo reflects chiefly the ambitions of its four empresses, who reigned almost continuously from 1724. The extravagant Empress Elizabeth (1742–62) successfully achieved the westernization of the arts that had begun under Peter the Great. She established manufactories of silks and fabrics, jewellery, porcelain and metalwork. All these decorative arts were predominantly French in character.

The early Rococo style was established by Frenchmen, including Pineau who worked at

Peterhof until 1727. His carved work was a sumptuous version of the French Régence. During the 1740s, the St Petersburg palaces were in the brilliant hands of Bartolommeo Rastrelli, the son of Peter the Great's principal sculptor, who had studied in Italy and France. He built or enlarged the Winter Palace, Peterhof and Tsarskoe Selo, and designed much of the furniture. Not a great deal of his Rococo is now to be seen, because some was replaced during the neo-classical period, and a great deal was destroyed during the Second World War.

Antonio Rinaldi came to Russia from Italy in 1752, and was employed by Catherine the Great who did not care for Rastrelli. Rinaldi's superb work can be seen at Oranienbaum (literally, the 'Orange Tree'), near Leningrad, and combines vigour and fluidity with a fine sense of colour. Katalnaya Gorka, a pleasure-lodge at Oranienbaum, is markedly Rococo within, and the furniture is characterized by its slender scrolled outlines. The most exciting example of Rinaldi's work is, perhaps, the Chinese Palace, which draws on both chinoiserie and European styles. Exotic motifs were used boldly, and the furniture, though basically European in form, makes use of Chinese frets and characters.

Denmark and Sweden

At this time, Sweden was an independent kingdom, though of less influence than formerly, and Denmark and Norway were united under the Danish crown. The long-standing trade with England in timber and iron ore helped to establish English influences in furniture simultaneously with the more enduring Dutch and German influences.

The early eighteenth-century chair with a hooped back and broad splat persisted to about 1760. English chairs were so popular in Denmark that in 1747 an order was made forbidding their importation. The Danes appreciated the economical lines of English furniture, however, and by the 1760s a light form of chair based on the 'Chippendale' type was made. Other imitations of simple English forms included clocks and bureau-cabinets. Mahogany was expensive, and walnut was more generally used, or pine which was painted or japanned. A delicate marquetry in stained woods can sometimes be found.

The guilds in both Denmark and Sweden were organized on German lines, and the traditional craftsman's piece, the cupboard, can be very similar to those from Germany. The north German commode or bureau with a bulbous, swollen front was made in Copenhagen. Sweden developed a distinct type of three-drawer commode, with pronounced bombé curves, a rather narrow top and base, and projecting feet. The drawers were separated by concave mouldings, the

Left: This bureau-cabinet shows how, in Denmark, the German style could reach the limits of extravagance. It was made for the Danish King by C F Lehmann in 1755, and is one of the most elaborate pieces of its type. The complexity of the commode base is matched by the exuberance of the Rococo carving in the cresting. The veneer and parquetry are principally of kingwood, and the corner panels are of bone and ivory on metal. The gilded mounts are partly of gilt-bronze, and partly of carved wood. (Rosenborg Castle, Copenhagen)

Above right: This Danish commode, made by C J Preisler in the early 1740s, is a courtly, luxurious piece. The restrained outline is broken by the arching mouldings on the front, which continue the curve of the feet. Many Danish furniture-makers were sent by the court to study their craft in Germany, and this piece shows more German than French characteristics. (Rosenborg Castle, Copenhagen)

Below right: Furniture in Sweden made in the international Rococo style, such as this table, indicated royal patronage. Like all European rulers, the King of Sweden wished to keep abreast of the latest Rococo fashions, and the court architect, Carl Harleman made several visits to Paris, where he studied under Vassé. The table, made in about 1750, is of carved and gilded wood, but the well-defined curves and solid construction give it more German character than French. (Royal Palace, Stockholm)

parquetry was in geometrical mosaic, and the ormolu rather sparingly applied.

French furniture was imported for the courts, and served as models for the royal palaces. Unfortunately, the palace of Christiansborg in Copenhagen was destroyed in a fire in 1794. In Stockholm the new palace was completed in the middle of the eighteenth century. Much of its furniture was designed by the architect, Harleman, and craftsmen were sent to study in Paris. Many pieces look very French, combining Parisian techniques with an admirable restraint in their design.

Holland

Dutch Rococo was not stimulated by the court, but was absorbed into traditional bourgeois forms. Chairs generally kept to the old-fashioned Anglo-Dutch forms with hooped backs and cabriole legs. Meanwhile, small pieces of furniture such as tea-tables and chests of drawers could be fine and well-proportioned.

The various forms of cupboard, whether wardrobes, bureau-cabinets or glazed display-cases, could be enormously wide. They were generally made in two parts, the lower

Below: Two-part cabinets were the show-pieces of eighteenth-century Dutch rooms. The commode base is of the Dutch bombé shape (the curves not being fully three-dimensional). The upper part has looking-glass painted with exotic water birds and plants, and just behind the Rococo carvings of the arched cornice there are five platforms for pottery or porcelain vases. The cabinet is veneered with burr-walnut, crossbanded with rosewood, and there are small marquetry panels of flowers. This fine piece shows the continuity of the best Dutch traditions. (Rijksmuseum, Amsterdam)

section being shaped in bulky curves. In the upper part, the panels or glazing bars were outlined by scrolling mouldings with carved Rococo leaves, and the arched cornices often had platforms for Delft or Chinese vases. Holland retained the claw-and-ball foot long after it had gone out of fashion in England, and on these cupboards it occurs in a massive form. The most pleasing veneer was of burr-walnut, but mahogany was also used. A marquetry tradition continued, but compared to the splendid work of about 1700 it became uninventive — though still distinctive — working flowersprays into the surfaces with tedious repetition.

It cannot be maintained that mid-eighteenth century Dutch furniture has a high place in European design. Perhaps their own traditions failed to develop because of the popularity of English and French furniture, and in 1771 all such imports had to be prohibited. Meanwhile, French chairs and commodes were imitated. A Dutch commode might easily be mistaken for French provincial work, but the marquetry

generally lacks vigour, and the ormolu mounts seem mechanical and repetitive.

England

By the mid-eighteenth century, the character of English furniture had become quite distinct from the rest of Europe. The standard of joiners' and cabinet-makers' work, which was already high in Queen Anne's reign, improved steadily, and the general excellence of London furniture was second only to that of France. This might not be expected from the *laissez-faire* state of the country. But if there were no guilds or central authorities to supervise the level of craftsmanship, the standards exacted by patrons and the competitive spirit among the makers themselves served equally well.

The established traditions made for logical construction, simplicity of outline, and classical ornament. When Rococo decoration came in, it was as though by the 'back door', and was not imposed by the taste of the court or the aristocracy. 'French' ornament, however, steadily increased in popularity from about 1740 until after 1760, and it could be lavish. Sometimes, as in the familiar 'Chippendale' dining-chairs, it was judiciously applied to the English style; at other times it seems uneasy, disjointed or even superfluous. The chinoiserie and 'gothick' variations were very popular as novelties. Since straight lines were much used in these styles, their ornaments could be more easily adapted to the English tradition than convoluting scrollwork. Furniture in the Chinese taste was more plentiful in England than in any other country. The eighteenth-century gothick style was almost totally confined to England.

Rococo in Europe was a courtly style. But in England the court had scarcely any power or prestige, and exercised almost no influence on the arts. Even George III, who was interested, never directed their course. The landed aristocracy, who governed the country, were predominantly Whigs whose wealth lay in their property. In both their town- and country-houses, they required comfort and convenience as well as a degree of splendour. Materially, England was now prospering as never before. With the growth of banking and colonial trade, merchant families could build and furnish houses as lavishly as any aristocrat.

The habits of society were not to change much until the Industrial Revolution. In contrast to France, English society was not noticeably dominated by women. Furniture remained masculine and functional, designed for its usefulness rather than for a luxurious indolence. On the other hand, through 'Beau' Nash's example at Bath, manners were more gentle, and the greater consideration given to women is reflected in their drawing- and dressing-rooms, which during the 1750s were

Right: This famous painting is the second from a set of eight, entitled Marriage à la Mode, in which Hogarth told the story of a disastrous marriage. The young couple, already bored with each other, are shown exhausted by their various dissipations of the night before. The room was taken from Lord Granville's house in London. Although it was painted in 1743, most of the furniture shown here might by then have been 20 years old. Notice the small tripod breakfast-table, moved close to the fire; the pole-screen on the right of the fireplace; and the arrangement of side-chairs around the walls of the room. (National Gallery, London)

decorated with gay fabrics and chintzes and Chinese wallpapers, and furnished with such pieces as china cabinets and small tables for use at tea gatherings.

The English attitude towards France, her traditional enemy, was somewhat equivocal. France was ruled despotically by king and church. Politically she supported the outlawed Stuarts, and economically she threatened colonial trade. These dangers were resolved by wars in 1745 and 1763 respectively. Meanwhile, certain cultivated Englishmen such as the Earl of Chesterfield mixed freely in Parisian society. French Rococo was taken up at first by those opposed to the Whig establishment, including the Tory aristocracy, the entourage of Frederick, Prince of Wales, and many London craftsmen who favoured the style as a welcome release from the tyranny of Palladianism.

There was no Baroque tradition in England comparable to the courtly styles of Europe. When Rococo appeared, it was a decorative novelty, not a logical development of what already existed. Rococo design was taught in London at the Academy of St Martin's Lane, which was founded by Hogarth. It came chiefly through H-F Gravelot, a French painter who came to England in 1732 and taught drawing and design at Hogarth's Academy. Rococo ornaments first appeared in engraving and silver work, and then, most suitably, on a large scale in the buildings at Vauxhall

Pleasure Gardens. It was probably at Vauxhall, too, that chinoiserie was first presented to the pleasure-seeking public.

Designs for furniture in the Rococo style can be seen in the engravings of an Italian, Gaetano Brunetti, published in 1736 and in those of some architects such as William Jones, who published a series in 1739. The details were handled with greater ease during the next decade. Rococo furniture was not normally designed by architects; rather, the style was left in the hands of the craftsmen, many of whom learned the important art of drawing at St Martin's Lane. English Rococo up to 1760 is often called the 'St Martin's Lane style'.

The best of the designers was undoubtedly the carver Matthias Lock. His drawings and engravings for looking-glasses and side-tables from 1740 show delight in the elaborate unclassical Rococo formula. In designs by Lock and others, one can see a progressive refinement and order of ornament, and by 1754, when Thomas Chippendale published his great folio volume, *The Gentleman and Cabinet-Maker's Director*, the style was fully mature. The book contained 161 plates illustrating nearly every type of furniture, and a third edition with 200 plates was published in 1762. It seems that he employed Lock and others as designers and engravers, but Chippendale's own contribution is likely to have been great, and he claimed to have

Above: Bed made for the Duke of Beaufort in about 1752 by the Linnells in the early chinoiserie style. It is japanned in red and green and gilded. (Victoria & Albert Museum, London)

Right: One of John Linnell's many designs for rooms. The decoration was to be carried out in pine. (Victoria & Albert Museum, London)

book of chairs (1765) was used in America, but appeared too late to influence the Rococo style in England. On the other hand, Thomas Johnson's designs for *girandoles* (published in 1755) and for other carvers' pieces—looking-glasses, side-tables and candlestands—(published between 1756 and 1761) are rather more elaborate than those in the *Director*. They include carved figures, both European and Chinese, and animal scenes from Barlow's engravings for Aesop's Fables. The girandoles are perhaps Johnson's best inventions, creating little worlds of their own, with rocky landscapes, mills and temples. The Rococo framing is quite asymmetrical, but exquisitely balanced. The designs may have been criticized as being too difficult, for in his second work he asserted that 'they may all be performed by a Master of his Art . . . I am well satisfied they can be executed by myself.' There are examples in existence which have been taken from Johnson's engravings, but we do not know if they were carved by him. William Linnell and John, probably his nephew, worked in London's fashionable Berkeley Square. They made excellent Rococo looking-glasses and chairs. John Linnell is known to have studied drawing in St Martin's Lane, and his very personal style is well known from the large number of his drawings which survive.

Since furniture was rarely signed, and few makers' labels have survived, we know very little about the craftsmen themselves. There were, however, an enormous number of them and the most distinguished, including Chippendale, William Vile—famous for the furniture he made for Queen Charlotte—and John Cobb, William Hallett, John Channon and Samuel Norman lived in or close to St Martin's Lane. Furniture-making included a number of different trades: the cabinet-maker, joiner (including specialized branches for chair and picture frames), carver, gilder and glass-grinder all made their contributions. Upholstery was carried out by the 'upholder', who also supplied curtains, carpets and wallpaper. A capable upholder supervised the entire business, and we may assume that Chippendale, Linnell and Norman acted as such. The work was often contracted out, however, to smaller specialist firms.

William Linnell, it seems, made the famous Chinese bed for Badminton in about 1754. Furniture in the Chinese taste had become the craze by the early 1750s in England. A room where tea is taken suggests oriental treatment, and cabinet-makers enthusiastically followed the fashion. The 'Barbarous gaudy *goût* of the Chinese', of which Mrs Montagu complained in 1749, included some japanned work copying imported screens and cabinets, while mahogany pieces of all kinds became Chinese by the inclusion of the orien-

invented and drawn a number of the pieces himself.

The long and distinguished list of subscribers to Chippendale's first edition is astonishing, and it was highly influential both in England and abroad. Some of the designs are plain and traditional, while others are of the wildest Rococo fantasy. Yet hardly a single piece of existing furniture made before 1764 can be attributed to him with certainty. All over the world, his name typifies the mature English Rococo style; yet his work after 1764, in a neo-classical idiom, was to be, if anything, finer.

None of the rival publications provoked by the *Director* approaches it in its comprehensiveness, and few do so in the quality of design and engraving. Ince and Mayhew's *Universal System of Household Furniture* (published in parts from 1759 to 1762) tells us more about their very reputable firm than about furniture styles. Robert Manwaring's

tal fret or paling, a temple roof, or a canopy. China cabinets naturally figured in such work, but so little attempt was made to understand true Chinese style that chinoiserie could be combined with Rococo or even classical details in a single piece.

English chinoiserie is seen at its best in carved looking-glasses. Pine could be carved into fragments of landscape, with Chinese peasants stepping delicately across palings, rocks, water and vegetation. The details that had originated in oriental lacquer and wall-paper underwent a transformation: peonies and bamboos became roses, acanthus or palms; dragons became cranes (ho-ho birds), dogs or other animals. Such exotic fantasies were essentially Rococo in spirit, and they quickly lapsed with the rise of Neo-classicism, to return with George IV's romantic work at Brighton Pavilion.

The gothick taste, which had appeared during the 1730s, was more enduring. The dream here concerned England's mediaeval past, and, when taken up by Horace Walpole and others, was allied to a kind of dilettante archaeology. Gothick was more masculine in character than chinoiserie, and well suited to a library. Chippendale illustrated gothick bookcases,

writing-tables, sideboards, hall-chairs, and a bed, but did not show the style in commodes or china cabinets, even though these occasionally were made. Furniture was gothick in detail rather than in form, with pointed arches, quatrefoil panels, balustrading and pinnacles. The resulting furniture bears no resemblance to the true mediaeval style in its construction or form.

English Rococo, then, presented a choice of the French, Chinese or gothick styles. But traditional or classical structure and proportions formed the basis of them all, and the amount of decoration could be varied according to the taste of the maker. Up to the 1760s, construction grew steadily lighter, and the ornaments more refined. The most obvious characteristic of mid-Georgian furniture is the universal use of mahogany, an expensive material imported from San Domingo or Cuba, which was strong and tough, and lent itself to fine and lively carving. It could also

129

be cut into wide sheets of veneer, either with a fine grain or, when cut from a root or fork, figured with a curl or flame. Walnut furniture was still made, but chiefly for bedrooms. Virginia walnut, imported from the American colonies, was sometimes used, as its grain is close and hard, resembling mahogany, and it was often stained red. Other materials included gilded pine for carved pieces (looking-glasses, side-tables and wall brackets), and japanned or painted furniture was used in Chinese rooms.

The different types of furniture were, with a few additions, much as before. Beds were of the four-poster variety with cornices often of carved mahogany. Bulky clothes-presses could be monumental when made with serpentine or bombé lower sections and carved corners and panels. Dressing-tables with fitted drawers were illustrated by Chippendale in plain styles as well as in the extremes of French Rococo. Dressing-cabinets, with bookcases above, look much like writing-cabinets, and served both purposes. In the dining-room, oval gate-leg tables tended to be made square in order to fit together more easily. Neither the dining-table nor the sideboard, as we know them, had developed as yet, and sideboard tables, though finely ornamented, seldom had drawers.

In the library, the pedestal writing-table became a piece of some magnificence, and there are famous examples by Vile and Chippendale. The bureau-bookcase had either mirrored or panelled doors above, or glazing bars carved delicately with Rococo or gothick details. During the 1750s a characteristic version developed with a diagonal pattern, which eventually took on the standard 13-panel formula. Many long bookshelves were made with glazed doors above and a projecting central part, surmounted by a broken pediment into which a plaster bust could be placed. In state-rooms and drawing-rooms there were gilded mirrors, side-tables, and candlestands which varied from simple rectangular shapes to the most elaborate fashions. The small and functional Pembroke table, named after the Countess of Pembroke, appeared by 1760, and was generally rather plain. The circular tripod table with a pie-crust top could be richly carved, and was accompanied by various forms of tea-table, including the rectangular type with a pierced gallery, raised on four elegant cabriole or columned legs, and kettle-stands — small tripod tables now erroneously called 'wine-tables' — which also could be of great delicacy. Other pieces for use in ladies' rooms included display-cabinets and hanging shelves for showing china.

Dining-chairs are, perhaps, the pieces that are most characteristic of the period. The type most conveniently described as 'Chippendale' has its top-rail shaped like a bow, forming sharp angles at the ends, and the delicate tracery of the back splat requires the strength of mahogany. This form developed by about

Below: This combined dressing- and writing-table is almost unique in English furniture for the profusion of its gilt-bronze Rococo mounts and the complicated swellings and recessions of the bodywork. It is attributed to John Channon, who worked in St Martin's Lane specializing in furniture inlaid with brass, and was made during the 1740s. There is obvious German influence in both the shape and ornamentation, but the interpretation of Rococo design has become rather confused. Note the inclusion of dolphins at the bottom centre. The pair to this table exists, and originally the two were designed to stand back-to-back when required to form a library table. (Victoria & Albert Museum, London)

Right: Probably made by William Vile of St Martin's Lane, London, who worked for Queen Charlotte after 1760, this bookcase shows the English tradition at its best. The classical form is a development from the Palladian style of William Kent, and the ornament, though chiefly classical, is carved with all the delicacy of the Rococo period. At this time mahogany was the wood used for most fine furniture. The flat surfaces are covered with veneers that show a curl, or 'flame' figure, and the carved work, the mouldings and frets, are glued over this. The platform at the centre of the pediment would have contained a bronzed plaster bust of a writer or philosopher. (Victoria & Albert Museum, London)

1750, and was imitated particularly in Scandinavia and America. Chippendale illustrated a large number of them, saying that more or less carving could be applied at will. The backs have occasional hints of gothick arches. Alternatively, the backs and arms might be formed of Chinese frets. The legs could be straight, with carved or applied frets (especially suitable for Chinese or gothick patterns), or cabriole, carved with acanthus leaves and cartouches. Although the claw-and-ball foot survived into the 1750s, Chippendale only illustrated the more fashionable rocaille or French scrolled types. Upholstered armchairs with cartouche-shaped backs were of the French form, but when made in England they tended to look disjointed and stocky. Sofas, too, made either of mahogany or gilded pine, were frequently made in the French style, and the tradition of forming the back of a settee out of several chair-backs persisted.

Commode chests of drawers, in imitation of the French, appeared by about 1750. They were made of mahogany with bold scrolling outlines, which in France would have been applied in ormolu, and their Rococo handles of gilt-bronze could be large and showy or small and delicate. Many of these commodes are rather ungainly, and demonstrate how England often failed to understand the principles of French Rococo construction. A revival of marquetry had begun by 1760, probably through the elaborate work of

Above: Solid mahogany armchair which closely follows a design dated 1759 in the Director for a 'French chair'. 'French' referred to the comfortable upholstery of back, seat and arms, and to the Rococo-style carving. (Victoria & Albert Museum, London)

Right: Pierre Langlois made this marquetry commode in England in about 1760. The carcase is made of pine in the English tradition (whereas the best French case-work was of oak), but a marble top to a commode is unusual in England. (Victoria & Albert Museum, London)

*Above: A delightful
informal 'conversation
picture' of the 1770s,
by Philip Reinagle,
entitled Mrs Congreve and
her Daughters, showing a
simply furnished lady's
sitting-room. The chairs
and tea-table look
provincial or 'country-
made'. They are in the
Rococo style, while the
looking-glass and side-
table are later. Pile
carpets like this one were
woven at the Axminster
Moorfields factories, but in
this case it was probably of
needlework. Note the
festoon curtains, which
were fashionable at the
time. (National Gallery of
Ireland, Dublin)*

Pierre Langlois. His commodes are ostentatious show-pieces, making great use of
ormolu in the French manner although tending to be rather heavy whan applied to the feet.
One of his typical designs in marquetry
included stems of flowers tied together by
ribbons. English commodes, whether made by
Langlois or others, almost invariably have
their tops of mahogany or marquetry veneer,
and rarely of marble as was used in France.

The neo-classical revival of the 1760s caused
Rococo decoration to die even more suddenly
than it had begun. The traditional logic of
English furniture moved by degrees into the
style of the 1780s known as 'Hepplewhite',
and the only legacy of the Rococo period was
the serpentine or bombé outline that can be
found on chests of drawers and Pembroke
tables up to the 1790s. However, an imitation
of the Louis Quinze chair in its most economical
form seems only to have been made right at
the end of the Rococo period, and it still goes
by the anomalous name of 'French
Hepplewhite'.

The quality of provincial furniture varied
enormously. At its best it was equal to London
work. When furniture was made of native
woods such as walnut, yew, fruitwoods or oak,
it had a provincial appearance, and is generally
known as country-made, even though it was

often made in cities. A dresser made of oak
may be quite in the style of about 1710, with
simple cabriole legs and panelled doors; yet
a later date is betrayed by the mahogany
crossbanding around the drawer fronts. Dressers, for displaying pottery and china, were
the show-pieces in the country, and other
forms tended to be simple. The bureau was a
popular country piece right through the
eighteenth century. Chairs and tripod tables
were made in great numbers, often in mahogany, and were simplifications of London types.

Windsor chairs were a distinct regional
type, and had been made in large numbers in
Buckinghamshire since the early eighteenth
century. It is not uncommon to find the legs
and rails of ash, the seat of elm, and the
hooped rail over the top to be of yew; but more
ambitious pieces could be carried out completely in mahogany. The back splat might be
shaped and pierced, showing a distant relationship with London chairs, and gothick
examples are known, standing on cabriole
rather than turned legs.

America
Although the English government did their
utmost to prevent it, the American colonies
became so prosperous during the eighteenth
century that they were able to defy the taxes,

133

Right: This is a room from the country-house built for a wealthy Philadelphia merchant, Edward Stiles, in 1762. The furniture, all of mahogany, shows both the sophistication of the Philadelphia 'Chippendale' style, and its close relationship to English models, though mostly it dates from the 1770s when this style was no longer practised in England. Note the luxurious and rare pair of sofas, the carved chairs in the style of Benjamin Randolph, and the mahogany and gilt looking-glass. The high chest of drawers, however, is a specifically Philadelphian piece, and was made by Michael Gratz in 1769. The magnificent flowered carpet is English, dated to about 1765, and the glass chandelier and lustres would also have been imported. (The Henry Francis Dupont Winterthur Museum)

134

openly to rebel, and to have their independence recognized in 1783. But English traditions survived in American culture, and their Rococo furniture was based on that of London. Sometimes an American chair or table can hardly be distinguished from an English one.

The 'Chippendale' period in America runs from the 1760s almost until the end of the century. In a country so large, where communications were difficult, innovations were naturally late in appearing. Rococo ornament was known for a long time in Philadelphia as 'the new French style', despite the fact that it came from England where by then it was far from new. The Chippendale style reached America in three ways. Immigrants occasionally included a cabinet-maker such as Thomas Affleck, who arrived in Philadelphia in 1763. Secondly, English furniture was imported, though in diminishing quantities as the century progressed. Third and most important were the pattern books, including Chippendale's *Director* (1754 and 1762) and the rival publications by Manwaring, and Ince and Mayhew. American Rococo carving often has a two-dimensional quality that suggests its having been copied from an engraving.

Colonial houses were neat buildings of brick and wood, combining the traditional Wren proportions with Palladian decorative features. The rooms were not large, and furniture tended to be narrow and taller than English works. The proportions were lean but crisp and stylish, and the top of a chair, settee or high chest was emphasized by shapely curves and finials. Although furniture from Philadelphia or Boston has style and beauty, and often a certain magnificence, it was practical and seldom luxurious. There were not a great number of forms. 'Chippendale' chairs were plentiful, as were upholstered settees, card-tables, and tea-tables, either of the round snap-top form with a bird-cage, or the rectangular tray top variety. Pembroke tables made their appearance rather late. There were firescreens, mirrors and tall clocks. The show-pieces were chests, high or low, and bureau-cabinets. Beds tended to be simple, with posts and draped testers, and low chests or kneehole writing-tables, when placed in bedrooms, served as dressing-tables.

The furniture industry was a thriving one. Just before American Independence, there were about 150 cabinet-makers, chair-makers and carvers working in Boston alone, and over 50 in Newport, Rhode Island. But apart from furniture and silver, no decorative craft was as yet properly developed, and all glass, bronze and brass, wallpapers and many fabrics had to be imported.

The American colonies, spread along 1,200 miles of coastline, may be divided conveniently into three areas. The South did not lead fashion at this time, and not much is known of the makers, although Thomas Elfe of Charleston had a large workshop. His account books show that he used the blind fret around his chests and bookcases. Many of the Southern craftsmen were, apparently, slaves. More than once there were complaints by white migrants against the employment of cheap labour.

In the middle region, Philadelphia was undoubtedly the most advanced and prolific centre. The makers included Affleck, Folwell, Savery, Gillingham and Shoemaker, whose trade labels occasionally appear on their works. Benjamin Randolph is probably the most famous, and his elaborate trade card was engraved in the style of St Martin's Lane. Philadelphia furniture could be very ornate, and looking-glasses, though not so large as English ones, could be almost as decorative. Tripod tea-tables with pie-crust trays, and card-tables with sharp angles and serpentine sides showed subtle variations of English types. Thomas Affleck is known for straight, solid 'Marlborough' legs, often with a blocked foot.

The cabriole leg with a claw-and-ball foot, though by now outmoded in England, remained popular. Dining- or side-chairs generally had cabriole legs, and the carved backs were based directly on English patterns, complete with gothick arches or Rococo carving. Among the popular types of chair was the ladderback with wavy pierced rails. While the chairs made in New York up to the end of the century were rather heavy in comparison with those of Philadelphia, New York card-tables generally are crisper and more stylish in their sheer, serpentine lines. The most famous Philadelphia piece was the high chest, now known as a highboy. Although it was the show-piece, and stood in the principal parlour, it appears generally to have been filled with family clothes.

Furniture was made in great quantity in the North, and was often traded for corn and tobacco grown in the South. New England furniture was less florid than that of Philadelphia, as though reflecting the puritan tradition. It also tended to retain the old Queen Anne styles, as for instance in dining-chairs with their hoop backs with shaped splats, and their cabriole legs with webbed feet. At Newport, Rhode Island, the furniture trade was dominated by the related families of Townsend and Goddard. The most recognizable feature of New England furniture, the blocked or 'swelled' style, is first known in a secretary desk signed by John Coit Jnr of Boston, but was most developed in Newport. The blocking, carved out of solid wood, resulted in raised or sunken panels with smoothed corners, and their heads were often given shell ornaments with the radials slightly

curved at the perimeters. In Boston, the blocked style generally occurs only on the lower part of a piece of furniture. The style travelled inland to New Hampshire where it can be seen in a rather less sophisticated form, and seems to be somehow related to north German work.

High chests were made in New England, but the more common show-piece was a two-part bureau or cabinet, raised on elegantly moulded bracket feet, or on sturdy claw-and-ball feet. Boston chests often had a swollen or bombé shape, which is generally associated with the name of John Coggswell. The bombé outline, though occasionally found in English furniture, probably reached America from Holland.

Small but interesting regional differences can be seen in claw-and-ball feet. In Philadelphia they were elegantly shaped, with the balls rather flattened. In New York they tended to be more sturdy, the back talon and lower leg being in the same upright line. The Boston form was quite distinct, and the side talons inclined sharply backwards giving an animated, nervous effect. At Newport, R.I., the claws were often undercut to show daylight between the talons and the ball.

The finest wood for furniture was mahogany, which came from the West Indies in most of the varieties that were used in England. However, it never quite displaced black walnut, which grew all along the Eastern seaboard and especially in Virginia. Other native woods were used, particularly in the north, such as maple, with a curly or bird's-eye grain, which was suitable for veneers, and cherry, which was popular especially in New Haven. Solid work or drawer linings might be of maple, cherry, tulip tree (a variety of poplar), white cedar, birch or pine. Other indigenous woods suitable for work in the country style

or on Windsor chairs included ash, chestnut and oak. Although regional traditions certainly existed, such as the use of oak for fine carcase work at Newport, these were seldom hard or fast, and one should not be dogmatic about defining local styles, the more so as both craftsmen and completed furniture tended to travel up and down the Eastern seaboard.

While fashionable Rococo styles adorned the houses of successful merchants, country furniture in established traditions continued to be made. The comfortable Windsor chairs and settees, often with a high arched back or shaped top-rail, were popular at all levels from the early eighteenth century through the nineteenth. In Pennsylvania there were a large number of German settlers who made their own furniture in what is now often known as the Swiss style. The chairs have block seats, splayed spindle legs, and carved backs made from single pieces of wood. These, and marriage chests, which were often painted, show a continuation of local traditions that derived from mediaeval and Renaissance Europe.

PURITY OF FORM
The neo-classical reaction

The neo-classical revival developed in the mid-eighteenth century and it was widely established throughout Europe by the 1770s. Like the Rococo which preceded it, it became an international style, although allowing less leeway for varying interpretation from country to country. Different national styles were united in the study of the same sources in Italy, Greece and Egypt, and, as a result, they inevitably developed along similar lines. Much emphasis, moreover, was laid on adherence to classical principles and this became more marked, as the movement gained momentum. A studied eclecticism was adopted after 1800 — leading to a more archaeological approach and creating even closer stylistic links between countries.

The ferment of intellectual ideas in late eighteenth-century Europe led to a stringent reassessment and questioning of many existing traditions. Numerous political, as well as artistic, changes took place in a striving toward an apparently attainable perfection. There was an accent on modernity, on sweeping innovation in an age of progress, yet classical antiquity was nonetheless still studied for guidance and inspiration. Winckelmann wrote: 'There is only one way for the moderns, to become great, perhaps unequalled: by imitating the ancients.' He drew careful distinction between imitation and mere copying, suggesting that classicism should be studied for its regenerative powers, and allowing for a romantic interpretation of the style.

In this world of high ideals and moral improvement, the frivolous Rococo would indeed appear decadent, and the reaction against it would become fierce, especially in France, the country of its origin. Abbé Le Blanc protested against it in his *Lettre d'un Français* of 1745, addressed to the Comte de Caylus, and Nicholas Cochin levelled another attack in the *Mercure de France* in 1754. But despite these publications, the Rococo lingered on for a number of years, especially at the conservative French Court, and Baron Grimm's remark of 1763 that 'tout à Paris est à la Grecque' may be taken with a pinch of salt at that early stage.

Paris was undoubtedly the most important centre for the promotion of the neo-classical revival, and among the many books produced there, the *Recueil d'Antiquités* by the Comte de Caylus was probably the most influential. Appearing from 1752 onwards, it illustrated his own collection of antiquities, making classical ornament familiar and laying the basis for the Louis Seize style. It also foreshadowed an important trend in stressing the simplicity of Greek classicism, which many would soon hold superior to that of Rome.

Another French writer of the day, the Abbé Laugier, supported this view in his *Essai sur*

l'Architecture of 1753, in which he presented a rationalist view of classicism and urged a return to primitive purity. 'Architecture' he wrote, 'owes all that is precious and solid to the Greeks alone.' It is not surprising that the first major work on Greek monuments — *Les Ruines des plus beaux monuments de la Grèce* by LeRoy — should have been published in Paris in 1758. This work had been preceded by the more intensive researches of two Englishmen, James Stuart and Nicholas Revett. They had visited Athens as early as 1751, and must take the credit for first showing an interest in Greece, even if their *Antiquities of Athens* did not appear until 1762.

In Germany, too, an interest in Greece developed through the writings of Johann Joachim Winckelmann, who was based in Rome as secretary to Cardinal Albani, but whose books were published at home. His *Reflections on the Imitation of Greek Art in Painting and Sculpture* of 1755 and his magnum opus *The History of Ancient Art* published nine years later, present a poetic account of Greek art, even though the moving descriptions of various masterpieces are more inspiring than instructive. In the words of Goethe, himself a vital force in German Neo-classicism, 'we learn nothing by reading Winckelmann, but we *become* something'.

The emphasis on Greece in preference to Rome not unnaturally sparked off a reaction within Italy, which was led by G B Piranesi.

He produced a splendid series of etched views of Roman remains to demonstrate, most effectively, the magnificence of Roman architecture. With their dramatic lighting and gargantuan representation of scale, these popular etchings played a part in the development of a Romantic brand of classicism within Europe. They served their purpose well, although visitors such as Goethe and Flaxman, familiar with Piranesi before visiting Rome, expressed disappointment with the tameness of reality when they arrived there.

Despite the swing towards Greece, Rome still exerted considerable influence during the late eighteenth century and remained the cosmopolitan centre of neo-classical Europe and the goal of both English and German Grand Tourists. Studies of the famous sites and collections were now reinforced by the discoveries at fresh excavations, such as that at Tivoli with which Piranesi was personally involved and which produced such important finds as the Warwick Vase.

With the Roman monuments recorded, distant sites were being explored: Palmyra and Baalbek were to become the subject of two books by Robert Wood in 1753 and 1757, while the young Robert Adam chose Diocletian's Palace at Spalatro in Dalmatia for his first book in 1764. Pompeii and Herculaneum in the south of Italy were much studied for they provided a wealth of evidence about Roman domestic architecture. Excavated in 1738 and

1748 respectively, at the instigation of the king of Naples, these two cities had survived miraculously intact under the laval dust of Vesuvius since the first century AD and thus provided a unique opportunity to study the interior decoration and furnishings of the Romans. There was, however, some confusion as to dating, and imitations of the decorations there were often mistakenly called 'Etruscan'.

Actual pieces of furniture were unearthed at these sites, but surprisingly, they were seldom reproduced accurately during the eighteenth century. Neo-classical furniture consisted at first of simple geometrical outlines, devised to carry the all-important classical ornament, and, with a few exceptions such as the tripod stand, the form of ancient furniture was rarely copied before the nineteenth century.

The ornament was derived mainly from Rome, at the outset, as illustrated in the new books. The Renaissance, especially the painted grotesques of Raphael at the Vatican, provided another source which was important to such designers as Adam in England and Clérisseau in France. Individual countries harked back to their own earlier classical revivals too; a nostalgia for the Grand Siècle of Louis XIV is thus noticeable in early French neo-classical pieces. But soon the heavy classical forms

Right: Mahogany armchair based on the Roman curule form. This is typical of the later work of Georges Jacob, with its fine, sweeping, simple lines and plain mahogany finish. It may well be after a design by Percier and Fontaine. The back has at some time been upholstered, but it now has a splat in the form of a classical incense-burner. (Musée des Arts Décoratifs, Paris)

would lighten, and the 1770s and 1780s saw an increasing delicacy and refinement in furniture.

After 1800, however, a marked reaction set in, with a craving for exactitude as the inevitable fruit of further researches. Vase paintings and bas-reliefs were closely studied for the clues they might provide as to antique furniture shapes, and many pieces were based on marble prototypes. Now the lessons of Pompeii and Herculaneum proved invaluable, and Greece was used as a source of ideas rather more than before, despite Napoleon's preference for the grandiose decoration of Rome.

Napoleon and his favourite designers, Percier and Fontaine, clearly played on Roman ideas for their associational value. The triumphal arches and classical temples of Paris were created with propagandist intentions, the French Empire being inevitably associated with that of Rome. This style was widely disseminated throughout Europe by Napoleon's campaigns, which also led to the development of an Egyptian revival after Napoleon had organized a programme of excavation in Egypt during his Nile campaign.

Egyptian antiquities, of which there were a number in Rome, had excited interest in the eighteenth century, and various advanced pieces of furniture with hieroglyphic ornament bear witness to a certain knowledge of Egyptian design. But this fashion was to accelerate after the publication of Baron Denon's *Voyages dans la Basse et Haute Egypte* in 1802 with Napoleon's encouragement, and thereafter Egypt joined Greece and Rome as a major inspiration.

The accurate character of this second phase of the neo-classical revival—which even affected fashions of dress—led to a decline in originality in due course, as the fervour of the revolutionary eighteenth century waned. The endlessly repeated classical forms became monotonous and Neo-classicism had subsided into a bland, even superficial, decorative style by the middle of the nineteenth century.

France

The decorative motifs of the classical revival in France, as everywhere, had their origins in antiquity, but the shape and proportions of the furniture were purely eighteenth century. It was not until the very end of the eighteenth century that furniture and decoration took on a purer classical form. The immediate inspiration for the revival is now difficult to trace. To a certain extent it was a return to the Renaissance, and also to the more severe, more classical Baroque of the time of Louis XIV, and, at first, there were affinities with the work of the Palladian designers in England.

The Rococo movement in France had powerful opponents from its start. Voltaire pilloried it in *Le Temple du Goût* in 1733, and the

Left: Bureau-plat and cartonnier designed by Louis-Joseph Le Lorrain for Ange-Laurent Lalive de Jully, and made in about 1756. The work was supervised by Caffieri, who also made the elaborate bronze mounts. This piece stood in Lalive de Jully's Cabinet Flamand and is considered to be the earliest example of French neo-classical furniture. (Musée Condé, Chantilly)

architect, Soufflot, in 1741, decreed that all right-minded people should look down on these frivolous products. Soufflot was later to accompany the Marquis de Marigny, in effect France's future Minister of Culture, on his tour of Italy during the years 1749 to 1751 — an important journey in the evolution of French taste.

The French Academy had a school in Rome, at the Palazzo Mancini, where, throughout the late 1730s and 1740s, French artists of outstanding talent were sent to further their studies. All these French artists met, at some time or another, the leading light of the Italian classical revival, Piranesi, and all were influenced by his work. Le Geay, for example, returned to Paris in 1742 from Rome with a widely publicized folio of work, and Saly, in 1746, published engravings of his designs for vases based on antique originals.

In 1745, Madame de Pompadour became the official mistress of Louis XV, and by 1749 was making plans for her brother, the Marquis de Marigny, to become the Director-General of the Arts. Accordingly she sent him on an extensive tour of Italy. His travelling companions became whole-hearted supporters of the classical movement, but Marigny seems not to have been quite so certain about the perfection of classical art at this stage and he was not completely won over until the 1760s.

Architecturally the Rococo movement had not had a tremendous impact. From the outside buildings, especially public buildings and churches, were still classical, although the use of columns, colonnades, pediments, and all the other classical devices had become noticeably lighter and fresher as the eighteenth century advanced. The interiors of houses at this time, especially the grand ones, had a sequence of rooms, used for entertaining, and it was usually only in the private apartments of the house where high fashion was allowed full rein, and therefore many rooms in Paris were still being decorated in the middle of the eighteenth century in a classical vein, this being a survival from the Baroque age rather than a revival of any antique style.

The only type of furniture from the Louis XIV period which was admired throughout the eighteenth century was that decorated with the Boulle technique. These were usually large sombre pieces of case furniture veneered in ebony, and with marquetry of brass and tortoiseshell, richly mounted in ormolu. The greatest exponent of this technique was André-Charles Boulle, hence its name. Boulle himself died in 1732, but his workshops continued under the direction of his son. Several cabinet-makers, trained in these workshops, branched out on their own, notably Etienne Levasseur, who became an independent cabinet-maker in 1760, and continued to work in the same style and technique so favoured by Louis XIV. Furniture by Boulle was already eagerly sought after and collected by the middle of the eighteenth century. Ange-Laurent Lalive de Jully, a man of taste and a collector, asked Louis-Joseph Le Lorrain, who had been in Rome in the 1740s, to design a suite of furniture for him in the Boulle tradition, consisting of a *bureau-plat*, a *cartonnier*, a cabinet and a clock. This Lorrain did, and the furniture, some of which is now in the Musée Condé at Chantilly, was finished in the mid-1750s, and is regarded as the earliest neo-classical furniture in France. Its ponderous architectural style and the technique used — ebony veneer inlaid with brass and richly mounted in ormolu — is certainly reminiscent of the furniture of Boulle, though the overall effect is very different. It was regarded as ultra-modern by Lalive de Jully's contemporaries, though reactions to it were mixed, some, like the Comte de

Caylus, having nothing but praise for it, and others, such as the designer and engraver, Cochin, being distinctly against it. The furniture was designed to stand in Lalive's *Cabinet Flamand*, decorated in the classical manner by the architect Barreau de Chefdeville, and it was after this that the taste for works *à la Grecque* or in the *goût grec* began to spread. These became catchphrases of the time, and anything remotely fashionable or in the new classical vein was immediately described as *à la Grecque*, regardless of the source of inspiration. The maker of Lalive's suite is not known, though the mounts were executed by the *bronzeur*, Philippe Caffieri. These pieces were in no way attempts to reproduce classical Roman or Greek furniture, the appearance of which was known to Lalive and Le Lorrain from contemporary publications. The furniture was something entirely new, and caused a sensation in Paris, where it seems to have been known by virtually everybody, as there are many contemporary references to the suite, and even advertisements for bureaux in the style of that of Monsieur Lalive, suggesting that everyone would know what style that was.

Oeben was another important maker of the transitional period from Rococo to Neoclassicism, and the early neo-classic period. Most of his later work, though less heavily architectural in appearance than Lalive's furniture, is in the new style; both he and Garnier, however, show their lack of architectural training by certain obvious mistakes such as including an even number of flutes in a pilaster. Floral marquetry, having returned to fashion in the late 1740s, was still popular, and Oeben, like many of his contemporaries German by birth, was one of its greatest exponents. Each of his flowers was usually identifiable, and most were probably copied from contemporary engravings. It was Oeben who started work on the *Bureau de Roi,* ordered for Louis XV in 1760, but he died in 1763 when the desk was still unfinished, and it was completed by his journeyman, Jean-Henri Riesener. Though the basic shape is still bombé and typically Rococo, much of the decoration is pure classical, and shows that, by the 1760s, the classical revival had gained quite a hold. Moreover, the desk was being constructed to stand in a room at Versailles with Rococo *boiserie* and furniture. Oeben's widow carried on her husband's workshop and used his stamp on pieces of furniture. In 1767 she married Jean-Henri Riesener, the most talented of her husband's journeymen, and thereafter Riesener used his own stamp on everything that was produced by the workshop.

The new rectilinear forms were obviously far more suitable for some pieces of furniture than others. *Secrétaires à abattant,* long-case or pedestal clocks and bureaux-plats were soon being constructed in an entirely classical fashion, but commodes were made well into the 1770s partially retaining the bombé shape of the Rococo, and still supported on cabriole

legs, as were smaller movable pieces of furniture, such as work- and writing-tables. Possibly it was felt that a totally classical interior, composed of heavy rectilinear furniture, would be too overpowering, and the necessity was still felt for the softening effect of curved forms. Work by most of the leading cabinet-makers at this time, such as Vanrisamburgh, Joubert and Riesener, all show this tendency to have classical mounts and sometimes marquetry on a commode with cabriole legs.

In 1769 François-Joseph Bélanger executed for Marie-Antoinette a design for a jewel cabinet. In form it resembled the cabinets on stands of the seventeenth century, having a pair of doors enclosing numerous small drawers, and supported on eight legs. This was the first piece of furniture with straight legs to be provided for a member of the royal family, and was quite different to the furniture of the mid-century.

In the early 1770s the Prince de Condé carried out radical redecorations in the Palais Bourbon, and the few pieces which are known to have been executed for him by Leleu at this time are in a totally classical style, though there are few, if any, datable examples extant. With chairs more than with veneered furniture, designers and makers clung tenaciously to the old lines, and chairs with voluted arm supports and cabriole legs were still being constructed in the 1780s.

Right: Jewel-cabinet presented to Marie-Antoinette by the City of Paris in 1787 and made by Jean-Ferdinand Schwerdfeger. The form of the piece is seventeenth-century, but the decoration is eighteenth-century. The mounts are probably by Thomire, one of the most famous bronze-workers of the day. The central bronze medallion symbolizes the arts, and the caryatid figures represent the four seasons. (Château de Versailles)

Below left: Writing-table made by Jean-François Leleu, possibly for Mme Victoire, Louis XVI's aunt. This is one of the few existing pieces which bears a resemblance to the more elaborate designs of De Wailly with its unusually convoluted legs. The maker's mark appears on the top of one of the drawer-fronts which is unusual in the eighteenth century, the most usual place being on the back or underneath.

145

An interesting connection between France and England at this time is provided in the work of Gravelot, who had lived for some time in England where it is known from contemporary references that he did designs for cabinet-makers and upholsterers. The content of these designs is unknown but at the time when they were done, about 1740, the Palladian style still held sway in England, and he would certainly have been conversant with it. By the 1760s Gravelot was back in France and was doing designs for ornament in the field of carpets and tapestries for the Savonnerie and Gobelins workshops. His familiarity, while in England, with the Palladian style must have made it easier for him to work in the vernacular of the classical revival.

By the middle and late 1760s the Marquis de Marigny was ordering furniture for his own use in the new style, though we can only judge this loosely from contemporary descriptions, as there is no visual record of the pieces he ordered. The Duc de Choiseul, France's first minister, also ordered pieces in what was to become known as the Louis Seize style. In

the late 1760s, Delanois supplied furniture to Madame du Barry — 208 pieces in all, both for her apartments at Versailles and for her Pavilion at Louveciennes. Most of this furniture is now either no longer identifiable, or no longer in existence, but some of the chairs do exist, and these favour the new classical style, and, from descriptions, so did most of her other furniture.

There existed in Paris at this time a ready-made market of furniture and objects in the establishments of the *marchands-merciers* and the *marchands-tapissiers*. The marchand-mercier was a middleman between the craftsman and buyers, and the best of them had shops in the Faubourg St Honoré. Lazare Duvaux, one of the most famous, died in 1758 — too early to have much effect on the decline in the taste for the Rococo. Simon-Philippe Poirier, however, does seem to have played a part. Already in the early 1760s he had in his stock several pieces of furniture and ormolu in the 'Greek' style, and persuaded several influential people into buying them. Poirier specialized in furniture set with porcelain plaques from the

Sèvres factory, and the carcases were often made by the ébéniste Martin Carlin. He usually made several pieces to the same design, and there are several versions of a ladies' writing-table which seems to have been a speciality of his — set with rectangular flower-painted Sèvres porcelain plaques, but still raised on elegant cabriole legs, a bow to convention. In 1777 Poirier's firm was taken over by his erstwhile partner, Dominique Daguerre, and its success continued.

The marchands-tapissiers specialized in seat furniture, beds, mirrors, and draperies of all kinds. At a time when rooms were usually decorated throughout in a co-ordinated style these entrepreneurs were of some importance, and many *menuisiers*, Louis Delanois for instance, sold more furniture to the marchands-tapissiers than to private clients. The marchands-tapissiers were actually craftsmen, most of them being upholsterers in their own right, and often had their workshops away from the smarter areas of Paris.

Many of the greater ébénistes of the latter half of the eighteenth century were German by birth. Oeben had secured royal patronage, thus also securing his position in Paris. Riesener, also a German, born in Gladbeck in 1734, took over Oeben's workshop, and, on the accession of Louis XVI to the throne in 1774, succeeded the aged Gilles Joubert as *ébéniste ordinaire du Roi*. His work for the Crown was ornate, full use being made of ormolu and marquetry, and his earlier pieces are heavy in appearance, typified by the commode, now at Chantilly, supplied in 1775 for the King's bedroom at Versailles. He also supplied a charming mechanical table to stand beside the Queen's bed. Made in collaboration with the mechanic, Merklein, this piece was constructed to answer all the Queen's needs. It was a dressing-table, writing-table, breakfast-table, and reading-table all in one. In the 1780s Riesener's elaborate pieces became too expensive for the royal family who were deep in debt, and many commissions went to the ébénistes, Stockel and Beneman. Riesener simplified much of his work, still retaining his individual style, and some of his later pieces, in plain, beautifully grained mahogany, free from marquetry and with simple ormolu mouldings, are among his most charming creations. He lived until 1806, working until 1801, but his major work after the collapse of the monarchy was to replace the royal arms and insignia on pieces of royal furniture with something which would be less offensive to the new order.

Another German working in Paris at this time was Adam Weisweiler, received as a *maître ébéniste* in 1778. Unlike Riesener, who seems to have designed his own furniture, Weisweiler worked almost exclusively for the marchand-mercier, Daguerre, who must have

Left: A cabinet and chest-of-drawers surmounted by a clock, veneered in tulipwood and lavishly mounted with ormolu and Sèvres porcelain plaques. Thirty of the plaques have the Sèvres date-letter N for 1766. This piece shows signs of having been altered at some time, and it is probable that it was made by either Martin Carlin or J-F Leleu. (Wallace Collection, London)

Right: A Japanese lacquer secrétaire en pente, made by Martin Carlin. Carlin made high quality furniture, particularly for the marchands-merciers Poirier and his successor Daguerre, who had a virtual monopoly on the importation of oriental lacquer into France, as well as on porcelain plaques from the Sèvres factory. This is one of the few sloping-front desks made in the late eighteenth century, as by then the bureau à cylindre had become fashionable.

dictated to him how the pieces he made should look, and probably provided him with designs. His creations are elegant and sometimes almost jewel-like. His richer pieces make use of Sèvres porcelain, on which Daguerre had a virtual monopoly, oriental lacquer, and sometimes *pietra-dura* panels, usually taken from seventeenth-century cabinets which had been broken up. His plainer pieces are often in mahogany with simple ormolu mounts, though on his finer works the mounts are often by the famous *ciseleur-doreur*, Gouthière. Certain decorative features are typical of Weisweiler's work, for instance interlaced stretchers, and *toupie* or top-shaped feet.

Martin Carlin was another German working in Paris who preferred to work for the marchands-merciers. His most famous pieces are those studded with porcelain plaques, supplied to him by Poirier, and later, by his successor, Daguerre. He also worked for Darnault, known to have supplied him with lacquer panels for furniture for the Château de Bellevue, where the aunts of Louis XVI had their home.

Very few new pieces of furniture made their appearance in the latter part of the eighteenth century. The secrétaire à abattant, the upper part of which falls forward to form a writing surface and to reveal drawers and pigeon-holes, became much more popular because it took up so much less space than a writing-table. Riesener made several fine and elaborately decorated examples for the royal family. The cylinder bureau *(bureau à cylindre)* also became more widely used in preference to the writing-table as, instead of clearing one's private papers away each time one

finished work, one just had to close the cylinder front to hide them from view. Commodes and corner cupboards *(encoignures)* were still as popular, and the *console desserte*, a type of sideboard with open shelves, made its first appearance. The more informal way of life favoured by Louis XV for his subjects was continued under Louis XVI, and many small movable tables for all sorts of uses were still popular. Reading-tables, writing-tables, worktables, *rafraichissoirs*—a kind of table with apertures in the top for ice-buckets for wine, *tables de chevet*—tables with a shelf and sometimes a drawer to stand beside the bed, *tables en commode*—small tables with two or three drawers in the frieze—were all still made in large quantities to satisfy the old aristocracy and the new rich.

In Paris and in the grander homes outside Paris, these pieces were nearly always veneered and often decorated with marquetry, sometimes, although rarely, with *vernis martin*, a kind of elaborate painting process built up in layers to imitate lacquer, invented and patented by the four Martin brothers. In the provinces, however, and in the not so rich bourgeois homes pieces were often made in solid wood, and were, of necessity, of much simpler form than the grander pieces they were imitating. Often the wood was simply polished and sometimes painted to match the decoration of the room for which it was intended. The Rococo style continued longer in the provinces and became more attenuated and elegant as the Louis Seize style spread. The charm of these provincial pieces is undeniable, and they are much sought after today.

Left: Secrétaire à abattant in lacquer and ebony, made by Jean-Henri Riesener. The plaque of the sacrifice to love and the mounts in the form of cornflowers appear on several pieces supplied by Riesener to Marie-Antoinette.

149

As was the custom earlier in the century there were still two types of chair in the late eighteenth century—the *sièges meublants*, which always stood against the wall, and the *sièges courants*, which were disposed about the centre of the room and could be moved about at will. The frames were, as earlier, of carved wood, either gilded, painted, or polished, the latter technique becoming noticeably more popular in grander establishments towards the end of the eighteenth century. The materials used to cover seat furniture were the same as earlier—damask, velvet, silk, brocade, printed cotton, embroidered silk, tapestry and needlework, with leather usually used for desk chairs.

Settees became more elaborate, and each variation had a different name. The reasons for these names, and the variations to which they referred are now difficult to trace. One does not know how a *sultane* differed from an *ottomane*, or a *turquoise*, and what the distinctive feature was of a *paphose*. Stools were still of the same basic types as before; the *tabouret*, the *pliant* and the *banquette*.

Beds were usually of carved wood, either painted or gilded, and with a canopy. They were nearly always placed with one long side against the wall, and the canopy was supported either by carved columns (*lit à colonnes*), metal supports hidden by the bed hangings (*lit à la polonaise*), or it was attached to the wall or ceiling behind or above the bed (*lit à la duchesse*).

The construction of furniture in France at this time, below the top level of craftsmanship, was not of the finest quality, and the parts that were not seen by the eye were often very badly finished indeed. Veneered pieces of furniture had carcases of oak or pinewood, and there appear to have been well over 50

Above: Armchair by Georges Jacob, made for Marie-Antoinette in 1787. The frame was carved by Triquet and Rode and painted by Chaillot de Prusse. (Château de Versailles)

Right: Commode made for Louis XVI's bedchamber at the Château de St Cloud, by Guillaume Beneman. The frieze has ormolu mounts symbolizing royalty—coronets, lilies, cockerels, and the crossed L's.

different types of wood, some native, some exotic, in use for marquetry work.

Most chairs were constructed from beech-wood or walnut, but fruitwoods and pinewood were sometimes used, and veneered seat furniture was sometimes made, though rarely. Later in the century chairs were made in mahogany *à l'anglaise*.

Georges Jacob, perhaps the most famous chair-maker of the time, became a *maître menuisier* in 1765, and by the 1780s had established himself as one of the leading chair-makers of Paris. He made pieces not only for the haute monde of Paris, but for influential clients abroad, such as the Duke of Zweibrücken-Birkenfeld, for whom he made a famous bed, now in the Residenz-museum, Munich, which caused quite a stir when it first appeared. He also made seat furniture for George IV of England and the Duke of Bedford, via the marchand-mercier, Daguerre, who was busy supplying pieces for both Carlton House and Woburn Abbey.

Jacques-Louis David, the painter, commissioned Jacob to make the furniture for his studio to his own designs. These pieces, direct copies of antique originals, were the first of their kind, and were in the style now associated with the French Empire. Hitherto only small decorative pieces, such as pedestals or *athéniennes*, had been modelled at all closely on Greek or Roman prototypes. At about the same time he made some chairs after designs by the painter, Hubert Robert, in what was known as the Etruscan style, for Marie-Antoinette's dairy at Rambouillet. These were only Etruscan in that some of the decorative motifs had been found on pots, probably of Greek origin, dug up in Etruria.

After the chaos of the Revolution in France, the advent of Napoleon brought, if not peace, at least a measure of order. Following their Emperor's example, the new rich were able to turn their attentions to patronage of the arts. There was a strong inclination towards purer and less fussy forms, and also a continuation of the trend towards antiquity, encouraged by the Emperor with his strong admiration for the art of Imperial Rome. Already in the 1780s certain architects, notably Charles-Louis Clérisseau, Jean-Demosthène Dugourc and François-Joseph Bélanger were designing interiors in the 'arabesque' or 'grotesque' style, culled from antiquity, which was favoured under the Directory and Consulate (1795–1804). At the beginning of the nineteenth century, a distinct return to the classical forms in all their purity became apparent. In 1798 Louis-Martin Berthault designed some bedroom furniture for the renowned lady of fashion, Juliette Récamier, and in 1801 Percier and Fontaine, the most important designers of the Empire period, published the first of their *Recueil de*

Décorations Intérieures. Other publications which strongly influenced taste and design at this time were *Plans, coupes et élévations des plus belles maisons et des hôtels construits à Paris et dans les environs* by the architect J C Krafft and the engraver N Ransonnette, 1802, *Nouveau Recueil en divers genres d'ornements et autres objects propres à la décoration* by Charles Normand, 1803, and *Fragmens d'architecture, sculpture, et peinture dans le style antique* by P N Beauvallet, 1804.

The painters of the day also dabbled in furniture design. As we have seen, Robert had provided chairs for Marie-Antoinette, and David, having designed his own studio furnishings, later designed furniture for the Emperor's rooms at the Tuileries, while Prud'hon designed a dressing-table for the Empress Marie-Louise and the cradle for the King of Rome. An important publication of the time was the periodical *Collection des Meubles et Objets de Goût,* the management of

Above: In this painting, La Consolation de l'Absence, the room is furnished entirely in the neo-classical style. The table is painted, probably in the technique known as vernis martin which imitated oriental lacquer, and behind it is a fire-screen. The mirror, console table, chair and cartel clock are all in the full late eighteenth-century Louis Seize style. (Musée Cognacq-Jay, Paris)

151

Left: Water-colour by
Auguste Garnerey of the
Music Room at the
Château de Malmaison.
The Empire-style suite of
mahogany and gilt
furniture, upholstered in
crimson and black to
match the curtains, bears
the maker's mark of Jacob
Frères, who carried out
most of the work for the
imperial family, often to
designs by Percier and
Fontaine. (Château de
Malmaison)

Above right: A tabouret
stool. Martial motifs
became very popular after
Napoleon's victories, and
this stool echoes his
penchant for anything
connected with imperial
Rome. (Château de
Malmaison)

Right: The Empress
Josephine's bedroom at
the Château de Malmaison
which is one of the finest
Empire interiors. The
Empress had the room
completely redecorated in
1810, and the carved and
gilt-wood bed with ormolu
mounts was made for her
by Jacob-Desmalter. He
made pieces of a con-
sistently high quality,
often to the designs of
Percier and Fontaine, and
carried out much work for
the imperial family.
(Château de Malmaison)

which was in the hands of Pierre de la Mésangère. What it was that prompted a former professor of philosophy to take over the running of a magazine must remain a mystery, but its importance was that it was seen by a large section of the public, to whom it showed the latest fashions in furnishings, and it was also seen by all the cabinet-makers who could then tell what the buying public would ask for, and have it ready for them.

The bible of designers of this time was the *Recueil de Décorations Intérieures* by Percier and Fontaine, containing 72 engraved plates, some showing designs which had already been executed. Charles Percier and Pierre-François-Léonard Fontaine met first at the studio of Peyre le Jeune, Inspector of the Royal Buildings. They met again when they were both in Italy, and in 1798 published their first work together, *Recueil des palais, maisons et autres édifices modernes dessinés à Rome.*

It was probably Georges Jacob who secured for the two architects their first official commission which was to design the furnishings of the Salle de Convention at the Tuileries in 1793. During the Consulate they were kept busy working on the restoration and redecoration of the old royal palaces, stripped by the revolutionaries, and which Napoleon now wanted to use. They worked at the Tuileries, the Elysée Palace, Saint-Cloud, the Grand Trianon, Compiègne, Rambouillet and Fontainebleau, and they also worked for the Empress Josephine at her country-house, Malmaison. In 1804 Percier and Fontaine designed the coronation throne for Napoleon

who, in 1805, in recognition of their services, gave them the title of Architects of the Louvre and Tuileries. In 1811 they became members of the Institut de France.

Their influence was strong throughout Europe, where their *Recueil de décorations* was widely read and followed, and spread to Russia, where Czar Alexander commissioned a series of water-colours with accompanying notes of the interiors and furnishings of the Tuileries.

The great arbiter of Imperial taste was Dominique Vivant, Baron Denon, the director of the Musée Napoléon, who supervised everything made in the *ateliers* of the artists and craftsmen working for the court; everything had to be given his approval. He had begun his career in the household of Madame de Pompadour, looking after her collection of engraved stones, and was sent as secretary to the French embassy in Naples. There he assembled a fine collection of vases, later acquired by Louis XVI for the Sèvres porcelain factory. In 1802 he was made Director of the Musée Napoléon and Master of the Mint, and advised the government in all artistic matters, busying himself with the smallest details of the furnishings, and sometimes even submitting designs himself.

Denon is most famous for his publication *Voyage dans la Basse et Haute Egypte*, a series of drawings done by him while following Napoleon's armies. He sketched many of the temples along the Nile, and architectural details as well, and the album of these achieved international fame, being published in

England, Germany and Italy by 1808. Cabinet-makers used many of the motifs he had sketched on furniture and in decoration, and there was a new wave of popularity for *le goût d'Egypte*. Denon commissioned Jacob-Desmalter, the most famous furniture-maker of the period, and Biennais, a goldsmith and sometime furniture-maker, to supply furnishings, using details from his drawings, amongst which were a bed decorated with Egyptian figures, and a medal-cabinet based on a portico in the ancient city of Apollinopolis Parva. Both Thomas Hope and George Smith, two important contemporary English designers, acknowledged their debt to Denon in their designs for rooms in the Egyptian taste.

Jacob-Desmalter was the son of Georges Jacob and was christened François-Honoré-

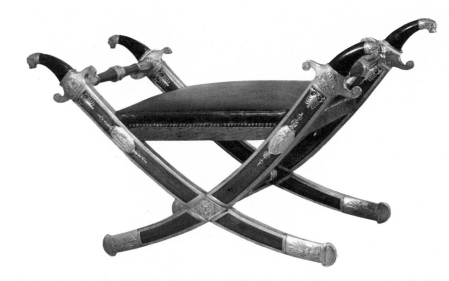

Georges Jacob — he took the name Desmalter from a family property. He received the best training possible in his father's workshop, which he took over on his father's retirement and ran until 1825. As we have seen, Georges Jacob already in the eighteenth century was an ardent exponent of what was to become the Empire style and his son must have been conversant with this at an early age. In 1798 Jacob-Desmalter married the daughter of Martin-Eloy Lignereux, the successor of the marchand-mercier, Daguerre, and an early exponent of the Egyptian taste.

Among his first commissions after his father's retirement was the re-furbishment of the house for General Bonaparte and his new wife, Josephine, and the execution to designs by Berthault of the bedroom furniture of Madame Recamier, which included a boat-shaped bed with swan's head scroll ends — an early example of a style of bed which became universally popular in the Empire period. Percier and Fontaine commissioned Jacob-Desmalter to carry out many of their designs for Napoleon, at Malmaison, the Tuileries and other former royal palaces. By 1807 Jacob-Desmalter had a sizable and successful firm. He employed about 350 workmen, and his annual output was worth 700,000 francs, one-third of which was for export. Despite his success he went bankrupt in 1813, owing to the tardiness of many of his clients in paying their bills and the slump in commerce caused

Above: Bathroom at the Château de Malmaison. The dressing-table is in burr-elm with ormolu mounts. Pieces like this with the mirror and table joined as one piece of furniture only became popular in the early nineteenth century. The wash-basin and stand is based on an antique incense burner. (Château de Malmaison)

Right: A bed which was part of a suite of furniture made for the bedroom of Pius VII at Fontainebleau. Although it bears no maker's mark, it is similar to work by Pierre-Antoine and Louis-François Bellangé, and Joseph-Marie Bénard. (Château de Fontainebleau)

Above: The bedroom of Comte Charles de Mornay painted by Eugène Delacroix. The tented room is very Empire in feeling, but the furniture is not formally arranged, and the cabinets and pictures are rather haphazardly placed. The furniture is in plain mahogany with no mounts or superfluous decoration of any kind — it is simple, solid and masculine, though still retaining the basic form so popular in the Empire period. (Louvre, Paris)

even their addresses as well, such as Biennais, though the necessity to do this had been removed with the dissolution of the guilds.

Napoleon went to great lengths to encourage the arts, and was much more than just a patron. He considered that luxury was a necessary adjunct to a healthy economy. He and Josephine visited the Gobelin and Sèvres factories, amongst others, and visited the leading cabinet-makers in their *ateliers*, as well as inviting many of them as dinner-guests. He was as much concerned with building the prestige of these establishments and the quality of their products as Louis XIV had been, and he also took a tremendous and almost finicky interest in the furnishing of his own living quarters. Despite the new accent on comfort and informality, strict protocol was still observed on public occasions, and the Empress and the Emperor's mother were the only people allowed to use an arm-chair in his presence — all others, including members of the Imperial family, used ordinary chairs or stools.

Although the style and decoration of furniture changed radically in the early nineteenth century, the only new type to make its appearance was the cheval-glass, sometimes called a *psyché*. This was a full-length mirror, pivoted between upright supports.

The exotic woods, particularly mahogany, satinwood and rosewood, were popular at the beginning of the Empire period, but the European blockade made these scarce, and native woods, such as maple, beech, walnut, oak and fruitwoods, were used much more. With the new fashion for large expanses of wood, the more highly grained examples became popular, such as amboyna and thuya, the attractive burr being obtained from the part of the tree close to the root.

After 1815 the quality and craftsmanship declined, and furniture became plainer and heavier. Louis XVIII's reign saw a revival of the Louis Seize style, and the Empire style lingered on in a watered-down plainer version through the reigns of Charles X and Louis-Philippe.

by Napoleon's later campaigns. The firm was soon running successfully again, though on a smaller scale, and when Jacob-Desmalter died in 1841 it was continued by his son.

There were other dynasties of cabinet-makers working under the Empire — the Bellangés, the Lemarchands and the Mansions were three of the most famous — but competition was much stronger now, since the Assembly had abolished the guilds in 1791. Increased industrialization caused more furniture of mediocre quality to be made, and the Continental blockade, started in 1806, made it increasingly difficult for cabinet-makers to import exotic woods or to export their finished wares to England.

Martin-Guillaume Biennais was one of the foremost makers and suppliers of the period. He came from Normandy, but settled in Paris in about 1790. He was appointed goldsmith to Napoleon and on his trade cards he described himself as a dealer in fancy goods, furniture, and fans, with a depot for display of his wares. His furniture was often to designs by Percier and Fontaine, and Denon, and his famous workshops, Au Singe Violet — 'at the sign of the purple monkey' — were in the fashionable Rue St Honoré.

Many cabinet-makers continued to stamp their goods with their names and sometimes

England

The 1750s saw the English Rococo at its height and, at the same time, the stirrings of the successive Neo-classicism all over Europe. In 1754, the very year of Chippendale's important *Director,* the young Scottish architect, Robert Adam, was embarking on the four-year Italian trip which would prepare him for a highly successful career as a classical architect. Within a few years he would have pioneered a revival, which would undermine the short-lived Rococo that preceded it and would lead to a clarification and discipline of design.

Right: The Dining-Room at Kedleston designed by Robert Adam in about 1761. The large scale of the neo-classical plaster-work decoration is typical of this early phase in Adam's career. With its inset paintings and neo-classical furniture, this room was evidently meant to present a unified whole, the sideboard apse forming the focal point, especially when the central floor space was cleared between meals. The complex sideboard group, on which the family plate was to be displayed in the traditional manner, may well have been inspired by James Stuart, and the vast jasper wine-cooler certainly belongs to Stuart's work in the house. (Kedleston Hall, Derby)

Although the Rococo years had been extremely productive as far as interior decoration and the decorative arts were concerned, the style was not necessarily universally followed. For those who disliked the wild extravaganzas of Rococo a conservative Palladian style was still employed into the mid-eighteenth century, and, certainly, Palladian principles still held good for external architecture.

With this continuing tradition of Italian inspiration — reinforced throughout the century by the Grand Tour — it was perhaps easier for the English to slip comfortably into the neo-classical revival than it was for their European contemporaries. The Rococo had been a fleeting fashion, and now, with Roman classicism stressed once more, architects and designers could develop effortlessly from a sound Palladian foundation. They were, after all, in many cases studying the same Roman sources as their Palladian predecessors; it was merely the interpretation that was to change in the late eighteenth century. It is not surprising, therefore, to find certain basic similarities between the interiors of William

Kent and Robert Adam, or between those tentative experiments towards neo-classical furniture of the 1760s and the pieces of 20 or 30 years earlier.

The Palladians, with their sound knowledge of important centres like Rome, were less adventurous than their successors, who now scoured Europe for uncharted sites. Hence the influential trips made by Dawkins and Wood to Palmyra and Baalbeck in the 1750s, and hence Adam's choice of Spalatro for the subject of his book. These studies, opening up new fields, would lead to a more serious imitation of classicism than that of the Burlington circle earlier in the century.

The most important work to be produced was undoubtedly Stuart and Revett's *Antiquities of Athens* of 1762, which with LeRoy's less extensive survey would ultimately lead to the new Greek revival. James Stuart, the more important architect of the two, put some of his Greek studies into practice on his return to England in 1755, but, unfortunately, he rarely carried out large-scale commissions, and was soon eclipsed by Robert Adam. His surviving decorations within Spencer House,

Above: Design for the Painted Room at Spencer House of about 1759 by James Stuart. This sketch is for one of the earliest neo-classical interiors in England. Much of the ornament is drawn from ancient Rome, while Raphael's sixteenth-century 'grotesque' decorations at the Vatican are another source of inspiration. The rectilinear furniture is far in advance of its time, the ormolu tripod being based on a Greek design, although the lion, crouching beneath the table-top, is reminiscent of Palladian furniture earlier in the century. (The British Museum, London)

158

St James, remind us of his importance, however, as the first great neo-classical designer in England.

Surprisingly the Painted Room at Spencer House, with its rinceaux, swags of corn husks, sphinxes, vases and classical figures, is more reminiscent of Rome — which Stuart had also visited — than of Greece. But Greek elements were introduced into the furniture designed by Stuart for this setting. Great winged lions, drawn from the Temple of Lysicrates in Athens, were incorporated, for example, into the sides of the splendid carved and gilded sofas, which survive with their matching set of chairs at Kenwood House today. The side-table included in Stuart's sketch of 1759 centred on another crouching lion, to relieve no doubt the severity of this advanced neo-classical piece with its fluted frieze and tapering, square-section legs.

The small ormolu tripod, visible in the sketch, was based on another Athenian monument, the Lantern of Demosthenes, and became a popular form in the late eighteenth century. Although shown equipped with branches, for use as a candelabrum, it could easily be adapted for incense-burning, which had become fashionable. Candelabra to this design were supplied to Lord Spencer in about 1759, with tall, painted and gilded *torchère* stands which were appropriately carved with griffins symbolizing fire. These are early examples of the type of torchère which Adam is erroneously credited with introducing into England.

Adam dismissed the decorations of Spencer House as 'pitifulissimo', and went on to describe Stuart's work for Lord Scarsdale as 'so ill done that [it] moves to pity rather than contempt'. However, he evidently learnt a lot from Stuart, and admitted later, in mellower mood, that he had 'contributed greatly towards introducing the true style of antique decoration'.

No doubt he benefited from the chance to study Stuart's technique at Kedleston, Derbyshire, when he succeeded him there in 1761. The severely classical sideboard group, although finally carried out under Adam's direction, seems to belong to Stuart's inspiration and to be in advance of Adam's neo-classical development at that date.

The Kedleston dining-room, with its shallow plasterwork decorations and inset paintings, serves as a reminder of the style of architecture with which Adam built up his reputation on his return in 1758. He completed Kedleston which had been begun by James Paine, and, indeed, many of his other early commissions were also for the completion or remodelling of existing buildings. Adam quickly proved himself to be extremely adept at coping with problems of 'conversion', as, for instance, at Syon, where he tackled the task of classicizing

a monotonous, long, low, Jacobean gallery with very successful results.

Enlivening rooms with apses and columnar screens, he transposed on to walls and ceilings the repertoire of ornament he had learnt in Rome. Piranesi had claimed that he had 'more genius for the true and noble architecture than any Englishman ever was in Italy'. This sound understanding of the antique, combined with a knowledge of the sixteenth-century vividly painted motifs of the Raphael School known as 'grotteschi', led to a balanced and confident arrangement of classical decoration. Sphinxes, griffins, caryatids, rams' heads, vases, tripods, classical shields were arrayed time and again amidst acanthus leaf scrolls, anthemions, palmettes, swags of ribbon or chains of corn-husks in ever changing combinations. Contained within squares, rectangles, semicircles or the popular oval, the stuccowork would frequently centre on inset medallions, painted with suitably classical subjects. At first used on a bold scale, these antique patterns were to dwindle to a great delicacy and over-refinement toward the end of Adam's life.

Above: Armchair designed by Adam in 1764 and made by Thomas Chippendale. Despite neo-classical sphinxes, anthemions and acanthus-leaf scrolls, Rococo and Palladian elements linger on in this early Adam chair design, which bears little relation to his later, more delicate work. When, in 1765, it was delivered as one of a set of eight such chairs, Chippendale charged the high price of £160 for the set.(Victoria & Albert Museum, London)

Above: The Library at Kenwood House, designed by Robert Adam in 1767. This barrel-vaulted library with its apsidal ends and columnar screens was intended, as Adam explained, 'for receiving company', and was accordingly impressive. The carved and gilded pelmet-boards, and the pier-glasses with their neo-classical crestings are original furnishings. The mahogany reading-desk is Rococo in design, but the set of chairs and sofas, although at first glance seeming to belong to the Palladian era, were in fact inspired by Greek sources.

but by the late 1760s he had developed a more suitable rectilinear style.

The mid-1760s were to see the return of the rectangular side-table, equipped with a top of marble, *scagliola*, or marquetried wood. Classical motifs decorated the carved and gilded or painted frieze, and the legs, which were generally arranged in pairs, were of tapering square-section or slender, baluster form. In the semicircular tables, which were soon to emerge as an alternative, decorative stretchers might also be included.

Side-tables — especially if intended for the pier between windows — would frequently be surmounted by a mirror in a rectangular or oval frame. The decorative crestings on mirrors and girandoles were reduced in scale as the 1770s advanced and a round-topped tripartite 'Venetian window' design developed during that decade.

Although the repertoire of classical ornament was adapted to a variety of uses, the lyre being a favourite device for the chair-back for instance, surprisingly few pieces of classical form were made. It would be some years before the recent discoveries at Herculaneum and Pompeii would bear fruit. Only in the urn-on-pedestal and torchère-stand were these archaeological tendencies foreshadowed, and both these forms had already appeared in Stuart's designs, before Adam's rise to fame.

The vases-on-pedestals which now flanked the sideboard-table were an elegant adjunct to the dining-room. Resembling the splendid marble urns sought by many a Grand Tourist on his travels, they served a practical purpose as well as a decorative one. The vase might be used as a knife-box, or provide a water-container. The pedestals, lined with tin and equipped with charcoal-burners, became useful plate-warmers — or else, to the horrified amazement of visiting foreigners, one pedestal was often found to contain a chamber-pot.

Tripod torchères, supplied in sets or pairs, for the support of candelabra and incense-burners, were based upon classical altars. Although Stuart had used this design as early as 1759, it seems that their great popularity in the 1770s was largely due to the French fashion for athéniennes.

French Neo-classicism made a great impact on the English now that the Seven Years' War had drawn to a close. Ideas were freely exchanged between the countries, and French goods — including furniture — were supplied to English clients. A number of Adam's patrons bought elegant tapestry hangings and matching upholstery sets from the Gobelins factory in Paris, and the furniture supplied to rooms of this type accorded closely with contemporary French taste. In chair design the similarities are particularly marked as with the oval-backed form popular on both

Adam intended his rooms to present a unified and harmonious aspect, with all components interrelating in the French manner. To this end, he designed floor-coverings to echo ceiling patterns, and even provided designs for such small details as the handles and keyhole escutcheons of the doors. Naturally enough, he would wish to supervise the furnishings of his interiors as well, and fortunately, through the survival of many of his drawings in Sir John Soane's collection, this aspect of Adam's work is very well documented.

Although Adam's first recorded furniture design is for a chair in the 'gothick' taste which was executed for Alnwick Castle in Northumberland, his pieces generally draw their ornament from Ancient Rome. Apparently rejecting the uncompromising severity of Stuart, Adam at first translates his classical patterns on to bulky forms, reminiscent of Palladian and Rococo fashions,

Left: Marquetry commode and torchère-stands by John Cobb, made in about 1771. The inspiration for this bombé commode comes from the Louis Quinze style in France although the deeper shape and marquetried top are typically English features. Despite the Rococo outline of the piece, its marquetry decoration is in the neo-classical taste and includes vases of flowers and swags of corn-husks. The unusual bombé pedestals were probably intended as torchère-stands, but within ten years white marble urns had been fixed to them. The set of furniture is completed by a pier-glass designed by Adam in 1772. (Corsham Court, Wiltshire)

sides of the Channel. Sofas followed French trends as well. The 'confidante'—with angle seats at either end—became so popular that in 1788 the firm of Hepplewhite considered an elegant drawing-room 'scarce complete' without one.

The commode played an important role in fashionable interiors of the late eighteenth century. It was generally veneered with a light coloured wood such as satinwood, according with the pale clear colours of the rooms better than mahogany, which tended to be relegated to the hall and dining-room. Classical patterns were introduced through marquetry—revived now in England as in France—and ormulu mounts were used in the French manner.

In the 1760s there was a belated vogue for bombé Louis Quinze commode forms, mounted with meagre Rococo mounts and decorated with the Adam repertoire of ornament. Pierre Langlois, a French-trained ébéniste practising in London, produced much work in this manner. Tailoring his French style to suit his English clientele, he reduced his mounting, generally employed marquetry in place of the marble tops used in Paris, and adopted the low form of commode—sometimes cupboarded —which the English preferred. John Cobb, formerly a partner of the Royal cabinet-

maker William Vile, and described by one of his contemporaries as the 'proudest man in England', also produced work of this incongruous Rococo-classical character.

The 1770s saw a growing preference for commodes of rectangular or semicircular shape. Sometimes these centred on delicate panel 'pictures' in the manner of Angelica Kauffman, which were carried out in a wide range of exotic woods and inset into the furniture in similar fashion to the Sèvres plaques of contemporary France. No doubt, these ambitious schemes were the work of specialist *marqueteurs*, and Fuhrlohg, a Swedish ébéniste who worked in London, is known to have produced some of the finest examples.

Many of the firms associated with the Rococo style through their publications distinguished themselves in the succeeding style. Ince and Mayhew were working in a sophisticated neo-classical manner at Croome Court within a few years of their *Universal System* and some of Chippendale's finest executed work is in the Adam taste. The rosewood- and mahogany-mounted sideboard group, the marquetried library desk, fall-front secretaire and dressing-commode delivered to Harewood in the early 1770s are generally considered to be amongst the most

Above: Japanned bedroom commode made for Harewood House, probably by Thomas Chippendale in about 1771. Several of the Harewood bedrooms were hung with India paper and appropriately furnished with japanned pieces. A combination of chinoiserie and neo-classical patterns was common at this time, and corn-husks, paterae and palmettes frame the oriental scenes on this example.

splendid pieces of furniture ever produced in Britain. They too, especially the secretaire, show a clear debt to France which Chippendale had visited in 1768.

The Harewood furniture, made for a house in which Adam and Chippendale were working simultaneously, was long assumed to have been made to designs by the architect. It is now realized that Chippendale — who was, after all, a competent and fashion-conscious designer — most probably designed the pieces himself. Adam, with his busy architectural career, can scarcely have had time to design all the furnishings in every house upon which he worked. No doubt he delegated work to other designers, or else his patrons consulted cabinet-makers independently. A firm of Chippendale's standing could be relied upon to marry up furniture with its setting, without the guidance of the architect.

A similar situation arose on several occasions between Robert Adam and the cabinet-maker, John Linnell, who had inherited his father's thriving business in 1763. Architect and furniture designer first collaborated at Kedleston, where Linnell's famous mermen sofa in 1762 still echoes the free-flowing Rococo, absorbed during his studies at the St Martin's Lane Academy. By the mid-1770s, when Linnell designed and made some of the furnishings for Osterley, he had developed a more classical style, which harmonized admirably with Adam's interiors.

Chinoiserie, like gothick, had certainly not died out with the advent of Neo-classicism, and japanned furniture was frequently provided for the bedroom, which, in the late eighteenth century, might still be hung with painted Chinese wallpaper. Two black and gold japanned commodes remain at Osterley today, while a green and gold colour scheme was preferred for the famous Chippendale bedroom suite of 1771 at Nostell Priory in Yorkshire. Mrs David Garrick planned her green and white bedroom furnishings round a present of Indian chintz in 1772, and Thomas Chippendale carried these out for her in the flat paintwork that was now preferred to the raised designs in imitation of relief lacquer.

Although Mrs Garrick's bedroom was in the Chinese taste, the bed itself was decorated with Adamesque motifs. Overall neo-classical painting was often done, in a variety of pale colours, although the 1770s saw the vogue for 'Etruscan' rooms, with striking Pompeian decorations in black, white and terracotta and furniture painted to match. An alternative to marquetry, it was not until the last decade of the eighteenth century that painting over veneers became standard practice.

Adam was the only late eighteenth-century English architect to publish any neo-classical furniture designs and he only included a few in his *Works of Architecture* of 1773. But he was by no means unique in his interest in furniture, and it was quite customary for

eighteenth-century architects to suggest furnishings for interiors, and even, on occasion, to provide silver designs.

The sketches by Sir William Chambers, Adam's rival, reveal an early appreciation of French Neo-classicism, with which Chambers had come into contact when studying in Blondel's Ecole des Arts in 1750, and through subsequent friendships with students at the French Academy in Rome. He appears to have been in close contact later with the Swedish contingent in London — he had himself been brought up in Sweden — and probably supplied them with designs.

James Wyatt returned to London from Italy in 1768 to find 'the public taste corrupted by the Adams' and complained that he was thus obliged to comply with it. Nonetheless, gaining widespread fame with his Pantheon in London's Oxford Street he went on to design a number of neo-classical houses and their furnishings, which were often painted to harmonize closely with the wall and ceiling decoration. James Paine, Thomas Leverton and Joseph Bonomi are among other architects known to have designed furniture for their interiors.

The 1750s had seen a spate of pattern books, which had helped to accelerate the widespread adoption of the Rococo, but there was to be a marked dearth of corresponding books in the neo-classical movement. In John Soane's words, 'Manufacturers of every kind felt as it were the electric power of this Revolution in

Left: The Library at Osterley Park. Adam's designs of 1766 for this room had been carried out by 1773, and the result is another excellent example of his interrelation of the component parts of a decorative scheme. The ceiling, recently restored to its intended clear pale colours, marries with the decoration of the architectural bookcases which would originally have been topped by vases or busts. John Linnell supplied the set of lyre-backed chairs, the library desk and pair of matching writing-tables, which he designed himself to harmonize with Adam's setting. The Vitruvian scroll pattern of satinwood on a rosewood ground echoes the carved patterns of the bookcases, and this, with the swagged mounting, reflects early French neo-classical designs. (National Trust, Osterley Park, Middlesex)

Right: Hepplewhite designs for shield-back chairs from his Guide of 1788. Hepplewhite's posthumously published book is a reflection of the neo-classical taste of the 1780s, and was criticized in its day for its conservatism. Even the shield-back chair design was probably not a new form. Nonetheless, the book served to disseminate the Adam style further afield and to a wider middle-class market.

Art', long before the major publications of the late 1780s.

Matthias Lock had produced some neo-classical pier-frame designs in 1769, Darly included one or two pieces of furniture in his *Ornamental Architect* of 1770, and a few impractical designs in the Piranesi style appeared in the *Builder's Magazine* from 1774 to 1778. But there was no book on the scale of Chippendale's *Director* before George Hepplewhite's *Cabinet-maker and Upholsterer's Guide* of 1788, and even then this posthumous publication tended to reflect the general taste of the decade rather than to propagate new ideas. Some of the designs for bedroom furniture hark back to Chippendale's plates, and a number of pieces illustrated were in the bowed serpentine curves of the 1760s. The cabriole leg is included in numerous designs.

The objects stated in Hepplewhite's preface —'to unite elegance and utility' and to avoid 'articles whose recommendation was mere novelty'—were fully realized, however, in a comprehensive range of practical pieces, intended to be of use to foreigners as well as 'our own countrymen and artisans whose distance from the metropolis makes even an imperfect or superficial knowledge of its improvement acquired with much trouble and expense'. Copious imitations both in England and abroad provide evidence enough of the success of the *Guide* which went into a second edition in 1789 and a third in 1794.

Thomas Sheraton wrote in a spirit of rivalry 'this work has already caught the decline, and perhaps, in a little time will suddenly die in the disorder'. His jibes, especially at the outmoded curves of Hepplewhite's chairs, were answered by the revisions in the 1794 edition, rectangular-backed chair designs of the Sheraton type replacing some of the more curvilinear designs of the first two issues.

Hepplewhite did much to popularize the shield-back, which, with oval and heart-shapes, was to be copiously used for chairs in the 1790s. His chair-backs were often decorated with neo-classical motifs of a less intricate nature than Adam's. The carved swag of material and Prince of Wales' triple feathers were favourite patterns. Simplified Adamesque ornaments were likewise included in the radiating marquetry designs for side-tables and for the popular Pembroke tables which had evolved from the hinged breakfast table of the mid-century. Some useful mechanical pieces included a neat tambour-fronted desk in the French manner, and practical storage space was provided in the compact deep-drawered sideboard, which now formed an alternative to the sideboard group with flanking pedestal cupboards.

Similar cabinet-furniture was illustrated in Thomas Shearer's smaller trade catalogue,

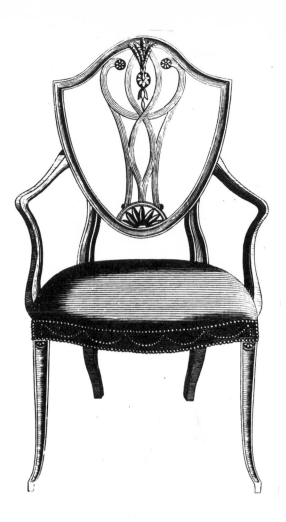

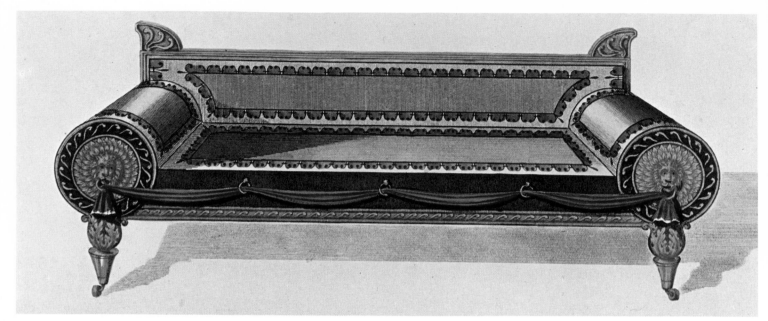

The Cabinet-Maker's London Book of Prices, also of 1788. Sheraton wrote that Shearer's designs were 'more fashionable and useful . . . in proportion to their number' than Hepplewhite's, although they tend to have been overshadowed by the greater fame of the *Guide*. As the title suggests, the book throws an interesting light on costs.

Little is known of the working life of Thomas Shearer and although Hepplewhite himself was a practising cabinet-maker, no furniture actually made by him has yet been authenticated. Hepplewhite is known to have worked with the firm of Gillow, which was based in Lancaster, opening a showroom in London in 1760. Although they did not produce a pattern book, the style of the firm can easily be assessed from the surviving cost-book sketches and through their practice, later on, of stamping their furniture.

Seddon & Company were great rivals of Gillow's in the late eighteenth century. Something of their importance can be gauged from the 1786 account of their workshop by Sophie von la Roche, which provides incidentally an interesting picture of the range of products within a fashionable cabinet-maker's of the day. Mr Seddon, she wrote, 'employs four hundred apprentices on any work connected with the making of household furniture — joiners, carvers, gilders, mirror-workers, upholsterers, girdlers — who mould the bronze into graceful patterns — and lock-smiths. All these are housed in a building with six wings. In the basement mirrors are cast and cut. Some other department contains nothing but chairs, sofas, and stools of every description . . . while others are occupied by writing-tables, cupboards, chests-of-drawers, charmingly-fashioned desks, chests both large and small, work- and toilet-tables in all manner of wood and patterns . . . chintz, silk, and

wool materials for curtains and bedcovers, hangings in every possible material; carpets and stair-carpets to order; in short anything one might desire to furnish a house . . .'

The 1790s were to see an increasing severity in the interpretation of classicism, which was reflected in the 113 plates of Thomas Sheraton's *Cabinet-Maker and Upholsterer's Drawing-Book* published between 1791 and 1794. The first two parts of this publication were given over to geometry and perspective and to drawing instruction which Sheraton practised professionally, the third being 'intended to exhibit the present taste in furniture, and at the same time, to give the workmen some assistance in the manufacturing of it'.

Although Sheraton had apparently trained as a cabinet-maker, he had clearly abandoned the craft by now, for he supplied the names and addresses of various firms where his pieces could be ordered, and he even implied that he had gleaned his ideas from associates in the trade. In describing his Harlequin Pembroke Table he wrote: 'In this I assume very little originality or merit . . . except what is due in the manner of shewing and describing the mechanism of it; the rest is due to a friend, from whom I received my first ideas of it.'

Although the categories of furniture illustrated correspond inevitably with those in Hepplewhite's *Guide*, the pieces are rather different in character. Flowing serpentine curves are replaced by rectangular forms — although some bizarre banana and kidney shapes are suggested — and elaborate classical marquetry patterns give way to geometrical banded borders and bold oval and lozenge insets in contrasting woods.

A vertical emphasis is lent to chests of drawers and commodes by the inclusion of slender colonette uprights which break into the frieze area. In chair designs, the front leg

Above: Sofa design by Thomas Sheraton, 1805. The decoration on the back is borrowed from Greek architecture and the cylindrical ends are probably adaptations from antique furniture. Many of Sheraton's later designs include sculptural animal forms, such as these gilded lion's masks. The swagging across the front of the sofa is an unusual feature which may relate to the brief, late eighteenth-century fashion for swagged drapes beneath the seat-rail.

Above right: Design for a sideboard from Thomas Shearer's London Book of Prices of 1788. Both Hepplewhite and Shearer illustrated these new deep-drawered pieces which were produced in the 1780s as an alternative to the sideboard group with pedestals.

Right: Library desk made by Thomas Chippendale the Younger in about 1804. With its monumental simplicity and sculptural decorations, this desk is an early example of fully-fledged Regency design. The Egyptian figures illustrate a new interest in the art of Ancient Egypt. (National Trust, Stourhead House, Wiltshire)

bonheur-du-jours and fall-front secretaires are clearly based on French ideas, even if they were intended to be carried out in less lavish materials.

The French influence — so constant in late eighteenth-century English furniture — had been reinforced for Sheraton by a visit to Carlton House, the London residence of the francophile Prince of Wales. Sheraton included a general sketch of the dining-room, and more detailed views of the Chinese drawing-room with its French pieces, probably supplied by the marchand-mercier Daguerre, who had opened a depot in London.

On this visit he was clearly struck by the sparing quality of the designs of Henry Holland, the architect in charge. Holland, whose 'august simplicity' was now widely preferred to the fripperies of Robert Adam, had started work on Carlton House in 1783, going on three years later to build the Prince of Wales' first Marine Pavilion at Brighton. He worked for several members of the Prince's political circle, including Lords Palmerston and Spencer and Mr Samuel Whitbread of Southill.

Like Adam he strove to create a sense of unity within his interiors, designing furniture as an extension of his clear-cut economical

soars upwards into the chair-arm support in an unbroken line. These features — and the spinning-top feet admired by Sheraton — relate to contemporary French fashions, and the work of such furniture-makers as Carlin, Weisweiler and Jacob. The commodes with curving open shelves at the sides, the delicate

style of architecture. Holland made constant use of rectilinear forms, and enclosed large-scale classical motifs within clearly defined outlines with bold colour contrasts. The recessed colonettes and concave quadrants of his boxy commodes reveal an understanding of up to date French design, and an admiration for the archaeological *style étrusque* in France led him to anticipate Regency development.

The severe classicism of David is echoed in the set of chairs which Holland designed for Southill in about 1796. Here already are the sabre-legs and bolt-head ornaments associated with the second, nineteenth-century phase of neo-classicism. They were probably carried out by the firm of Marsh & Tatham, who had worked extensively for the Prince of Wales.

Charles Heathcote Tatham (1772–1842), the brother of one of the cabinet-making partners, was a pupil of Holland, who sent him to Rome in 1794. Over the next three years, Tatham built up a collection of classical fragments for his master, and, more importantly, supplied him with sketches of Graeco-Roman ornament, which Holland incorporated into his designs. Among these was the monopodium which soon became widely used as a sculptural support in England. Tatham eventually published his researches in 1799 in his *Etchings of Ancient Ornamental Architecture drawn from the Originals in Rome and Other Parts of Italy*, which led to his being credited with the rise of the 'Anglo-Greek Style' in Joseph Gwilt's *Dictionary of Architecture* of 1842.

The sculptural forms suggested by Tatham play an important role in the more accurate Neo-classicism of the 1800s, when much of the furniture takes on the appearance of carved stone. No longer content with the mere adaptation of classical ornament, designers now sought to recreate the furniture of antiquity. Bas-reliefs and vase paintings were studied for guidance, and Pompeii and Herculaneum naturally provided a fount of ideas. The classical daybed, X-frame stool, deep-yoked klismos chair and tripod monopodia table or stand came into popular use. There was an emphasis on monumentality, in contrast to the fragile femininity of the 1790s, and dark colours — mahogany, rosewood, ebonizing and bronzing — were used in preference to the pale gold of satinwood.

Rome was no longer the chief source of inspiration. In the 1790s Tatham had already noted that the Grecian taste was gaining ground, and now the purity of Greek classicism was held by many to be superior to the ornamental Roman style.

Tatham had foreshadowed another shift in taste when he illustrated some of the Egyptian antiquities in Rome, in his correspondence with Holland, although this was of course

given tremendous impetus by Napoleon's Nile Campaign and the subsequent publications of Baron Denon. Canopic jars, scarabs, lotus leaves, winged discs of the sun, and the jackal and hawk-headed figures of Egyptian mythology were rapidly seized upon by the furniture designers. The tapering outline, based on the famous Pylon gateway, was widely popularized and the swathed and headdressed figure of the mummy-case was translated into side-terminals for bookcases, commodes and desks, like that supplied to Stourhead by Thomas Chippendale the Younger in about 1805. Mary Russell Mitford writes in *Our Village* of a library 'all covered with hieroglyphics and swarming with furniture crocodiles and sphinxes' — incongruous features that were to become commonplace in English settings.

The first designer to publish Egyptian motifs alongside Greek and Roman in furniture was Thomas Sheraton, whose *Cabinet Dictionary* of 1803 was followed by *The Cabinet-Maker, Upholsterer and General Artist's Encyclopaedia*, still incomplete at the author's death in 1806. Sheraton was living in considerable penury at the end of his life and his incipient insanity has been read into

Below: Armchair of about 1803 designed by Thomas Hope. Painted black and gold to relieve the pale yellow and bluish green of the Egyptian Room in his mansion at Duchess Street, the chair is appropriately decorated with Egyptian motifs. The jackal-headed Anubis and hawk-headed Horus feature in the hieroglyphic panels beneath the couchant lions, and sacred scarabs ornament the feet. The Greek bracket decoration above the feet is, however, hardly consistent with the other Egyptian motifs and reveals the mixture of traditions which sometimes creeps into Hope's work. (National Trust, Buscot Park, Berkshire)

Left: Sketch of the Flaxman Room, Duchess Street, designed by Hope in about 1800. Decorated to enshrine the sculpture of Cephalus and Aurora which was commissioned from his friend, Flaxman, in 1790, this room embodies Hope's principle of 'symbolical and narrative ornament' which made a great impact on the character of nineteenth-century design. The X-frame chairs and accompanying footstools, monopodia and caryatid-supported table plinths are close to classical originals, and reflect the growing archaeological interest of the 1800s. The dramatic combination of hangings and mirror, to reflect the sculpture from different angles, illustrates the romantic vein in Hope's neo-classicism.

these wild impractical designs so far removed in character from those of the *Drawing Book*. But, in the ghoulish animal forms which lend a nightmare quality to many of the pieces, Sheraton had already sensed the sculptural emphasis of the high Regency, and he illustrated such advanced pieces as the classical chaise longue.

He had possibly been inspired by the furnishings of Thomas Hope's famous house in Duchess Street, which, acquired in 1799, was completed around 1804. The house could be viewed by appointment, and imitations of its contents had already 'started up in every corner of the capital' by 1807 when Hope published views of it in his *Household Furniture and Decoration*.

The house had been planned to enshrine the great classical collection of its dilettante owner, built up on his travels in Europe, Asia and Africa, and each room had decoration carefully selected to create an appropriate setting for its treasures. In the Flaxman Room with its sculpture of Cephalus and Aurora, for example, the entire programme of decoration centred upon 'these personages and the face of nature at the moment . . . the goddess of the morn is supposed to announce approaching day . . . The bird consecrated to night perches on the pillars of the black marble chimney-piece, whose broad frieze is studded with golden stars. The sides of the room display, in satin curtains, draped in ample folds over panels of looking-glass, and edged with black velvet, the fiery hue which fringes the clouds just before sunrise . . . The broad band which girds the top of the room contains medallions of the ruddy goddess and of the Phrygian

169

Above: Gothic design for a state bed designed by George Smith in 1807. The 'gothick' style had never completely died out in the late eighteenth century. This design employs an elaborate Perpendicular Gothic, a style which gradually gave way to an Early English revival as the century advanced.

youth, inter-mixed with the instruments and the emblems of the chase, his favourite amusement. Figures of the youthful hours, adorned with wreaths of foliage adorn part of the furniture, which is chiefly gilt in order to give relief to the azure and black and the orange compartments of the curtains.'

This description gives some idea of the brilliance of colouring used throughout the interiors which included an Indian gallery and an Egyptian room described by West-macott as Hope's 'little Canopus'.

In the cold linear engravings, Hope outlines an orderly arrangement of carved and sabre-legged chairs, X-frame stools and chimera-ended banquettes, of caryatid or monopodia tables, tripod torchères, shield-shaped wall-sconces and spirit-lamp chandeliers. One may agree with George Dance's comment that it 'excited no feelings of comfort as a dwelling' despite the warmth of colour.

Hope also included large-scale furniture designs in the antique manner, alongside his

general views. Several of the pieces from which these designs were taken still survive — despite the later demolition of Duchess Street and the Deepdene, Hope's country-house. Boldly carved and painted or gilded, they bear some resemblance to the furniture of Napoleon's designer, Charles Percier, whom Hope knew.

Hope's pedantic designs were of prime importance but there was probably more direct imitation of those of George Smith. Smith's *Collection of Designs for Household Furniture and Interior Decoration* came out in 1808, drawing heavily on Hope's inspiration but diluting and coarsening the classicism to such an extent that his proud claim of 'the most flattering testimonials from Mr Thomas Hope' is difficult to believe. If less scholarly, however, his comprehensive range of designs was infinitely more practical.

Although classicism predominated in the early nineteenth century, other Romantic revivals existed alongside. Amongst the 158 plates of Smith's book several are 'after the Gothic or old English fashion and according to the costume of China'. Perpendicular Gothic forms lived on, now given a heavier treatment than during the mid-eighteenth century, as the designs of A C Pugin show.

Chinoiserie had become fashionable once more through the Prince of Wales' use of it at Carlton House, and later for the Brighton Pavilion. Lacquer and japanning were popular, as were Chinese-inspired designs used in painting and the now fashionable penwork. With the importation of Chinese furniture, bamboo became the rage and was painstakingly copied in European woods.

In the 1820s a Rococo revival emerged, no doubt as a result of mid-eighteenth century French furniture flooding the market in the years after the Revolution. Louis Seize cabinet forms continued to be reproduced, and a fashion for Boulle led to the metal and shell marquetry of Le Gaigneur and Bullock and to the widespread vogue for brass inlay in mahogany or rosewood.

Mounting was copiously used now, and metal grilles set in commode doors. Galleries ran round shelves on desks and cupboards were frequently inset with mirror glass which played an important part in the Regency interior. The convex mirror in a circular frame topped with eagles or dolphins was a regular feature.

Many new pieces of furniture made their appearance during these years: the what-not, the davenport, the circular bookcase, the sofa-table, which, with its end-flaps, was a useful accessory to the sofa or chaise longue. A spate of tables, large and small, but usually at this date on heavy bases, bears witness to the more informal room arrangement now favoured. 'I think', wrote Fanny Burney in

1801, 'no room looks really comfortable, or even quite furnished without two tables — one to keep the wall and take upon itself the dignity of a little tidyness, the other to stand here there and everywhere, and hold letters . . .' At last the rigidity of eighteenth-century rooms had given way to a cosy clutter which in turn would soon lead to crowded interiors. Already in the pattern books of George Smith, the heavily fringed and tasselled window-draperies of the Victorian era were being shown.

The term 'Regency' is used as a label for a style which far exceeded the political limits of the period of George III's reign from 1811 to 1820, extending over the first 30 years of the nineteenth century. Associated with classicism, the style also encompassed various other undercurrents as we have seen, which were later embodied within the Victorian

mélange of styles. Classicism did not die out as the nineteenth century progressed, but already in the design books of Richard Brown, Henry Whitaker and Peter and Michelangelo Nicholson in the 1820s and in the instalments of Ackerman's *Repository*, a coarseness crept in which diminished the power of both the elegance of Adam and the archaeological exactitude of Hope.

Germany

German furniture design in the latter part of the eighteenth century was dominated by the work of David Roentgen, the only German designer at this time to have any international influence. In 1769 he organized a very successful sale of furniture by lottery in Hamburg, and, in 1772, on his father's retirement, came into full control of the Neuwied workshop. David Roentgen quickly realized that he would have to widen his horizons if he wished to continue making high quality furniture, and in 1774 he visited Paris. In 1779 he went back to Paris with several loads of the best furniture made at Neuwied, and set up a depot there. His success was astounding and he was soon making furniture for the royal family. He was appointed *ébéniste-mécanicien du Roi et de la Reine* and, during the 1780s, was paid more by them than Riesener, the

Left: Writing-table by David Roentgen, the most celebrated and successful ébéniste of the late eighteenth century. This is typical of Roentgen's plainer work, being beautifully made and finished in fine quality, well-figured wood, and discreetly mounted in ormolu. The drawers and cupboards have elaborate mechanical fittings, a feature of much of Roentgen's work. (Bavarian National Museum, Munich)

172

official Royal ébéniste. The Paris guild of menuisiers and ébénistes, jealous of his success, forced him to join them and he became a maître ébéniste.

In 1783 Roentgen made the first of several visits to St Petersburg where he had an introduction to the Empress Catherine the Great, who, in 1785, wrote to Baron Friedrich Melchior Von Grimm 'David Roentgen and his two hundred cases have arrived safely and at the right moment to satisfy my gluttony'. Several pieces he supplied to her are still in the Winter Palace in Leningrad.

Roentgen also travelled around Holland, Italy and parts of his native Germany, but the French Revolution robbed him of his French clientele, his Paris depot was confiscated and his Neuwied factory was destroyed by Republican troops, and, despite being appointed Court furnisher to the erratic Frederick-William II of Prussia, he was ruined.

Roentgen's success had been spectacular, and he had been paid unprecedented sums by Louis XVI and Catherine the Great for his more elaborate pieces, the mechanisms of which were made with the help of Peter Kintzing. Roentgen's furniture was always flawlessly executed, as beautifully finished inside as out, and the style and quality of his marquetry, sometimes floral, sometimes pictorial and often to the designs of Januarius Zick, was unsurpassed by any of his contemporaries. He retired to Berlin after the Revolution, but returned to Neuwied in 1802 to try to re-establish his workshop. He was unsuccessful in this, and died when travelling in 1807.

Apart from the work of Roentgen, the new classical style took a long time to find favour in Germany, and the Court furnishers in Potsdam and Berlin were still working in the full Rococo style well into the 1770s. The first neo-classical designs for furniture were not published in Germany until about 1780 by Franz Heissig of Augsburg. In Weimar the *Journal des Luxus und der Moden*, established in 1787, finally published designs for fully classical furniture based on English and French prototypes. In Austria also it was not until the 1780s that furniture became less florid, with the influence of English designs becoming clearly discernible.

What has come to be known as the Louis Seize style was never favoured to the same extent in Germany as elsewhere, and, by the time it had found a hold in Germany, the Empire style was spreading quickly from France, and soon superseded the clumsy adaptations of Louis Seize furniture. The severe lines of the Empire style and the use of dark woods, usually mahogany, and the more exact knowledge of antique forms appealed to German taste.

During the reign of Jerome Bonaparte in Westphalia a French architect and pupil of Percier, Grandjean de Montigny, re-furnished the castle at Kassel and the Palace known as Wilhelmshöhe, then temporarily known as Napoleonshöhe. Some of the furniture for these magnificent rooms was commissioned from Jacob-Desmalter and other pieces, in much the same style, were made by the native craftsman, Friedrich Wichmann.

In Bavaria, the Empire style was most popular at Munich and Würzburg. On the eve of the Battle of Jena in 1806, Napoleon occupied the new apartments in the Empire style in the Baroque Residenz at Würzburg. Much of the early nineteenth-century furniture in the Residenz was copied directly from French originals and supplied by Johann Valentin Raab.

In Prussia King Frederick-William III openly embraced the French style and had the designs of La Mésangère's publications slavishly copied. In Austria, M Seuffert, Elias Weinspach, Thomas Hoss, and J W Sohn were all working in the French Empire style, with a leaning towards the new Biedermeier style, soon to become so popular. At the same time, Johann Haertl of Vienna started to make his ingenious secretaires shaped like lyres or drums.

This grander type of Empire furniture was soon found to be too expensive and out of keeping with the new Germany, impoverished by warfare, and the simpler Biedermeier furniture quickly found favour with the middle classes. Based on the classical style, it was simple and functional, and the darker heavier mahogany was often replaced by the lighter coloured elmwood or fruitwoods. The accent was on comfort and simplicity, and interiors were less formal.

With the plainer interiors came a stress on the importance of seat furniture, and pieces that were decorative rather than functional disappeared. Most rooms had a large comfortable sofa, probably with a table in front of it, and a suite of chairs grouped around it. There would often be a worktable or two for the ladies of the house, a mirror on the walls, and cabinets for writing and the display of china.

Vienna was a great centre of middle-class affluence and housed a number of cabinet-makers. The most famous of these was Josef Danhauser who ran a factory from 1804 until his death in 1830.

In Berlin Karl Friedrich Schinkel, with his work for the Prussian royal palaces, introduced a new Neo-classicism to the German states. Born in Neurippen in 1781, he began to study architecture under Friedrich Gilly at the age of 17 and later at the Berlin Academy. In the early 1800s he travelled around Europe, but by 1809 he had returned to Berlin and was considered important enough to design furniture for Queen Luise's rooms in the Charlottenburg Palace. His most famous work was as an architect, but his furniture, ultra-modern in its day, foreshadowed the Biedermeier style and, less immediately, much Art Deco furniture of the 1920s. His furniture was strikingly simple in design and had neither the fussy prettiness that epitomized the English Regency, nor the uncomfortable correctness of Thomas Hope's classicism. It was distinctive and functional, but sneered at by contemporary designers in France and England, who often sacrificed comfort and elegance to achieve archaeological correctness.

Right: Interior by Johann Erdmann Hummel. The furniture is in the simplified Empire style known as Biedermeier, which was very popular with the middle classes in Germany. Here it is arranged in a semi-formal style, soon to disappear in all but state-rooms. The cheval-glass was an early nineteenth-century innovation. (Museum für Kunsthandwerk, Frankfurt)

Below right: Pair of chairs made for the Queen's throne-room in the Munich Residenz to a design by Louis Von Klenze. Von Klenze was appointed Supervisor of Court Buildings to Crown Prince Ludwig of Bavaria in 1816, and by 1824 was head of the Building Authorities for Bavaria. (Residenz-museum, Munich)

Below: Bed veneered in pearwood and designed by Friedrich Schinkel for the bedroom of Queen Luise in the Charlottenburg Palace, Berlin. The clean lines of this piece contrast with other late Empire furniture which tends to be much heavier. (Schloss Charlottenburg, Berlin)

Another architect, Leo von Klenze, also designed furniture. Working in Munich, he was influenced by Percier and Fontaine, and his designs made full use of motifs and forms taken from Greek architecture and decoration. His most famous patron was Ludwig II of Bavaria, who shared his enthusiasm for antiquity, and he was appointed Supervisor of Court Buildings, and later head of the Building Authorities of Bavaria.

The Empire and Biedermeier styles continued in Germany well into the mid-part of the nineteenth century, though by then they had become very heavy and ponderous and ran concurrently with the newer historic styles.

Russian furniture in the late eighteenth century and early nineteenth century had been a compromise between the contemporary English and French styles, but, by 1815, the strongest influence came from Germany, and much Russian furniture of this time, if it is not known to be Russian, is described as German Biedermeier.

175

Above: Reception-room at Haga Slot, Sweden, designed by Louis-Adrien Masreliez. The chairs, based on the ancient klismos and known as senator chairs in Sweden, are the work of Erik Öhrmark and were carved by Jean-Baptiste Masreliez, the designer's brother. The side-table at the back, known as a console-desserte, is typically French in form. (Haga Slot Pavilion, Stockholm)

Johan Hartwig Ernst Bernstorff, whose residence in Copenhagen was being redecorated in the semi-classical transitional Louis Quinze/Louis Seize style. Jardin's first commission in Denmark was the dining-room in the palace of the Lord High Steward, Count Moltke, at Amalienborg. In 1759 and 1762 he worked on another Moltke house, Marienlyst, much of which was rebuilt and redecorated in the classical taste after Jardin's designs. In 1760 he was appointed Surveyor of the King's Works and his first royal commission was to replan the park at Fredensborg and redecorate Count Moltke's apartments. In the winter of 1762 Jardin went back to Paris, and, on returning to Scandinavia, redecorated the Banqueting Hall at Christiansborg in preparation for the wedding of the future King Christian VII. He continued to carry out royal commissions in the Louis Seize style until his dismissal in 1770.

Jardin's position as Court architect was taken by his pupil, Caspar Frederik Harsdorff, who continued carrying out royal comissions, including some painted mirrors, decorated *en arabesque* at Frederiksberg. He used the full repertoire of classical decoration, including fasces, laurel wreaths, cornucopia and portrait medallions and executed work for many private clients, including Countess Moltke.

In 1754 the name of Joseph Christian Lillie first appears in the royal accounts for providing furniture, and, by 1790, he was the Court decorator and furniture designer. Working with Harsdorff he carried out much important work, including the suites at Christiansborg for Crown Prince Frederik and Princess Marie, and rooms at the Amalienborg. He also carried out various commissions in Norway, and, at the beginning of the nineteenth century, moved to Lubeck where he died in 1827. Jardin and Harsdorff had both been strongly influenced by the French neo-classical style, while Lillie was influenced by English as well as French taste. Two other designers of some importance at this time in Denmark were G E Rosenborg (designer for the Royal Furniture Emporium from 1771 to 1781) whose designs Harsdorff sometimes used, and Nicolai Abildgaard, who carried out many interiors in the same manner as Lillie.

The most important Swedish cabinet-makers of the late eighteenth century were undoubtedly Georg Haupt and Christopher Fuhrlohg, both of whom worked in France and England, Fuhrlohg remaining in England. Both showed strong European influence in their magnificent marquetry furniture. Georg Haupt, born in Stockholm, was apprenticed in 1754 to Johan Konrad Eckstein. He became a journeyman in 1759, and left the next year with Christopher Fuhrlohg to study cabinet-making in Germany, Amsterdam and Paris.

Most Polish furniture of the late eighteenth and early nineteenth centuries derives from the French Directory and Empire styles. With the work of the brothers Friedrich and Johann Daniel Heurich and the 'Simmler furniture', the influence of the German Biedermeier style is much more apparent, though often linked to the Polish love of carved decoration.

Scandinavia and the Low Countries

The new classical taste came to both Sweden and Denmark at quite an early date—the Swedish country-house, Akerö, had a classical room designed by a French architect in 1754. In 1755 Nicolas-Henri Jardin, the French architect, was invited to Copenhagen by Frederick V's Minister for Foreign Affairs,

Haupt lived and worked in London from 1768 to 1769, and returned to Sweden in 1770 to take up his appointment as *ébéniste du roi* and to submit his masterpiece to the Guild. He remained in Sweden as head of a large work-shop until his death in 1784, and produced furniture in a transitional and later a full neo-classic style, strongly influenced by the techniques of Oeben and Riesener.

During the latter part of the eighteenth century, the Scandinavian countries had enjoyed almost total non-involvement in the European conflicts, but the rise to power of Napoleon and the ensuing wars began to affect them, their trade being severely diminished by the English blockade of Continental ports. Denmark's fleet and parts of Copen-hagen were destroyed by the British, who were afraid their alliance with Russia might change to an alliance with France and by 1813 the Danish government was bankrupt. The more circumspect Swedes made no pacts, and kept their neutrality, and, despite having invited one of Napoleon's marshals to become Crown Prince, eventually sided with England.

In the middle and late eighteenth century English influence had been strong on functional middle-class Scandinavian furniture, but Scandinavia was isolated by the war in the early nineteenth century. English and French forms came to Scandinavia via Germany which was the strongest influence at this time, and there emerged a simple Empire style, partly necessitated by the economic situation. This first appeared in Denmark, and soon spread throughout Scandinavia and with it, because of the difficulty in obtaining mahogany, came a liking for the paler native woods such as birch, ash and maple.

The classical revival survived in Denmark almost until 1850, under the influence of Gustav Friedrich Hetsch, who had studied under Percier in Paris, and still favoured the French Empire style. He was Professor at the Academy and a leading decorator and designer who wielded great influence. In Sweden the Empire style gave way much more quickly to the revival styles which reached their peak in the middle and latter part of the century.

English and French furniture enjoyed such popularity in eighteenth-century Holland that in 1771 the Amsterdam guild forbade the importation of furniture made outside the Netherlands, and all furniture had to be branded with the mark of the Amsterdam Joseph's Guild, the letters J G flanking the arms of Amsterdam.

French furniture was popular, and was much copied by contemporary Dutch makers, such as Andries Bongen, and the ban on imports encouraged the Dutch makers to improve and experiment with the new classical style. The plainer pieces were made in mahogany, and

Left: One of a pair of Swedish secretaires made for Princess Sophia Albertina by Georg Haupt, who studied cabinet-making in Sweden, as well as in Germany, France and England. The marquetry and mounts on this secretaire, based on French originals, are typical of much of Haupt's work. (Tullgarn Palace, Stockholm)

Below: Opflagtafel or Dutch serving-table. This kind of serving table was made only in the Nether-lands. The overall shape with chamfered corners and short square tapering legs is typically Dutch. (Rijksmuseum, Amsterdam)

177

curves were more or less eliminated. The more elaborate pieces were made in exotic woods, often satinwood, and were usually inset with panels of either floral marquetry or oriental lacquer.

The shape of the furniture at this time in Holland was based on English or French originals, though the resulting pieces, often with canted corners, bands of inlay and tapering legs or feet, are closer to Italian models.

In 1808 King Louis-Napoleon gave orders for the Town Hall in Amsterdam to be converted into a royal palace, and refurnished by Dutch craftsmen. The most important of these was Carel Breytsspraak, who provided furniture in the French Empire style, using plain mahogany veneers and simple shapes, often with classical ormolu mounts. The seat furniture was mostly provided by the upholsterer, Joseph Cuel.

The inspiration for most early nineteenth-century Dutch furniture came from France in the form of Percier and Fontaine's *Recueil de décorations intérieures* — and even more obviously La Mésangère's *Meubles et objets de goût.*

After 1815 the Royal Palace in the Hague was partly redecorated at the behest of King William I. The style was noticeably Napoleonic in its splendour, with large suites of gilt-wood chairs. One of the most important suppliers was G Nordanus, who worked in mahogany often incorporating panels of floral marquetry in his work.

The classical style persisted in the Netherlands well into the second quarter of the century, becoming noticeably simpler and closer to the German Biedermeier style. This well-proportioned functional furniture, often made in lighter native woods, such as ash or maple, was eventually ousted by the emergent revival styles, soon to become so popular.

Italy

Despite the researches in Greece and the criticism levelled at the 'debased' classicism of Rome, Italy still remained the centre of Neo-classicism in the mid-eighteenth century. Rome attracted a great number of foreigners, and, within her cosmopolitan itinerant society, the foundations of the neo-classical revival were laid.

That they were laid by foreigners has already been stressed; indeed, it could have been argued that eighteenth-century Italy contributed virtually nothing to the initiation of the movement, were it not for Piranesi, whose romantic vision of the splendours of Rome redressed the balance in the Graeco-Roman controversy, and served as a major catalyst in the international advance of neo-classical architecture.

Born in Treviso in 1720, Giovanni Battista Piranesi had studied architecture and theatri-

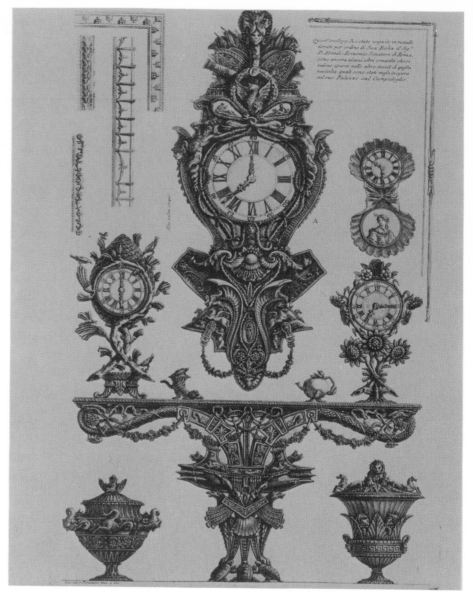

cal design in Venice, before visiting Rome in 1740, where he decided to settle permanently five years later. Having studied etching under Giuseppe Vasi, he produced his *Prima Parte dell' Architettura e Prospettiva* in 1743, with its theatrical visions of reconstructed ancient Rome and its evocative views of ruins.

Over the next 33 years, Piranesi was to etch more than 1,000 plates, which would do much to aggrandize his adopted city and fire the imagination of architects all over Europe. The views shown in his dramatic *Vedute di Roma* were far removed from the standard topographical views of the day, and, if exaggerated and distorted, were, in Robert Adam's words, designed to 'inspire and instil invention'. Piranesi's major four-volume *Antichità Romane* of 1756 did indeed leave a marked impression on the French students of the Academy in Rome, and on visiting English architects such as Adam.

The more controversial character of Piranesi's work in the 1760s was due to his

Above: Design for clocks, vases and table by Giovanni Battista Piranesi, 1769. The crowded mixture of classical motifs is less an attempt to recreate antique forms than a means of producing original outlines. Although the large cartel clock was executed, it is doubtful whether many of his eccentric, unbalanced designs — which almost evoke Rococo — were actually carried out.

involvement in the dispute over Greece and Rome. As champion of Roman supremacy, he produced *Della Magnificenza ed Architettura dei Romani* in 1761 — in which he also praised the Etruscans — which led to a dialogue with the Greek protagonist, Mariette. At first dry and rationalistic, he abandoned this approach in *Parere sull' Architettura* of 1765 to urge a free adaptation of classical elements, which would also be applied to his furniture designs.

In the meantime, Piranesi was working for Carlo Rezzonico, Pope Clement XIII. For Clement's nephew, the Cardinal Giovanni Battista Rezzonico, Piranesi executed his only building, the church of the Knights of Malta in Rome, Santa Maria del Priorato, and decorated an apartment in the Palazzo Quirinale. Some of the designs for the apartment were included in *Diverse Maniere d'Adornare i Camini* of 1769, a folio largely given over to fireplace designs which show 'what an able architect may make of the ancient monuments by properly adapting them to our manners and customs'. Half a dozen furniture plates were also included, which, like Piranesi's other unpublished furniture designs, bear little relation to classical Rome as far as form is concerned but are loaded with Roman, Etruscan and Egyptian ornament. Winged chimeras, sphinxes, vases, masks and caryatids crowd the sedan chair, commode, side-tables and outsize clocks in Piranesi's illustrations, and are outlined with a metallic precision reminiscent of the bronze furniture excavated at Pompeii in the succeeding years. Piranesi's *Parere* motto 'They scorn my novelty, I, their timidity' seems appropriate to these fantastic, exaggerated essays, which, with their sweeping sarcophagus curves, veer, at times, close to the dying Rococo.

Piranesi later published a book devoted to *Vasi, Candelabri e Cippi*, and already in 1769 he revealed a sound knowledge of the classical vase in his urn designs, which he incorporated into his furniture plates. This is, no doubt, the result of his studies as a restorer and agent in the sale of antiquities.

His influence was to be far-reaching, and especially important for the English development, even if later generations came to disapprove of his tendency, in Tatham's words, to 'sacrifice accuracy to what he conceived the richer productions of a more fertile and exuberant mind'.

179

Piranesi had illustrated Egyptian motifs in his etchings and he used the Egyptian style for his Caffè Inglese decorations of 1765. Mengs was simultaneously executing Egyptian paintings in the Vatican, and some late eighteenth-century Roman furniture carries decoration drawn from the Egyptian antiquities in Rome, thus anticipating the French 'goût Egyptien' by several decades. For instance, in the 1777 Pécheux portrait of that great blue-stocking, the Marchesa Gentili Boccapaduli, a table with hieroglyphic ornaments and Egyptian caryatid legs is clearly visible in the background. But this is surprisingly advanced taste for the 1770s, a decade which saw, on the whole, a mingling of Rococo and classical elements all over Italy. In certain centres, such as Venice, Neoclassicism had barely taken root.

The sculptural tradition of Italian furniture lent many neo-classical pieces a positively Baroque appearance, as with the massive bronze table, for example, made for the Vatican in 1789 which has been described as perhaps the finest piece of furniture produced in late eighteenth-century Rome. Its Herculean supports were modelled by Vincenzo Pacetti and cast by Giuseppe Valadier, and the giltbronze reliefs and inscriptions of the frieze inset commemorate the important events of the pontificate of Pius VI. The Egyptian granite top was cut from a block discovered in the wall of the Pantheon of Agrippa during

the 1740s; thus the table provides a marriage between genuine antiquity and the Romantic evocation of the classical world.

The Italian intarsia tradition carried on also into the late eighteenth century. Marquetried furniture in the neo-classical taste was made in Rome, most notably by Rosario Palermo, but Milan is generally recognized as the most important centre for this technique. Although a number of cabinetmakers practised it in Milan, they tend to be eclipsed by Giuseppe Maggiolini, who became official *intarsiatore* to the Archduke Ferdinand, Governor-General of Milan. Maggiolini's work is well documented, both through his signed works and through the careful records of G A Mezzanzanica whose father had worked with him.

Born at Parabiago near Milan, Maggiolini had been trained nearby and moved to Milan in 1771. With archducal patronage, he quickly established a great reputation and could command the highest prices. He produced rectilinear furniture in the Louis Seize manner, without, however, the rich mounting favoured by the French. His severe tables and commodes were decorated with profile heads in roundels, military trophies, and ivy tendrils in different woods. Some of the more ambitious marquetry designs were provided by the Milanese painters, Andrea Appiani and Giuseppe Levati. He disapproved of the use of ivory or stained woods, and in 1765 had woods of 86 different

Far left: Mechanical desk by Giovanni Socchi, made in about 1810. Socchi made several versions of this ingenious desk, which when closed forms a compact oval table. Mechanical furniture had been very popular in late eighteenth-century France and Germany, but this piece is more ambitious than most French examples.

Left: Writing-cabinet by Giuseppe Maria Bonzanigo, made in 1775. This sculptural piece is one of the best known works by the famous Turin wood-carver, Bonzanigo. Although Louis Seize in inspiration, the carved carcase is typically Italian in its cluttered elaboration. It was probably made to celebrate the marriage of Maria-Clotilde of France with Vittorio Amadeo's son, Carlo-Emmanuele IV, and the billing doves at the top appear to relate to this theme. (Hunting Lodge, Stupinigi, Turin)

181

colours in his workshop, which gives some idea of the subtle colour variations in the intricate neo-classical panels.

With the French invasion and subsequent expulsion of the Austrians, Maggiolini worked under the new Napoleonic viceroy, Eugène Beauharnais, although he does not appear to have adapted to the Empire style before his death in 1814.

Ignazio and Luigi Revelli worked in a similar vein in Turin, where there was also a close stylistic link with France, even if the Louis Seize themes were treated with a free exuberance when executed here. Giuseppe Maria Bonzanigo, who worked for the Court in Turin from 1773, was famous for his exquisite carving, which led to a Court appointment as woodcarver to Vittorio Amadeo III in 1787.

Born at Asti, Bonzanigo came of a family of woodcarvers who specialized in organ-cases. He produced a wide range of furniture, with delicate deep-cut carving, which was, however, often too small in scale for the piece it adorned. For this reason A L Millin commented in 1811 that his pieces showed 'more dexterity than taste'. His fragile swags of flowers have the appearance of meticulously carved ivory, and, not surprisingly, 1803 saw Bonzanigo attempting to set up a gallery and workshop 'to perfect the art of carving in wood and ivory'.

After the French occupation of Piedmont in 1796, Bonzanigo turned increasingly toward portrait sculpture, carrying on his carving in the Louis Seize style after the restoration of the monarchy. He, like Maggiolini, seems to have made few concessions to the heavier Empire style of classicism then in vogue.

Although French fashions were reflected in the commode and chair designs of Italy, English pattern books also played their part in the absence of Italian equivalents. Simplified versions of Chippendale, Hepplewhite and Sheraton chairs are to be seen throughout Italy as a reflection of this English influence. It was French taste, however, that predominated in the early nineteenth century, with the establishment of the Bonapartes as rulers of the different states of Italy. There was little opportunity for private patronage now, but the Napoleonic taste was stamped on Italy so effectively by the members of his family that the Italians continued to imitate it for many years to come, long after the liberation.

The Bonapartes had little faith in Italian craftsmanship, a sentiment that was shared by much of Europe. In 1805, the German dramatist, Kotzebue described the furniture at the Villa Borghese, the Roman house of Napoleon's sister, Pauline, as 'magnificent and tasteful for which circumstances a visitor immediately guesses that it is not an Italian lady who rules here'. They imported most of their furnishings from Paris, although they sometimes made a public-spirited endeavour to promote local industry: for example, Elisa Baciocchi, another Bonaparte sister, commissioned pietra-dura table-tops for the Pitti palace in Florence and helped the Opificio there to flourish once again. She also trained Italian craftsmen in the French manner, and set up a *manufacture royale* under the direction of a Parisian ébéniste named Youf. At first, their activities were concentrated in her principality of Lucca where she was redecorating the Palazzo Signoria, but when in 1809 Florence was annexed to Lucca she turned her attention to furnishing the Pitti, where a number of her pieces survive.

Some of them were made by Giovanni Socchi, who had already worked for her in Lucca. He supplied the unusual drum-shaped commodes

Left: Stool designed by Pelagio Palagi in about 1836. Palagi's Palazzo Reale furniture of the 1830s combines the controlled classicism of the French Empire style which was still popular in Italy with the natural flowing exuberance of Italian furniture. (Palazzo Reale, Turin)

with gilt-wood mounts and marble tops, which stand in the Sala dei Tamburi, and he made a series of ingenious mechanical desks, shaped like oval tables, which, when fully opened, reveal a chair and desk with sliding top and rising pigeon-hole section. Although these pieces are unlike any documented French work, their inspiration clearly stems from Paris, and we know that some Italian cabinet-makers were using imported French mounts at this time, as well as studying imported pieces of furniture.

The same process was carried on, albeit in a shorter space of time, by Elisa's sister, Caroline Murat, in Naples. The heavier Neo-classicism was more readily accepted there, however, for quite an archaeological tradition had already been established in Neapolitan furniture in the late eighteenth century; fragments found in the excavations at Pompeii and Herculaneum had often been incorporated into court pieces, in the same way that sections of the local lava were inset decoratively.

Extensive redecoration in the French taste was carried out under the new régime, which

Above: The Throne-Room at La Granja. Situated near the Escorial, this palace was built during the eighteenth century. The carved and gilded throne combines Rococo curves with an early neo-classical medallion-framed head. The other mahogany and gilt furnishings reflect the Spanish Empire style of the early nineteenth century when French influence far outlived the Napoleonic occupation. (La Granja, Spain)

greatly pleased the Bourbons when they eventually returned. 'If only we had been away for another ten years' one of the princes is said to have remarked as he looked at one of the altered palaces. Far from defacing the Napoleonic emblems, the restored monarchs of Italy chose to continue the style of their conqueror after 1815. Eagles, caryatids and lions' masks found their place in a style of debased classicism, which long remained in currency. The 1830s were to see a gradual increase in the inevitable carving which had been suppressed during the severe classicism of the Empire years. This is reflected in the florid style of an Anglo-Italian furniture-maker called Peters, who worked in Piedmont, and in the work of the influential Pelagio Palagi (1775–1860), who designed the interiors of the Royal palace in Turin for Carlo Alberto from 1832, employing Empire and Baroque elements in his showy 'palace' furniture. As Director of the School of Ornamental Design in the Accademia Albertina in Turin, Director of the Academy in Rome, professor of the Milan Academy, and a member of the Academy

of St Luke, Palagi's ideas were widely imitated. But although remembered for his neo-classical work, Palagi chose to decorate the royal summer palace of Racconigi in the Gothic taste, a reminder of the stylistic choice that confronted architects all over Europe as the nineteenth century advanced.

Spain and Portugal

The same development from light and graceful Neo-classicism in the eighteenth century to the ponderous Napoleonic style of the 1800s took place in both Spain and Portugal.

In Spain the French influence, strong through the Bourbon link, led to a popularity for chairs in the Louis Quinze manner at least until the 1770s. French fashions for veneered furniture tended, however, to come indirectly, via Naples. Charles III had ruled there before he came to Spain, and it was from Naples that he brought Gasparini, who became director of the Manufactura Real in 1768. Thereafter many advances were made in Spanish techniques as well as in fashions.

Gasparini was largely responsible for the

183

importance of the commode, which now tended to replace the *vargueño* as a show-piece. At first of flowing Régence form, it took on a more severe rectangular outline in the 1770s. Pompeian painting, mirror insets, Wedgwood or Buen Retiro porcelain plaques, or white marble inlays were used, but many commodes were decorated with elaborate *trompe l'oeil* marquetry worked in the Italian manner.

English pattern books were to lead to elongated versions of Chippendale and Sheraton chairs, although the English influence was more marked in Portugal on the whole, where it coexisted with French and Dutch tendencies. The Portuguese commode, like the Spanish in shape, differed in decoration, being marble-topped, and marquetried with simpler geometrical patterns, with enamelled handles in the Dutch style. In the late eighteenth century semicircular commodes on tall, tapering legs were also popular.

Although Portugal and Spain both fell prey to the Empire style, English Regency influences were apparent at the time of the liberation in 1811 of Portugal, whereas the the Spaniards clung to the French style until about 1830. Heavy mahogany furniture with coarse carving and mounting in the classical taste continued to be in vogue until the Gothic and neo-Baroque revivals.

America

The advent of Neo-classicism in America dates historically from the time that the 13 colonies emerged as an independent nation. The small writing-box, now in the Smithsonian Institute, on which Thomas Jefferson set out the Declaration of Independence in 1776 was one of the first pieces to give an intimation of what was to come. Made by Benjamin Randolph with a simple line inlay it was a harbinger of what was to become known as the Federal Style. American cabinet-makers were quick to take advantage of the growth and expansion brought about by the new peace and the advance of trade and commerce.

By 1788, the date of the adoption of the Federal Constitution, Chippendale furniture was out of style in England, but still the fount of fashion as far as America was concerned. In the same year Hepplewhite's *The Cabinet-Maker and Upholsterer's Guide* and *The London Cabinet-Maker's Book of Prices* were published, and shortly afterwards Sheraton brought out his book of designs. These were widely used in America as the basic material

Right: The Phyfe room at Winterthur. Duncan Phyfe, son of a German immigrant was one of the most successful American cabinet-makers. His version of English Regency taste, conservative but stylish, became increasingly popular, and he soon owned three houses in the centre of New York as his showroom and workshop with over one hundred men working for him — the first American workshop to operate on a factory scale. (The Henry Francis du Pont Winterthur Museum, Delaware)

for cabinet-makers who gave the pieces their individual and regional interpretation.

The apprenticeship system in America was strictly adhered to, and supervised not only by the guild concerned but also by the local civil authority. In 1660 in Boston the period of apprenticeship in a trade was laid down by law to be seven years, but in the eighteenth century, especially in the later years, the period of apprenticeship became progressively shorter as the demand for furniture, and thereby journeymen to fulfil this demand, increased. Repairs were a major part of the business of any cabinet-maker in the eighteenth and nineteenth centuries; for instance Samuel Ashton of Philadelphia made 120 new pieces of furniture in the year 1801, and repaired 70 old pieces. In the smaller cities one cabinet-maker would undertake to make and finish all kinds of furniture, while in the more important centres work was carried out by several different specialists. These were very similar to the divisions in Paris at the time, and consisted mainly of cabinet-makers, chair-makers, inlay-makers, carvers and gilders, turners and upholsterers. Usually these people all had separate establishments though sometimes they worked under one roof; the best instance of this being the

workshop of Duncan Phyfe, who had a virtual factory employing over 100 men. Because there were no separate guilds to supervise the different branches, as was the case in Paris, one man was often capable of carrying out several or all of these jobs, though the increased demand for furniture, and the new fields of expansion in the late eighteenth century tended to encourage people to specialize. The setting up of larger workshops in the more important centres, such as those of Thomas Affleck, Benjamin Randolph, Thomas Tuffts and William Savery in Philadelphia, the Burlings in New York and the Townsends and Goddards in Newport, Rhode Island, also tended to encourage the journeymen and apprentices to specialize in one branch of their work.

Men became apprenticed at about the age of 15, and were usually journeymen by the age of 21. They would then work for many different establishments for the next few years, until they had enough money and experience to set up either in a business of their own or in partnership with another cabinet-maker or upholsterer, at which time they would take on apprentices of their own. In a large city the cabinet-maker would purchase his inlays ready-made from a specialist such as Thomas Barrett of Baltimore, who sold panels of inlay, veneers of satinwood and purplewood, window cornices, brass and iron rods for stairs and blinds, hair seating, gold leaf, composition, glass-paper and mahogany knife-cases, much of which was imported.

Cabinet-makers living near the coast or a waterway would use mahogany as their principal wood though inland the native walnut was more widely used as mahogany was difficult to come by, and cherry wood was used extensively, though especially in Connecticut. The carcase of the furniture was constructed in soft wood, usually a variety of pine. Haircloth was the most popular material for upholstery, and leather was often used, dyed to suit the client's taste. Horsehair, being hard-wearing and durable, was popular, and the grander house had silk and wool velvet, often imported from Europe. Printed cottons were used to make covers.

An important insight into the lives and work of the cabinet-makers is given by the price-books. These set out suggested prices for particular items of furniture and wages for journeymen, and also gave engraved designs for furniture. These price-books and the restrictions they imposed eventually led to great strikes in Philadelphia in 1796 and

New York in 1802, which were eventually resolved by the employers agreeing to a 50 per cent advance on the current stated prices in the London price-books.

Samuel McIntire, born in Salem, Massachusetts in 1757, was an architect and furniture-maker, most famed for his carved decoration, which he often added to pieces of furniture made by other craftsmen, as well as carrying out the carved details for the rather simple houses he designed. This mixture of accomplishments was the norm rather than an exception in America.

Duncan Phyfe, considered by many as the greatest of all American cabinet-makers, began a new tradition in the field of furniture manufacture in America. Born in Scotland, his family emigrated to America in the early 1750s when he must have been 15 or 16 years of age. They settled in Albany, and his father started work as a cabinet-maker. By the early 1790s, Duncan had gone to New York and changed the spelling of his name from Fife to Phyfe. By 1815 he owned three adjoining houses which were his workshops, warehouse and showroom. His designs for furniture never

Above left: Commode by Thomas Seymour of Boston, made in the early nineteenth century. This piece is again based on English originals. The radiating pattern on the top is inlaid, but the shell half-medallion at the back is painted. (Museum of Fine Arts, Boston)

strayed far from those in Sheraton's design books, and in the early nineteenth century he faced stiff competition from immigrant French craftsmen working in the fashionable Napoleonic style, such as Charles-Honoré Lannuier and G J Lapierre.

Lannuier arrived in New York in 1803 and set up business working in what came to be known as the American Empire style, based on the French Directory and Napoleonic styles. His pieces were more elaborate than other New York contemporary work and made use of gilt-metal mounts imported from France.

European styles now reached America much sooner than in the eighteenth century because of improved communications. George Smith's *Cabinet-maker and Upholsterer's Guide* had tremendous influence after its publication in 1828, as did the French Restoration style, giving rise to heavy, late classical pieces either in plain wood or sometimes stencilled with classical fruit or floral decoration. The leading manufacturer of this plainer furniture was Joseph Meeks and Son, and this soon developed into the heavy, early Victorian style.

THE MACHINE AGE
The nineteenth century

A number of new factors radically affected the development of furniture design during the nineteenth century, and these make a study of this period unusually complicated. It is therefore necessary, before embarking on any kind of historical survey, to try to isolate new influences and to see how they changed the progress of taste throughout the Western world.

The major social change was the growing ascendancy of the middle classes, and it is not unreasonable to suggest that they, or their values, completely dominated aesthetic development from the early 1800s to 1914.

Before the nineteenth century, artistic innovations were usually initiated through the agency of either a feudal or a monarchical-aristocratic *élite*, and the end-products of the attitudes that such groups normally display are very different from those which result from the values of a bourgeoisie. The traditional assurance of inherited continuity in an aristocratic society gives to its members a sense of stability, and this in its turn produces an emotional climate that can accept change, progress or innovation. The members of such a group, surrounded by all the advantages of stability, have the self-confidence which is needed to promote a developing culture. While traditional continuity is maintained, there is time, and room, for experiment. The middle classes, on the other hand, have little of this sort of self-confidence. Rising bourgeois societies are not usually artistically creative, and their uncertainty pushes them constantly to copy their 'betters', and to seek reassurance in the well-tried and the familiar. The desire to make every object seem better and more valuable (which we find evidenced throughout the nineteenth century) expresses such aspirations with poignant clarity, and it is thus easy to explain why during the nineteenth century, soft wood was grained to simulate hardwood, cast-iron was painted to imitate bronze, wallpaper was printed to look like silk or velvet, plaster was marble-ized, stucco was colour-washed in stone tints and houses were paired to look twice as large.

The life-style of a middle-class reflects its members' middle-of-the-road social and financial status, as they conform anxiously to their particular nostalgic ideal. On the other hand, as the members usually make up the major part of the mercantile community, they will also wish to obtain best value for money, and to avoid aristocratic frivolity and monarchical extravagance. Austerity has little attraction for the bourgeoisie, and solidity, conformism and comfort are the qualities that are most appreciated.

The universal 'embourgeoisement' of society took place in every western country and at most social levels during the nineteenth

century, and whilst the poorer sections of the community aspired to all the benefits of middle-class life, the breakdown of the old hierarchical systems led the monarchs and the old aristocrats to modify their attitudes to agree more closely with those of the new middle classes. An English politician remarked of Queen Victoria, 'If I want to know what the middle classes are thinking, I ask the Queen.'

It is within this context, therefore, that we can begin to understand the numerous 'revived' styles that were popular throughout the century, and to appreciate how each of them fulfilled a particular aspect of the

bourgeois desire for reassurance through familiarity. At the same time, elaboration of workmanship and apparent costliness were essential elements in the display which a primarily materialistic society demanded.

Another vital influence on the development of the domestic arts during the nineteenth century was that of a rapidly expanding technology. Not only did mechanical methods of production allow for the manufacture of vastly increased amounts of furniture, but it also provided the means of reproducing cheaply and easily the elaboration of workmanship that had hitherto been available only to a privileged few. The inevitable loss

Above: The novelist Charles Reade in his London study, painted by C Mercier in the 1860s. This shows an 'Elizabethan' chair (in fact it resembled a Charles II piece), a bobbin-turned occasional table at which Reade is writing, and a standard kitchen chair of a type that persisted unchanged for some 40 years, on which Reade is seated. (National Portrait Gallery, London)

190

of artistic spontaneity caused by the erosion of craft techniques was easily overlooked by a market which was dominated by a desire for richness, novelty and value for money. Technological processes were also directly responsible for radically changing the appearance of furniture, and, for example, the invention of the coil-spring, the perfection of methods of laminating and shaping timber and the introduction of metal parts all permitted the production of pieces in new forms, and with new functions.

Technology changed the very quality of life itself throughout the nineteenth century, not only by facilitating the introduction of devices which immensely increased the comfort and hygiene of seating and sleeping furniture, but by bringing about the development of efficient lighting systems, drainage and sanitary appliances, cooking stoves and heating arrangements. It must be accepted,

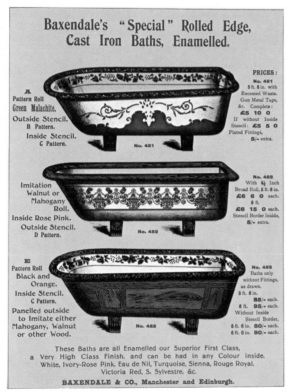

Above Right: The nineteenth century concern with enhancing apparent value extended to objects which hardly required this attention. In the early 1900s, Baxendale & Company, a firm of Birmingham ironmongers and suppliers of plumbers' ware, offered a range of cast-iron baths which were stencilled with patterns that suggested fresco painting, or grained to simulate wood.

too, that in certain ways technology retarded progress; the pollution and squalor that accompanied industrialization led many advanced thinkers to retreat into a dream limbo, based on a past when life was supposed to have been simple and happy, and to attempt to revive historic styles and ways of life to accord with their vision.

There were various further influences on the development of furniture in the nineteenth century which had not previously been felt, but it will suffice to mention three of the most important. One was the role played by the collectors of antique furniture. Here was a type of person who seems not to have existed

before the nineteenth century, for although 'Cabinets of Curiosities' and collections of relics had been put together by rich men throughout Europe since the early Renaissance, it was not until the early 1800s that collectors began to acquire pieces of old furniture and to introduce them into their houses for everyday use. Three key figures stand out — the first is King George IV, who bought seventeenth- and eighteenth-century furniture from France at the time of the Revolution, thereby not only setting a fashion that has persisted up till the present time, but also becoming a major promoter of the 'neo-Louis' styles. The second figure is the Empress Eugénie of France, whose fascination with Marie-Antoinette led her to seek out and replace in the royal apartments any pieces of eighteenth-century furniture that had not been sold by the revolutionaries. She also put in hand the redecoration of several of the imperial palaces in a revived Louis Seize style and commissioned pieces of new furniture to complete the ensembles. The third person is, of course, William Morris, whose passion for old craftsmanship and admiration for pre-industrial ways of production led him to surround himself with objects from the past. Although in many ways we might consider him as a progressive, who was outside the middle-of-the-road course of majority taste, he was certainly influential over a large number of people connected with the arts, and a whole generation of collectors in the last third of the nineteenth century followed where Morris and his circle had shown the way.

Loosely connected to the idea of collecting, another impetus relates to the rise of nationalism that affected the worldwide political scene toward the end of the century. The Franco-Prussian war, the unification of Germany and of Italy and the American Civil War were all in their way responsible in each of these countries for stimulating a search for national identity, and this in its turn brought about a new enthusiasm for what were believed to be 'national' styles. Colonial furniture in America, furniture in eighteenth-century England, Renaissance and even Biedermeier furniture in Germany all became the objects of nationalistic pride, and in the absence of sufficient original pieces to meet the new demand, they were copied in large quantities, but with more conscious accuracy than had ever been the practice in the earlier part of the century.

The third significant influence which must be accepted is that of increasing female emancipation. In England and in America this culminated in the achievement of women's suffrage immediately after the First World War, but the changing status of women was an important issue all through the nineteenth

century, and was inevitably reflected in the appearance of the home.

It is noticeable that throughout the century there was a constant breaking-down of formality in the arrangement of furniture; whereas in an eighteenth-century house it was lined up round the walls, and individual pieces were brought out for use and then replaced, by the beginning of the nineteenth century chairs, sofas and tables were placed permanently in the centre of the floor. By the end of the century the rooms over which the lady of the house exerted her dominance (the drawing-room, the boudoir, the bedroom) were often cluttered to such an extent that it was difficult to walk without collision.

Dr Siegfried Giedion describes this phenomenon as 'the devaluation of space', and relates it closely to the devaluation of aesthetic symbols which he traces to the French Empire. He also admits, however, that the romantic lounging attitudes that it became fashionable for women to adopt in the early 1800s required large pieces of comfortable and conveniently placed furniture to support them, and that the encroachment of the furniture into the centre of the room

expresses the breakdown of formality which accompanied the rise of the middle classes and the gradual disappearance of an aristocratic society. The busy emerging bourgeoisie and its ladies had little time for the kind of etiquette prevalent in eighteenth-century France, where much of the seat furniture was not even meant to be sat on.

The gradual breakdown of the old formality took place in many ways, and many of them can be directly attributed to feminine attitudes; the introduction of flowers and plants into living-rooms, the proliferation of small objects and ornaments, the increasing attention which was paid to physical comfort and *bien-être*, all confirm the tendency for the women of the family to take over more and more of the decisions relating to the household. Towards the end of the century much of the output of the new, popular periodicals contained endless information about how to make feminine surroundings more 'dainty', 'pretty' or 'cosy', in a manner that was obviously intended to appeal to a specifically female readership.

Before looking in detail at the various furniture styles which were popular between

Above: The Waterloo Gallery at Apsley House in London was added onto the existing building for the Duke of Wellington in 1828, and the architect was Benjamin Dean Wyatt. It was intended to provide an appropriate setting for the annual Waterloo Banquet, and the decoration seems to be one of the earliest examples of 'neo-Louis' in Europe, although the furniture was still in the current 'fat-classical' style. (Wellington Museum, London)

the early 1800s and the Great War of 1914, it is also essential to realize that, unlike previous centuries, nineteenth-century taste did not follow a development of continuous progression. The introduction of a style did not immediately cause all those that had previously existed to become unfashionable, and practically all the major nineteenth-century stylistic expressions co-existed to a greater or lesser degree throughout the hundred years.

It became customary early in the century to furnish the different rooms in prosperous households in different styles, each of which was considered to be appropriate to their function. Thus a large house decorated and furnished in, say, 1865, might have a neo-Rococo drawing-room, an Elizabethan dining-room, a Gothic library, a Moorish billiard-room. The bedrooms might have 'fat-classical' pieces while the boudoir could be neo-Louis Seize. This practice makes the precise dating of much nineteenth-century furniture extremely difficult, particularly that which was made in styles such as neo-Rococo or 'fat-classical', since they retained their popularity for almost the whole of the century. Furniture catalogues of the early 1900s still offered pieces, especially those intended for bedrooms or the less showy rooms, in styles which had first originated in the 1840s.

The enormous increase in the number of people who made up the buying public during the nineteenth century meant that taste operated over a wider variety of social levels than ever before. The new rich were no longer

necessarily progressive, the progressives were often not rich. This overlapping and confusion has tempted many historians to simplify their task by concentrating on the 'advanced' designs, and to leave the vast bulk of nineteenth-century production largely undocumented.

The intricacies of the Arts and Crafts movement or the wilder fantasies of Art Nouveau have been examined in detail, whilst the 'middle-of-the-road' expressions of middle-class taste have been contemptuously ignored. Whether or not such expressions appeal to us is largely irrelevant; they are a major part of the stuff of history, and it is proposed in this chapter to try and chart the course of 'middling' taste in furniture from around 1830 until 1914.

The Louis styles

Of the many revived styles which were popular during the nineteenth century, the interpretations of the French styles of the seventeenth and eighteenth centuries survived the longest. Indeed if one were to look for the 'real' nineteenth-century style, the Louis revivals could lay the most convincing claim.

Examples of one or another of the Louis styles appeared in every country in the civilized world from the 1820s to the 1900s, although the neo-Rococo enjoyed the greatest popularity in furniture. Curiously, there is strong evidence that the idea of reproducing the grandeur that surrounded the French monarchy originated in England rather than in France.

The interiors at Lancaster House in London that the architect Benjamin Dean Wyatt designed from 1825 to 1826, the Waterloo Gallery that he designed for the Duke of Wellington at Apsley House in 1828 'in brilliant mimicry of Oppenordt, Boffrand and Verberckt', and the state reception room at Windsor that Sir Jeffry Wyatville built for George IV in the late 1820s, were all of them well in advance of any similar revivals in the country of their origin. These interiors, with their strongly monarchical associations, must have concisely expressed the mood of the establishment at this time, when many people hoped to return to the old ways, as they had been before the French Revolution and the wars with Napoleon.

The furniture trade did not catch up with the new fashion for some ten years however, and these rooms were all furnished with pieces in the prevailing 'fat-classical' style, although in the case of the royal palace they were so enriched as to be hardly describable as classical at all. George Smith, in his *Cabinet-Maker and Upholsterer's Guide* of 1826, showed a design for decoration of 'The Age of Louis XIV', together with several suggestions for curtains, but there was no

DRAWING. ROOM.   CURTAIN. VI.

Right: By the end of the first quarter of the nineteenth century there was a very evident growing interest in the styles of the French seventeenth and eighteenth centuries. George Smith's book of patterns entitled The Cabinet-Maker and Upholsterer's Guide, published in 1826 in London, contained several suggestions for decoration and curtains in the Louis styles. This one was described as being in the 'manner used in France during the lifetime of Louis XIV'. The book showed no complementary furniture however.

furniture to match, and he no doubt intended that the movable pieces should be in the 'fat-classical' style. Indeed, in the 1830s a modified type of 'fat-classical' began to appear, which had leafy naturalistic carving and was described as 'Louis Quatorze'. By the mid-forties however, neo-Rococo furniture was being made by virtually every firm in the country, although it is often difficult to identify the manufacturers as few of them signed or labelled their productions.

William Smee & Sons showed typical mid-nineteenth century Rococo chairs with sprung, deep-buttoned upholstery in their catalogue of 1840 (described as 'superior lounge chairs'), and Miles & Edwards, who were in business at 134 Oxford Street, London between 1822 and 1846 also made pieces in the neo-Rococo style. It is interesting that this firm would also undertake any sort of work in the home, apart from the supply of furniture, and we may cite this organization as typifying a tendency, which began at the start of the nineteenth century, for furniture and upholstery firms to take over many of the functions which had previously been the province of architects.

The increasingly numerous well-to-do families who were setting up house in the new suburbs were hardly likely to consult a first-rank designer for advice, yet they all wished for a background which was showy, durable, respectable and not too startlingly unusual. The neo-Rococo style filled all these requirements admirably, but it remained very much a 'decorator's style', never much favoured by architects or progressive designers. The curving shapes of the furniture, with its scrolls and volutes, provided a luxurious product which could nonetheless be executed by indifferent craftsmen, and it also lent itself successfully to machine production and the mechanical carving techniques which were being developed to answer the demands of the expanding markets.

It was during the 1840s and 50s that two developments occurred which were to set the character of so much mid-nineteenth century furniture, especially pieces made in the neo-Rococo style. The first was the appearance, round about 1850, of the 'balloon-back' chair, in which the back uprights were merged into the top-rail in one continuous curve. This design was obviously based on the French Louis Quinze panel-back side-chair, but the upholstery and filling in the back were omitted, and the general form was much more flowing than that of the French original. Some of these chairs had turned front legs and a more solid frame for use in the dining-room, but the most typical examples were the cabriole-legged drawing-room chairs, which usually formed part of a suite.

The other particular mid-nineteenth century development was the introduction of coil-springing and deep-buttoning, and these not only revolutionized the comfort of seat furniture but also produced a new shape of chair.

Patents for coil-springs had first been taken out in England in the 1820s, but by the 1840s and 1850s their use was universal in chairs that were meant for comfort. The typical comfortable mid-century chair either had a show-wood frame with neo-Rococo detail, or was completely overstuffed with the form being derived entirely from the presence of the coil-springing. This was usually combined with deep-buttoned upholstery, the use of which one writer has tried to ascribe to psychological forces, comparing the button with the navel, which he suggests is the emotional centre of a bourgeois and domestic society! Be that as it may, deep-buttoning was also a clever commercial device for using up the short-staple cotton and wool combings which are the by-products of mechanical spinning, and it served to hold in position the large quantities of filling required in overstuffed sprung furniture.

Neo-Rococo furniture was designed for use in every room, but its principal popularity was in the drawing-room or the boudoir, where feminine influence was strongest. The style was infinitely adaptable however, and was used for carcase furniture as well as for chairs. (The term 'carcase' furniture applies to any pieces that are basically a shell such as wardrobes, commodes and chests of drawers.) It was also very popular for a type of fully gilded console table with marble top, and for overmantel glasses, and the ornament in the cheaper versions was often executed in plaster composition on wire armatures.

By the mid-1860s neo-Rococo had begun to go out of fashion, to be superseded by a more rectilinear and more controlled Louis style with much closer affinities to Louis Seize, but although popular enthusiasm for it diminished over the last thirty years of the century, neo-Rococo never disappeared completely.

Towards the end of the century the demand seems to have split two ways, and the typical mid-Victorian 'free-Rococo' vanished somewhere in between. At the upper end of the market, a knowledgeable clientele was requiring really good copies of eighteenth-century French furniture which could be mixed indistinguishably into collections of genuine pieces. Indeed some of the furniture made by firms like Gillows in the early 1900s was of such quality and so close to the models that, at a distance of 70 years, it now requires an expert to say whether or not they are genuine eighteenth-century pieces.

Many great collections of French seventeenth- and eighteenth-century furniture

were assembled during the latter part of the nineteenth century; Baron Ferdinand de Rothschild used his to furnish the great house that he had built at Waddesdon near Aylesbury in the late 1880s. Even as far back as the mid-1850s, Lord Hertford found nothing strange in commissioning a copy of the famous eighteenth-century 'bureau du roi', to place among his collection of original French furniture. He paid Pierre Dasson, the Parisian furniture-maker, the huge sum of £3,600.

At the lower end of the furniture market the trend towards fussiness and spindliness, which became very pronounced in the 1890s and early 1900s, had the effect of making the end-products barely recognizable as having any relation at all to eighteenth-century France.

In the early years of the twentieth century many firms making lower priced furniture had given up describing their wares with any degree of precision, and any piece with 'frenchified' cabriole legs, curving shapes or a Rococo fret was just called 'Louis', or merely 'fancy' if the French connection seemed too tenuous. Much of this furniture was constructed in a very dark mahogany with a highly polished surface, which gave it even less of a French look.

The Edwardian period did, nonetheless, witness a considerable revival of interest in Louis Quinze and Louis Seize, and many decorating firms made a renewed speciality of such interiors and furniture for wealthy houses. The styles also enjoyed a considerable success in the commercial world, one of the most famous examples being the interiors of the Ritz Hotel in London, completed in 1906.

Far left: Baron Ferdinand de Rothschild furnished the Grey Drawing Room of Waddesdon Manor with French Rococo pieces in 1889, but the ensemble retains an indefinable late nineteenth-century atmosphere. (National Trust, Waddesdon Manor, Buckinghamshire)

Left: One of the neo-Rococo pieces designed by Philip Hardwick for the drawing room at Goldsmiths' Hall in London, on which he was working in 1834. (Goldsmiths' Hall, London)

197

At this time every store had to have its
'French Dress Department', and every Grand
Hotel or Atlantic liner its 'French Grill Room'
or 'Trianon Bar'.

The neo-Louis Seize manner always found
much more favour with the top-class furniture
manufacturers than the Rococo, and pieces
in this style were made throughout the 1860s
and 70s by Wright & Mansfield, Johnstone &
Jeanes, Holland & Sons, Gillows, and Jackson
& Graham, although these last two had
shown lavish examples of neo-Rococo furniture
at the Great Exhibition of 1851. Whilst the
firm of Gillows, which was originally founded
in 1695, is perhaps the most famous of all
English furniture manufacturing firms,
Holland & Sons enjoyed a very high reputation
throughout the nineteenth century, but more
especially for the 'fat-classical' pieces that
they supplied to the great new clubhouses,
and to some of the royal palaces.

France was somewhat behind England in
taking up the neo-Louis styles, although the
brilliant Aimé Chénavard made designs for
neo-Rococo chairs in 1835, and some manufacturers' catalogues even showed details in
this style as early as 1830.

It was not really until the beginning of the
Second Empire in 1851 that the neo-Louis
styles made much impact on French taste.
In fact, as soon as the Prince-President
Louis-Napoleon Bonaparte became Emperor,
he embarked on a series of official building
projects and public works which were specifically designed to promote the new régime and
to remind Frenchmen of their glorious past.

French official architecture, decoration and
furnishing were launched immediately into a
full-scale neo-Louis revival, and the emphasis
in furniture was towards Louis Quinze and
Louis Seize. Neo-Rococo furniture was made
for the new Louvre, the palace of Chantilly,
and for the theatre and some of the private
apartments at Fontainebleau, but the Empress
Eugénie's enthusiasm for Marie-Antoinette
led her to order the redecoration of the
apartments at her favourite château at St
Cloud in a neo-Louis Seize style. The existing
interiors were gone over and 'heightened',
and although a great deal of coil-sprung
seating furniture was introduced, much of
the remainder was genuine eighteenth-
century. New pieces were added in a
'matching' style however, (later to be known
as 'Louis Seize Impératrice'), and full rein
was allowed for the current desire for rich
display. Indeed it even came to be considered
permissible to add extra decoration and
enrichments to historic pieces in order to
make them as acceptable as the new ones.

Pictures of the St Cloud interiors also
show what might be described as the second
phase of the 'devaluation of space', if we
accept that the first phase merely entailed

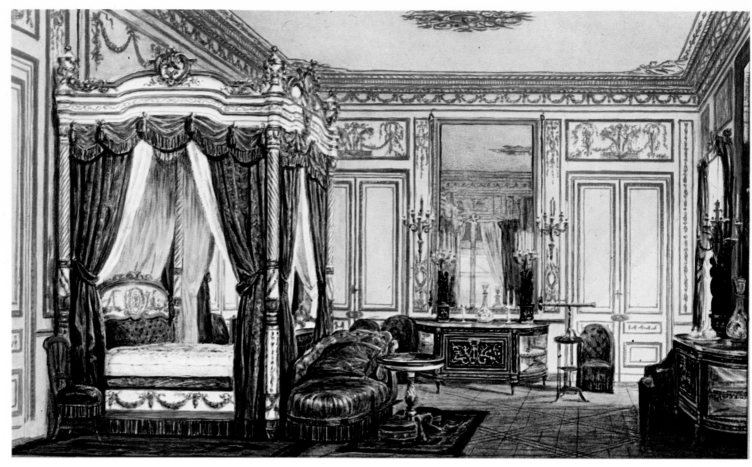

moving furniture away from the walls; for, by the late 1850s and during the 1860s, basic furnishings were being supplemented by a whole series of new pieces which were introduced extraneously. Most of these were usually given one of the prevailingly popular Louis styles, since their market was essentially middle-class, and they were intended for the rooms where such styles were most likely to have been adopted. Occasional tables, 'whatnots' and étagères, stools, poufs, fireside chairs, worktables for embroidery and sewing, screens—the list is endless, and the general effect relates directly to the visual breakdown of formality, where this had traditionally been expressed by symmetry and balance. It is very tempting to interpret the whole tendency as a manifestation of extending feminine influence, especially in France where women's social position had always been stronger than in other European countries.

Round about the middle of the century the 'Chiavari' chair, or 'chaise volante' (literally, 'flying' chair) first appeared, and these seats were made in lightweight woods so that they could easily be moved by a guest who wanted to move from group to group. They became very popular in drawing-rooms and libraries, where the user himself might need to move his seat frequently. The increasing practice of fitting castors to chairs and tables also added to the mobility of furniture, and showed

a definite intention to break away from static arrangements. So great did the clutter and mobility eventually become in many of the rooms in the Imperial Palaces that the duc de Morny remarked that one had to move about with as much caution as a ship avoiding shoals of rocks!

Numerous important Paris furniture-makers worked in the various Louis styles during the Second Empire; L A A Beurdeley, A G Fourdinois, Henri Dasson, G Grohé, L E Lemarchand were some of the most famous, and many of them supplied the palaces. The firm of Krieger, who began production in 1847 and continued until the 1930s, and Sormani (also in business by 1847 and continuing until 1934) both enjoyed a reputation for high-quality production, but Jeanselme probably had the highest prestige.

In 1847 J P F Jeanselme took over the famous company of Jacob and became one of the leading makers of fine furniture in France. The various partnerships and amalgamations of the Jeanselme family are rather difficult to sort out, but the firm produced a steady output from 1824 until the 1930s, although their greatest fame seems to have been under Napoleon III.

After the doldrums of the 1830s and 1840s, the French furniture industry moved back into an international position during the fifties and sixties. At the Great Exhibition of

Above: The Empress Eugénie's enthusiasm for Marie Antoinette initiated a change in taste towards a neo-Louis Seize style, and in 1863 J B Fortuné de Fournier portrayed this in a series of watercolours showing the interiors of Eugénie's favourite palace at St Cloud. In the Empress' bedroom, two original eighteenth-century pieces by Guillaume Beneman (first intended for use as sideboards) are shown in an interior largely furnished with typical mid-nineteenth century over-stuffed and deep-buttoned easy chairs. The ensemble is dominated by a huge four-poster bed of a type unknown in the eighteenth century, and in the style which came to be known as 'Louis Seize Impératrice'. (Château de Compiègne)

Above: The neo-Rococo fashion was universally accepted from the late 1830s. A watercolour by H F C ten Kate of the Reception Room at the Plein Palace in the Hague, painted in 1849, shows a late neo-classical room arbitrarily and unsuitably filled with a suite of ebonized neo-Louis furniture. A great ottoman occupies the centre of the close-carpeted floor, and a huge L-shaped seat, designed for comfort rather than elegance, has been forced into a corner, completely blocking a door. (Oranje-Nassau Museum, Delft)

1851, French furniture had already carried off several major awards, and Queen Victoria bought various pieces from leading Paris manufacturers when she visited the Imperial family in 1855.

The defeat of the French armies by the Prussians in 1870, and the ensuing unrest, administered a severe setback to every part of French industry, but by about 1876 it was well on the way to complete recovery, a fact which was triumphantly underlined by the Paris International Exhibition of 1878.

The neo-Louis styles, with their unfortunate associations, underwent a temporary lapse from public favour, although they never completely fell from fashion. The firm of Beurdeley, which had always been famous for its furniture in the Rococo style, did not close down until 1895, but its later productions showed the tendency towards elongation and fragility that characterized contemporary work throughout the world. Henri Dasson did not die until 1896, but although he was capable of copying original pieces to a high degree of accuracy, many of his 'free' interpretations from the 1880s showed the typical spindly elongation of the time. The firm of Zweiner, also producing fine furniture in the neo-Rococo manner, was principally active between 1880 and 1895, but it seems evident that much of the traditional French fondness for curved forms (which is so

brilliantly expressed in the Rococo) had been diverted towards the sinuous shapes of 'Art Nouveau' by the turn of the century.

As a final pointer to the persistence of neo-Rococo taste however, we may note that even the London firm of Maple, which opened a branch in Paris in 1896, was still offering the French public a large range of 'Meubles Louis XV et Louis XVI' in their catalogues up until the First World War, and even after.

Most other European countries took up the neo-Louis styles as enthusiastically as England and France, although, of the German-speaking nations, Austria was the first to do so. The mid-eighteenth century traditions had never wholly died in conservative Vienna in spite of the revolutionary pressures of the first quarter of the century, and the haute bourgeoisie and the Court eagerly accepted a fashion which suggested a monarchical tradition so clearly.

The neo-classical severity of Austrian Biedermeier had been becoming more and more softened throughout the 1830s, and by the mid-1840s neo-Rococo was firmly established. The firm of Karl Leistler received praise for their furniture at the Great Exhibition of 1851 in London (amongst which were some chairs of extremely curvaceous form), but they had already supplied a large number of neo-Rococo pieces from 1842 onwards for the Palais Liechtenstein in

Vienna, together with the Thonet company. Heinrich Dubell, another noted Viennese furniture-maker, provided tables and desks for the re-furnishing of the Hofburg in 1853, and, unlike England and France where neo-Rococo was often confined to certain specific rooms, the Hofburg seems to have been completely done in this style. Even Michael Thonet, famous for his invention of bentwood furniture, made numerous pieces in the most lavish neo-Rococo style in the late 1840s and early 1850s, and it must be admitted that the celebrated bentwood itself has a strong affinity with neo-Rococo in its curved forms and convoluted, interlaced structure. As late as 1902 the architect Otto Hofer was designing neo-Rococo chairs for the Vienna State Archive, and we may take the continued popularity of bentwood throughout the second half of the nineteenth century and on into the twentieth as an indication of the deep affection that Rococo enjoyed in western Europe.

The other German-speaking countries were slightly slower to take up neo-Louis, probably due to the continued influence of the two great exponents of Neo-classicism, the architects Karl Friedrich Schinkel in Prussia, and Leo von Klenze in Bavaria, both of whom remained staunch upholders of Neo-classicism throughout their working lives. Neo-Louis came a little sooner to Prussia than to Bavaria, but by the late 1850s and during the 1860s neo-Rococo enjoyed as much popularity in Germany as elsewhere in the world, and much of the output came from Mainz in the Grand Duchy of Hessen. This was one of the most important centres of the German furniture trade throughout the entire nineteenth century, and a large export trade to foreign countries was conducted from there.

The most famous manufacturer in Mainz was Anton Bembé, who not only made furniture which reflected the various changes in fashion in Germany throughout most of the century, but also provided designs for decoration and hangings and for complete rooms. The firm was already making pieces in the neo-Rococo style by the early 1840s, and continued to do so during the 1850s and 60s.

Another famous Mainz firm, that of Wilhelm Kimbel, was promoting neo-Rococo even earlier than Bembé, and from 1835 onwards Kimbel produced three famous pattern books in numerous instalments containing many designs in this style. Anthony Kimbel, a member of the same family, set up in business in New York, thereby extending German influence far beyond the usual range of export markets.

Although the popularity of the neo-Louis styles, as in most other European countries, tended to slacken after 1870, it received the most unexpected renewal under the influence of King Ludwig II of Bavaria, whose increasing eccentricity drove him to commission several extraordinary architectural extravaganzas. The king's disenchantment with the nineteenth-century world bred in his mind an obsessive worship of the absolutism of the French seventeenth- and eighteenth-century monarchy, and this, combined with his desire for solitude, was the reason for the building of two country retreats in a romanticized French style.

Schloss Linderhof, built between 1870 and 1886 to the designs of Georg Dollmann, looks to our eyes rather as though the Petit Trianon had been redesigned by Charles Garnier, the architect of the Paris Opera. On the other hand, at Schloss Herrenchiemsee, which was constructed between 1878 and 1886, Dollmann reproduced accurately many features of the palace of Versailles.

Each of these buildings required suitable furniture, and this was provided in a style of luscious excess which matches exactly the exaggeration of the architecture. Seat furniture, tables, beds, desks, a pianola-organ, were all designed in a riotous elaboration of neo-Rococo. At Linderhof the principal supplier seems to have been the Munich firm of Anton Possenbacher, working to designs by Adolf Seder, and delivery took place during the mid-1870s. At Herrenchiemsee most of the furniture was designed by Julius Hofmann — helped by Adolf Seder — who worked under Dollmann and succeeded him as architect to the building in 1884. Delivery continued during the 1880s until work was stopped in 1886 when the king was confined for insanity, but it is certain that Ludwig's commissions greatly encouraged craftsmanship of every order among the fine-art manufacturers in Bavaria at this time. It is tragic that he bankrupted himself and the country in the process.

It is certain that no comparable neo-Rococo furniture was made, either before or since, but it must be admitted that German Rococo furniture always had a certain measure of excess, which may be appreciated by comparing the productions of Nahl, Spindler or Kambly with those of, say, Cressent, Oeben or Tilliard. The vogue for neo-Rococo continued until the end of the nineteenth century in Germany, and on into the twentieth, becoming in the process almost a revival of a revival; as late as 1898 the firm of Julius Zweiner was supplying rich Rococo bedroom furniture for the Royal Palace in Berlin, whilst at the lower end of the market A & L Streitenfeld were offering thin neo-Rococo in their collection of *Reiche und Elegante Sitzmöbel* published in Berlin by C Claeson.

Trends in Scandinavia and Russia followed those in Germany very closely, and neo-classical enjoyed a long spell of popularity in these countries, but by the 1850s and 1860s

neo-Louis was firmly established. During the 1840s Russian furniture, whilst it still retained the basic neo-classical forms, had become considerably softened by the introduction of naturalistic carved foliage and curving leg shapes, and by the late 1840s neo-Rococo was already popular.

It is probable that the architect A I Stackenschneider designed a set of neo-Rococo furniture for the Pink Drawing Room at the Winter Palace in St Petersburg on which he was working in 1846 and 1847. He certainly provided designs for the furniture in the Gilt Drawing Room in 1850, and this suite was executed by Vasily Bobkov who, with Peter Gambs and Andrey Tour, was one of the leading furniture-makers in St Petersburg.

In 1894, Robert Melzer designed a complete neo-Rococo scheme for the Private Dining Room in the Winter Palace, and the white-painted furniture was made by Friedrich Melzer. This displayed none of the improper elongation and spindliness that was so prevalent at the end of the century, and possibly the Czar and his family were sufficiently discerning to demand a fairly accurate and convincing product.

Italy was the most important of the Latin countries in matters of design during the nineteenth century, and supported her own Louis revival in spite of the long-lasting Napoleonic influences in favour of Neoclassicism.

As we have seen in the previous chapter, Filippo Pelagio Palagi (1775–1860), a designer of great importance, continued to work in the neo-classical style until the middle 1840s, and, had it not been for the sequence of political events which overtook the whole country between 1849 and 1860, its popularity might have continued much longer.

It seems very likely that the neo-Rococo style was adopted by the new régimes, and by the progressive forces that were working towards the eventual unification of Italy that took place in 1861. Count Camillo Cavour, for example, one of the principal politicians who brought about unification, is shown in an engraving of 1861 standing in his study in Turin, surrounded by neo-Rococo furniture and decoration.

Italian furniture-designers had in fact been flirting for a long time before the mid-century with ideas that were far from strictly neoclassical. Giuseppe Borsato re-published his *Opera Ornamentali* in Milan in 1831, and, unlike the 1822 edition, it contained a number of suggestions for furniture in eclectic and Gothic styles. Giuseppe Cima's *L'Addobatore Moderno* however, published in Milan round about 1840, showed a whole series of furniture designs in the most fully developed neo-Rococo style, and such influences soon began to be reflected in production. Another work

showing a large amount of neo-Rococo designs was *L'Artista Italiano*, published in 1854, which had contributions from, among others, C Invernizzi and A Sidoli. The architect Alessandro Sidoli was a prolific producer of engraved designs, and even after his death some of his proposals in a type of revived Louis Quatorze were shown in *L'Arte Illustrata* published in Turin in 1870.

The firm of Ferdinando Pogliani in Milan made a great deal of neo-Rococo furniture during the 1850s, and gave it an Italian flavour all its own. Curving backs were often combined with straight square legs in the seat furniture, and many of the carcase pieces and desks showed a curious amalgam of Renaissance elements. Most of their furniture was beautifully inlaid and decorated with veneers of contrasting woods, and turned finials and

Above: The universal popularity of neo-Rococo was reflected in the furnishings of the study of Arthur Hazelius, one of the founders of Stockholm's Nordiska Museet, in 1870. The balloon-back chairs, the Rococo sofa, the scroll-legged table, might have come from any mid-century bourgeois interior. (Nordiska Museet, Stockholm)

Above right: Count Camillo Cavour, one of the leading figures in Italy's unification, was frequently depicted in neo-Rococo surroundings, and it is possible that the style was considered to suggest a forward-looking attitude, in contrast to the associations of Neo-classicism with the old Italian monarchies. (Musei Civici, Brescia)

open frets were also used to achieve the desired richness. Pogliani's work received special praise at the Vienna Exhibition of 1865, together with that of Ferri and Bertolazzi of Siena, Frullini of Florence and Pazzi of Rome.

Neo-Rococo appears, nevertheless, to have had a relatively short life in Italy, and it may always have seemed a rather foreign importation. After the Risorgimento had become an established political fact, middle-class taste tended to turn towards styles that suggested the great periods of Italian history, and away from the frivolity of Rococo.

The style remained popular in certain Italian circles however, especially those dominated by the Italian royalty and aristocracy. The salon in the apartments occupied by Queen Margherita in the Palazzo Pitti in Florence had already been completely redecorated and furnished in a rather Bavarian Rococo style in 1860, and when the state-rooms in the Quirinale Palace in Rome were re-furbished for King Umberto in the last years of the century some rooms were given a complete neo-Rococo scheme. The villa Pignatelli in Naples, originally built in 1829, was completely redecorated in neo-Rococo when that family acquired it just before the end of the century, and in this case the furniture, whilst following the original French and Italian models fairly closely, included many pieces which were unknown in the eighteenth century.

America's contribution to neo-Louis was perhaps the most interesting of any in the world, and the American furniture industry developed the forms to a much greater degree than was customary in Europe, making use of technology in ways that were relatively unknown in other countries.

The neo-classical style remained popular for building until well into the 1860s (although by about 1855 it was permissible to vary this by the introduction of other building styles), but furniture in the more rigid classical manner was being rapidly abandoned in favour of neo-Rococo by the early 1850s.

Neo-Rococo furniture of a fairly standard type was available from a number of American firms by the mid-century, of which a typical parlour set was that provided by Elijah Galusha of Troy in 1853 for the Robert Milligan House at Saratoga Springs, and which is now at the Brooklyn Museum.

The unique development of American neo-Rococo furniture resides in the work of John Henry Belter (1804–63), who perfected revolutionary techniques for laminating timber

Right: Many firms copied Belter's technique and style with varying degrees of success. Prudent Mallard, who worked in New Orleans at almost the same time as Belter, produced large pieces of high quality, such as this bed in a New Orleans bedroom, 'suited to the cavernous splendour of ante-bellum mansions'. (The American Museum in Britain, Bath)

which allowed the formation of sweeping curved shapes, which in their turn could be elaborately carved. Belter's furniture was usually executed in rosewood, and he was able to achieve a remarkable degree of strength. The firm that he founded in New York in 1844 enjoyed a great success producing parlour and bedroom suites, and chairs and tables, and many other firms imitated his designs. Prudent Mallard and François Seignoret in New Orleans, Ignatius Lutz of Philadelphia, Charles A Baudouine, Alexander Roux and even the Meeks Company all made similar elaborate pieces during the 1850s, but none of them seems to have achieved the technical virtuosity of Belter. Baudouine was said to have pirated Belter's patent, and indeed whilst the Belter firm went bankrupt in 1867, Baudouine prospered.

The American Civil War (1861–65) brought radical changes to the American furniture industry, and many of the smaller firms were forced to close for financial reasons. The form taken by the eventual economic recovery completely revolutionized the industry, and mechanical processes overtook many of the traditional skills of the craftsmen.

By the 1870s manufacturers in the Mid-West

had virtually eliminated the smaller East Coast firms, and Grand Rapids, Michigan, and Cincinnati, Ohio, had become the centres of production for the middle-of-the-market trade, supplying their goods from highly mechanized factories to the whole of the American continent. New York still remained the centre of the upper end of the market however, and it is noticeable that taste had begun to turn away from excesses of neo-Rococo by the mid-1860s (much as it did in Britain) and a much more rectilinear and restrained style with strong affinities with the Louis Seize style became popular. Ebonizing, emphasized with ormolu mouldings and gilt-incised lines, was used on many pieces, and foremost in this quality field was the firm of Léon Marcotte.

By the mid-1860s the company had become New York's leading decorators, and although they also made furniture in the neo-Renaissance manner, the output of neo-Louis Seize continued well into the 1870s. Several other firms worked in this style — Thomas Brooks

and Herter Bros in New York, Jelliff of Newark and Henkels of Philadelphia — and its popularity continued until the early twentieth century, although, as the nineteenth century drew to a close, the pieces were made to look progressively more like the original prototype and less of an interpretation.

On both sides of the Atlantic, the market seems to have divided, the higher end demanding copies of convincing accuracy, whilst the lower was flooded with spindly pieces on which any addition of swirling fret would label them 'Louis Quinze'.

In the 1890s the Kimbel company of New York and the Brooks Household Art Company of Ohio were turning out neo-Rococo furniture that bore a close resemblance to the original article, and a growing market was developing in the importation of copies from France, where they tended to be made with even greater accuracy. Some were obviously intended for sale to the gullible as genuine antiques, to satisfy the growing snob appeal of collecting.

It will be seen from this brief survey that the neo-Louis styles were universal throughout the Western world during the nineteenth and early twentieth centuries. There was a vigorous interchange of import and export between countries which served to disseminate new fashions and their regional variations. Furthermore there was a constantly growing market during the nineteenth century for furniture and decorative items in the new colonies that were being opened up in every remote corner of the globe.

Many London firms, right from the beginning of the century, concentrated specifically on colonial markets, and, within the limitations imposed by the necessity of using the furniture both on board ship and of it being easy to stow, metropolitan fashions were adhered to as closely as possible. Special suites of parlour furniture and dining-chairs in the neo-Rococo style were made in London for export to Australia and New Zealand from the 1850s to the 1870s and although they were provided with easily removable arms and legs, they were very like the London models.

Other contemporary styles

It is, as has already been mentioned, a particularly confusing aspect of nineteenth-century furniture history that numerous styles enjoyed popularity at the same time, and that various different styles might be considered appropriate to express different functions within the same building. Whilst the neo-Louis styles were generally the most persistent throughout the last two-thirds of the century, several others were held in almost equal esteem.

Whilst it was usual to adopt a neo-Rococo or neo-Louis Seize style in the rooms over which the women of the family had most influence, from as early as the 1820s it was also believed that the masculine preserves of the household should be treated rather differently. Gothic or Renaissance were often adopted for the library, study or dining-room, and neo-classical also continued to be favoured in these rooms for many years — and even, sometimes, for the drawing-room, boudoir and bedrooms as well. Indeed a kind of 'utility classical' of almost indeterminate date survived in the humbler rooms of most domestic establishments right up to the end of the century, and even into the twentieth. In order to identify the most important styles

Left: The furniture made in New York by John Henry Belter's firm between 1844 and 1867 is perhaps the most interesting variant of the neo-Rococo style. Whilst the pieces are loosely based on Louis Quinze models, the shaped, laminated backs, the deeply pierced naturalistic carving and the exaggerated proportions are all characteristic of the nineteenth century. (The American Museum in Britain, Bath)

contemporary with the neo-Louis, we may perhaps divide the main ones under the four headings of 'fat-classical', neo-Gothic, Elizabethan and technological.

Fat-classical Furniture that is still basically neo-classical in form and inspiration, but which has been 'fattened' by an increasing amount of rich, carved ornament, often of naturalistic form, and by the adoption of a more flowing form than was normal in strictly neo-classical pieces, is termed 'fat-classical'; almost invariably such furniture, however elaborate, had turned legs.

The type appeared in England early in the nineteenth century, and in 1812 Morel & Hughes supplied suites of the richest kind for the Prince Regent at Carlton House. Similar seat furniture, all with beautiful matt and burnished gilt show-wood, was made by Morel & Seddon for Windsor Castle in 1828.

All the important furniture-makers used this style, and it may be studied in all its rich diversity in pattern books like George Smith's *Cabinet-Maker and Upholsterer's Guide* of 1826, or *The Practical Cabinet-Maker* by Peter and Michael Angelo Nicholson of the same date. Its popularity lasted until at least the 1860s, and fine examples were provided for the new London clubhouses during the 1840s and 1850s, notably those made by Holland & Sons for the Reform Club in 1838. Indeed this style, in simplified form with very little ornament, became classic for furniture in rooms where no display was deemed necessary, and catalogues of the early 1900s still offered timeless, rectangular, functional carcase pieces of the sort that first appeared in the 1850s.

The equivalent in French furniture was remarkably similar, and the enriched Empire style of the Restoration and Louis-Philippe gave way to straightforward functional pieces, usually in fine 'plum-pudding' mahogany like the English counterpart, with little carved enrichment and no metal mounts. French pieces often had slightly more panelling and raised beading than was to be found in English examples, and sometimes the top of a wardrobe or the side of a bed would be given a small sweep which had something of a neo-Louis suggestion. These pieces were nearly always made anonymously, especially in the 1860s and 1870s, as they were seldom intended for display. Similar furniture may be found in Germany, although there appears to have been a stronger tendency for the German-speaking countries to adopt the 'romantic' styles.

In Italy, furniture with fattened Empire forms was produced from the 1830s onwards, and the panelled components, the absence of metal ornaments, the 'fat' carving and the fine, opened veneers, were all used in a manner that followed contemporary European practice very closely. Paolino Moselini of Cremona enjoyed a reputation for the quality of his furniture in the 'fat-classical' style in the 1830s and 40s, and much of it was decorated with subtle, contrasting inlays. Giuseppe Cairoli and Speluzzi of Milan were two other firms who made this type of furniture in the 1850s and 1860s, and an Englishman named Peters, who had a factory in Genoa, made pieces that were almost indistinguishable from English productions. Undoubtedly the most remarkable Italian 'fat-classical' furniture, however, was designed by Pelagio Palagi for King Carlo Alberto at the Royal Palace in Turin. Some of the beautiful neo-Etruscan furniture that Palagi designed for the King's palace at Raconigi was exhibited at the Great Exhibition in 1851, and was judged to be '. . . deserving of a place in the palace of any sovereign'.

America's 'fat-classical' furniture was of a rather simple kind, which reflected the country's relatively undeveloped economic state in the 1830s and 1840s. It is clearly

Below: An Aristocrat's Breakfast, painted by P A Fedotov in 1849, shows a room which is completely furnished with 'fat-classical' pieces that might have been made 20 years earlier — the only concession to modernity being the over-stuffed easy-chair. (Tretyakov Gallery, Moscow)

exemplified in the early output of the firm of Joseph Meeks & Sons of New York and there were many references to the French Louis-Philippe style in their production. The use of the newly invented steam sawing machinery to cut large, flat members, which were covered with mahogany veneer, enabled a fairly showy product to be made without resort to too much carved work.

Duncan Phyfe, who is usually associated with the late eighteenth-century style, turned out a considerable amount of 'fat-classical' furniture, and in 1840 an English immigrant working in Baltimore, named John Hall, published a pattern book called *The Cabinet Maker's Assistant*. It contained 198 plates showing suggestions for pieces in the simplified French form, and it provided a whole repertoire of massive but practical furniture. Some American late-Empire furniture was decorated with designs which were stencilled onto the flat surfaces in a gold-dust mixture, and this seems to be a uniquely American practice. The 'fat-classical' style hardly survived the 1840s in the United States, and the growing fashion for neo-Louis was adopted in a much more wholesale manner than was customary in most European countries; the survival of the earlier style in the humbler rooms was therefore rather more rare.

The 'fat-classical' style was very popular in Russia, and some of the furniture produced by Andrey Tour in the 1840s was very similar to contemporary English pieces. Peter Gambs executed a magnificent set of full-gilt furniture for the Winter Palace in St Petersburg in 1830 to the designs of Montferrand, but the most outstanding suite was made by Andrey Tour from 1850 to 1852 to the designs of Leo von Klenze. It was intended for the Hermitage Museum, and it was remarkably like the furnishings provided in London for Carlton House 40 years earlier.

Neo-Gothic This furniture seems to have originated in England as a direct descendant of the pieces that were made for the dilettante collectors of the eighteenth century, who required furnishings for the romantic fantasy dwellings that they had had built.

King George IV gave encouragement to yet another branch of artistic creation, in his decision that a number of the interiors that were being re-furbished at Windsor Castle should be decorated and furnished in the neo-Gothic style. His architect, Sir Jeffry Wyatville, was able to make use of the unusual talents of a young designer named Augustus Welby Northmore Pugin (1812–52) to help him with a style in which he lacked confidence.

Pugin was a key nineteenth-century figure, and although he practised as an architect, his flair for publicity gave him great influence over the taste of his contemporaries. His passionate religious faith led him to believe that Gothic architecture was the only true style, and he expressed his views in forceful and highly controversial writings.

Although he was only 15 at the time of his commission at Windsor, Pugin made numerous designs for decoration and furniture during 1827 and 1828, working directly for Morel & Seddon, who eventually were to supply the furniture. All of it displayed a remarkable, precocious talent, and a certain frivolity that had great charm, but Pugin was later to express extreme dissatisfaction with his early work. Whilst it is possible to attribute some of the design faults to Pugin's youth and inexperience, the chairs, side-tables, sideboards and stools that he produced merely underline his basic difficulty in creating furniture in a Gothic style, since there was no precedent which allowed sufficient sophistication to appeal to early nineteenth-century taste.

Such mediaeval furniture as still existed looked extremely crude to nineteenth-century eyes, and so all early neo-Gothic pieces made

Below: Pelagio Palagi and Carlo Bellosio carried out alterations to the Castello di Raconigi near Turin in 1834, and a rich, late neo-classical style was maintained throughout. The Etruscan Room served as a dining-room, and the chairs were awarded special praise when they were exhibited in London in 1851. (Castello Reale di Raconigi, Turin)

use of purely architectural details and ornaments, which were grafted, more or less successfully, onto the basic functional furniture shapes. Although Pugin's later designs (for instance the many pieces that he produced from 1844 onwards for the new Houses of Parliament in London) displayed much more understanding of mediaeval precedent, the original difficulty still persisted, and he was driven to such anomalies as the use of linenfold panelling to decorate the doors of writing-desks, or ogee — S-shaped — arches to brace the legs of tables. Pugin was, nonetheless, an exceptional designer, and most commercial neo-Gothic furniture remained unashamedly impure in its detail. It was not until much later in the century, under the influence of Bruce Talbert and Charles Eastlake that neo-mediaeval began to lose its fancy-dress look, and came to look much less 'neo-Gothic' in the process. This trend really formed part of the Arts and Crafts movement however, and is covered in the following chapter. The kind of honest, basic furniture proposed in Talbert's *Examples of Ancient and Modern Furniture* (1876) or Eastlake's *Hints on Household Taste* (1868) never appealed very strongly to the middle-of-the-road market.

Most countries produced neo-Gothic furniture at some period during the nineteenth century, although its popularity had generally waned to a very large degree by the 1870s. The style had a long life in the German-speaking countries of central Europe, where it had become romantically fashionable to build country houses in mediaeval style, or

Above left: The exaggerated quality of most neo-Gothic French furniture is certainly apparent in this chair 'à la cathédrale' of about 1840. (Musée des Arts Décoratifs, Paris)

Left: One of the hundreds of neo-Gothic pieces that A W N Pugin designed between 1844 and 1852 for the new Houses of Parliament in London, providing a remarkable testimony to his ability. (Victoria & Albert Museum, London)

Above: A W N Pugin turned out an enormous amount of work during his relatively short life, and his furniture ranged from the frivolity of his early style at Windsor Castle to the scholarly and thoughtful character of the interiors of the Houses of Parliament in London.

France had but a brief flirtation with 'faux gothique' or 'stile cathédrale', and this mostly took place between 1830 and 1850. Aimé Chénavard made designs for Gothic furniture and decoration round about 1830, and Pierre-Antoine Bellangé, the influential Empire furniture-maker, had made Gothic furniture for Count Esterházy as early as 1811. But in most cases French neo-Gothic merely consisted of the addition of a few vaguely Gothic shapes in shallow mouldings onto pieces of basically late-Empire form; the furniture designed by Eugène-Emmanuel Viollet-le-Duc (1814–79) for Roquetaillade in the 1860s, or for the reconstructed interiors at Pierrefonds was far too archaeological for the average French market.

In Italy, however, quite a considerable fashion developed for neo-Gothic furniture, and this is somewhat surprising in that the true mediaeval Gothic only touched the edge of the mainstream of Italian architecture. In about 1850, Alessandro Sidoli published a number of engravings of neo-Gothic furniture and decoration, but as far back as 1818 the versatile Palagi had worked in this style at the Tempietto of the Villa Tittoni at Desio, and various Gothic architectural designs had been published by L F Basoli in 1826. Many houses in the Gothic style did not have special furniture, and the extraordinary painted interior of the Villa Amalia at Erba, completed in 1843 to the designs of the painter A Scrosati, seems to have been mainly furnished with neo-Renaissance (or 'Dantesque') pieces, as was the equally incredible castle at Carimate. The architect Celeste Chierichetti of Milan did, however, design neo-Gothic furniture for the interiors of the Villa Litta at Vedano in the 1850s, but it is noticeable that it was round Trieste (ruled by Austria until 1919) and the parts of northern Italy which came under Germanic influence that the neo-Gothic style was most popular.

Neo-Gothic furniture was made sporadically in Italy right through the century however, but towards the closing years such pieces were designed much more consciously to look like original mediaeval ones. At the Turin Exhibition of 1898, the Carlo Zen firm showed several Gothic items which were relatively close copies, including a carved and canopied throne, but these were accompanied by other pieces in the Moorish style and even some Empire Revival chairs.

A certain amount of neo-Gothic furniture was made in America, imitating the European fashion, but the style had no particularly strong emotional connection with America's past, in the way that it was felt to have in some parts of Europe. Many of the important furniture-makers turned out pieces in the neo-Gothic style during the 1830s and 1840s however — notably Joseph Meeks of New

to emphasize the Middle Ages in houses that already existed. Designs for neo-Gothic furniture had appeared in Germany as far back as the end of the eighteenth century, and they were put out from all the main centres of the German furniture trade during the 1830s and 1840s. Kimbel of Mainz made neo-Gothic furniture, as did the Leistler firm in Vienna, and this company submitted an enormous Gothic bookcase to the Great Exhibition of 1851. The Rhine castle of Stolzenfels was restored, and filled with neo-Gothic furniture, some designed by Franz Xavier Fortner in 1842, some by Johann Wilhelm Vetter in 1844. Fortner also designed furniture for Schloss Hohenschwangau in 1835. Schloss Sychrov near Prague was given an incredible neo-Gothic interior, which, although designed by Josef Pruvot in 1847, was not actually completed until 1862.

After 1880 German taste turned much more to the Renaissance, and the solemn Gothic furnishings that were made to the designs of Julius Hofmann and Peter Herwegen for King Ludwig of Bavaria at Neuschwanstein in 1883 were no longer very much in accord with contemporary German interest.

York, John Jelliff of Newark and Richard Byrnes — but most of their productions were either merely standard plain neo-classical carcase pieces with a little 'blind' Gothic ornament tacked onto them, or wildly spiky fragile examples of fret-cutting, especially in chair-backs; even at the time these were recognized as being totally impractical.

The Elizabethan style 'Elizabethan' is a term that was particularly favoured in England during the first half of the nineteenth century, and it tended to be used fairly indiscriminately to describe any furniture which was neither classical nor Gothic. Many pieces in this loosely-named style had strong Renaissance affinities, since the Elizabethan period itself adopted many details of Continental Renaissance art, but free use was also made of the seventeenth-century Jacobean and Caroline motifs, especially bobbin or corkscrew-turned legs and stretchers. It was a style which was particularly popular for the re-furnishing of existing historic houses, and was also used for dining-rooms, libraries, halls, and in fact for all the rooms which were considered to have formal functions.

In England, the Elizabethan style was the precursor of the neo-Renaissance style which in its turn eventually became one of the most popular furnishing types during the second half of the nineteenth century. All the architects who favoured the Old-English fashions wished to use furniture that could be considered appropriate to their buildings; furthermore the large legacy of dwellings throughout England which dated from the fifteenth to the seventeenth centuries evoked an immediate response amongst the early nineteenth-century middle classes who wanted instant ancestry to bolster their social position.

Most leading furniture firms promoted one version or another of the Elizabethan or Old English style, and there are numerous designs by Gillows dating from the 1840s. Shaw's *Specimens of Ancient Furniture*, published in 1836 and Robert Bridgen's *Furniture with Candelabra and Interior Decoration* of 1838, were two influential works which contained many plates that were widely copied.

The architect Anthony Salvin made a speciality of the design of 'Olde Englyshe' furniture for many of his houses, and both at Mamhead in Devonshire and at Scotney Castle in Kent there were fine bedroom suites

Left: The furniture that Carl Leistler of Vienna showed at the Great Exhibition of 1851 in London received considerable acclaim. This great bookcase, in which elaboration of workmanship was pushed to its ultimate, was described at the time as doing 'infinite credit to those who have produced it'.

Right: Although the first part of Lyndhurst near Tarrytown was designed by Alexander Jackson Davis in 1841, the dining-room was not added by him until the mid 1860s. The furniture, which also dates from that time, makes an interesting comparison with the pieces that Davis produced 22 years earlier, and clearly shows how much more heavy and 'serious' the Gothic Revival had become, although the same inappropriate use was still made of architectural elements. (Lyndhurst, Tarrytown, New York)

Right: The architect Anthony Salvin made a speciality of houses in the Elizabethan or Jacobean styles, together with appropriate furniture. This bed, for which the design drawing still exists, was based on Jacobean models. (Private collection)

and other neo-Elizabethan or neo-Caroline pieces dating from the 1840s. By the late 1860s, the so-called Elizabethan style was beginning to merge into the neo-Renaissance style, which eventually superseded it in the 1870s.

Technological advances The development of technology precipitated many important changes during the whole of the nineteenth century, and technological processes were applied to many aspects of furniture manufacture. Experiments were constantly being made with new materials, sometimes purely in order to provide novelty, and these were not always a success. Into this category must be placed the macabre chairs made of horn and antlers, which were made in England, Germany and America in the middle years of the century, or the chairs and tables made of coal, which created a mild sensation in the 1850s.

Papier-mâché furniture was perhaps the most appealing of all the oddities. It was first made in England, from about 1830 but became popular all over the world. Papier mâché-panels, combined with wood framework and supports, were used as chair-backs. table-

tops, and as decorative elements on carcase furniture. The papier mâché itself was usually japanned in black, and this was in turn decorated with mother-of-pearl inlay, naturalistic paintings of flowers or scenes, and stencilled patterns of gilding. Jennens & Bettridge of Birmingham was the principal firm which turned out these decorative objects, and they were in business from 1816 till 1864, although some other firms continued working until the early twentieth century. The style was usually some form of neo-Rococo, since this allowed full expression to the curvaceous shapes into which papier mâché could be moulded. Complete sets of furniture were

rare, but occasional chairs in varying degrees of elaboration, side-cabinets, light tip-top tables, firescreens, desk-sets, were all introduced into fashionable homes to help give that air of variety, contrast and novelty which was considered to be so appealing.

The main technological innovation that took place during the nineteenth century was, of course, the introduction of metal parts where only wood had previously been used. The invention of the coil-spring and its effect on the appearance of comfortable seat furniture has already been noted, but metal came to be employed in many ways that had hitherto been unknown. Furniture made completely

of metal (usually cast-iron) first became commonplace in the 1840s, and was mostly produced in the expanding metal manufacturing
centres of the English Midlands. Before this,
most metal furniture had been made of
wrought iron, and out of doors, where such
pieces had their principal use, it required
constant painting to prevent rapid deteriora-
tion through rusting. Cast-iron, sometimes
combined with wood-slat seats or marble
table-tops, became very popular for garden
furniture, or for furniture which was likely
to be subjected to hard usage (in pubs or
cafés), and many delightful designs were
invented. The Coalbrookdale Company made
the famous 'fern' seats from 1858 onwards,
and hall-stands, umbrella-stands, 'door
porters', fenders and flower-pot stands were
all popular. In accordance with the nineteenth-
century taste for a 'valuable' appearance,
these objects were painted to simulate either
brown or patinated green bronze.

A great amount of cast-iron furniture was
exported from Britain in the middle years of
the century, but most countries soon developed
their own centres of production. M Dupont of

Paris exhibited a cast- and wrought-iron bed and a child's cot at the Great Exhibition of 1851, and the bed had sheet-iron ends and a side formed by a cast-iron panel ornamented with naturalistic foliage and hunting scenes in relief. Peyton & Harlow of London exhibited iron bedsteads, one of them with a beautiful domed canopy frame rising to a cast-iron corona. Tomás de Megne of Madrid also exhibited an iron bed, with cast ornament in relief. Cast-iron, combined with iron rod, was used extensively in the production of beds from the 1830s, for metal beds afforded a most welcome alternative to the wooden beds of the time, so many of which were infested with vermin, even in rich households. The cold strength of iron must have provided a miraculous release from the massive wooden bed of nineteenth-century legend, with its thick dusty hangings, oppressively hot feather mattress and lurking bed-bugs.

By the 1870s beds were being made of brass which looked much more light and cheerful than black-painted iron, and which would permit a higher standard of ornamental work. The complete tester had almost disappeared by the second half of the century, and even the half-tester had been replaced by small hinged side-screens, over which a little thin material or muslin could be draped.

In England it was the Arts and Crafts Movement, especially as expressed in the productions of Liberty's and Heal's, that brought wooden beds back to popularity after their eclipse during the last 30 years of the nineteenth century, although brass still remained popular into the next century. The later brass bedsteads were without any particular style and with virtually no ornament. They were often made of square brass tubing which relied merely on a small curved sweep or turned finial for decoration. The first brass beds of the 1860s, on the other hand, were formed out of circular tubes of varying sizes, and enriched with castings, plaques of mother-of-pearl and massive knops in order to achieve as rich an effect as possible.

Cast-iron furniture, especially the outdoor type, was also made in the United States during most of the century, and many patterns continued to be marketed for over 50 years. A set of cast-iron garden seats with members romantically shaped to imitate twigs and rustic logs was advertised by the Boston Ornamental Iron Works in 1857, and the identical pattern was being sold in the 1890s. Many firms made cast-iron furniture in America, based in Cleveland, Boston and New York, and the styles moved from rustic and neo-Rococo through Gothic to neo-Renaissance, although the most consistently favoured always incorporated a sort of naturalism, made up of elements of realistic plant forms, presumably as this was felt to fit in best with the usual open-air use.

There were, however, two particular areas where America specialized in 'technological' furniture: firstly in that which had particular provision for comfort; secondly in mechanical pieces which were transformable in some form or other. These two furniture types are closely related, and it is tempting to see American interest as connected at least partly, with that country's early development of long-distance rail travel. Trains which could be lived in for several days and nights required kinds of space-saving devices which were unknown even on ships, together with provisions for extra comfort in adjustable and well-sprung seating. The general American travelling public was able to become familiar with these advances rather before they had become usual in Europe, largely due to the considerably more democratized nature of the country's social structure.

In England, and in Europe generally, most mechanical and 'patent' furniture was intended for the use of invalids, and much American 'comfortable' furniture was of a kind which had little parallel in Europe.

Numerous devices were invented for 'digestive' chairs, smokers' chairs, adjustable chairs and rocking-chairs, and most of them made use of metal springs, ratchets, levers, cast-iron bases or revolving supports. The railway connection is obvious, and many of the later pieces might have come straight out of a contemporary Pullman Drawing-Room Car. By the very end of the century, however, American enthusiasm for gadget furniture seems to have waned, and the market gradually faded.

The second uniquely American development in furniture design was that of transformable

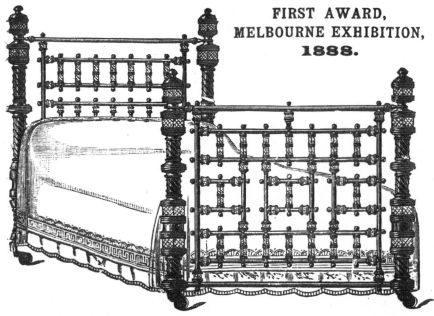

pieces. In the small flats in the rapidly expanding cities that were the homes of so much of the American population during the second half of the nineteenth century, devices with space-saving properties became necessary; the typical 'dumb-bell'-shape apartment house plan, which was common building practice at this time, shows vividly the cramped layouts which gave rise to the development of dual-purpose furniture. (Whilst the population of London multiplied by four during the nineteenth century, that of New York multiplied by 80!)

The item upon which most ingenuity was expended was the bed, and although sleeping-frames which folded, either vertically or horizontally, into a cupboard had been known

in Europe since the mid-eighteenth century, no country ever took the practice of bizarre fantasy further than America. The most extraordinary device was that which allowed a bed to be given the appearance of a piano when not in use, and perhaps in this we can see the ultimate in the expression of nineteenth-century middle-class pretension — the suggestive bed was finally transformed into the appearance of the very object which came to symbolize most of the aspirations of the growing bourgeoisie. The fact that this piano could not be played was probably largely irrelevant.

Experiments also took place in the use of certain organic materials for the manufacture of furniture. Cane, rattan and wicker were all used with varying degrees of success, and rattan and wicker were to achieve results which expressed engaging fantasy. Some-

times the materials were imported from their country of origin to the industrialized countries to be made up, sometimes the pieces would be made up near their source and exported complete. The usual basis was a wood frame over which the material would be formed in various shapes, and rattan furniture became very popular in conservatories and winter gardens, from about 1850. Towards the end of the century the ever-increasing number of unrelated elements in the middle-class drawing-room was further swelled by the introduction of basket chairs, with chintz covers and backrests. They undoubtedly helped to promote the feeling of cosiness and informality which expressed the increasing influence of women over every aspect of life in the developed countries, and in America in 1886 it was stated that a few such pieces were 'indispensable in modern apartments'.

Above left: Chairs and tables made of cane, rattan and wicker were first made round about 1850, and enjoyed a considerable vogue for furnishing conservatories and winter gardens.

Above: The interior of the Café Griensteidl in Vienna, painted by Rudolf Vokel in 1890, includes typical Thonet bentwood chairs in the surroundings for which they were admirably suited. (Städtische Museen, Vienna)

218

Probably the most famous technological furniture of the nineteenth century, and certainly that which had the longest life, was the bentwood furniture developed by a German named Michael Thonet. Thonet first started a small factory for making conventional furniture at Boppard, on the Rhine, and in 1830 he began experimenting with methods of economizing on labour and materials. He tried to make use of the techniques of bending veneers, already well known to the Biedermeier furniture-makers, and also to develop this practice further by gluing various parts together with their grain running in different directions so that curved shapes could be held in tension. Thonet's early productions were not particularly successful, but he was able to interest Prince Metternich in the ideas, and he moved to Vienna under the Prince's protection in 1842.

Thonet set up a factory in Vienna in 1849, and by this time he had given up his experiments with shaped, laminated sections, and was concentrating on bending solid wood. At the Great Exhibition of 1851 he showed pieces made of solid, bent rosewood, which were the precursors of the famous bentwood furniture which the Thonet factories were turning out in huge quantities by the 1860s, making use of mass-production and industrial techniques.

The opening-up of the United States in the second half of the century, together with the development of the colonial countries, provided a huge market for furniture which was cheap, strong, light and easily transported, and Thonet's bentwood pieces fulfilled all these requirements. Furthermore, the pieces themselves, (mainly chairs—including the famous 'American' rocker—but also tables, stools, hat-stands, sofas, and even artists' easels) all displayed a delightful, inventive elegance. The snaky convolutions of the

Right: This advertisement by Thonet Brothers, issued in 1862, gives an indication of the variety of the firm's products that could be manufactured from the same basic components.

circular sections—and their relation to neo-Rococo must not be overlooked—exerted an appeal to the eye which, combined with qualities of strength and durability, have ensured the popularity of this furniture up to our own time. It was Thonet, not the idealist William Morris, who created something approaching the 'decorative, noble, popular art' which Morris hoped to produce.

The remarkable success of bentwood seems to lie in its classless simplicity, which found acceptance at every social level. Thonet products could be seen at the end of the century in middle-class English drawing-rooms, in popular Viennese restaurants and cafés, in Australian mining towns and in American hotels.

Thonet's company remained very flexible in its commercial attitude, and a certain number of pieces were made in the early 1900s which had specifically neo-Louis details, and which became popular for use in the ladies' departments of big stores and in exclusive tea-rooms.

Neo-Renaissance

By the late 1860s and early 70s the fashion for the neo-Louis styles had been caught up, if not overtaken by that for the neo-Renaissance in most countries of the western world. The style varied considerably in interpretation from one country to another, but certain characteristics and details were common to all. It was generally based on the use of ornament derived from the sixteenth and seventeenth centuries, but this allowed for a considerable amount of variation in different countries. Furniture now exhibited a rectangular outline unlike the neo-Rococo, together with massive forms ornamented with areas of rich carving, turnery, or contrasting inlays. Few pieces, if any, were painted, and the obvious intention was always towards a weighty and impressive richness.

The possibility of national variations, which could express through slightly different detail the past of the country of origin, may well have been one of the reasons for its rise to popularity, and it could be used to help satisfy the trend towards nationalism which marked the progress of taste, as the nineteenth century moved into its final third. The striving for national identity which accompanied the struggle for unification in Italy and Germany was one of the influences which had an important bearing on the course of late nineteenth-century middle-class preferences.

Britain was of course not subject to the strong emotional impulses that the style evoked in some other countries, and the English variant was somewhat less 'serious'. It is perhaps best known as 'Free-Renaissance', since few pieces followed the originals very closely; it has also been called, rather contemptuously, 'the bracket-and-overmantel style', and this does suggest the marked tendency towards spindly fussiness that characterized much English furniture towards the end of the century.

Many architects designed furniture in the Free-Renaissance manner, including Robert

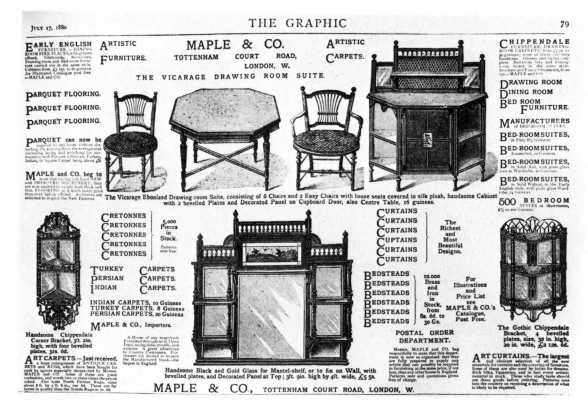

Left: Maple & Company of Tottenham Court Road, London, issued this advertisement in the Graphic in 1880. The firm conducted a middle-of-the-market trade for many years, and the goods that they offered are typical of bourgeois English taste of the time.

Right: The American neo-Renaissance style could be extremely impressive when used for a whole scheme of decoration. The members of the Hatch family were painted in the library of their Park Avenue mansion in New York by Eastman Johnson in 1871, and the richness of the interior was as closely portrayed by the artist as the likenesses of the sitters. (Metropolitan Museum of Art, New York)

Edis and T E Collcutt, and many of the plates of Edis' influential *Decoration and Furniture of Town Houses*, first published in 1881, showed not only furniture in this style, but also fireplace surrounds, overmantels, fixed cupboards and panelling. Indeed it is difficult to draw the line between good Free-Renaissance furniture and that which was designed by other important figures who were more closely tied to the Arts and Crafts Movement than to the popular market.

The influence of two Arts and Crafts architects, Eastlake and Talbert, can be traced in the development of the English Free-Renaissance style, although their work was much more consciously mediaeval in the manner of William Morris, and showed links with the neo-Elizabethan of the first half of the century. Charles Eastlake gave his name to a whole style of furniture in America, through the publication of his *Hints on Household Taste* in 1868, which found an eager public on both sides of the Atlantic. In fact, the American interpretation of the Eastlake style was much closer to the designs of Bruce Talbert, whose *Gothic Forms Applied to Furniture* (1867) and *Examples of Ancient and Modern Furniture* (1876) contained designs of a less austere kind than Eastlake's, and suggested a logical development of the work of Pugin.

Furniture firms at all levels of the market made pieces in the Free-Renaissance style, and in the upper bracket, Gillows, Collinson & Lock and C & W Trapnell consistently maintained a high level of quality. Panels incorporating carving or inlays based on north Italian ornament of the sixteenth century, designs based on Flemish strapwork or François I or Henri II ornament were freely used, and all of them were drawn together within a framework of rectangular and architectural character. The interior of Scott's new St Pancras Hotel in London was furnished in the richest neo-Renaissance manner by Gillows in the early 1870s, and this type of decoration came to supersede Gothic or Elizabethan for dining-rooms and libraries. Edis even recommended neo-Renaissance for drawing-rooms and bedrooms.

Although the better firms maintained their quality output as the end of the century approached, the cheaper and more commercial furniture-makers steadily bastardized the neo-Renaissance style. Papers like the *Furniture Gazette*, and the trade catalogues of the 1880s and 1890s, offered pieces that were becoming increasingly fussy in design and flimsy in construction. Carcase furniture took on a profusion of shelves and brackets, often supported on small turnery, and panels of bevelled glass or mirror, together with elaborate inlays of contrasting woods. All these features were included to give an effect of elaboration

223

on pieces whose basic form was thin and unsatisfactory. Some makers turned to a more specifically reproduction style, and catalogues at the turn of the century carried ranges made in oak, which was given a dark, fumed finish, and elaborate carvings and strip ornament.

An interesting variant of neo-Renaissance was the furniture which emanated from the United States. This had a much looser relationship with the style of origin than its European counterparts, and seems to us, therefore, to belong much more truly to the nineteenth century, as well as being strongly American.

Gaining popularity rapidly after the end of the Civil War in 1865, furniture in the American neo-Renaissance style exactly matched the attitudes of that period of commercial expansion and development which extended over the next decade. Massive, rich, rectangular, this furniture was decorated with projected panels of contrasting veneers, gilded incised linear patterns, and a profusion of turned ornamental knobs. Rosewood, burr-walnut, ebonizing, gilding, porcelain plaques and ormolu mounts might all be combined on one of the more costly examples, to produce an effect of magnificent opulence, which was often carried through the decoration of the whole house. Such interiors became the visible expression of men who had 'arrived', and they must have reflected exactly the ideals of railway magnates, expanding frontiers, industrialization and progress.

Most of the New York furniture-makers worked in this style, and Alexander Roux ('ever the tasteful proponent of the latest style') made a great amount of Renaissance revival furniture. Leon Marcotte made typical pieces during the 1860s and 1870s, together with others that were much closer to the original European models. John Jelliff of Newark, and Thomas Brooks & Company of Brooklyn were also known for their fine pieces, but it was the highly mechanized Grand Rapids firms that usually produced this essentially middle-market style.

The Berkey & Gay firm of Grand Rapids, and Mitchell & Rammelsberg of Cincinnati virtually dominated the furniture section of the Philadelphia Centennial Exhibition of 1876 with huge Renaissance revival pieces. These firms, together with the Phoenix Furniture Company, and Nelson Matters & Company, of Grand Rapids, took over a large part of the middle and lower ends of the market with products that ranged from near exhibition standard down to the humblest three-part bedroom suite for the newly-married small-time farmer.

By about 1880, however, the popularity of Renaissance revival was beginning to wane, and one of the reasons was undoubtedly the

Left: The American neo-Renaissance style took a somewhat different course from the European equivalent, in that the pieces displayed even less similarity to genuine Renaissance models. Indeed, in this rosewood cabinet made by Alexander Roux of New York in 1866, a highly eclectic collection of ornaments has been grafted rather arbitrarily onto the basically monumental neo-Renaissance form. (Metropolitan Museum of Art, New York)

Right: Whatever the function of any piece of furniture, it had to be given the fashionable style of the day, and this 'patent' desk was turned out with American neo-Renaissance details. Such desks, made in this case by the Wooton Desk Company of Indianapolis, were very popular in the United States in the second half of the nineteenth century. Apart from their undoubted usefulness, we must also see them as an expression of the American love of gadgets. The example dates from 1874, and belonged to Jay Gould, the financier. (The National Trust for Historic Preservation, Washington DC)

poor-quality bastardized versions that were manufactured in huge quantities by the less reputable Grand Rapids factories. Furthermore, a new generation of the buying public was growing up in the United States by the last two decades of the century, and its members had not the same inclination for the ostentation and massive display that their parents required to demonstrate the position they held in society.

The development of the neo-Renaissance style divided in the late 1870s. On the one hand, there was the appearance of a sophisticated simplicity which tended to eliminate much of the lavish applied ornament, whilst retaining the rectangularity and the incised linear decoration. On the other hand, a slightly self-conscious trend led towards 'honesty' and 'reform' which in turn encouraged a renewed interest in the more rugged woods, like oak, and oiled rather than french-polished finishes. Both these trends came to be known as the Eastlake style, although the products were

as much akin to those proposed by Bruce Talbert as by Eastlake himself.

One of the principal firms which made the more sophisticated type was Herter Bros, of New York, and much of their output had a great deal in common with the 'Art furniture' being made in England at about the same time. Great use was made of ebonizing, which was enlivened by stencilled gilt designs and inlays with a distinctly Japanese flavour. But these beautiful, bland pieces were never intended for a mass market, nor could such quality be produced in sufficient quantity.

The simpler aspects of the so-called Eastlake style were more in line with developing popular taste, and Kimbel & Cabus of New York, and Mitchell & Rammelsberg specialized in this furniture during the late 1870s and the 1880s. An important influence on the continuance and development of the Eastlake style's concern with 'honesty' was the work of the architect H H Richardson; his brilliant ideas on decoration had a great impact, and his pieces

often relied on the use of local woods, which might carry some judiciously disposed carving, but no applied ornament. Although Richardson died in 1886, a talented band of contemporaries carried on his theories in Chicago and on the Pacific Coast during the remaining years of the century, and could be said to have been achieving a truly national furniture style.

The development of neo-Renaissance furniture in the countries of the European mainland proceeded in a much less unconventional manner than in the United States. The style followed fairly closely such models as were felt to be appropriate from the historical furniture of each country, and there was little attempt at any departure from precedent.

In Germany and Italy, a return to what was dimly seen as the 'glorious past' had a considerable appeal in the upsurge of nationalism which took place in each of these countries at the time of their unification—which in both cases was during the 1860s and 1870s; the neo-Renaissance style appeared to be exactly what was required to provide an acceptable background. In Germany the final effect suggests a kind of Wagnerian late Middle Ages, whilst in Italy it is the world of Dante or the Medicis.

In Germany and Austria, neo-Renaissance furniture had first appeared in the 1840s, and a number of the highly praised pieces that Carl Leistler sent from Vienna to the Great Exhibition of 1851 were quite distinctly neo-Renaissance in character. In the 1870s and 1880s, the style was eagerly adopted by the increasingly prosperous German bourgeoisie, and the dark, elaborate character to which it lent itself so easily became completely associated with German late nineteenth-century middle-class life.

During the latter half of the 1870s, and throughout the 1880s and 1890s, neo-Renaissance remained popular all over the German-speaking countries. Most of the new official buildings were decorated in the style, and the interiors of the Reichstag in Berlin, designed by Paul Wallot in 1884, but not completed until 1894 with furnishings from the Munich firm of Pössenbacher, were totally given over to neo-Renaissance. Hugo Stamman and Gustav Zinnow designed interiors and furniture for the new Hamburg Town Hall in 1897 in the neo-Renaissance style, and Karl Köchlin provided interiors in 1884 for Heinrich von Ferstel's new neo-Renaissance Vienna University.

Many architects designed neo-Renaissance furniture all over Germany, such as Gustav Kachel of Karlsruhe, Hans Grisebach of Berlin, Rudolf Feldscharek and Alexander Wielemans von Monteforte of Vienna and the Munich architect George Hauberisser, who also worked in a rather Puginesque Gothic at the new Munich Town Hall in the early 1880s.

Above: The neo-Renaissance style appealed strongly to the prosperous bourgeoisie of newly united Germany, and it helped to suggest a deeply-rooted and continuing national tradition. Many favourite elements can be identified in this design for a living-room by the architect H Kirchmayr of Munich, 1890.

Right: Some of the most lavish neo-Renaissance interiors in Italy were created and furnished for the bachelor nobleman, Gian Giacomo Poldi-Pezzoli in Milan, and these rooms were intended as a setting for his considerable art collection. Much of the furniture, including the monumental bed, was made by Speluzzi and adorned with carving by Ludovico Pogliaghi. (Museo Poldi, Milan)

Middle-class demand continued to be served by firms like Bembé of Mainz, who not only made furniture but also designed complete interiors like the one published in *Building*, the English magazine, in 1883.

Neo-Renaissance furniture was made throughout Germany and Austria by such firms as Würfel or Franz Michel of Vienna, the Pallenbergs in Cologne, Philipp Niederhöfer of Frankfurt, Ziegler & Weber of Karlsruhe or George Schölte of Stuttgart.

Napoleon III's revivalistic ventures in French official building involved the use of the neo-Renaissance style, based on the architecture of the time of François I or Henri II, and appropriate pieces were required to furnish both new work and restorations.

The palaces with original Renaissance interiors were in a number of cases refurnished, notably the palace of Fontainebleau. Massive neo-Renaissance pieces were provided by Guillaume Grohé in 1860, typical of which was a magnificent set of chairs enriched with fine carving, which were made to designs by Ruprich-Robert. Even before this, in 1856, Grohé had executed the cradle, designed by Froment-Meurice, that the city of Paris had presented to Napoleon and Eugénie for the Prince Imperial, and this was made in the richest neo-Renaissance manner.

It has been claimed that this style first appeared in France at the exhibition of 1839, and that Aimé Chénavard (whose neo-Rococo exercises we have already noted) merely led a whole group of designers and decorators, but it still seems that the style did not become generally popular before the early years of the second Empire.

Grohé, who became official supplier to the Imperial Court, was perhaps the most spectacular exponent of the neo-Renaissance, but many of the other contemporary furniture-makers that we have already noted as working in the neo-Louis styles were also producing neo-Renaissance pieces. Fourdinois, Jeanselme, Krieger and many other lesser firms all turned out their own interpretations. Neo-Renaissance decoration and furniture were, of course, frequently used in conjunction with other styles in the same house; Baron James de Rothschild's Château de Ferrières, completed in about 1860, had a neo-Renaissance dining-room, sitting-room and central hall, but also a neo-Louis Seize music-room and a neo-Rococo study. The house that Mme Paiva, one of the richest and most notorious figures of the late 1860s, had built for herself on the Champs Elysées in Paris was almost entirely decorated in neo-Renaissance. It took 11 years to build, and the house-warming party did not take place until 1866; the interior is a monument of French neo-Renaissance taste. All the important artists of the day worked on the house, and Carrier-Belleuse even provided a bronze and silver neo-Renaissance console table.

Paul Mauguin, the architect, also designed much of the special furniture, which was ornamented with gilt-bronze plaques set into ebonized surrounds.

The upheavals brought about by the Franco-Prussian war, and France's defeat and the ensuing political troubles, curtailed the development of taste for a time, but Henri Havard, in his influential book *L'Art dans la Maison*, published in 1884, obviously still believed neo-Renaissance to be perfectly acceptable, mingled with a judicious amount of neo-Louis in rooms where he considered it appropriate.

The Exposition Universelle of 1889 was somewhat of a turning-point in French bourgeois taste in that it was firmly forward-looking. The Galerie des Machines and the Eiffel tower served as symbols of a changing cultural attitude, and the revival of floral decoration and the emerging Art Nouveau style were much in evidence.

It should not of course be overlooked that Art Nouveau itself had deep neo-Rococo origins and that these must make it appeal strongly to the public in a country where Rococo was an integral part of its historic culture. Neither should it be assumed that it superseded previous fashions at any one specific moment in time — certainly the neo-Renaissance style continued with gradually diminishing popularity in France until the 1914 war.

Italian interest in neo-Renaissance tended (as might be expected) to favour a sort of 'Dantesque' vision of Italy's past. Again, as might be expected, this style also became associated with the Risorgimento and its own emphasis on Italy's glorious history. As far back as 1840, Cima had proposed designs in a neo-Renaissance style in his *Addobatore Moderno*, and Allessandro Sidoli published examples of his versions of it in the 1850s.

Andrea Baccetti made rich furniture in Florence during the 1860s and 1870s, and received much critical acclaim at the various exhibitions to which he submitted his work.

The Italian furniture-makers usually turned their attention towards the richness of the later Renaissance, and the carver Luigi Frullini was almost alone in following his rather sixteenth-century inspiration. His pieces had a quality of restraint that was noticeably lacking in the productions of his contemporaries, and this was combined with a very architectural character. He was much acclaimed at various exhibitions, including that of 1862 in London.

Enthusiasm for the neo-Renaissance amongst the middle classes continued unabated after Umberto I ascended to the throne of united Italy in 1878, and most bourgeois households had at least one neo-Renaissance room. None of the artistic collections that

228

many Italians were putting together at this period could be considered complete if it did not contain a large proportion of so-called Renaissance objects, many of which of course turned out later to be fakes.

Every European country produced its own version of the neo-Renaissance style; the castle of Peles in Rumania, for example, was started in 1875 and furnished and re-furnished for the royal family in the most elaborate manner right up to 1914. Friedrich and Robert Melzer made neo-Renaissance furniture for the Winter Palace in St Petersburg in 1894. Ibsen's study in his home on the Abendsgate in Oslo, where he lived from 1895 until his death in 1906, contained neo-Renaissance bourgeois furnishings, mixed with overstuffed easy chairs of a more typically mid-century appearance.

The Exotics

The Moorish style A type of decoration which was loosely based on the vocabulary of near-eastern design was popular all through the nineteenth century. Known variously as 'Moorish', 'Turkish', 'Saracenic' or 'Arab', its main characteristics involved the use of the Moorish arch form, highly patterned walls in the manner of Persian tiles, and amorphous pieces of furniture of rather undefined shape, covered with cushions.

The popularity of this exotic fashion is intriguing, but it appears that any function which was considered foreign to conventional nineteenth-century bourgeois ideas was felt to be satisfactorily absorbed when it was in such unusual surroundings. Smoking rooms (with obvious connections), billiard rooms (male preserve), bathrooms (Turkish), were all decorated with versions of near-eastern

Left: John D Rockefeller had a magnificent 'moorish' sitting-room in the house in which he lived on West 54th Street, New York, in the 1880s, but the effect was mostly achieved by the rich joinery (with ivory and mother-of-pearl inlay) and the brilliant colouring. The furniture, although ebonized and splendidly upholstered with embroidered covers, was nevertheless hardly distinguishable from the prevalent neo-Renaissance-cum-Eastlake styles of the period. (Brooklyn Museum)

Below: The 'turkish' style was popular all through the nineteenth century. A typical divan covered in carpet, and with the frame completely concealed, was included in an album of designs for Reiche und Elegante Sitzmöbel by A & L Streitenfeld of Berlin.

229

detail, and the style was also applied to boudoirs (harem?), garden retreats and, in Lisbon, even a railway station!

During the first half of the nineteenth century, the Moorish style was still mostly employed on follies, pavilions and garden features, and very little furniture was made for such buildings.

In England, Owen Jones, an influential architect and designer, was an enthusiastic exponent of near-eastern decoration, and his *Plans, Elevations and Sections of the Alhambra*, published from 1836 to 1845, created great interest in Islamic practices of polychromy and pattern. Although he designed a lot of buildings and decorative schemes with Moorish details and colours, little evidence survives that he ever produced any furniture. In fact, apart from the overstuffed divan, little furniture in this style seems to have been attempted anywhere much before 1860. Even the famous Arab Hall that the painter Lord Leighton had constructed in his house in London in 1880 had only some fixed seating.

A few pieces with Moorish details were designed by Andrea Baccetti in Italy however,

and the incredible Moorish interior of the villa Crespi on Lake Orta, designed by the architect Giovanni Colla in the last years of the century, does seem to have been completely furnished with pieces that made use of near-eastern elements in their design.

The Turkish drawing-room at the Rumanian palace of Peles also had stools and occasional tables with near-eastern decoration, but the specifically oriental look was achieved by the use of overstuffed sofas, and it was upon these objects that most of such schemes relied for their effect, together with coverings of brilliantly patterned carpet and embroidery.

In New York, A A Vantine and Company made a speciality of supplying 'everything that belongs to a genuine Moorish interior' during the 1890s, and the increasing popularity of overstuffed couches, divans and 'Turkish corners' probably reflected the liking for comfort and relaxed informality which were to become such a characteristic of American life. Not that designers in the United States were alone in this trend in the closing years of the century, for firms like Holland & Sons in London were offering a complete 'Turkish' smoking room in one of their catalogues, which had fixed overstuffed divans set on either side of the fireplace and provided the total environment for 'a chamber specially furnished for wakeful rest'.

The Japanese Style The arts of the Far East have fascinated the Western world since the close of the Middle Ages, and during the eighteenth century it became fashionable in most European countries to construct follies and garden buildings in what was loosely called the Chinese style. The English architect Sir William Chambers, in his *Designs of Chinese Buildings, Furniture etc.*, published in 1757, showed suggestions for a number of chairs and tables in his interpreted far-eastern styles, and this kind of piece became extremely popular between 1770 and 1830.

It was not until the opening of Japan to foreign trade in 1854, however, that Japanese art came to be much known in the West, but as soon as this event took place its popularity grew rapidly in Europe and America. While the more advanced aspects of Japanese influence were to be found in the Arts and Crafts movement (to be described in the next chapter), a great many elements of the Anglo-Japanese style filtered down to the middle-level markets during the last 20 years of the century, so that many a bourgeois drawing-room was decorated with 'Japanese' fans, and every suburban boudoir had its 'art' pot containing a spray of peacock feathers.

By the 1880s and 1890s the furniture trade was producing large amounts of Japanese-influenced pieces, some of it using real bamboo for legs and frames (unlike most

Left: Although the celebrated 'Peacock Room' that the painter James McNeil Whistler decorated in 1877 had a strong Japanese flavour, the furniture was either neo-Louis or neo-Renaissance, with a few eighteenth-century antiques. (National Monuments Record, London)

Below: In 1882 Herter Bros of New York provided a complete 'Japanese Parlour' for the 5th Avenue mansion of William H Vanderbilt, including special neo-Japanese furniture.

231

earlier products which were made of wood with a simulated bamboo finish) and panels of woven grass to decorate doors and table-tops. Most of these pieces were intended as occasional furniture, appreciated for its quaint character, and few rooms would contain more than one or two. Vantine's Emporium in New York imported large amounts of bamboo furniture from China and Japan in the late years of the century, and companies like Nimura and Sato of Brooklyn made up bamboo into furniture in America itself.

Although by 1886 *The Decorator and Furnisher* was able to state that bamboo furniture was always in demand 'among people of artistic tastes', few of these went so far as W H Vandebilt, who commissioned Herter Bros, to design a complete Japanese Parlour in his 5th Avenue mansion.

'National' and 'Old-World' revivals from 1880 to 1914

The increasing nationalism in politics throughout the world towards the end of the nineteenth century, which culminated in the Great War of 1914, was reflected in many aspects of the cultural scene. In furniture design, the trend towards a search for a style which suggested the actual past of the nation concerned, which we have already noted as an aspect of the Renaissance revival, became canalized into revivals which were even more specifically related to national styles, and the production of pieces of furniture intended to reproduce actual antiques with considerable fidelity. In England, from approximately 1880 and certainly at least up until 1914, a con-siderable market grew up for reproductions of English eighteenth-century furniture, and some of these were copied so accurately that it is now very difficult for anyone other than an expert to tell that such pieces are not genuine.

At the upper end of the market, firms like Gillows made so-called Chippendale, Adam, or Sheraton furniture which followed the originals very closely, and in which the standard of craftsmanship was equally high. Indeed this firm had in any case made many of the originals themselves during the eighteenth century (as they pointed out in their catalogues) and their productions might therefore be claimed not even to be copies! Even such a progressive firm as Morris & Company, could turn out furniture in a completely eighteenth-century style, and the bergère chair designed for them by George Jack round about 1895 followed late eighteenth-century precedent so closely as to be indis-tinguishable at first glance from its model. It is also apparent that the snob element in-herent in the increasingly popular activity of collecting antique furniture formed part of the rising demand for accurate copies.

A firm like Maples would have a large show-room in which they offered genuine antiques for sale, mingled with their own reproductions.

At the lower levels of the market, the com-mercial copies of English furniture made by English firms were naturally more convincing than those of Continental styles, but a lot of the output at the end of the century had the curious characteristic of increased size com-bined with a reduction in the individual members. This gave so much late nineteenth-century furniture a strangely spindly look, although the detail might be copied from the model with understanding and accuracy.

The same trends were apparent in America at that time, although 'eighteenth century' across the Atlantic was interpreted as Ameri-can Colonial. By 1884 *Cabinet Making and Upholstery* was able to report that 'the making of antiques has become a modern industry'. The Centennial Exhibition held in Phila-delphia in 1876 to commemorate 100 years of American independence may well have helped to promote a nostalgic interest in a specifically American past with such emotive exhibits as 'a New England kitchen', and in 1888 the *Ladies Home Journal* was telling its readers that 'nice old-fashioned chairs . . . make a parlor look very cosy and old-time'; the centre of the American furniture industry in Grand Rapids soon responded to the demand, and, for instance, Barnard & Simonds of Rochester advertised in the *Grand Rapids Furniture Record* in 1902: 'Furniture of our Forefathers — Colonial Reproduction Chairs'.

Left: Robert W Edis' influential Decoration and Furniture of Town Houses, first published in 1881, contained numerous engraved plates showing suggestions for furnishings. Most of these were either in the neo-Renaissance or Arts and Crafts styles, but, prophetically, there were also two plates of eighteenth century revival pieces of the type that became increasingly popular as the nineteenth century drew to its close. This view shows the 'Adams Style' boudoir, decorated by Gillows, for the Princess of Wales' Pavilion in the 'Street of Nations' at the Paris Exhibition of 1878.

Above right: By the start of the twentieth century, and at the upper end of the market, many firms were making reproductions of antique furniture of a very high standard. Gillows offered a large selection of copies from many periods, with especial emphasis on the French and English eighteenth-century styles.

Right: At the lower end of the furniture market, commercial production and a less discerning clientele resulted in the end-products often falling far short of the intention. This plate from Sadgrove's catalogue of 1904 shows a typical commercial interpretation of the mid-eighteenth century style, but it could never be mistaken for the genuine article.

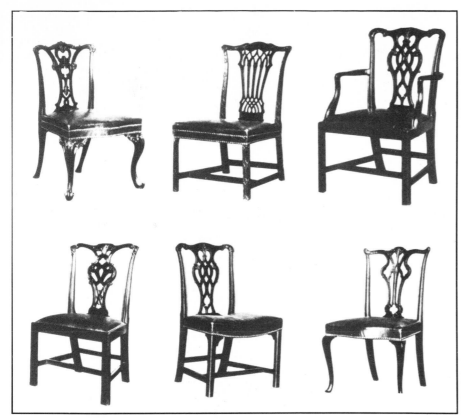

By the turn of the century, some firms were even turning out more or less accurate copies of American Empire pieces of the 1830s.

Germany experienced a Biedermeier revival in the last years of the nineteenth century which lasted into the 1920s. Nevertheless, although much use was made of the blond woods and contrasted ebonizing that was such a characteristic Biedermeier feature, and the pieces themselves exhibited a classical severity, the wholesale copying of actual antiques was not nearly as widespread as was the current practice in England or America.

The Munich architects H Helbig and C Haiger designed some furniture between 1898 and 1900 which was almost a neo-Biedermeier pastiche, and even Peter Behrens (a darling of the Modern Movement) produced similar imitations in 1908. In 1913, another architect, Gustav Halmhuber, produced designs for furniture in a neo-German Empire style, reminiscent of the work of Thouret, Raab or von Klenze of 80 years earlier.

In all the German-speaking countries, however, the influence of manufacturing and design associations like the Deutscher Werkbund and the Wiener Werkstätte had, from 1900 or so, begun to turn the course of general

CHIPPENDALE LIBRARY

233

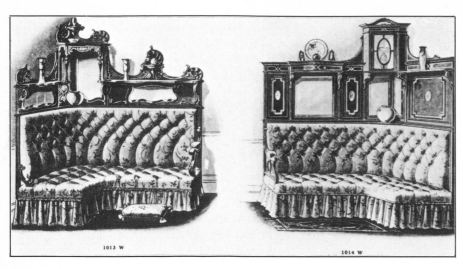

Above: Maple & Company always provided solid and restrained taste, and their catalogues are an essential source of information. In about 1910 they were offering 'cosy corners' in the fashionable neo-Adam style, together with the still popular Louis Quinze.

Right: The neo-Renaissance furnishings, the rich upholstery and the 'informal' arrangement of this interior painted by Solomon J Solomon in 1884, all create a fascinating evocation of the atmosphere of a prosperous middle-class English home towards the end of the nineteenth century. Display, elaboration, possessions, culture, comfort, all appealed strongly to a predominantly bourgeois society, and their various expressions made up the nineteenth-century style. (Leighton House, London)

taste towards a spare, rectangular style which, whilst it had little similarity to Art Nouveau, owed hardly more to nationalistic revivalism. It was a style which was later to be brilliantly exploited by the great French designers of the 1920s and 1930s like Ruhlmann and Leleu, but which was hardly appreciated outside Germany before 1918.

A curious side-effect of nationalism took place in several of the European countries that had a strong tradition of agrarian culture however, and this was a revival of self-consciously 'peasant' styles of furniture. The main features were a wilfully 'primitive' construction, allied to a lavish use of fairly historically accurate, naïve carved and painted ornament, and the principal period of inspiration was usually the late seventeenth century and the eighteenth century. A few such pieces, expressing a highly sophisticated unsophistication had made their appearance in some of the Germanic states as early as the 1850s, but it was not really until the 1880s that the work of designers like J A Malmström in Sweden or Shutov in Russia came to be much appreciated; certainly in Russia this kind of rather self-conscious primitivism had a considerable success.

In certain areas of central Europe peasant furniture had never ceased to be made in accordance with traditional practice until well into the twentieth century, and it was therefore easy for the Hungarians Róberttöl Nádler or Lajos Kosma to take up the tradition where true peasant craftsmen were already abandoning it at the turn of the century. It is an interesting insight into late nineteenth-century trends to realize that such pieces would have been considered to be beneath the notice of an educated clientele until the basic peasant tradition which had produced them was dying, and that the social changes of the nineteenth century seem eventually to have brought a total reversal of aesthetic intention, which has remained with us until the present day.

234

THE REBIRTH OF DESIGN
Arts and Crafts and Art Nouveau

The later part of the nineteenth century saw a succession of attempts to revitalize the applied arts. While the established furniture manufacturers produced their pastiches of traditional or exotic styles, a small number of innovators in both Europe and America tried to break free from bourgeois taste.

In historical terms, Art Nouveau was but one conclusion to the search for originality, unity and moral authority which had begun with designers and theorists such as A W N Pugin in England and Viollet-le-Duc in France during the 1840s. Pugin (1812–1852), the prime mover in the development of a progressive Gothic style in English architecture and design, was aware of the damaging results of uncontrolled mass-production on aesthetics and it was his aim, and the aim of those who followed, to harness the intellectual and material resources of the times to the service of art.

The Aesthetic Movement
Throughout the nineteenth century in England, there were two parallel streams of production and theory. The development of industrial methods caused the mass-production of furniture, metalwork and ceramics in styles borrowed from the past and often debased. As early as 1841, Pugin, in one of his major polemics, *The True Principles of Christian or Pointed Architecture*, could refer in tones of deep disgust to 'those inexhaustible mines of bad taste, Birmingham and Sheffield'.

Six years after this book was written, Henry Cole (1808–1882), using the pseudonym Felix Summerly, founded the firm of Summerly's Art Manufactures, which survived until 1851. During the time this existed, Cole gathered round him a group of men who were to preach the gospel of 'Fitness for Purpose'. This group included Richard Redgrave, Matthew Digby Wyatt, Owen Jones and Ralph Wornum; their aim was, as Cole wrote later in his autobiography:
'To revive the good old practice of connecting the best art with familiar objects in daily use. In doing this, Art Manufactures will aim to produce in each article superior utility, which is not to be sacrificed to ornament; to select pure forms; to decorate each article with appropriate details relating to its use and to obtain these details as directly as possible from nature.'

This view was propounded in the magazine founded by Cole in 1849, *Journal of Design and Manufacture,* which ran until 1852 and in several books written by his circle following the commercially successful but aesthetically disastrous Great Exhibition of 1851. Of this event, Owen Jones remarked in his *Lectures on the Results of the Great Exhibition:*
'No unity; the architect, the upholsterer, the

paperstainer, the weaver, the calico-printer, and the potter, run each their independent course; each struggles fruitlessly, each produces in art novelty without beauty, or beauty without intelligence.'

In his *Manual of Design*, published in 1876, Richard Redgrave put it thus:
'The design for a work must have regard to construction, and consequently to proper use of materials ... *Utility* must have precedence of decoration.'

Thus, the basic principles behind the movements of the last two decades of the nineteenth century were firmly laid in the 1850s. We recognize instantly the sources of their belief, when William Morris, for example, wrote in 1880, 'Have nothing in your house that you do not know to be useful or believe to be beautiful', or when Ford Madox Hueffer described his father's work in the Arts and Crafts Exhibition Society catalogue produced in 1896: 'Adaptation to need, solidity, a kind of homely beauty and above all absolute dissociation from all false display, veneering and the like. . . .'

Any discussion of new design in English

Left: Pugin's talent is perhaps best expressed in the consistency which unified every part of his work. In the library of the House of Lords at the Palace of Westminster, where he collaborated with Charles Barry between 1844 and 1852, his furniture is exactly matched by the panelling, the bookcases, the ceiling, and even the carpet pattern, to produce that totality which is the peculiar characteristic of a masterpiece. (Palace of Westminster, House of Lords)

238

furniture in the latter part of the nineteenth century must, therefore, go back to Pugin and the Gothic revival. Of course, 'gothick' had been an obvious feature of English design from the mid-eighteenth century but the Gothic of Pugin, Burges and others differed from this earlier manifestation by virtue of its truth to archaeological sources. Victorian progressive Gothic designers did not seek to romanticize their design but to use its best features as essential points of reference. This can be seen by comparing A W N Pugin's book *Gothic Furniture* of 1835 with the work of the same title by his father Augustus Charles Pugin, published in 1820. Pugin's most famous group of furniture was made for the House of Lords in the 1840s in collaboration with the architect of the new Palace of Westminster, Charles Barry. A recent report by the Victoria & Albert Museum, London, says:

'Pugin's greatest involvement was from 1844 onwards in the design of every aspect of the interior decoration and furnishing. During the next eight years, Pugin literally worked himself to death, providing designs for the entire internal decoration and all the furniture of major importance. It was Pugin's labours and attention to the smallest details of ornament that gave the tremendous sense of unity to the interior of the Palace, and at the same time gave each area its distinctive character and each room its particular status.'

There is a great contrast between the sturdy, beautifully functional oak furniture of the House of Lords and Romantic Gothick, of which Pugin himself had once been a disciple. In *The True Principles* he wrote:

'. . . your modern man designs a sofa or occasional table from details culled out of Britton's Cathedrals, and all the ordinary articles of furniture, which require to be simple and convenient, are made not only very expensive but very uneasy. We find diminutive flying buttresses about an armchair; everything is crocheted with angular projections, innumerable mitres, sharp ornaments, and turreted extremities. A man who remains any length of time in a modern Gothic room, and escapes without being wounded by some of its minutiae, may consider himself extremely fortunate . . . I have perpetrated many of these enormities in the furniture I designed some years ago for Windsor Castle.'

The majority of the House of Lords furniture was made by the two leading firms of commercial cabinet-makers, Holland & Sons of Mount Street and Gillow's of Oxford Street. Other pieces, including some of the most important, were made in the workshops of John Webb and Johnstone & Jeanes, both of Bond Street.

Pugin's furniture had considerable influence on English design in the mid-century. His sons, E W Pugin (1834–1875) and Peter Paul Pugin (1851–1904) produced somewhat watered-down pieces based on their father's style. The architect G E Street designed some spectacular pieces for Holland & Sons in the 1860s, and also taught many of the later Gothic designers, who in turn taught the leading members of the Arts and Crafts movement. Another designer, Charles Bevan, was employed by the firm of Marsh & Jones, later Marsh, Jones & Cribb, for whom he designed fine Gothic furniture with inlaid geometric decoration, a typical feature of High Victorian Gothic. The architect William Butterfield designed a small amount of domestic furniture in the Gothic style in the 1850s, usually in walnut inlaid with ebony and sycamore.

In the 1860s, however, there was a revolt against Pugin's ideas and his use of commercial firms. The leader of this counter-movement was William Morris. It would be specious, however, to suggest that the various ideas and motives current at the time are necessarily easy to differentiate or indeed that the matter was in the least clear-cut. For side by side with Morris was the Art Furniture movement, which was itself a reaction, however partial, against Pugin but which departed from Morris's ideas on many points. And

Left: Carved, painted and gilt oak washstand designed by William Burges. Made for the Guest Chamber of the Tower House, Melbury Road, London, this piece is signed and dated 1880. The top, bowl and soap dishes are of marble, the back is inset with small mirrors and the taps and fittings are of bronze. (Victoria & Albert Museum, London)

239

somewhere in the middle is the figure of William Burges, who would appear to have had some sympathy with everybody's point of view, but who managed to remain idiosyncratic and unrestricted by any particular movement.

Like most of the leading nineteenth-century furniture designers, Burges was trained as an architect. He had been a pupil of Matthew Digby Wyatt, from whom he would have imbibed many of the principles of the Cole circle, although there is little evidence that they made any great impact on him. He designed many small churches in the thirteenth-century style and the interiors

and furnishings of Cardiff Castle and Castell Coch for the Marquis of Bute, who lavished a vast fortune on these two projects. Burges also designed some remarkable furniture for his own house in Melbury Road, London, which he built between 1875 and 1881 as 'a model residence of the fifteenth century'. Some of the pieces for this house are similar to the ornate painted furniture produced by Morris & Company in the 1860s; the most remarkable of the Burges pieces is the bookcase, now in the Ashmolean Museum, Oxford, executed in 1862 and decorated with painted panels by Edward Poynter, Edward Burne-Jones, Simeon Solomon, Thomas Morten, N H J Westlake, W F Yeames, Henry Holliday, Albert Moore, J A Fitzgerald, Frederick Walker and H Stacy Marks. Burges differs from Morris in the strictly archaeological nature of his designs and in his use of commercial manufacturers. None of his designs was marketed commercially, however, and he did lay strong emphasis on craftsmanship.

Burges was also one of the earliest designers in England to appreciate the qualities of Japanese art, drawing a parallel between the honesty of Japanese craftsmanship and that which existed in Europe in the Middle Ages. In much of his work, Japanese motifs mingle with Gothic and Burges forms a natural link between the traditional Western style of Victorian Gothic and the new aesthetics of 'Japonisme'.

The 1860s, then, saw the development of two concomitant approaches to the design and production of furniture and, indeed, to the applied arts in general. The Art Furniture movement developed out of the Gothicism of the 1840s and 1850s and out of the philosophic and practical concerns of Sir Henry Cole and his circle. William Morris, however, took another path, that of a return to a mediaeval idea of individual craftsmanship, although towards the end of his life he recognized the futility of trying to ignore the existence of machinery in the machine age. From the Art Furniture movement developed the Aesthetic movement and from Morris's socialist idealism, the Arts and Crafts movement.

The Art Furniture movement grew naturally out of the philosophy of Henry Cole. It saw the birth of a new breed of artist, the freelance industrial designer. The most famous of these were Bruce Talbert (1838–1881) and Christopher Dresser (1834–1904). Talbert trained as an architect but in 1862 began designing furniture for Doveston, Bird & Hull of Manchester; in later years, he designed for many of the leading commercial manufacturers, including Collinson & Lock, G S Lucraft & Son, Holland & Son, Marsh, Jones & Cribb and Jackson & Graham. Although evidence is lacking, it seems likely that the group of furniture supplied by

Gillow's to Bradford Town Hall in 1873 is based on Talbert's designs.

In 1867, Talbert wrote *Gothic Forms applied to Furniture* and followed this seven years later with *Examples of Ancient and Modern Furniture, Tapestries and Decoration*. Like the other leading designers of the Art Furniture movement, Talbert's training in the Victorian Gothic school of architecture was to affect even his most original designs.

Perhaps the most influential critic of this period was Charles Eastlake, whose book *Hints on Household Taste* of 1868 caused a design revolution. He was the first to use the term 'Art Furniture' although, ironically, no piece actually designed by him is known. His ideas for furniture, as seen in his often reprinted work, are in fact more than a little dull. The designer J Moyr Smith, himself a distinctly minor figure, wrote in his *Ornamental Interiors* of 1887 that Eastlake's furniture was 'in construction too much like a packing case'.

The furniture which we would now associate most immediately with the Art Furniture movement is usually of a dark wood, either black or ebonized baywood, basswood or walnut. It has painted decoration and a fair quantity of gilding and brass fittings. The

best known firm of commercial manufacturers was Collinson & Lock. This type of furniture was produced in massive quantities throughout the 1870s and 1880s and, as Charles Handley Read pointed out, was largely inspired by the extraordinary cabinet, now in the Victoria & Albert Museum which was designed by the architect T E Collcutt for Collinson & Lock. The eclecticism of the Art Furniture movement is revealed in this piece which betrays Gothic, Japanese, Renaissance and Queen Anne influences but which is nevertheless the first example of an entirely new approach to furniture design in the nineteenth century. It is all the more remarkable for the break it marks with Collcutt's earlier furniture; designed in 1871, this piece is in total contrast to the simple oak furniture which, under the influence of Philip Webb and Bruce Talbert, Collcutt had been designing in the previous years.

The Art Furniture movement produced one furniture designer of outstanding genius, William Godwin (1833–1886). Like Christopher Dresser, Godwin had been one of the first to appreciate the functional, architectonic qualities of Japanese design. Throughout the late 1860s and 1870s, he produced one of the most consistent and convincing bodies of

Left: Oak wardrobe designed by Philip Webb and painted by Edward Burne-Jones with scenes from Chaucer's Prioress's Tale. This was Burne-Jones's first completed oil painting, the piece being made from 1858 to 1859 as a wedding present for William Morris. (Victoria & Albert Museum, London)

work of any major designer of this period. His most famous piece remains the ebonized buffet of 1867, which was re-made commercially by the firm of William Watt in 1877. The latter pieces were inset with embossed Japanese leather paper first imported by Liberty's in 1876; the angular design of this piece marks a total and radical break with hitherto accepted European styles.

Godwin designed for a number of firms. He collaborated with Whistler on William Watt's stand for the Paris Universal Exhibition of 1878; the previous year he had designed Whistler's house in Tite Street, Chelsea, and the pieces for Watt were painted with a theme by Whistler called, characteristically, 'Butterfly Suit, Harmony in Yellow and Gold'. He had designed the so-called 'Greek' chair for Watt in 1875 and in 1877 he designed a 'Jacobean' chair for the firm of Collier & Plunckett of Warwick, England. One of his earliest domestic commissions was for the furniture of Dromore Castle, County Limerick, which was designed and built between 1867 and 1869. Godwin's chairs are in oiled wainscot oak with natural calf upholstery; they were made by Godwin's own Art Furniture Company, the first organization of its kind. Apart from the firms already mentioned, Godwin designed for Gillow's, Green & King, W A Smee and Collinson & Lock. Many of his later pieces, as Elizabeth Aslin remarked, were in 'mahogany also ebonized and decorated with a few gold lines in the panels'.

Thomas Jeckyll (1827–1881) was also an Aesthetic movement designer of great individuality. He favoured padouk wood and walnut for his furniture and designed some superb cast-iron and brass for the Norwich firm of Barnard, Bishop & Barnard. The two projects with which Jeckyll was connected which have brought him lasting fame were the woodwork for Whistler's Peacock Room, designed for F R Leyland in 1877, the epitome of rich, decorative 'Japonisme', and the furniture for the London house of Alexander Alexander Ionides, one of the leading patrons of the Aesthetic movement. Jeckyll's metalwork shows that he had absorbed the decorative aspects of Japanese design. Some of the roundels in the brass and iron fireplaces closely resemble tsuba (sword-guards). An earlier commission than the two previously mentioned, the furniture for Heath Old Hall, Wakefield, designed and executed from 1866 to 1870, shows that, even at this early date, Jeckyll was using Japanese patterns in relief on furniture of fairly traditional shape.

William Morris and the Arts and Crafts Movement

The firm of Morris, Marshall, Faulkner & Company was founded in 1861. William Morris (1834–1896) had been articled to the architect

G E Street in 1855, where he met Philip Webb (1831–1915), who was to become one of the most important designers for Morris's firm. Prior to entering Street's practice, Morris had been at Exeter College, Oxford, where he had met another significant figure in the history of the firm, Edward Burne-Jones (1833–1898). Through this latter friendship, Morris was brought into contact with two leading members of the Pre-Raphaelite Brotherhood, Dante Gabriel Rossetti and William Holman Hunt.

In essence, Morris's ideas about the quality of design, and his philosophy of improvement, were not much different from those of other leading Victorian figures. He defined two types of furniture, one being 'necessary . . . workaday . . . simple to the last degree' and the other 'state furniture . . . sideboards, cabinets and the like . . . as elegant and elaborate as we can with carving or inlaying or painting'.

Morris's firm first showed its work publicly at the International Exhibition in London in 1862. The pieces exhibited fell into Morris's second category — extraordinary, elaborate, richly painted objects. The King Renée Cabinet, designed by the Gothic architect

Above: Walnut cabinet designed by William Godwin in 1876 for his own use. The four panels of carved boxwood inset into the upright drawers, and the ivory handles, are of Japanese workmanship and were probably purchased by Godwin from Liberty's. (Victoria & Albert Museum, London)

J P Seddon, was painted with imaginary scenes of *The Honeymoon of King Renée*, based on Walter Scott's *Anna von Geierstein*. The artists who undertook this scheme were Ford Madox Brown, Edward Burne-Jones, Dante Gabriel Rossetti and William Morris himself (Morris, it should be emphasized, is not known to have actually designed any furniture). In 1858, Burne-Jones painted the Chaucer cabinet with scenes from *The Prioress's Tale* and in 1861, two further examples, the Chess Player Cabinet and The Saint George Cabinet, the latter painted by Morris, were made by the firm.

Other pieces produced at this early date are more in keeping with the simple idealism which lay behind Morris's socialist principles. As early as 1857, Holman Hunt had made a simple oak table. He designed pieces for the firm in plain shapes, and is credited with the introduction of a green stain which was the sole decoration used on oak tables designed by Philip Webb. Webb also designed the so-called 'Morris' chairs, simple pieces based on rush-seated Sussex chairs.

A report on the Manchester Jubilee Exhibition of 1887 remarked with reference to Morris & Company '. . . it requires a long purse to live up to the higher phases of Morrisean taste . . . .' This comment was certainly true of many of the firm's productions; in general, their clients were drawn from the aristocracy and the rich merchant classes; between 1868 and 1890 they undertook decorative schemes at St James's Palace, at 1 Palace Green for the Earl of Carlisle, at 1 Holland Park for Alexander Alexander Ionides, at Rounton Grange, Northallerton for Sir Lowthian Bell, at Clouds, East Knoyle for the Hon. Percy Scawne Wyndham and at Stanmore Hall for W D'Arcy. Sadly, none of these interiors has survived, but the list makes the point that while Morris may have preached the doctrine of art for everyone, the practical consequence of his idealistic revolt against the machine age was that none but the very rich could afford his work, and, except for the well-educated upper classes, few could appreciate his lofty aestheticism.

The firm began production in 1862 at 8 Red Lion Square, London, moving in 1865 to 26 Queen Square. In 1875, the firm's name was changed to Morris & Company, and two years later showrooms were opened in Oxford Street. In 1881, the workshops were transferred to Merton Abbey, and in 1890, the Pimlico cabinet-making workshops of Holland & Company were taken over. In 1890, George Jack, who had entered Philip Webb's architectural practice in 1880, became chief furniture designer and in 1896, following Morris's death, the designer William A S Benson, who with Morris's encouragement had set up his own workshop in Hammersmith to produce metalwork, became chairman of the firm. Another designer, Mervyn McCartney, produced work for Morris & Company at this time, reverting to eighteenth-century taste. The later pieces were decorated with elaborate marquetry and employed a variety of woods.

Under Morris's influence, the 1880s and 1890s saw the founding of numerous craft guilds and small private bodies dedicated to hand-built furniture and artifacts. One of the first of these was the Century Guild, founded in 1882 by A H Mackmurdo (1851–1942). Typically, it announced its aim as being 'to render all branches of the arts the sphere no longer of the tradesman but of the artist. It would restore building, decoration, glass-painting, pottery, wood-carving and metal to their right place beside painting and sculpture.' Although neither Mackmurdo himself, nor any of the other designers associated with this venture, notably Selwyn Image, Herbert Percy Horne or Clement J Heaton, ever claimed allegiance to that movement which 18 years after the founding of the Guild was to become known as Art Nouveau, at least one of their contemporaries, the designer Reginald Blomfield, pointed out in the *Magazine of Art* of 1904 that many of the stylistic roots could be found in the Century Guild's work: '. . . it [Art Nouveau] started in England some 20 years ago, with the ingenious experiments of

Left: Cabinet in rosewood inlaid with purplewood and ebony, with light metal ('oldsilver') mounts designed by William A S Benson and made by Morris & Company after 1896. Although superbly made, the ornateness and commercialism of this piece is in contrast to the Morris ethos. (Victoria & Albert Museum, London)

Right: William Morris's bedroom, Kelmscott Manor, Oxfordshire. The ornate mediaevalism of this interior typifies Morris's approach to art and design. The bed is sixteenth century, but the embroidery is by Janey and May Morris. The curtains are 'Vine' pattern and the wallpaper 'Willow', both first produced in 1874. (Kelmscott Manor, Oxfordshire)

Right: Oak writing-desk with pierced copper hinges designed by C F A Voysey in 1896 and made by W H Tingey. One of several pieces of furniture designed by Voysey for W Ward Higgs between 1896 and 1900. The plain functionalism of the woodwork is in contrast to the ornate metal mounts, a consistent feature of Voysey's furniture. (Victoria & Albert Museum, London)

Below right: Dining-chair in mahogany designed by Mackmurdo for the Century Guild from 1882 to 1883 and made by Collinson & Lock. Apart from the fretwork back, the design of this chair is unremarkable. The back itself looks forward to the swirling, linear style of Art Nouveau. (William Morris Gallery, Walthamstow)

two young architects [Mackmurdo and Horne] with an uncommon share of eccentric ability, who for the first time revealed the numerous possibilities of the "swirl" and the "blob".' Certainly the famous title page of *Wren's City Churches*, or the equally extraordinary chair-back of approximately the same date are prophetic of the 'whiplash' style prevalent on the Continent a few years later but never fully developed in England.

In general, Mackmurdo's significance in nineteenth-century design is a result of his progressive attitude to the aesthetics of his day, rather than to any particular brilliance as a designer. Most of his furniture, in satinwood decorated with inlay, with carved ornament by Herbert Horne, painted panels by Selwyn Image, and hinges by Bernard Creswick, was made by the two firms of Goodall & Company of Manchester and Wilkinson's of Bond Street. Mackmurdo sought his inspiration in past styles, predominantly those of the Italian Renaissance and Queen Anne. His founding of the Century Guild in 1882 was followed by commissions to design a music-room for the International Health Exhibition of 1884, and for a stand with furniture for a firm of tobacco importers, Cope Bros, at the Liverpool International Exhibition of 1886. In 1887, he designed the entrance hall for the Manchester Jubilee

Exhibition, at the same time decorating the interior of Pownell Hall, Cheshire, for Henry Boddington. He also designed wallpapers for Jeffry's and fabrics for Wardle's.

The Queen Anne style had been popularized in the 1860s by the architect Richard Norman Shaw who had been a pupil of G E Street. Shaw designed Gothic furniture in the early 1860s, and had later become a very successful architect as well as a designer of fabrics and wallpapers for a number of different firms. Shaw's most famous piece of furniture, indeed the only one that can be attributed to him with absolute certainty and a landmark in the development of nineteenth-century Gothic, is a combined writing-desk and book-case which he designed in 1861 and which was executed for him by the sculptor James Forsyth.

As we said earlier, the founding of the Century Guild in 1882 was the first of many such events, which attempted to perpetuate the spirit of William Morris and John Ruskin. In 1883, pupils of Norman Shaw founded the St George's Art Guild, followed in 1884 by the founding of the Art Workers' Guild and in 1886 by the Art Workers' Guild of Liverpool. In 1888, the same year as the Arts and Crafts Exhibition Society showed its members' work for the first time, the most famous of these groups, the Guild of Handicrafts, was founded by C R Ashbee.

The best known and most gifted designer connected with the Art Workers' Guild was Charles Francis Annesley Voysey (1857–1941). Not surprisingly, he had, like most of his contemporaries, been articled to a Gothic architect, in his case J P Seddon. He had set up his own practice, and with the advice of his friend, Mackmurdo, designed wallpapers and fabrics. In 1884, he was a founder member of the Art Workers' Guild. It is important to emphasize that Mackmurdo remained the greatest single influence on his style, and, like Mackmurdo, Voysey is considered one of the English designers who pioneered that style which became known internationally as Art Nouveau. His own attitude to this distinction remained ambivalent. He wrote in the *Magazine of Art* in 1904: 'I think the condition which has made Art Nouveau possible is a distinctly healthy development, but at the same time the manifestation of it is distinctly unhealthy and revolting.'

Voysey's wallpapers, such as *Cereus* (1886), *Water Snake* (c.1890), *Deer and Trees* (1908), and chintz patterns such as *Trees and Birds* (1895), were obviously close in feel, though flatter and more decorative, to those of William Morris. They were known widely, as were Voysey's architecture and designs for furniture and metalwork, in the rest of Europe and the United States, having con-

siderable influence on many designers. His furniture and metalwork, the former usually of oak and the latter of copper and brass, display a similar use of light, sinuous shapes, particularly tree and heart motifs. Voysey was opposed totally to the somewhat drab aspects of the Aesthetic movement, combining his use of delicate motifs with an airy functionalism considerably before its time.

The Guild of Handicrafts, founded by Charles Robert Ashbee in 1888 with a capital of £50, was the organization which was, and remained, truest to Morris's ideals of honest workmen producing honest work by hand, to the spiritual and physical well-being of the community. In 1890, the Guild leased 'Essex House' in London's East End and in 1902 moved to the village of Chipping Campden in the Cotswolds, a move which many other craftsmen followed and which makes this area of Gloucestershire still active today in many branches of the applied arts. The Guild itself went into voluntary liquidation in 1908, although many of the craftsmen carried on working independently, and produced metal-work based on Ashbee's designs until well into the 1930s.

The Guild's most famous product was unquestionably metalwork, more specifically silver. It did produce some furniture, in a somewhat Gothic English-country-furniture-

via-William Morris style. The principal cabinet-maker employed by the Guild was J W Pyment, and much of the furniture is decorated with embossed leatherwork by Statia Power. More important was the group of pieces the Guild made to the designs of Mackay Hugh Baillie Scott. Baillie Scott had been active as an architect and interior designer in the Isle of Man since 1887, having previously been articled to an architect. In 1898, he was commissioned to furnish the interior of the Grand Duke of Hesse's Palace at Darmstadt, one of the focal points of the Art Nouveau movement in northern Europe, and the most important commission received by any English designer of this period. In terms of his reputation, it placed Baillie Scott on a level with Walter Crane, Voysey and Mackintosh as one of those who had most impact on German and Austrian designers. The furniture and metalwork was executed by the Guild of Handicrafts which itself became revered among German designers.

Baillie Scott, like Voysey, is seen as one of the most important English contributors to the Art Nouveau style; furniture designed by Baillie Scott after the Darmstadt commission and made by J P White of the Pygtle Works, Bedford, in mahogany or oak and inlaid with contrasting woods and metals, is certainly closer in the style of its surface decoration to Continental Art Nouveau furniture than most English designs of this period. In collaboration with Broadwood's,

Baillie Scott designed many 'Manx' pianos, small upright pieces, usually with a plain oak case decorated with elaborate and beautifully designed burnished steel and brass fittings.

The influence of the High Victorian Gothic movement was strong in the firm of Kenton & Company which was founded in 1890 by a number of young architects. Ernest Barnsley and Ernest William Gimson had been pupils of John Dando Sedding, and Sidney Barnsley and Alfred Powell had been pupils of Richard Norman Shaw, while William Richard Lethaby had been principal assistant in Shaw's office. Both Sedding and Shaw were, like Philip Webb and William Morris, pupils of G E Street. These four, together with Mervyn McCartney and Reginald Blomfield, formed Kenton & Company, each putting up £100. They employed four craftsmen but despite producing some splendid pieces, the venture failed in 1892. Lethaby became, with the sculptor George Frampton, first principal of the London County Council Central School of Arts. Gimson and the Barnsleys moved to the Cotswolds. After this move, Sidney Barnsley concentrated mainly on furniture, while Gimson and Ernest Barnsley practised architecture on a wider scale than previously. Nevertheless, Gimson set up a small furniture workshop in Cirencester, which moved to Daneway House, Sapperton, in 1902. Sidney Barnsley designed and made all his own furniture, in a strong rustic style which usually used oak. Gimson designed his pieces only, the manufacture being left to skilled craftsmen, one of whom, Peter Waals, became a cabinet-maker in his own right. Gimson used a variety of rich woods, veneers and inlays. Lethaby's furniture was similar to that of Sidney Barnsley, in oak and firmly rooted in the Arts and Crafts tradition. McCartney and Blomfield were inspired by the eighteenth century, using rosewood and mahogany.

One of the most obvious features of Gimson's furniture is its stylishness, the combination of a beautifully modulated use of form with rich and glowing woods and metal mounts often in silver. In the designs of Charles Rennie Mackintosh (1868–1928), we have the same approach to style, although the use of materials does not play an important part in the work of the Scottish designer, the form always speaking for itself.

Mies van der Rohe described Mackintosh as 'a purifier in the field of architecture', and the influential Art Nouveau dealer and critic Julius Meier-Graefe, in his book *Modern Art* published in 1908, described Mackintosh's

interiors as 'intellectual chambers garnished for fair souls not for corporeal habitation'. Both descriptions are true; Mackintosh's use of space, incorporating white furniture embellished with sculptural decoration, sinuous lines and inset with panels of pale enamels or stained glass are at once ethereal and functionalist. One uses that last word advisedly for although Mackintosh's work does make a total break with previous design in England, and looks forward to a modern mode of light colours and clean lines, the furniture is frequently by no means 'functional'. It is often poorly made and should be considered more as sculpture.

Mackintosh studied at the Glasgow School of Art under Francis H Newbery. Fellow pupils included Herbert MacNair and the sisters Margaret and Frances Macdonald. Frances married MacNair and in 1900 Margaret married Mackintosh. Mackintosh's early career was remarkably successful. In 1889 he entered the architectural firm of Honeyman & Keppie; in 1896 this firm (although all the designs and plans were Mackintosh's work) won the commission for the new Glasgow School of Art. This magnificent building, unquestionably Mackintosh's finest work, was completed in 1909. In 1897, the designer received the first of his many commissions from Miss Kate Cranston (Mrs John Cochrane) for the decoration of the tearooms in Buchanan Street, Glasgow, the furniture being designed in this instance by George Walton. This was followed in 1901 by the commission to design the interior and furniture for the Ingram Street tearooms, and in 1904 by a similar commission for the Willow tearooms, the last of which was perhaps the most successful of these decorative interiors. From 1902 to 1903, Mackintosh designed and furnished Hill House, Hellensburgh, for Walter W Blackie, the publisher, to whom he had been introduced by Talwin Morris, art director of Blackie's firm and himself the designer of some interesting metalwork in the Mackintosh style. Other important commissions for private houses included Windyhill, Kilmacolm, in 1899, and between 1904 and 1906 the interior of Hous'hill, Nitshill, Glasgow, the home of Miss Cranston. In 1916 and 1917 Mackintosh executed his last important commission, the Bassett-Lowke House in Northampton, but after about 1905 he was ignored by the public and his work was virtually forgotten in Britain.

In his day, Mackintosh's reputation probably stood higher in Germany than it did in his own country. His work was shown widely throughout Europe in the years around 1900, including Vienna in 1900, Turin in 1902, Budapest, Munich, Dresden, Venice and, in 1903, Moscow in an exhibition organized by Sergei Diaghilev. In 1901, he entered the

Left: Upright cabinet in dark stained oak, with stained glass and mother-of-pearl insets, designed by Charles Rennie Mackintosh in about 1905. The geometric quality of the Scottish designer's furniture was the one feature which impressed designers in Austria and Germany.

exhibition organized by Zeitschrift für Innen-Dekoration of Darmstadt, called Haus eines Kunstfreunds. As a result, Mackintosh's work had a considerable influence upon many of the leading northern European designers and architects, including Hoffmann, Olbrich and Behrens in Germany and Austria, the De Stijl group in Holland, and Frank Lloyd Wright in the United States. His style contrasts with the hot, florid forms of French Art Nouveau, but is nevertheless an important part of that movement, rooted in symbolism, which the Germans called Jugendstil.

Most of Mackintosh's furniture is of oak, but some of the later pieces — for instance a table commissioned by W P Douglas in 1912 — were made by the firm of Guthrie & Wells of Glasgow in mahogany. The furniture for the Basset-Lowke House is in both mahogany and ebonized wood, while the fittings for the Glasgow School of Art are in Baltic pine. After 1918, Mackintosh designed some textiles but these were not well received. He also designed carpets for some of his interiors, these being in a style far in advance of its time.

Another leading designer of furniture in Glasgow was George Walton (1867–1903), the brother of the painter, E W Walton. George set up a business as an interior decorator in Glasgow in 1888, and between 1896 and 1897, designed the furniture of Miss Cranston's Buchanan Street tearooms, which was followed in 1897 by a commission to design the interior and furnishings for a café belonging to William Rowntree in Scarborough. He designed a number of domestic interiors, opened a branch of his business in York in 1898, and in the same year moved his headquarters to London. In 1897 and 1898, he designed 'Clutha' glass for the Glasgow firm of James Couper & Sons, as did Christopher Dresser. In 1897, he met George Davison, head of the European division of Kodak and designed a chain of Kodak shops throughout Britain, Belgium, Italy and Austria. His furniture, which comes in a variety of woods including walnut, birchwood, mahogany and ash, is simple in style, close to the English Arts and Crafts tradition, but influenced by Mackintosh. Walton also designed some furniture for the London store of Liberty's.

English furniture in the pure Art Nouveau style, with whiplash lines and flowery inlay, is mainly commercial, produced by such

251

firms as Liberty's and J S Henry. E G Punnett designed good quality pieces for these firms as well as for another firm of commercial cabinet-makers, William Birch. Punnett's pieces are in a geometric style derived from Scottish and Austrian examples. The furniture of the Scottish designers E A Taylor and George Logan, usually in mahogany and often inlaid, is again greatly influenced by Mackintosh. In many English pieces of this type, there is a profusion of inlay — marquetry panels, pewter, mother-of-pearl, enamel, stained glass, and repoussé copper panels. Although some of it is extremely elegant and of fine quality, the majority is obviously of cheap manufacture in a much debased style. Liberty's, which had been founded by Arthur Lasenby Liberty in 1875, commissioned a number of outstanding designers including George Walton, Lindsay Butterfield, Walter Crane, Voysey and Archibald Knox. Their furniture, of which the most famous example is probably the Thebes stool, based on an Egyptian original and first marketed in 1884, is, however, not of the same high level of artistic excellence as their metalwork and fabrics. Ambrose Heal, a member of the Heal furnishing family, designed some excellent

pieces with inlaid metal and wood of contrasting colours.

New Design in the United States
In the United States of America, the development of new design at the end of the nineteenth century followed the same stylistic paths as

Above: Glazed cabinet in satinwood by Liberty & Company. Although the designer of this elegant piece is not known, it reflects, together with a table and three chairs en suite, the influence of a 'Cabinet in walnut glazed with clear bent glass' designed by George Walton and illustrated in the 1901 Special Summer Number of the 'Studio'. The present piece is dated to about 1905. (Victoria & Albert Museum, London)

in Britain but with considerable chronological elision. Most of the various styles which had taken some 50 years to mature in England and Scotland were telescoped into roughly 20 years between 1890 and 1910 in the United States. The influence in the three predominant areas of progressive aesthetics in America — New England, which for the purposes of this essay is taken to include New York State, the Middle West, and the West Coast — was strongly English, with the protagonists of the Arts and Crafts movement, William Morris, Voysey and Ashbee having the greatest impact. Many of the leading American designers had visited England and some of the foremost English designers, including for instance C R Ashbee and Walter Crane, visited America, and some of them finally settled there.

On the Eastern seaboard, the influence of the Gothic revival and the Aesthetic movement was definite but muted. At least one designer, Isaac Scott, made good pieces in walnut in a style closely based on Pugin's, but this work was done in the 1870s, at a time when it would have been anachronistic in England. More interesting is the work of the Herter Brothers of New York, led by Christian

Herter, and Henry Hobson Richardson, who worked in the same city. The Herter Brothers' pieces are of very fine quality, usually in ebonized cherry wood, with gilding and marquetry inlay. As with similar furniture in England, the Herter Brothers' work shows a deep awareness of Japanese design.

Henry Hobson Richardson's work was influenced by Richard Norman Shaw, Bruce Talbert and Charles Eastlake. He designed good pieces, usually in oak, with an element of Gothic and Queen Anne. After his death, his firm was taken over by Charles A Coolidge who continued in the same style. One of his major commissions was to furnish the Chicago residence of John J Glessner who was also a patron of Isaac Scott. The Coolidge furniture, in oak, was made by the Boston firm of A H Davenport.

Unquestionably, the most important development was the rise of a mature Arts and Crafts school of furniture-makers and craftsmen, a development which followed the founding of the Boston Arts and Crafts Society in 1897. A number of designers are associated with this movement in the Eastern states, the best known of whom are Elbert Hubbard and Gustav Stickley.

Hubbard (1856–1915) started his professional life in the somewhat unpromising capacity of soap salesman. His transition from this occupation to a leading member of the American Arts and Crafts movement was extraordinarily swift, for in 1893 he was a soap salesman and in 1895 he was the publisher of an edition of *The Song of Songs* printed on his own press, modelled on William Morris's Kelmscott press. This was the first work of Hubbard's newly named Roycroft works of East Aurora, New York; needless to say, he had visited England in 1894 and met Morris. The production of books led to that of leather bindings, which in turn led to the foundation of a general workshop for hand-made leather goods, and in 1901, the first furniture was made, mostly in oak, but occasionally in mahogany, and

Left: Walnut and inlaid bookcase designed by Isaac E Scott in 1875. Commissioned by Mr and Mrs John G Glessner of Chicago, this is one of the most impressive American examples of neo-Gothic furniture. Influenced by the English Gothic Revival and by Charles Eastlake it shows none of the provincialism associated with the early arts and crafts movement in the United States. (Chicago School of Architecture Foundation)

stamped with Hubbard's own orb and cross mark.

Hubbard's idea of furniture was that category which Morris termed 'workaday' and 'simple'; Hubbard described his work as 'severe and rarely beautiful' and in the recent exhibition catalogue of the Arts and Crafts movement in America, the designer is referred to as having 'popularized a sincere, if somewhat plebeian, version of the ideals of William Morris'. He employed a number of skilled designers, including David Hunter, who had visited Austria and was impressed by the work being done in Vienna. Hubbard's chief metalwork designer, Karl Kripp, was in fact a Viennese who brought a touch of Austrian austerity to the factory's products in copper, brass and other metals.

Gustav Stickley (1857–1942) must be considered the single most important figure in the development of new approaches to design in the United States. One of six brothers, he, and four of his family, produced good quality furniture in the Arts and Crafts style but more significantly, between 1901 and 1916, he edited the *Craftsman*, the magazine which more than any other propagated the ideas of the Arts and Crafts movement throughout America. Thus Stickley's influence in the Mid-West and on the West Coast was about as strong as it was in his own state of New York.

Trained as a stonemason, Stickley started making furniture with his uncles and other relatives in the 1880s. In 1898, he founded the Gustav Stickley Company in Eastwood, Syracuse, New York; he employed two of his brothers, Leopold and J G Stickley, both of whom left in 1900 and set up a company of their own at nearby Fayetteville making furniture closely based on that of their brother. Through the pages of his magazine, Stickley was the most vocal of all the progressive designers active in the United States. His furniture is almost always of oak, since he felt that this wood was above all others '. . . adapted to the massive simplicity of construction'; most pieces are stamped with the Stickley motto *Als Ik Kan* (All I Can), a suitable mediaeval boast borrowed from Jan van Eyck via William Morris. Stickley was not a good businessman and in 1915 his firm went bankrupt, the *Craftsman* ceasing publication the following year. Ironically, Leopold and J G Stickley showed a greater measure of adaptability to public demand and were in a position to take over their brother's workshops; the re-organized firm was called the Stickley Manufacturing Company Inc., and still exists today.

Surprisingly, the designer who received the most attention outside the United States was Charles Rohlfs. Rohlfs opened a workshop in Buffalo in 1890, employing eight workmen. His style was simple and functional, but the work was of very high quality and, unlike other purist Arts and Crafts designers, he decorated the strong outlines of his oak furniture with delicate carving and marquetry inlays, this work being executed by one of his craftsmen, George Thiele. It has been said that this ornament was largely suggested by Sullivan's exterior decoration for the Buffalo Guaranty Insurance Building. Rohlfs exhibited a substantial quantity of his furniture at the Turin exhibition of 1902; the German, Austrian and English critics were very enthusiastic, and the American was elected a member of the Royal Society of Arts in London. He was also commissioned to provide some furniture for Buckingham Palace. His mark on furniture is an 'R' within the rectangular frame of a wood saw.

Whereas the Arts and Crafts movement in the East faded out during the First World War, that in the Middle West, centred in Chicago, led to one of the most significant architectural movements of the twentieth century, the Prairie School. The reason for this is self-evident. Chicago produced two men of outstanding genius, Louis H Sullivan (1856–1924) and his one-time employee Frank Lloyd Wright (1867–1959), around whom the Prairie School was centred and who gave it impetus and strength. Without Wright, the Arts and Crafts movement in Chicago would probably have suffered the same fate as in New York.

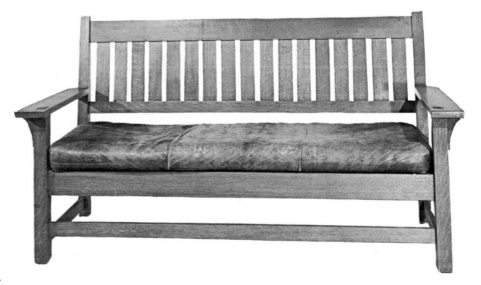

Below: Oak settle with leather cushions designed by Gustav Stickley and made in the Craftsman Workshops, Syracuse, New York, in about 1908. This piece first appeared in Stickley's catalogue of 1909 priced at US $50. It is interesting to compare its uncompromising rectilinearity with the Frank Lloyd Wright library table. Nothing could demonstrate more clearly the lack of real imagination apparent in the majority of East Coast arts and crafts design. (Art Institute of Chicago. Gift of Mr and Mrs John J Evans Jnr)

The period between 1895 and 1905 was an exciting one for designers in the Middle West. In the former year, the Chalk and Chisel Club was founded — later the Minneapolis Arts and Crafts Society — arguably the first organization of its kind in the United States. This was followed by the Chicago Arts and Crafts Society in 1897, the Industrial Art League in 1899, the Society of Arts and Crafts of Grand Rapids, Michigan, in 1902 and the William

Right: Mahogany and
brass long-case clock
designed by George Grant
Elmslie in 1912. Standing
7 feet 4 inches high (nearly
2¼ metres), this is one of
eight pieces commissioned
from the firm of Purcell,
Feick and Elmslie by Henry
B Babson of Riverside,
Chicago. Elmslie had
designed Babson's house in
1907 while working for
Louis Sullivan. The style
of this piece, especially the
finials, is typical of Prairie
School work and is strongly
influenced by Frank
Lloyd Wright. The face-
plate was made and
engraved by Kristian
Schneider and the hands
were made by Robert
Jarvie of Chicago; the
nine-chime movement was
imported from Germany.
(Art Institute of Chicago)

Morris Society of Chicago, which was founded
by an Englishman, Joseph Twyman, in 1903.
Twyman was a critic and apologist for the
English Arts and Crafts movement, lecturing
extensively in Chicago and the Mid-West on
Morris and his followers. Walter Crane
lectured at the Art Institute of Chicago in
1892, and Ashbee visited Chicago twice; in
1911 he wrote the introduction for a volume
of Frank Lloyd Wright's work published in
Germany. A number of Chicagoans visited
England, and fabrics, wallpapers and furniture
by Morris & Company were sold in the major
Chicago department stores.

The style and quality of the Prairie School
was formed in the late 1880s and early 1890s.
The two architects, Louis H Sullivan and
J S Silsbee, taught a number of brilliant
students and employed a young generation of
draughtsmen and designers, which included
Frank Lloyd Wright, George Grant Elmslie,
Louis J Millet, George L Healey and George
Washington Maher. Sullivan had been trained
at the Massachusetts Institute of Technology
(MIT) and the Ecole des Beaux Arts in Paris.
He settled in Chicago in 1875 and formed an
architectural practice with Dankmar Adler.
Louis Sullivan's conception of bold, stylized
ornament as an integral part of his buildings
was to have a profound effect on the young
designers who worked in his office, and through
whom his ideas were carried out. Louis Millet,
who was himself trained at the Ecole des
Beaux Arts, and George Healey were in
partnership from 1881 to 1899, and from 1890
to 1918 Millet was the head of the Decorative
Design department at the Art Institute of
Chicago.

The characteristic which binds together
George Grant Elmslie, George Washington
Maher and Frank Lloyd Wright was just this
conception of the building and its interior as
'proceeding from main motif to minor motifs,
interrelating and to the last terminal all of a
piece' and Frank Lloyd Wright, in a famous
passage from *In the Cause of Architecture* of
1908, wrote: 'The most truly satisfactory
apartments are those in which most of all the
furniture is built as a part of the original
scheme. The whole must always be considered
as an integral unit.' In part, this idea sprang
from the notion of the furniture extending
and reflecting the lines of the building, and
thus emphasizing its essential features but,
especially in the case of Lloyd Wright, the
concept of the structural importance of the
furniture in relation to the whole unit sprang
from a deep love and understanding of
Japanese art and design, which he had seen
for himself when he visited Japan in 1905.

Elmslie was born in Scotland, emigrating
to the United States in 1884. In 1887, he entered
the office of J S Silsbee, where he met Frank
Lloyd Wright and Maher. He moved to the

firm Adler & Sullivan two years later, becoming chief designer in 1895. He opened his own practice in partnership with William Gray Purcell and George Feick in 1909, and after Feick's death in 1913, he and Purcell carried on until 1922. Elmslie did not design furniture for all of his interiors, only for the most important ones. His designs were less rectilinear and geometric than those of Lloyd Wright, his ornament being more organic and closer in style to that of Sullivan. Most of his furniture is in oak, but occasionally he made more elaborate pieces in different woods. In 1907, he designed the Henry B Babson house in Riverside, Illinois, the furniture being simple and in oak. Five years later, however, when he had his own practice, he designed a further group of furniture for the Babson House in mahogany, including the famous long-case 'Grandfather' clock now in the Arts Institute of Chicago. It is interesting to note that Babson also owned furniture by Gustav Stickley.

After a short period in the office of J S Silsbee, George Washington Maher started his own practice in 1888. He travelled to Europe in 1892 and remained there for five years, absorbing the major stylistic movements in England, France, Austria and Germany. On his return to the United States he received a number of important commissions for private residences, the significant characteristic of which was his conception of the interiors based on a single organic theme. His interior for the John Farson house in Oak Park (1897) was based on the theme of the lion, that of the James A Patten House in Evanston (1901) was based on the thistle, while the hollyhock was the theme used for the Harry Rubens house, Glencoe (1902–3). The use of these thematic designs, which extended through the furniture and fabrics used in the house, was one way of achieving that sense of unity the Chicago designers required. In 1908, Maher designed the Ernest Magerstadt house, in which the furniture is more geometric and the organic designs more schematic, showing the influence of Frank Lloyd Wright.

After a period in the office of J S Silsbee, Frank Lloyd Wright became chief draughtsman in the firm of Adler & Sullivan in 1888, remaining in this capacity until 1893. Two of the earliest groups of furniture Lloyd Wright designed were for his own house in 1895 and for the Isidore Heller house in Chicago in about 1897. Between 1897 and 1908, when he built and designed the interiors of two of his greatest works, the Frederick C Robie house and the Ray W Evans house, both in Chicago, Wright moved away from the fluid, organic ornament of Sullivan to a strictly geometric, functional style based on rectangles, slats and flat surfaces. As the Princeton Arts and Crafts catalogue remarked, Lloyd Wright's furniture 'must be regarded as architectural sculpture rather than merely utilitarian objects — a part of a larger sculptural whole'.

Not surprisingly, the West Coast of America was a little behind the mid-West and the Eastern states in its appreciation of the Arts and Crafts movement, and the craftsmen and designers who were its main practitioners in California were active between about 1900 and 1910. It would be true to say that, in the regions we have discussed so far, the English style was predominant — at least initially, but on the West Coast, influences from Chicago and New York were probably more decisive. In 1878, the Herter Brothers of New York had designed the interior of the Mark Hopkins house on Nob Hill, San Francisco, and the firm's representative, Edward F Searles, came to San Francisco, married Hopkins' widow and subsequently donated the house to the University of California, when it became the Mark Hopkins Institute of Art. Irving Gill, who had worked in Sullivan's office, settled in San Diego in 1893, the architect Ellsworth Storey of Chicago came to live in Seattle in 1903, George Wharton James, who had been associate editor of Stickley's *Craftsman* in 1904, settled in Los Angeles and in 1909 published the short-lived *Arroyo Craftsman* (only one edition appeared). In 1909, Frank Lloyd Wright undertook his first commission on the West Coast, the George C Stewart house at Montecito.

Below: Oak Library table designed by Frank Lloyd Wright. Made for the Ray W Evans house in Chicago in 1908, this piece is exactly contemporaneous with the stylistically similar furniture of the Frederick C Robie house, also in Chicago. The open geometricity of Wright's style at this time is almost entirely without precedent, although like Godwin's buffet, it owes much to Japanese architecture and design. (Art Institute of Chicago)

The most important firm of craftsmen on the West Coast was Greene & Greene of Pasadena. The brothers Charles Sumner Greene and Henry Mather Greene were born in Cincinnati, and studied architecture at MIT. They would, thus, have been aware of the new developments in aesthetics both in their native city, the centre of the Art Ceramic movement in the United States, and in New England. The Greenes moved to Pasadena in 1893 and in 1901 Charles went to Europe. He was influenced by a strange combination of styles including the English Arts and Crafts movement, Swiss chalet architecture, Japanese designs and the domestic Mission style of architecture, as found in the cool white-walled Mission houses of Spanish America.

In just two years, between 1907 and 1909, the brothers created their major work, four houses in and around Pasadena, for Robert C Blacker, David B Gamble, Charles M Pratt in Ojai Valley, and William R Thorsens in Berkeley. The furniture in Thorsens' house was made by a Scandinavian craftsman in Peter Hall's workshop in Pasadena, and the furniture of all four houses, usually in walnut or teak and inlaid with ebony, fruitwood and semi-precious stones, gave the Greenes a reputation which spread far beyond the boundaries of California. Ashbee visited the state in 1909, and wrote in his memoirs:
'I think C Sumner Greene's work beautiful; among the best there is in this country. Like Lloyd Wright, the spell of Japan is on him, he feels the beauty and makes magic out of the horizontal line, but there is in his work more tenderness, more subtlety, more self-effacement than in Wright's work. It is more refined and has more repose. Perhaps it loses in strength, perhaps it is California that speaks rather than Illinois, . . . as work it is, so far as the interiors go, more sympathetic to me.'

Following the disastrous earthquakes in California in 1906, which destroyed vast areas of building, there was great scope for new ideas in architecture and furniture design. In 1906, the architects Lucia Mathews and her husband Arthur Frank Mathews opened their furniture shop in San Francisco, which lasted until about 1920. Their pieces are in a variety of woods — oak, mahogany, walnut, beech — and are decorated with painted or carved ornament, the former being largely the work of Lucia Mathews herself. The shop, which employed between 20 and 50 craftsmen at a time, undertook both large interior schemes and single commissioned pieces. The style of decoration was influenced by English Arts and Crafts design, but also by French Symbolism and oriental art.

Art Nouveau

In the period between 1890 and 1910, we see the development in Europe of a style which has become known uniformly as Art Nouveau. In fact, this is a term which has been much abused and taken for granted. In strictly historical terms, the *Maison de l'Art Nouveau* was a shop founded in Paris in December 1895 by a dealer-entrepreneur called Samuel Bing. The shop showed work by young, mainly French, designers, in many different media —glassware, furniture, metalwork, prints,

Right: Upright cabinet by Eugène Gaillard, exhibited by Samuel Bing at the Paris, Exposition Universelle of 1900. Gaillard was inspired by French furniture of the Louis Quinze period. This example is of exceptional quality, with well-chiselled bronze fittings following the flowing lines of the wood. (Danske Kunstindustrimuseet, Copenhagen)

Left: Gilt-wood and upholstered sofa designed by Georges de Feure for Samuel Bing and included by the latter in his display at the 1900 Paris Exposition Universelle. Obviously inspired by Louis Quinze furniture, de Feure incorporated rhythmic Art Nouveau forms without relieving the piece of its essential impracticality. (Danske Kunstindustrimuseet, Copenhagen)

paintings, ceramics — as well as selling newly imported work from the Far East. The shop was similar to Liberty's in London, although on a smaller and more specialized scale. Bing himself later expressed surprise that his shop should have given its name to a stylistic movement. He wrote: 'At its birth Art Nouveau had no pretensions to being a generic term. It was simply the name of an establishment opened as a rallying point for youth keen to show their modern approach.' And in 1896, the French critic Victor Champier wrote: 'Art Nouveau has only one thing against it; its unduly pretentious precision. It simply indicates an effort.'

In England, the term was, and is still, used largely to describe stylistic developments during the period we have indicated in Europe, and more specifically, France. In Germany, the style is known as *Jugendstil*, in Austria, *Sezessionstil*, in Catalan *Modernista* or *Arte Joven* and in Italy, the London store Liberty gave its name to *Il Stile Liberty*. It is interesting to note that the French periodical *L'Ameublement*, with the furniture of Mackmurdo, Baillie Scott and Voysey in mind, referred to certain characteristics of new furniture design as the *Genre Anglais*. All this might imply that every country was aware of a uniform style but was giving it a different name. In fact, the reverse was true. Every country was indeed aware that the end of the nineteenth century saw a renaissance of artistic ideas, which they naturally wished to characterize by a unifying term but they were also aware of differences. The Austrians and Germans, tied by historic, geographic and linguistic bonds, developed a very similar style, the main characteristic of which is geometricity. They had little apparent sympathy or contact with developments in Paris or Nancy, while France herself maintained an historically consistent insularity towards the development of new styles.

The term Art Nouveau, therefore, can be understood in two ways. It can either be taken as a generic expression of a widespread renewal of artistic ideas in Europe at the end of the nineteenth century, without necessarily implying a stylistic unity, or it can be taken to mean a specifically French and Belgian style of decorative design, characterized by its flowing organic forms, swirls, blobs and whiplash motifs. It is not justifiable historically to use the term Art Nouveau to describe a uniform late nineteenth-, early twentieth-century style in the decorative arts, since it is obvious that no such unified style actually existed. In England and the United States, Art Nouveau in the French style was hardly seen at all.

In France, the major designers of Art Nouveau furniture were Eugène Gaillard, Eugène Vallin, Louis Majorelle, Alexandre

Left: Writing-desk in oak and fruitwood marquetry designed by Emile Gallé of Nancy. Exhibited in the Paris Exposition Universelle of 1900, this piece is a typical mixture of French eighteenth-century forms and late nineteenth-century symbolism. The lid bears an inlaid inscription from a poem by Baudelaire.

Right: Reconstruction of the Pavilion of the Union Centrale des Arts Décoratifs designed by Georges Hoentschell for the 1900 Paris Exposition Universelle. The furniture is by Louis Majorelle and the large painting, L'Ile Heureuse, is by Albert Besnard. (Musée des Arts Décoratifs, Paris)

Charpentier, Emile Gallé, Georges de Feure, Hector Guimard, Georges Hoentschell, Rupert Carabin, Eugène Colonna and Tony and Pierre Selmersheim. There were two distinctive groups of designers, those working with Gallé at Nancy and those who worked in Paris, revolving around Bing. It should not be thought, however, that the new style was accepted in French intellectual circles; in describing the Salon d'Art Nouveau in 1895, Edmond de Goncourt wrote about the 'delirious rantings of ugliness'.

The School of Nancy numbered among its adherents Emile Gallé, Louis Majorelle, Eugène Gaillard and Eugène Vallin. Their work is characterized by a rich use of floral and pictorial marquetry, but is often somewhat commercially made, which reflects adversely on the quality. Also, as several critics have pointed out, the style of the furniture is not particularly original, being closely modelled on Louis Quinze and early Louis Seize Rococo. Much of the naturalism of the Ecole de Nancy's imagery derives from the asymmetrical quality of Japanese art, which influenced French designers in other areas of the applied arts, combined especially in Gallé's case with an affinity with the French Symbolist movement. Maurice Rheims, in his book on Art Nouveau, quotes a long passage written by Gallé to accompany a piece of his furniture made in 1902, called 'Autumn Pathways'. It gives a picture of the inspiration behind much of the School of Nancy's work: '. . . The sense of decoration in this sideboard is extensively based on the deliberate con-

trast between the representation of tangible things and the vision of certain lofty realities, those mysteries which we desire and must divine if we can . . . *Patina*! I have emphasized the antithesis between realistic representation and symbolic adornment by applying a waxy patina only in certain places, where the relief has been heightened by the use of encaustic. Elsewhere, on the other hand, I have taken a daring course which is without precedent in the cabinetmaker's art; the surface of the wood has been left in its natural virgin state without varnish or patina.'

Right: Cabinet designed by Hector Guimard, part of a suite executed in 1900. The rhythmic asymmetry of this piece, derived in part from Japanese naturalism, is typical of the best French Art Nouveau of this date. (Musée des Arts Décoratifs, Paris)

262

Gallé did not in fact design much furniture, although his first pieces date from about 1885. The major furniture-maker of the School of Nancy was Louis Majorelle (1859–1929), who, although producing many pieces in what might be described as the 'standard' Nancy style, designed a number of magnificent pieces in dark, highly polished woods with ormolu mounts which, both stylistically and in terms of quality, may be compared with the finest eighteenth-century craftsmanship. Most of the Nancy School designers used local fruitwoods, though Majorelle favoured mahogany. Two craftsmen who specialized in pictorial marquetry panels designed by Gallé and Majorelle for use in their furniture, as well as for independent decoration, were Victor Prouvé and Jacques Grüber.

The designers who worked for Bing, including Georges de Feure, Georges Hoentschell and Eugène Colonna, were more eclectic and Symbolist in style than those of the Nancy School and had less interest in naturalism. De Feure and Colonna produced delicate, spidery pieces, the former's being predominantly seat furniture in gilt-wood and with delicate, embroidered silk upholstery. They were somewhat impractical pieces, attempting as they did to emulate the ethereal qualities of Symbolist painting and poetry. De Feure's favoured wood was Hungarian ash. Hoentschell's furniture was more substantial, with a heavier use of sculptural ornament. Many of his pieces were in Algerian plane.

Two French designers of great individuality were Hector Guimard and Rupert Carabin. Guimard was primarily an architect who, as a follower of Viollet-le-Duc, was fascinated by the possibilities of exposed skeletal metalwork in buildings. His architecture aside, he is best known for his brilliant use of such apparently unmalleable materials as cast-iron, which he designed to flow with ease and plastic liquidity. He did, however, create a considerable amount of furniture and *boiserie* (panelling) for his interiors, which show the same concern with fluidity and motion. He tended to use dark woods, such as mahogany. Rupert Carabin was possibly the most Symbolist of all French furniture designers. Just as the work of Mackintosh and Frank Lloyd Wright can be experienced as abstract sculpture without any necessary reference to function, so Carabin's furniture goes to the opposite extreme of vertiginous reality, with that overtone of eroticism which is elemental to the French Symbolist movement. The heavy rich mahogany which Carabin used was sculpted with twisted nudes, masks and foliage with a brilliant, almost oily, patina.

A concern with line similar to that of French architects such as Guimard was apparent also in Belgium. Victor Hortá (1861–1946) designed his first major building, the Maison Tassel in

Brussels from 1892 to 1893, of which one contemporary critic wrote, 'no detail derives from anything at all in existence'. This was followed in the 1890s by the Hôtel Solvay, the Hôtel Van Eetevelde, the Hôtel Deprez, the Maison du Peuple, and his own house, now the Musée Hortá. Both the exteriors and interiors of these buildings are allowed to show their iron, skeletal structures which thus became integral parts of the decorative schemes. The rhythmic flow of the designs, drawn from botanical forms, demonstrates at once the influence of Symbolist art and French eighteenth-century ornamentation. The furniture for some of these houses was also designed by Hortá and is frequently petaloid in form. The majority of Belgian Art Nouveau furniture was designed for specific interiors and was not meant to stand in isolation. The woods most frequently used were, initially, beech, birch and oak, with mahogany and citrus woods imported from the Belgian Congo becoming popular in later schemes.

Gustave Serrurier-Bovy (1858–1910) was a furniture designer who used mahogany and who, apart from occasionally employing stencilled patterns, left his furniture unornamented. Significantly, Serrurier-Bovy had a retail furnishing shop in Liège which

Above: Project for a living room by Bellery Desfontaines, dated 1905. Architect, painter and designer, Bellery Desfontaines in this scheme shows an awareness of current English styles, as well as an obvious respect for designers such as Guimard. (Bibliothèque Doucet, Paris)

Left: Carved mahogany three-legged table designed by Hector Guimard in about 1908. All of Guimard's furniture was made as part of an architectural entity yet its quality allows it to stand alone. The carving on this piece typifies the smooth fluidity associated with the architect's use of organic motifs. (Musée des Arts Décoratifs, Paris)

263

showed English Arts and Crafts furniture. In 1900, he designed collapsible pieces in beechwood.

Henry van de Velde (1863–1957), who spent most of his active life in Belgium, designed beautiful flowing furniture often painted white. He exhibited with Mackintosh on at least two occasions and the Scottish designer's influence was strong in his work. This manifested itself in the general shape of van de Velde's early furniture, his use of white enamelling, his unpainted case furniture, which was frequently inset with pale stained glass, and the chairs he designed, with pale upholstery by the Belgian Symbolist painter, Johann Thorn Prikker. Thorn Prikker also designed chairs himself, in an insubstantial, spidery style. Other Belgian designers whose work was shown at the Salons of *La Libre Esthétique* founded by Octave Maus, which showed the applied arts side by side with painting and sculpture, were Paul Hankar, Paul Cauchie, Georges Hobe, Georges Antoine Peereboom and Antoine Pompe.

Designers in Holland, as in Scandinavia, were influenced equally by the functionalist style of Austria and Germany and the more restless Art Nouveau of France and Belgium. The Netherlands architect, H P Berlage executed his major commission, the Amsterdam Stock Exchange, in 1903, and also designed furniture. His ideas were closest to the Arts and Crafts ethic of William Morris, and his theories on the importance of logical construction and integrity of workmanship enjoyed respect and authority. K P C de Basel, who had been apprenticed to a joiner in The Hague, later worked as an architect in Amsterdam; he designed some furniture which, like his architecture, shows the influence of Assyrian and Egyptian art. C A Lion Cachet was a designer whose work shows one of the strongest influences on Dutch Art Nouveau: batik design from Indonesia. He used woods of contrasting colours, and collaborated with two artists, G W Dijsselhof and Theodoor Nieuwenhuis in founding a studio in Amsterdam.

Below left: Armchair designed by Henry van de Velde, with upholstery by Johan Thorn Prikker, of about 1895 to 1900. The leading Dutch symbolist painter, Prikker was greatly influenced by Javanese batik designs, although the angular design on the present fabric is in harmony with van de Velde's style. (Nordenfjeldske Kunstindustrimuseum, Trondheim)

Below right: Armchair in veneered mahogany, of about 1898 to 1904, designed by Antoni Gaudí for the Casa Calvet, Barcelona. (Museo Gaudí, Barcelona)

The influence of French and Belgian Art Nouveau, although strong, was not completely dominant in Italy either. In Turin, Pietro Fenoglio was inspired by Victor Hortá, as were a number of other Italian designers whose work nevertheless tends to vulgarize the original purity of the style. In the same city, however, Giacomo Cometti worked in a style based on the furniture of Mackintosh as interpreted by the Wiener Werkstätte and Eugenio Quarti of Milan, whose strong functional pieces, in mahogany inlaid with mother-of-pearl and metal, show the same stylistic roots.

Pietro Fenoglio's buildings in Turin display the search for unity throughout the architecture, interior metalwork, *boiserie* and furniture that can be seen in the work of Victor Hortá. The Casa Fenoglio has a most restrained and attractive use of flowing metalwork in the balustrades which is echoed on the delicate carvings on the doors and the finely modelled brass fittings. Eugenio Quarti's furniture shows similar restraint, but his is more geometric. There are pieces bearing carved, floral motifs obviously inspired by the style of French furniture which Quarti had seen and admired in the 1900 Paris Exhibition, combined with a geometricity of outline close to Viennese and German types. Such work shows a keen interest in international developments. In contrast, the work of Ernesto Basile of Palermo is idiosyncratic, with little reference to Art Nouveau or Jugendstil. Massive pieces in mahogany, made by the firm of Ducrot of Palermo and often embellished with sculptural metalwork by Antonio Ugo and painting by Ettore Maria Bergler, seem to hark back to the Italian Renaissance, or even further back to Roman and Etruscan furniture. Not surprisingly, in view of these stylistic antecedents, they are also prophetic of that style of Italian architecture and design which was popularized in Italy during the 1920s and 1930s under Mussolini.

One Italian designer whose work cannot be categorized in this way was Carlo Bugatti (1855–1940). Trained as a painter, Bugatti won a prize for his furniture at the Italian exhibition in London in 1888. The style was extraordinary, being a mixture of Middle Eastern fantasy and Japanese naturalism. Certainly nothing like it had been seen before and, in the Art Nouveau movement as a whole, Bugatti's work remains an amazing eccentricity. Bugatti himself described his furniture as being 'of no special style', although in the Turin exhibition of 1902, the tassels and brass inlays gave way to a more simple, curved style obviously based on the Art Nouveau furniture he had seen in Paris in the 1900 exhibition, in which he was represented. Apart from his use of metal inlays, usually of copper or brass, Bugatti relied for his decorative effects on the inlaying of contrasting woods, ivory and vellum.

Der Jugendstil

The designers and architects of Germany and Austria were in sympathy with the aesthetic ideals of William Morris and his followers, although they were champions of industrial methods. It might also be said that while the more socialist elements of Morris's philosophy — in other words the political aspects of his work — were largely, and probably purposely ignored in the United States, they reached sympathetic ears in Germany and Austria. Between 1890 and 1905, the whole direction of design in northern Europe was changed by a group of exceptionally gifted designers. In Munich, Hermann Obrist, August Endell, Joseph Maria Olbrich, who founded the 'Artist's Colony' in Darmstadt in 1899, Richard Riemerschmidt and Peter Behrens formed a brilliant artistic community and from 1897 to 1898 established the Vereinigte Werkstätten of Munich and Dresden. It is also significant that Henry van de Velde settled permanently in Germany in 1899.

In Vienna, Josef Hoffmann (1870–1956) created the Wiener Secession in 1897 and, in 1903, he collaborated with Koleman ('Kolo') Moser in the founding of the Wiener Werkstätte. In the eighth exhibition of the Wiener Secession, work by the young Austrian designers was shown together with whole rooms designed by Henry van de Velde, the designers of the *Maison Moderne,* a shop in Paris similar to that of Bing which had been founded by Julius Meier-Graefe in 1898, and the British designers Ashbee, Charles Rennie Mackintosh and Mackintosh's wife, Margaret Macdonald. Ashbee and van de Velde had both shown with *La Libre Esthétique* in Brussels in 1894. Ashbee and Mackintosh became firm friends with Hoffmann and Moser, and the Austrians visited England and Scotland; their deep appreciation of the workshop system of the Guild of Handicrafts did much to inspire the formation of the Wiener Werkstätte.

The most significant work of this latter group is the splendid Palais Stoclet in Brussels, built between 1905 and 1911. One critic, Wilhelm Mrazek, has written recently:
'This house . . . is a *Gesamtkunstwerk*; the *Werkstätte* gave its best there, and made it a monument of *Jugendstil* in applied art. Josef Hoffmann and his co-workers Czeschka, Klimt, Löffler, Powolny, Metzner and Luksch created a house which presents perfect unity in style. Money was no object and they feasted on precious materials. With its play of flat surfaces, the building is a triumph of the geometric principle and of ornamentalism combined with *Sachlichkeit*. All things in the exquisitely furnished interior, vitrines, cup-

boards, chairs, lamps, silver and china combine to create an environment which is one great homage to geometric beauty.'

When we read this, and remember the search for unity which dominated the Arts and Crafts movement, the work of Mackintosh and the Glasgow designers and the great architects and designers of the Prairie school, we see this element as one which binds them close to the similar preoccupation of Belgian and French architects such as Guimard and Hortá. We can also appreciate, when we recall Owen Jones' criticism of the Great Exhibition of 1851, quoted earlier, how much had been achieved in the second half of the nineteenth century.

THE TRIUMPH OF STYLE
Art Deco

During the first decade of the present century following the decline of Art Nouveau there was little encouragement for the development of design in furniture. Two main factors for this decline can be found in the writings of contemporary critics of the decorative arts.

The family as an institution was still as potent a social force as it had been in the previous century and proved a strong deterrent, although an unconscious one, against innovations. The average well-to-do family in Europe and America lived in a fairly spacious and comfortable house filled with the accumulated furniture of the last hundred years and the tradition of keeping family furniture with its sentimental associations and comfortable familiarity proved stronger than any desire for novelty. Largely uneducated in artistic matters — there were few magazines with a widespread circulation devoted to interior design in the early years of the century — the buying public was distrustful of investing in anything out of the ordinary and relied largely on the persuasiveness of the salesmen in the big decorating firms in London and New York who through laziness or ignorance found it easier to sell pastiches of Tudor, Queen Anne or Chippendale styles.

The other and perhaps more important factor was adequately summed up in the words of the architect Charles Spooner writing in

The British Home of Today published in 1904. 'During the last few years', he commented, 'there has been a very large growth in the admiration for old furniture and in the desire to collect it. The admiration is widespread and often uncritical. There is no real desire on the part of many people to buy beautiful things for their daily use, and one is not surprised to find such people turning to old work. It is indeed difficult at the present time to buy a piece of modern furniture with which it would be pleasant to live. The art of furniture making, like many a craft today, is in a depressed condition. It is being carried on by a very few people, and there is as yet but a small demand for it. The great bulk of furniture made today is without art and as long as it is made under the present conditions will remain so.' These conditions Spooner explained as being due to the poor wages paid to men with little or no training. In addition, because the work was subdivided, it became monotonous and deprived the workmen of any pride in their craft. Poor workmanship was concealed by thick coats of French polish and 'what happens afterwards is the purchaser's affair'.

It is noticeable that from this time many firms of reputable antique dealers on both sides of the Atlantic included the significant word 'reproductions' in their advertising. The taste for antique furniture which Spooner

Above: One of a pair of pinewood cabinets veneered with boxwood, mother-of-pearl and ebony designed by Josef Hoffmann from 1910 to 1914. Hoffmann, the leading figure of the Wiener Werkstätte, was a versatile designer of works of great elegance, who was strongly influenced by Voysey, Ashbee and Mackintosh. Following William Morris in avoiding the use of the machine, Hoffmann and his Viennese colleagues specialized in hand work with a consequent high cost of production — but he found no lack of wealthy patrons with an appreciation of the quality and distinction of his creations. (Museum für Angewandte Kunst, Vienna)

recorded obviously could not be satisfied by the comparatively few genuine antique pieces which had survived from the sixteenth to the eighteenth centuries — Regency furniture was considered to be unworthy of collection and was dismissed as 'gimcrack rubbish' — and in consequence both in England and America, and on the Continent, the greater part of the furniture trade was devoted to the production of 'reproductions' of the antique. In many cases these were skilful enough to deceive even an expert eye and in 1906 the firm of Bartholomew & Fletcher advertised that their 'specialité' (sic) was 'reproduction from fine old models'. A coffee-table, or, in the twenties, a radiogram or cocktail cabinet for which there were no historical precedents would have deceived no one, but as late as the 1930s there were many firms like Bartholomew & Fletcher or Nicholls & Janes of High Wycombe whose output consisted of copies, often exact to the last detail, of the eighteenth-century furniture illustrated in Macquoid's *Age of Mahogany* and Macquoid and Edward's *Dictionary of English Furniture* — and in some instances the pieces reproduced were themselves of doubtful authenticity. At the most modest estimate half the antique furniture extant today was actually made in the first three decades of this century both in England and France.

The Demise of Art Nouveau

The Studio Year Book of Decorative Art, an annual publication devoted to the best design in England, America, France, Germany,

Austria and Hungary, made its first appearance in 1906. As far as the English section is concerned, the record of advances in design for many years was a melancholy one. Almost without exception the newly-built houses illustrated were versions of Tudor or Queen Anne originals and, where shown, the interiors were filled with antiques or furniture of so nondescript a character that it is difficult to ascribe it to any particular style. There were a small number of English designers who were making valiant efforts to produce furniture which was not shackled to tradition, but in the absence of any definite contemporary idiom the results were too often timid and unadventurous. Despite their determination to break with the past their forms of furniture were pared-down versions of traditional pieces sparsely decorated with inlaid lines of ebony, boxwood or pewter which did little to enliven the over-simplification.

Ambrose Heal Jnr experimented with hitherto little used woods such as chestnut and, in a number of pieces, used sunken handles on drawer faces or revolving wooden handles, set in circular panels, which when turned released sliding bolts on the inside of drawers. His designs had a refreshing simplicity although on the debit side his side-table for a dining-room illustrated in *The British Home of Today* had no less than 14 legs.

For a few years following its founding in 1893 the Arts and Crafts Society had looked as though it might play a decisive role in improving standards of taste in England and the United States, but by 1906 the quality and originality of its annual exhibitions had deteriorated to the extent that the *Studio* correspondent viewed them with 'a certain feeling of melancholy' with only the furniture of Ernest Gimson giving any hope for the future. Gimson emerged as possibly the most original designer of this period but even his work has echoes of the seventeenth century in its conception. His virtues were simplicity of design with an emphasis on the beauty of the natural grain of the wood accentuated by handwrought handles and decorative hinges by E G Halton and A Gardiner. His use of projecting panels on doors and drawer fronts became almost a signature and in some cases a rectangular panel has an octagonal panel superimposed — in one piece this has a smaller rectangular panel applied to its face with an even smaller octagon superimposed. His seeming lack of invention could have been due to a natural reticence or to the demands of his clients, and the inlaid decorative panels of differently coloured woods and pewter with which he occasionally enlivened an otherwise plain piece of furniture were obviously inspired by Elizabethan and Jacobean embroideries. Although far from being reproductions of the antique, Gimson's furniture could be placed without incongruity into one of the Tudor interiors fashionable at the time and comply with the 'English reticence' so often quoted as an ideal — probably in reaction to the exuberance of French Art Nouveau furniture which had so outraged the traditionalists a few years before.

The influence of Gimson, Sidney Barnsley, George Jack, Peter Waals and others designing in this manner was slight as their output, being entirely handmade, was necessarily small and, in comparison with more commercial products, expensive. Furthermore they tended to work in rural areas where craftsmen with traditional skills could be found and this in turn gave little opportunity for the buying public to become familiar with their work.

In 1908 Aylmer Vallance, writing in *The Studio Year Book*, commented on the developments in cane and wicker-work furniture which had 'arrived at an eminent degree of attainment' at the hands of German and Austrian designers. Very different from the creaking chintz-covered armchairs to be found in many English houses, the new versions of chairs, tables and plant-stands designed by Josef Hoffmann and Wilhelm Schmidt for the Prag Rudniker Werkstätte and by Nicholai in Dresden had a taut elegance which justified their use in drawing-rooms and the winter gardens of hotels. In England the craft of basket-weaving had been centred round Leicester and from basket-weaving the making of cane furniture was a natural progression. Furniture similar to that made on the Continent was made by the Dryad Craftsmen from designs by B J Fletcher. Light and easily cleaned whether left in its natural state or painted, cane furniture became extremely popular for use in restaurants, cafés and public rooms.

The wholesale reproduction of antiques flourished in France to an even greater extent than in England and if anything the skill with which these facsimiles were made was greater. Similarly, there were persuasive and unscrupulous dealers eager to sell for vast sums these spurious antiques — the same dealers who had conducted a campaign of vituperation against Art Nouveau which they considered

Left: Oak dresser designed by Ambrose Heal in 1914. In the early years of the twentieth century English furniture designers strongly resisted such trends as Art Nouveau, and turned for inspiration to the simpler furniture of the sixteenth and seventeenth centuries. Without being a pastiche of an antique, Heal's dresser acknowledges the past while being unmistakably of its time and would harmonize with earlier pieces. Decoration is restrained — a simple carved motif on the edges of the shelves — while the pull-out slide above the drawers provides extra working space. The wooden handle recessed in the circular panels works a concealed fastening.

271

a threat to their livelihood—and remote country-houses were furnished by them with 'family heirlooms' which were sold with a show of reluctance to unsuspecting visitors.

By 1908 Art Nouveau had become so discredited that the critic Achille Ségard described it as 'bizarre, pretentious, abnormal, overwrought and inadequate to any practical object' though *The Studio Year Book* showed that in a modified form several designers remained faithful. Most of the original Art Nouveau designers had abandoned the style very soon after the 1900 Exhibition and its subsequent commercialization. Taste then reverted to an attenuated version of Louis Seize furniture painted white and upholstered in shades of old-rose, which was soon to be found not only in private houses but also in the public rooms and bedrooms of the new hotels which were springing up in the capitals of Europe during the first decade of the century. Irreverently known as 'Louis the Hotel', this type of furniture was popularized by the big decorating firms of Mercier Frères, Maple—which had branches in London and Paris—and Waring & Gillow.

The Advent of Art Deco

In 1910 two events in Paris had a decisive effect and led to the creation of a style which has acquired the recent title of Art Deco. The first was the appearance of Sergei Diaghilev's Ballet Russe and especially the *première* of the ballet *Scheherazade*. Contemporary writings and memoirs abound with descriptions of the astonishing effect this ballet had upon

Left: Chair in white painted oak designed by Charles Rennie Mackintosh for the Rose Boudoir shown at the International Exhibition of Decorative Art, Turin 1902. The chair (and its black painted companion) met with both vitriolic abuse and ecstatic praise. Amid a welter of safely traditional or grotesquely eccentric contributions, the Mackintosh designs were awarded a diploma of honour. (University of Glasgow)

Below left: One of Paul Poiret's contributions to the 1925 Paris Exhibition was the decoration of three barges moored on the Seine. This interior shows Poiret's lasting fondness for the brilliant oriental colours of the Ballet Russe combined with simple shapes reminiscent of the work of the Wiener Werkstätte.

Right: Cupboard veneered in lemonwood forming part of a suite of furniture made in 1907 by Niedermoser of Vienna to the design of Koloman Moser. Moser, together with Hoffmann, was one of the guiding spirits of the Wiener Werkstätte and was similarly interested in designing anything from a complete decorative scheme to a lady's handbag. His work demonstrates the strong links between English and Scottish designers and their Viennese contemporaries. (Museum für Angewandte Kunst, Vienna)

its audiences who were transported by the combination of an erotic and sadistic libretto, sensuous music and choreography and, above all, the dazzlingly brilliant *décor* and costumes by Léon Bakst. This sensation was repeated to only a slightly lesser degree when the ballet had it *première* in London in the following year. The pale and subtle nuances of Art Nouveau were superseded by the brilliant oriental colours which were applied to furniture as well as to its upholstery and a

craze for all things Persian pervaded the decorative arts. Large elaborately decorated cushions became a recognized article of furniture piled in heaps in lieu of settees in imitation of those on which Zobeïde, the heroine of *Scheherazade,* and Thamar, the central figure of another exotic ballet designed by Bakst, reclined between orgies.

The second event was the exhibition of decorative arts from the Münchener Werkbund at the Salon d'Automne of 1910. Although badly received by the critics it proved so popular that mounted police had to be brought in to control the crowds clamouring for admission. Little information is available as to the actual exhibits and judging from photographs of other work from the Werkbund it seems improbable that French designers could have been inspired by the rather heavy and characterless interiors — apart from the fact that German taste had never been highly regarded in France and memories of the disasters of the 1870 Franco-Prussian War were still too fresh for many Frenchmen to take an unbiased view. It is more likely that the concept on which the Werkbund was founded — a group of artists and designers working together in conjunction with manufacturers and holding joint exhibitions of their work — appealed to French designers as a practical solution to their artistic problems. The influences which found expression in the pre-war version of Art Deco stem more from the light elegant artifacts of the Austrian Wiener Werkstätte than from the German movement.

During the opening years of the twentieth century the designs of William Morris, Baillie Scott, Charles Voysey, C R Ashbee and Charles Rennie Mackintosh had had considerable influence on German and Austrian designers especially on those of the younger generation desirous of a break with the prevailing taste for ponderous versions of historical styles. Mackintosh, whose work had aroused little interest in England and even less in France, found new admirers particularly in Vienna and his interiors inspired Josef Hoffmann, a brilliant designer of subtle and refined taste. The eccentricities of much of Mackintosh's furniture which tend to give the impression that it was meant more to be admired than used in everyday life were reduced and, combined with reminiscences of the Biedermeier style, resulted in simple and extremely elegant pieces.

In Germany the influence of English designers and critics was tempered by a more practical realization that if furniture of good design were to be brought within the reach of all incomes the slow processes of hand crafts had to give way to the most modern methods of machine production. The Deutscher

Werkbund or German Craft Union was formed in 1907 and within two years had enrolled the active support of 360 designers, 267 manufacturers and 95 influential critics and writers working with the common aim of improving the quality of industrial production. According to *The Studio Year Book* for 1910, the Werkbund was so well organized that its influence had led to a decline in the import into Germany of French and English art productions and the position of Paris as the arbiter of taste in Europe was threatened. The influences which evolved into the pre-war version of French Art Deco can be directly traced, however, to the light, elegant productions of the Wiener Werkstätte rather than to the heavier German counterparts. Just as the Austrian decorative artists had referred back to the Biedermeier period so the French designers, in reaction against the sinuosities of Art Nouveau, returned to the tighter and more disciplined idioms of French furniture of the 1820s — significantly a time when the links with tradition had begun to loosen as a result of the Romantic absorption with the past. In Austrian, French and Italian designs for furniture, textiles and other forms of decoration, the same repertoire of motifs emerged around 1910. Baskets or bowls of formalized flowers appear in oval panels — the oval shape was extensively used for table-tops, mirrors incorporated in dressing-

Left: Dressing-table chair by Follot, about 1910. He was first associated with the French Art Nouveau movement, but by about 1904 he had developed an individual style and was an early pioneer in Art Deco, designing single pieces characterized by the use of precious materials and fine carving. (Musée des Arts Décoratifs, Paris)

Below left: Small commode in shagreen and ebony designed by Paul Iribe. One of the most versatile of Art Deco designers, Iribe first attracted attention with the fashion illustrations he did for Paul Poiret in 1908. Until his departure for the United States in 1914, he created an enormous collection of work for interiors, wallpapers, furniture, fabrics, jewellery and graphics. His favourite motif of a conventionalized rose — the 'rose Iribe' — became the signature of early Art Deco when it was borrowed by other designers. (Musée des Arts Décoratifs, Paris)

Right: French escritoire of about 1920. A typically delicate piece of furniture designed for a boudoir and showing in its lacquered decoration typical Art Deco motifs of oval panels enclosing baskets of conventionalized flowers. This form of ornament shows striking similarities to the work of Italian and Austrian designers; the original inspiration is demonstrably that of Charles Rennie Mackintosh. (The Martins Forrest Collection)

tables or simply as wall-mirrors. Carving in low relief of roses, zinnias and pendant bell-shaped blossoms was applied to the exposed frames of chairs and to mirror frames or used as panels set in doors. A chair by Paul Follot, for example, has an oval panel in the back framing a basket of fruit carved in low relief — the combination of blond fruitwood with ebony reverts to a fashion of about a hundred years before.

The new Art Deco style found an immediate response from the public and its slightly exotic charm which combined novelty with a certain regard for the past was realized to the full by such designers as Paul Follot, Maurice Dufrêne, Clement-Mère, Armand Rateau and others who had previously been in the forefront of the Art Nouveau movement through their association with either Siegfried Bing or Julius Meier-Graefe. Plans were made for an exhibition to be held in 1915 of the decorative arts of all countries, but this had to be postponed indefinitely after the outbreak of the First World War.

Immediately peace was declared the idea was taken up again, for France needed to assert her position as leader of taste in Europe in view of the importance of fashion in every field of the decorative arts to the national economy; and although Europe was shattered and near bankruptcy as a result of the war

there were new markets in both North and South America and even eastward in India. Many of the leading French manufacturers threatened to boycott the exhibition if Germany, so recently the bitter enemy of France, were invited to participate. Financial reasons also delayed the International Exhibition of Decorative and Industrial Art until 1925, but in the intervening years the lessons of the Deutscher Werkbund had been driven home, with groups of designers collaborating to present their work in a number of the big Parisian department stores and thus increasing the popular interest in the newest developments of Art Deco.

Twice a year at the Salon d'Automne and the Salon des Artistes Décorateurs, fully furnished rooms were exhibited to the public. These were either actual schemes already commissioned or they could be bought outright and installed in the client's house. These exhibitions were as much discussed and featured in the press as the collections of the leading couturiers some of whom, Paul Poiret and Jeanne Lanvin for instance, combined dressmaking with the design of interiors. Paul Poiret's *Atelier Martine* was the direct result of his pre-war fashion tours in Germany where he visited the studios of the Werkbund and was so impressed that on his return to France he opened an establishment for the sale of decorative accessories — furniture was not greatly featured in his schemes and where it appears it was obviously inspired by the Wiener Werkstätte.

The 1925 Exhibition
Many critics objected that the furniture at the 1925 exhibition was more a display of luxury and fine craftsmanship than a true reflection of the state of the furniture trade of each country. In fact, a number of the exhibits dated from before the war when the idea of the exhibition had first been put forward. In the meantime, however, Art Deco had undergone modification, was becoming unfashionable and was shortly to disappear in favour of the essentially anti-decorative 'Modernism'.

The designer who had the greatest impact on press and public was Jacques-Emile Ruhlmann whose working life was to span a brief 20 years between his first exhibited work in 1913 and his death in 1933. The Ruhlmann exhibit was spectacularly luxurious and reflected his avowed intention to work only for the richest clients, using the most precious materials and with complete control of the final decorative scheme. As his taste was extremely cultivated and the standard of craftsmanship he exacted from his workers unsurpassed by any standards he found no lack of appreciative clients. His favourite materials were the rarest woods and veneers

combined with shagreen, fine leathers, tortoiseshell and ivory, and he used these to clothe the simple but subtle forms of his perfectly proportioned pieces. The individuality and style of his designs were above fashion and consequently changes in taste made no difference to the lavish commissions he received for the decoration of private houses and embassies. The forms of Ruhlmann's furniture were in the tradition of the First Empire or of the Boulle pieces which were popular during the reign of Louis XIV.

In contrast with Ruhlmann's designs, those of André Groult and J Leleu were pared-down versions of the Louis Quinze style with the difference that, instead of intricate inlay and bronze-doré mounts, both these designers veneered the simplified *bombé* — convex — forms with tortoiseshell, macassar ebony or blond shagreen harmonizing with the paintings by Marie Laurençin which Groult included in many of his decorative schemes. Ruhlmann's sombre, rich veneers, relieved by ivory handles and discreet inlays of the same material, were essentially masculine in feeling while Groult and Leleu created interiors and furniture which were eminently suitable as backgrounds for elegant women. Together with Paul Follot, Maurice Dufrêne and Léon Jallot they can be said to be the original exponents of Art Deco in its initial phase.

Working in less conventional materials and often in collaboration with these designers were a number of fine craftsmen whose talents were applied to furniture. Edgar Brandt, Raymond Subes and Paul Kiss, the most esteemed metalworkers of the day, created console tables, the small occasional tables known as 'guéridons', standard lamps, radiator cases and pedestals which interpreted the linear forms of Art Deco in wrought iron. Armand Rateau, whose collaboration with the couturière Jeanne Lanvin has already been mentioned, created bronze furniture which was less inspired by the current Art Deco than by the classical models of Greece, Rome and the Near East, setting them against lacquered walls and screens with the same motifs of birds and flowers.

In the current taste for rich surface textures the techniques of Chinese and Japanese lacquer were revived by Jean Dunand — also a metalworker and acknowledged to be the finest craftsman in contemporary France — and by Eileen Gray and Evelyn Wild. Dunand's

furniture, simple in form, was decorated with as many as 20 coats of lacquer and enhanced with geometrical designs in gold, silver and inlaid eggshells—a revival of a Japanese technique. The lacquer pieces of Eileen Grey and Evelyn Wild were plainer, relying on the mirror-smooth surface of the material for effect. After a career as the foremost jeweller in Europe working in the Art Nouveau manner, René Lalique devoted his attention to working in glass and there are extant dining-tables made entirely of etched plate-glass held together by almost invisible metal framings. His glass and marble dining-room was one of the rather more remarkable exhibits.

If the interiors and furniture by these and many other designers in the different French sections reflected a taste for luxury and fantasy, the English contribution was in comparison sober, earning only faint, polite commendation from the compilers of the official French catalogue who regretted that the inheritors of the traditions of Ruskin, William Morris and Walter Crane could not have produced something with more originality. They did, however, praise the kitchen furnished by Messrs Easiwork Ltd, and the ensembles arranged by Mrs Maufe which included a desk finished in silver leaf by Edward Maufe. On the other hand the spokesman for the English committee found Ruhlmann's furniture heavy and inclined to overpower the nature of the wood, although it was admitted that Ruhlmann's technical

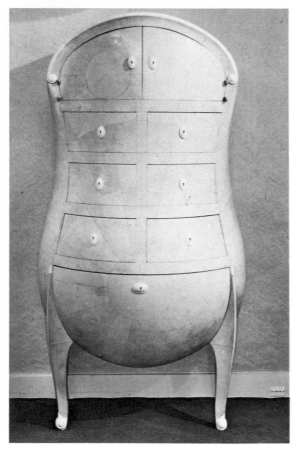

skill and craftsmanship were unsurpassed. This adverse criticism did not prevent several English designers from producing direct imitations of his work shortly after. The exhibition gave visitors the opportunity of seeing work from a number of European countries whose productions were little known outside their own borders. It is noticeable that in most cases the trend in design was a pastiche of early nineteenth-century styles with the accent upon national characteristics and trends.

This reversion to the cult of historicism stems from the early years of this century when Italy, politically and economically at a low ebb, had offered little or no encouragement to original furniture design. The only notable name to have survived from this period is that of Carlo Bugatti whose creations, eccentric and frequently grotesque in conception, combined elements derived from sources ranging from North Africa to Japan, executed in inlays of pewter and vellum with lavish use of silk tassels. Very poor as a country, Italy was largely living on tourism and its past glories, selling its many antiques to foreign collectors and replacing them with skilful replicas, the whole of the furniture trade being engaged in this practice. The Milanese designers Emilio Lancia, G de Finetti

Above: Cabinet in palisander wood decorated with repoussé tinted leather and gilt-bronze mounts designed by Clément Mère in about 1920. Clément Mère began to exhibit furniture from 1910 which combined simplicity of form with a highly wrought surface texture. This cabinet has as its main decoration panels of fine leather embossed and coloured in semi-abstract designs with a strong Japanese influence. (Collection, Galerie Félix Marcilhac, Paris)

Left: Chest of drawers in ivory and shagreen designed by André Groult and shown at the 1925 Paris Exhibition. Shagreen was one of Groult's favourite materials and in this piece he devised a form both sensuous and untraditional. (Manoukian Collection, Paris)

and Tomaso Buzzi, the latter working for the firm of Labirinto, exhibited furniture with a strong neo-classical influence often with details more or less directly copied from those found on metal furniture excavated at Pompeii and Herculaneum. Giulio Richard, designer for the porcelain firm of Richard-Ginori, inclined more to decorations, inlaid or painted, taken from architectural details of Renaissance buildings, interpreted in a somewhat surrealistic manner. The avant-garde art movement of Futurism which flourished briefly before the First World War was devoted entirely to painting and the issue of vehement manifestoes, both of which involved little financial outlay on the part of indigent reformers. Furniture and the decorative arts necessarily involving craftsmanship and financial investment on the part of the artist were ignored. During the 1930s interest turned to the furniture of the eighteenth and nineteenth centuries which had formerly been despised as falling below the standards of the Renaissance and although genuine pieces of these periods were in plentiful supply, contemporary design was generally limited to copies.

In Denmark Kay Fisher, Aage Rafn and Kai Gottlob also were strongly influenced by the neo-classic furniture of the late eighteenth and early nineteenth centuries. The Swedish exhibit was characterized by the simplicity of the basic forms of the furniture which betrayed influences of a provincial version of Louis Seize and Empire styles. From the work of Carl Malmston, Carl Bergsten, Horvick, and the firms of Nordiska Kompaniet and Svenska Möbelfabrikorna, critics deduced that the market seemed to be more for a prosperous democratic middle class than for a rich aristocracy.

There were two notable absentees, the United States and Germany. The American designer Paul Frankl wrote in 1930: 'The only reason why America was not represented was because we found that we had no modern decorative art. Not only was there a sad lack of any achievement that could be exhibited but we discovered that there was not even a serious movement in this direction.' Contemporary periodicals give every indication that

279

taste in America was almost exclusively directed toward antiques or reproductions. The early experiments of, for instance, Frank Lloyd Wright, whose 1904 prototype for a revolving writing-chair is now in the Museum of Modern Art, received little encouragement. Advanced contemporary design was confined to architecture — interior decoration was not yet the potent force it was later to become — and the innovations of sky-scrapers which were mainly intended for commercial use were only too often furnished with indifferently

designed stock office furniture. With considerable foresight the Metropolitan Museum of Art in New York acquired some of the best of the French exhibits including several fine pieces by Ruhlmann. It was possibly as a result of the display of these objects within a very few years that an interest in contemporary furniture arose in America.

The reasons for the absence of Germany were more complex. The economic situation of a ruined and defeated country was the main cause and the threatened boycott by French manufacturers also played a large part. Added to this, internal difficulties prevented an entry from the Bauhaus which at this time was the only organization of importance which could have represented the new spirit in Germany, working on similar lines to the De Stijl in Holland.

The De Stijl movement, named after the magazine which was the mouthpiece of its various members, had been founded in 1917 by Theo van Doesburg and Piet Mondrian to advance revolutionary theories of 'neoplasticism' or the stress on horizontal and vertical elements in a design combined with a limited use of primary colours, red, blue and yellow and three neutral colours, black,

Left: Chair designed by Gerrit Rietveld. The avantgarde periodical 'De Stijl' advocated neo-plasticism — a theory of delineating spatial dimension by the use of horizontal and vertical planes combined with the use of only red, blue and yellow and the non-colours, black, white and grey. The early paintings of Mondrian are examples of this theory. Rietveld realized this doctrine in a number of pieces of furniture of which the chair illustrated is the best known example. Although lacking comfort and stability, it represented a genuine attempt to break with outworn traditions. (Victoria & Albert Museum, London)

Above right: Boudoir designed by Louis Sognot for Primavera, the decorative art department of the Parisian store Au Printemps, which was exhibited at the Paris Exhibition, 1925.

white and grey. The 'Berlin' chair designed by G T Rietveld shows the application of these theories to furniture with the various elements of construction joined only by screws and painted to accentuate their individuality. It is easy to see why this chair, known at that time to a limited number of people, should have found little response from the manufacturers for whom it was intended as a prototype for not only was it uncomfortable — as Rietveld himself admitted — but its appearance gave the impression that a single unwary movement would be sure to topple it.

A more modified version of the theory could be found in the furniture designed by S van Ravensteyn which formed part of the Dutch exhibit in 1925. Less aggressive than Rietveld's chair the suite of bedroom furniture appeared to be composed of planks of wood, haphazardly painted in black and white, propped one against another and earned the comment from an Italian critic that it was the 'height of modernistic snobbery . . . mere curiosities'. *De Stijl* was published in Paris in 1920 and the theories it put forward had a considerable influence on the avant-garde designers reacting against Art Deco.

Right: Chair in steel and leather designed in about 1928 by Le Corbusier and Charlotte Perriand. Contemporary with the Bauhaus, a group of French designers were reacting against Art Deco by advancing revolutionary concepts of the relationship between art and the machine, producing interiors and furniture which were often too starkly functional for general acceptance. (Musée des Arts Décoratifs, Paris)

Overleaf: As an architect, Frank Lloyd Wright was an original and highly controversial figure, designing buildings which aroused either fervent admiration or acute dislike. His furniture was often less aesthetically successful than his buildings; Wright tended to think of furniture in terms of architecture, of wood in terms of stone or concrete — with a resulting heaviness. (Victoria & Albert Museum, London)

281

The International Style

The writings and work of William Morris and his followers had had a great impact on a number of designers in Germany and were one of the contributory causes for the founding of the Deutscher Werkbund in 1907. Its founder, however, Herman Muthesius, after spending several years in England, held the conviction that only by a close collaboration between artists, architects and particularly manufacturers could a new rational style be evolved and that the potentialities of the machine must be utilized rather than ignored as it had been by Morris and his disciples.

In 1919 a programme for training in this integration of art and commerce was realized by the formation of the Bauhaus at Weimar by the architect Walter Gropius with Function and Construction as the keywords of the movement. The anti-academic basis of the training meant a virtual abolition of any decorative ornament in favour of abstract geometrical shapes. Tuition was conducted on two complementary courses, one devoted to techniques and materials, the other to the study of form, both courses being combined in the production of prototypes which could be used by manufacturers in terms of mass-production. In the turbulent political atmosphere of post-war Germany the aims of the Bauhaus, running contrary to established academic standards, were bound to engender hostility and accusations of socialism, and in 1925 the Weimar Bauhaus was closed by the authorities but reopened at Dessau where

it attracted some 600 students from many countries including Japan. Before its final closure by the Nazis in 1933 two directors succeeded Gropius after his departure in 1928 — Hannes Mayer and Mies van der Rohe; the latter, together with Marcel Breuer, was responsible for experimental prototypes of tubular steel furniture from 1925 onward. Mart Stam, a De Stijl associate, had designed a tubular steel chair in 1924, but his version was constructed from lengths of straight tubing joined by curved sections — the Bauhaus types had more elasticity with one continuous piece of tubing bent into shape with no joints at all. The most notable Bauhaus versions were Breuer's 'Cantilever' chair of 1928 and Mies van der Rohe's 'Barcelona' chair dating from 1929.

At the same time a number of French designers were working along similar lines in rejecting the concept of 'Decorative' in favour of 'Functional' furniture. Le Corbusier, Charlotte Perriand, Robert Mallet-Stevens and Pierre Chareau were among those in the forefront of the same movement which the Bauhaus was propagating. The rapid spread of chromium-plated tubular steel furniture throughout Europe was mainly due to the

Another extremely significant factor in furniture design in the twenties was the growing use of plywood. This consisted of thin layers of wood with the grain of each layer at right angles to that of the next, glued together under pressure to form a solid board which, if properly made, had none of the disadvantages of a comparable piece of natural wood. It had no tendency to split, warp or twist, was lighter in weight and could be made in sizes far greater than had previously been possible. A heavier version called laminboard or ibus consisted of strips of timber glued together and faced on each side with layers of veneer. Made in even larger sizes than plywood it was used for the sides and doors of large pieces of furniture. Experiments in making plywood had been made in America during the nineteenth century, but the results were unsatisfactory as the adhesive tended to be affected by humidity and the thin sheets of wood, sliced lengthwise across the tree trunk, displayed unsightly joins. A French invention of the 1870s, the rotary cutter, enabled the ply to be cut in a continuous sheet, the log being firmly held at each end and revolved slowly against a long cutting edge gauged to obtain the thickness of veneer required. The development of water-resistant cements in 1890 led to the manufacture of plywood in Russia and Finland. By 1912 Finland was the principal supplier in Europe.

The lightness and great tensile strength of plywood had been utilized in aeroplane construction during the First World War and subsequently in the building of commercial vehicles. During the timber shortages and a consequent scarcity of properly seasoned wood in the twenties, plywood was increasingly used in the construction of domestic furniture and panelling. Employed at first in its natural state it proved invaluable for the backs of large pieces of furniture and mirrors and for drawer bottoms where its resistance to splitting kept out dust. Subsequent technical improvements in facing plywood and laminboard with veneers of rare woods greatly extended its use and by reducing the costs enabled manufacturers to market furniture at far lower prices than hitherto possible. The British Empire Exhibition of 1924, while doing little to advance furniture design in England, had aroused interest in the many rare coloured woods grown in the colonies and extended the range of decorative finishes which had previously been restricted to oak, mahogany, walnut and satinwood. The cut edges of laminboard which exposed the rough inner construction when used for shelves were masked by strips of ebony or rosewood which contrasted with the paler veneer covering the horizontal surfaces and formed a decorative motif characteristic of much furniture of the 1930s.

old-established firm of Thonet which had pioneered the manufacture of bentwood furniture, mass-producing light, elegant and cheap machine-made furniture which could be found in both palaces and cafés. The Thonet techniques were adapted to the manufacture of metal furniture with ease and in fact many of the new pieces bore a striking resemblance to wooden originals created independently over 50 years before.

This new concept of furnishing aroused great controversy when, in addition to chairs, metal was used for tables and cupboards; its detractors claimed it was noisy, uncomfortable and fit only for the surgical wards of hospitals, while its admirers maintained that in an age when the machine was becoming more and more a part of daily life metal furniture was an appropriate symbol of the times. French designers claimed the credit for its invention and softened its starker effects with additions of wooden elements decorated with lacquer or exotic veneers and with upholstery in leather or fur. Introduced in England by the firms of PEL and Cox it was at first marketed as a luxury item, but mass-production reduced its cost and by the early 1930s was a commonplace in hotels, restaurants and canteens.

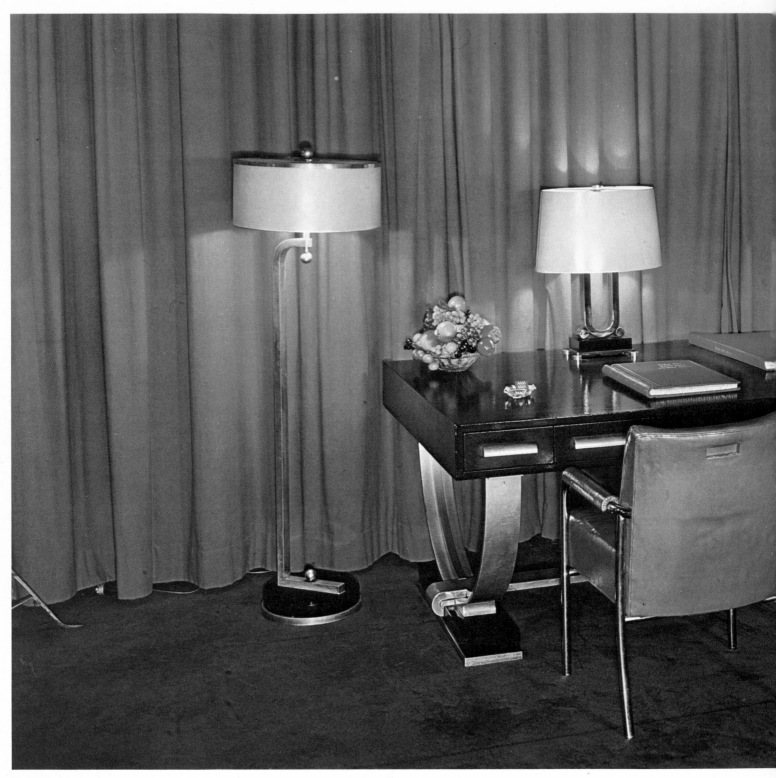

A radical change in domestic furniture design was the result of social changes which followed from the First World War. As a contemporary writer observed, the family pattern was broken up and whereas before the war the tendency was for a family to remain in the same house surrounded by accumulations of furniture and only moving when financial circumstances or a growing family made it imperative, the shortages of money and employment during the twenties forced families — smaller now — to move more often and usually into increasingly smaller houses or flats. Housing shortages forced the splitting of large family houses into as many apartments as possible, and as domestic help became scarcer the tendency was to have the minimal amount of furniture and to avoid a dust-collecting clutter of ornaments. This trend was even more marked in the thirties when, with the increase in cars and outside entertainments, less time was spent in the home.

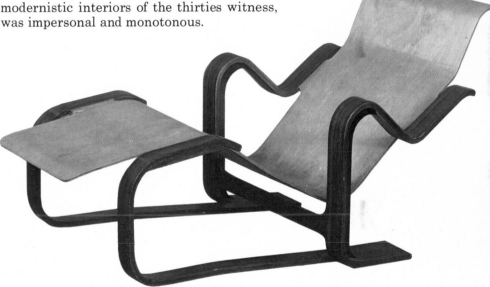

cupboards made the monumental wardrobes of the nineteenth century unnecessary. Impoverished families could no longer entertain on the lavish scale of the past and, if there were a dining-room at all, it was exceptional to find a dining-table designed to seat more than six people and in some flats no provision was made for dining at all. Dinner parties gave way to cocktail parties—alcohol and particularly gin was inexpensive—and the cocktail cabinet became an important feature of domestic furnishing. Furniture, except in the homes of the very rich, became smaller, lighter, easier to clean, and more importantly became cheaper. A series of bookshelves incorporating a writing-desk and a cocktail cabinet, for instance, were grouped round a divan which also served as a bed and, apart from a low coffee-table and one or two easy chairs, this was the sole furnishing. The design was minimal, block-like and with no unnecessary decoration to collect dust; ornaments and pictures were reduced to a minimum, and the total effect, as photographs of modernistic interiors of the thirties witness, was impersonal and monotonous.

After the Wall Street crash of 1929 and the years of depression which followed until about 1935 the furniture trades of Europe and America suffered as the nouveaux-riches of the twenties were replaced by the 'new poor'—a description which appeared with monotonous frequency during the following decade. The cult of Modernism which had finally ousted the ornamental fantasies of Art Deco in the late twenties was as much a matter of necessity as one of fashion. Catchwords of 'functionalism' and 'fitness for purpose' were really euphemisms for the required low price which put any extraneous ornament out of the question. The 'Great Dullness' as Maurice Dufrêne describes it in his introduction to the 1931 issue of *The Studio Year Book* was the result of 'the uniformity and simplicity of international art'. Dufrêne continued with

Left: Group of furniture designed by Donald Deskey in 1932 for the private suite of S L Rothafel in Radio City Music Hall. Deskey, one of the leading American decorators of the time, designed this handsome ensemble for the creator of the most palatial, and often outrageous, movie houses ever built. The restrained design reveals the main influences on contemporary American design—Chinese, French and Austrian. (Rockefeller Center, New York)

Above: Shaped plywood chaise-longue designed by Marcel Breuer in 1936. The upholstery has been removed to show more clearly the basic form. Using similar techniques to those employed by Thonet nearly a hundred years before, designers in the twenties and thirties shaped plywood under steam pressure in their search for new forms capable of cheap mass-production. (John Cox Collection, Brighton)

As rooms in newly-built houses and apartment blocks were smaller than before, less furniture was needed and very often some was built in as part of the structure. The functions of the dining- and living-rooms were combined and consequently the bulky and ornate sideboard, without which no dining-room had been considered adequately furnished, just about disappeared. Similarly technical improvements in plumbing made the antiquated washstand quite superfluous, while built-in

the apt comment that if the photographs in the volume had been presented without captions it would have been impossible to make a correct attribution for the designer or even the country of origin. Two years later John de La Valette, a writer much concerned with the questions of art and industry, claimed in the same publication that in 1933 'we touched bottom in the matter of decorative art'.

Manufacturers were faced with recurring economic crises and the ever present fear of bankruptcy, and they had to produce furniture at the lowest possible cost. Often dispensing

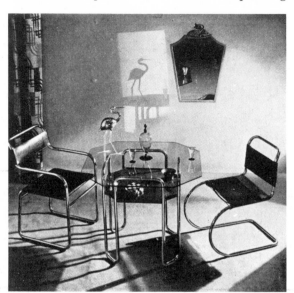

with designers to save money, they made versions of pieces which were themselves anaemic adaptations of originals from the Bauhaus or from avant-garde French designers. The tubular steel chair, now mass-produced and selling at remarkably low cost, appeared in interiors from Austria to California and its over-exposure occasioned caustic comments from writers in decorating magazines. Alternatively, extremely bulky easy chairs upholstered in tweed—one was advertised as capable of seating five people—would provide the only seating accommodation. Another international feature was the use of sycamore as a veneer relieved by machine fluting or by contrasting bandings of a darker wood, ebony or rosewood. In an attempt to relieve the enforced monotony of these pieces, manufacturers resorted to making asymmetrical furniture, for instance a writing-desk with drawers on one side balanced on the other by a plain wooden support.

There were several reasons for the spread of this international and uniform style in interior decoration and furniture. The big decorating firms which had enjoyed great prosperity in the post-war years were severely affected by the depression. Although there were still a considerable number of rich clients their numbers were decreasing as the slump continued with no signs of a return to normal and, in addition, the very lucrative orders for what was termed contract work (decoration

of boardrooms, ocean liners and palaces in the Near East) more or less disappeared. Consequently the big firms were obliged to cater for a less wealthy clientele, one both younger and less interested in period *décor*. Their design studios, considerably reduced in number, were forced to work in an unfamiliar idiom and had to acknowledge the hitherto despised modernism.

The increasing number of exponents of the comparatively new profession of interior decorator further threatened the large decorating firms. With little or no professional training — there were no schools of interior decoration as such in the twenties and few in the thirties — they could undercut the big firms and, by using social connections, impose their personal taste on their clients. Very few had the technical ability to design furniture and the majority encouraged the new taste for Regency and Victorian furniture and decorative objects which were considered 'amusing' with the added advantage of being plentiful, owing to the breaking up of many large houses, and, most important, of being extremely cheap. Baroque furniture from Italy and Spain, equally cheap, plentiful, and genuine, was exported in vast quantities to England and the United States where it was ruthlessly stripped of its polish or paint and bleached to harmonize with the currently fashionable pine panelling. It is true to say that a Baroque, Regency or mid-Victorian interior was as typical of taste in the thirties as a modernistic room.

The surrealistic exhibitions in Paris and London extended the trend against modernism and many decorators were quick to utilize its less macabre aspects. Jean-Michel Frank, working in Paris and California, created deceptively simple interiors which were nevertheless very costly. He used furniture in basic shapes completely unadorned but finished in the richest materials — vellum, shagreen or fine lacquer — and to these he added surrealist touches in the form of lamps, tables and ornaments cast in bronze and plaster from designs by Giacometti. Perhaps the most widely known piece of surrealist furniture was the 'Mouth' settee created by Frank after a drawing by Salvador Dali of an interior which metamorphosed as a portrait of Mae West.

Diversity of Styles
The later years of the decade saw a return to more decorative interiors as Europe and the United States gradually recovered from the effects of the depression. The growing number of interior decorators working in intense competition, each relying on the constant presentation of a new concept as much as any couturier in Paris, led to a wide diversity of styles. In practical terms a piece of antique decorative furniture was easier to sell to an unimaginative client as a basis for a building scheme of interior decoration than an idea conveyed by a drawing as the latter always carried the risk that the client might not approve of the furniture when actually made. Although still considerably reduced in size, the furniture trade at both ends of the market probably catered for a wider range of taste than at any time before. On both sides of the Atlantic deplorable versions of Tudor and Georgian originals — anything with a cabriole leg of the Queen Anne style was automatically labelled Georgian — were still mass-produced

Below: Cocktail cabinet in maple, made in England about 1935. The use of plywood and the lack of carved ornament are both measures of economy. The vertical fluting is found in much early thirties furniture and the design of the base shows French influence. (Royal Pavilion, Art Galley & Museums, Brighton)

289

for the hire-purchase trade, and these were so shoddily made that their disintegration after a few years' use was a certainty.

For those with 'taste but limited incomes' — a description much used in advertising in the thirties — there was the birchwood furniture mass-produced by Finmar Ltd, after designs by Alvar Aalto, the Finnish craftsman. This had the attraction of simplicity and lightness, owing to its construction from plywood which was steamed and moulded into pleasing shapes, and was extremely inexpensive. In England Duncan Miller, Betty Joel, Arundell Clarke, Hayes Marshall, Gordon Russell and Alistair Maynard were responsible for furniture which stressed simplicity, good proportions and the use of figured veneers.

From 1935 onwards small occasional tables and cocktail cabinets were covered with sheets of peach-coloured mirror sometimes contrasted with bandings of sapphire-blue faceted mirror. These were indicative of the growing trend to more decorative effects as was buttoned upholstery, a revival of a Victorian fashion, which was extensively used on shaped bedheads, settees and chairs. Endless variations were made on the draped dressing-tables with their skirt of gathered satin or taffeta concealing the drawers and cupboards each side of the kneehole, the fabric-covered top being protected by a sheet of plate-glass. The most popular colours for these were a pale mushroom pink, aquamarine blue and celadon green.

Syrie Maugham, erroneously credited with the invention of the 'all-white' room, originated a number of pieces of furniture which were versions of simple eighteenth-century French pieces altered to suit modern needs, including stands for a telephone with spaces for directories, book tables with sunk compartments for plants and bedside tables to take a lamp and a breakfast tray. These were painted with the crackle finish which was her trademark and were intended to harmonize with the antique French and Italian painted furniture which she included in most of her interiors.

In the thirties there is curiously little mention of the many French designers who had exhibited the fine pieces in the Art Deco manner during the twenties and only a few new designers, André Arbus, Jacques Adnet and Marcel Champion, carried on in the tradition of Ruhlmann (who had died in 1933) — but their furniture is often heavy and inclined to rely on novelty. Taste in France as elsewhere was veering to the antique and decorative.

Many designers had already emigrated from Germany before the advent of the Nazi régime in 1933 and the closing of the Bauhaus in that year saw the exodus of most of its teachers and students to England and, notably, the United States where they had a considerable

influence on modern American design. Here, as in England and France, the predominant taste among the richer sections of society was for the past but in the rapidly growing cities modernist decorations and furniture were considered more appropriate in the new buildings. Interior decorators were more highly organized with design studios than in Europe, and Donald Deskey, Gilbert Rhode, Walter Dorwin Teague, Paul Frankl and Hugo Gnam, to mention only a few, designed variations on the limited modernist repertoire of streamlined, veneeered furniture. Their designs made use of asymmetrical forms, curved corners and thick plate-glass tops and shelves with an occasional concession to ornament in the form of lacquered details and motifs derived from Chinese and Japanese sources. It cannot be said that the thirties was a decade remarkable for high standards of originality or invention in furniture or that representative pieces will be as eagerly collected as those of the previous decade.

Left: Dressing-table and stool designed by Paul Frankl. The decorative motifs on the mirror and the supports for the table show a curious throwback to the already outmoded Art Deco. Frankl did much to propagate a distinctive American style at a time when American manufacturers were solely concerned with reproductions. 'Skyscraper' furniture — cupboards and bookcases piled in vertical shapes echoing the masses of the buildings seen through the windows — illustrated his statement that skyscrapers were the only original works of contemporary art to be found in America. (Sybarites Gallery, New York)

Above right: An example that derives from a French eighteenth-century original of the painted furniture designed in about 1930 by Syrie Maugham. Her interiors achieved their effect by a mixture of furniture of different periods sometimes stripped and bleached but more often painted in off-white or pastel colours with a crackled finish. (Royal Pavilion, Art Gallery & Museums, Brighton)

Right: Syrie Maugham's own drawing-room in about 1933. The stark modernist décors of the depression years gave way to more ornate and decorative designs and under the influence of Syrie Maugham and her celebrated white rooms, the way was opened for more romantic and surrealist interiors. Her use of simple French and Italian furniture combined with off-white walls, mirror screens and masses of white flowers and a sophisticated chic which ensured their imitation.

291

INNOVATION
Furniture to the present day

In the 1970s, we are nearer than we ever have been to achieving one recognizably international style of modern furniture. The credit or blame, depending on whether one considers uniformity boring or a reassuring sign of general agreement on what is right for our times, can be given partly to the increased efficiency with which international communications have pierced geographical boundaries and partly to a co-operation permitted by the relative lack of political tension between countries in the West since the Second World War. National styles persist, certainly, but they are now much less clearly defined, and attitudes towards them much less chauvinistic. Yet this is a situation that has only come about since the war, for in the 1940s and 1950s, one could still analyze quite clearly the separate, concurrent movements which have each subsequently contributed to the look of international furniture today. The majority of these movements were well under way by the end of the 1940s, and those with the strength and validity necessary for survival can be seen to have become fused into the Italian furniture revolution of the 1960s, which set the pace for over a decade.

The 1940s
The outbreak of war in Europe in 1939 halted the development of furniture design and manufacturing techniques on that continent, but it also forced several changes of emphasis and direction at an international level, the results of which are only now, with the perspective bestowed by time, beginning to become clear. Western furniture might have been very different today had not, for example, Mies van der Rohe and Marcel Breuer been forced to emigrate from Germany to the United States by the increasing intolerance of their ideas in Hitler's pre-war Germany.

In Germany itself, the simple, functional and somewhat aseptic principles of the Bauhaus (which shocked German bourgeois taste in the 1920s and which Hitler described as Bolshevik art) were supplanted by the earthy realism of Hitler's 'Blood and Soil' style — at its most vehement in heavy wooden furniture carved with Nazi propagandist symbols. Its more innocuous relative, the 'Heimat' style of rustic, cottage modernism spread throughout the whole of occupied Europe (infiltrating even the two neutrals, Sweden and Switzerland) where it took root and flourished long after the war was over. Although in the late 1940s there was some evidence in Germany of a return to pre-war design standards, it was not until the establishment of the Hochschule für Gestaltung at Ulm in 1955 (inaugurated by Walter Gropius) that any real national concern about the direction of furniture design became apparent. Even then, many of the principles which gave

the Bauhaus its meaning were re-examined and deliberately rejected, and it took more than 20 years from the outbreak of the Second World War for the work of the Bauhaus designers to be appreciated internationally — and copiously imitated. In the meantime, their principles of functional simplicity were suddenly and rudely imposed on the world by practical necessity, in the form of the material shortages and drastic economies of wartime. The furniture that was produced in this emergency situation had neither the classic elegance nor the impact of, say, Breuer's 'Wassily' chair, but it nevertheless made a substantial contribution to the progress of furniture design.

The British response to necessities imposed by the war shortages is summed up by Richard Sword in *Utility Furniture and Fashion 1941–1951* (published by the Inner London Education Authority, 1974).

'. . . . that furniture should be strong and serviceable, not in any way temporary and it should use the minimum of raw material. Only hardwoods — oak or mahogany — were to be used and all joints were strongly mortised or pegged. Because plywood was unobtainable, veneered hardboard had to be used for panels. Characteristically, most of the cabinet furniture stood on plinths rather than legs; wood sections were relatively thin and panels were often sub-divided. Plastics were needed for the war effort, so that knobs and handles were of wood, but, in spite of the shortage of steel,

screws were specified in the construction, contributing greatly to the strength of the finished piece. Wardrobes were deep enough for clothes to be hung sideways; this was certainly not always a feature of pre-war wardrobes and is an example of the thought that went into the way in which the furniture would be used. Springing in the easy chairs was minimal, one pound of steel wire having to do the work of seven pounds. Partly because of this particular shortage, no settee or three-piece suite was designed, although a bed-settee was made for those who had to combine their living and sleeping accommodation.'

In Britain, the war provided a unique opportunity for a group of idealistic design reformers to impose good design on an entire population. The bulk of Britain's timber had always been imported, and the acute shipping shortage in 1939 had an immediate effect on supplies. Other imported goods could be rationed, but there were special problems in controlling both the production and consumption of furniture. There was plenty of furniture around when war broke out, but more would undoubtedly be needed for the services, for those who were bombed out and for those who, despite the war, were marrying and setting up home for the first time. But even if the ability to buy furniture was limited to those in real need, there was still the problem of who should make it, and what kind of furniture should be made. The huge, ornate, expensive pieces so prevalent before the war were of

course out of the question, but if manufacturers were to be asked to make cheap furniture, there had to be some system of quality control to protect the consumer.

Various measures were tried during the early years of the war. In the summer of 1940, furniture came under price control and timber supplies to the furniture industry were suspended. Early in 1941, the Government issued specifications and contracts for the making of 'Standard Emergency Furniture' — an inferior predecessor to Utility. Although many manufacturers had now switched their production to war work, the others could still make what they liked — if they had the timber. But by the end of that year, furniture manufacture had been restricted to 20 specified items and, in June 1942, the Board of Trade announced its Utility Furniture Scheme, under which only furniture of specified design and price was to be produced, under licence, from October 1942 onwards.

Under the scheme, Hugh Dalton, the new President of the Board of Trade, aimed to 'secure the production of furniture of good, sound construction in simple but agreeable designs and at reasonable prices, ensuring the maximum economy of raw materials and labour'. Among those on Dalton's advisory committee was Gordon Russell. Russell, still possibly the foremost furniture designer/manufacturer in Britain, had already proved that he could adapt to the times, and that he believed in 'furniture for the people'. Although

the tubular steel of the pre-war Modern movement had never entered a piece of his furniture, he had, in the 1930s, recaptured for England a position in the forefront of furniture design by progressing from individual decorated pieces strongly influenced by the Arts and Crafts movement to batch-production of beautifully proportioned, strong, simple, undecorated sets. He was already involved in trying to spread his design ideology still further by setting up a 'Good Furnishing Group' of retailers when war broke out, his Broadway showrooms were half-destroyed by an incendiary bomb and his workshops and factory taken over for wartime production . The brief for the Utility Scheme, 'to ensure a supply of furniture of the best quality available at controlled prices to meet a real need', represented an opportunity to prove to a whole country, with government endorsement, the truth of what he and a few other pioneers of design reform had been saying for years, unheeded by public and manufacturers alike. Eleven designers were asked to submit drawings but, in the end, Edwin Clinch, H T Cutler and L J Barnes — all from High Wycombe, which was still the centre of the British furniture-making industry — appear between them to have been responsible for the first Utility range of 20 items.

The production of this first range was by no means the end of the Utility story, as Russell saw in it the seeds of a method from which could grow an overall improvement in the

Above: Bedroom furniture from the British Utility ranges of 1947. Most manufacturers were restricted to designs in these ranges as materials were still subject to controls of all kinds, and therefore goods were made with the available rather than the most suitable materials. Thus manufacturers hastily turned their war-time technology to peace-time use by employing surplus war materials not previously applied to furniture, such as aluminium and steel. This tubular metal bed displays in practice many of the theories of low-cost functional simplicity advocated in the 1920s by the Bauhaus.

standard of mass-produced furniture that would benefit the post-war, de-controlled situation. A panel of designers duly worked through the war and in March 1946, nearly a year after the end of the war, a Board of Trade exhibition showed fifty pieces of Utility furniture, which were produced and bought tax-free through the successive stages of de-control until 1952. It was also after the war,

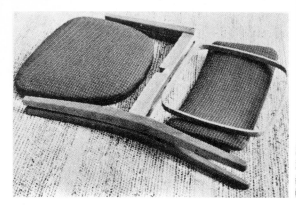

when freedom of design was allowed, although still under Utility specifications, that some of the best pieces of Utility appeared — notably those by Christopher Heal for Heal & Son, which demonstrated that sensitivity and ingenuity could manipulate strict limitations on dimensions and materials into unexpected elegance. When freedom of production was eventually permitted, some firms reverted to their old ways. But as Gordon Russell has himself said: 'Some of the good manufacturers were very anxious not to return to pre-war standards. They genuinely wanted to make a decent product.' Sufficient impact was certainly made by the Utility Scheme to ensure that British furniture was never quite the same again.

While the British were getting Utility furniture rammed down their throats, during the early 1940s, like it or lump it, a revolution of comparable importance was stirring in Denmark. It was less immediately all-embracing, since it was not nationally imposed by an authority of governmental stature, but its ultimate influence was far greater internationally, as it led to the great Scandinavian furniture export boom of the 1950s and 1960s. The furniture, usually in birch, beech or teak, was superbly made, spare-framed and undecorated in an elegant, sophisticated and totally new style, neither aggressively modern nor, on the other hand, nostalgically countrified.

During the last years of the war, and despite the war, a housing research programme was carried out in Copenhagen in which several hundred flats were measured and photographed to record current family living habits. The analysis of the material showed that, in an urban environment at least, many flats had

two rooms or less, and that the layout of the flat revolved around specific sets of furniture — a dining-room suite, a drawing-room suite and a bedroom suite. These were packed in until there was virtually no room to move and, as if that were not sufficiently claustrophobic, the furniture tended to have opulent curves and exaggerated carving. Boldly-coloured, flower-patterned curtain and upholstery fabrics further burdened the eye.

A reaction to all this had already set in, however; the young architects were in the vanguard, supported by a sympathetic press and the Copenhagen Cabinet-makers Guild, which had already shown alternative furnishing solutions at its annual exhibitions. The suggested alternatives came in the shape of smaller, lighter pieces of furniture, single items instead of sets, and they were grouped round the walls to give maximum floor space. In 1944, these alternatives reached the public when the Danish Co-operative Society opened a furniture shop in Copenhagen. Almost all the furniture in the shop was designed by Børge Mogensen, a young designer who had been Head of the Danish Co-operative Society's Furniture Design Department since 1942 and who, with his assistants, had spent the two intervening years concentrating on this project. All the items were single pieces of furniture, but had a simplicity and harmony of style which allowed them to work well together. Denmark had never before seen anything like this furniture, yet its origins were clear, for Mogensen had studied with Kaare Klint, whose basic demands for function and quality dismissed novelty for its own sake and rooted design principles in classic pieces such as the English Windsor and the Swedish stick-back chairs. But Mogensen's furniture

Above: Priva knock-down chair designed by Elias Svedberg for the Nordiska Kompaniet, Sweden, in 1949. This piece of furniture came with the basic components supplied finished and with nuts and bolts for easy home assembly.

296

was also in tune with the times—it had real purpose and met real needs. It appeared stark when compared with heavy, ornamental period furniture, but it took advantage of the war-induced shortage of materials by using Danish birch and Swedish beech, it was adapted to current production methods and it was geared to contemporary living conditions, taking up relatively little space and being easy to handle and easy to clean.

Mogensen's theories were ratified for, in spite of grim warnings from the established, traditional manufacturers that people would always want suites, the new furniture was received enthusiastically by the Danish public. Other designers, inspired by Mogensen, made classic contributions which, of their kind, have still to be bettered. Hans Wegner's first significant 'Chinese' chair was made by Fritz Hansen in 1944 and indicated a decisive move away from the Klint school in its freer, more sculptural treatment, an obvious signature being the method by which he linked the back

and arms of a chair with a single, curved, elegantly turned rail. Finn Juhl's style was more individual and obviously influenced by contemporary abstract sculpture in the way that structural form was elaborated far beyond the demands of function. In the early 1950s, Juhl worked as an ambassador for Danish design by creating many of the international travelling exhibitions, but the furniture sold itself. By 1950, Denmark had an annual furniture export of 3 million kroner (£155,000), by 1960 it had risen to 146 million kroner (£7,601,000) and in 1973 it was 725 million kroner (£49,000,000). This export bonanza resulted in widespread plagiarism, notably the highly successful G-Plan in Britain in the fifties and sixties. The rapid reorganization of the Danish furniture industry after such a crippling experience as the Second World War has been attributed to the fact that it was never fully industrialized, thus retaining flexibility in production. A nation of cabinet-makers, Denmark's production has always

been best described as 'mechanized craft', which made, and still retains, its unique reputation on uncompromising quality.

Finland's reputation for timeless, simple, well-made modern furniture had been made by Alvar Aalto in the 1920s, and continued to survive. It could be said that only in the 1940s was the rest of Scandinavia beginning to catch up with Finland and certainly one other Scandinavian country followed Denmark's lead, for in 1949 the big Stockholm furniture store, Nordiska Kompaniet, opened a completely separate department to sell well-made, inexpensive, simple designs by the architect, Elias Svedberg. His knock-down/home-assembly Priva range was one of the earliest examples of a manufacturing-marketing principle which changed internationally the image of furniture retailing in the 1960s. In France, too, there was a growing sympathy for simple furniture, for although the annual Paris exhibition was filled with huge, painted, inlaid, over-carved and over-polished pieces (probably intended for export), by the late 1940s the city's stores were beginning to stock furniture which was light in both weight and colour. By the early 1950s France had re-discovered cane and wicker furniture, which became as popular in the 1960s and early 1970s as it had been in the twenties and thirties.

The concern of the Danish designers in the 1940s was to update their traditional methods of making furniture to suit the rapidly changing contemporary needs in the home, and indigenous supplies of wood permitted them to carry out this programme without having to resort to the research and development of suitable new materials. Designers in other countries were being forced to look beyond solid wood by the international timber shortage, and this war-induced situation can once again be seen to have had a significant influence on long-term developments. In Germany, the firm of Edwin Behr, faced with a shortage of solid, quality timber for its wall-storage systems, developed a special type of chipboard made from resin and woodchip waste material. This material has been widely adopted over the years as a wood-substitute, laminated with wood veneers or plastic to give an acceptable finish, and is now produced under licence by more than 50 chipboard factories all over Europe.

In Britain, a manufacturer named Noel Jordan, realizing that there would be little future for his small, light-engineering firm after the war, decided that his production could be adapted to furniture and advertised for a designer who would create 'furniture for today in today's materials'. The chosen designer, Ernest Race, devised a chair, the BA, which used re-smelted aluminium alloy from aircraft scrap. This chair was first shown at the 'Britain Can Make It' exhibition

in London's Victoria & Albert Museum in 1946 and earned an international reputation for its innovatory design and technology. It sold more than a quarter of a million units during its 23-year production run, during which time some of the earlier, wear-worn models were re-sold for their aluminium content at a net profit on current prices. This was Ernest Race's first production design (he had no formal design training, but had studied interior decoration before the war), and for the next 20 years until his death in 1964, both he and the firm, re-named Race Furniture, became known for simple and unpretentious furniture of great technical ingenuity. As he used materials which were mostly new to furniture, his work was without precedent, and it represents one of the most important milestones in the history of British furniture design.

For the milestones of truly international stature in the 1940s and 1950s, one looks to America. In 1940, the Museum of Modern Art (MOMA) in New York held a national competition for 'Organic Design in Home Furnishings'. In the furniture section, two

Left: Pedestal range by Eero Saarinen for Knoll International, United States, 1956. Visually, the chair has a sculptural unity of form, but in practical terms it was found impossible to make the item in one piece. The plastic shell of the chair, upholstered in wool, is mounted for strength and stability on a slim, waisted cast-metal base with a fused plastic finish. The tables have similar bases and tops in either marble, plastic laminate or wood veneer.

Below left: BA chair designed by Ernest Race for Race Furniture, England, in 1945. After the war and with no formal design training, Race joined a small engineering firm which was looking for peace-time products to make and someone to design them. As neither wood nor fabric were yet available, they at first tried, without success, to adapt a range of unit furniture to aluminium sheeting, resmelted from aircraft scrap, until Race casually produced a set of drawings he had done for a chair and table in cast aluminium. First shown at the Britain Can Make It exhibition in 1946, more than 250,000 chairs were produced before the model was finally discontinued in 1969.

young architects, Charles Eames and Eero Saarinen, won first prizes for seating and other living-room furniture. Among the items was a chair that introduced totally new concepts in both design and production. Seat, back and arm sections were united in a single, three-dimensional shell form, made of wood-veneer strips and glue, which had been shaped over a cast-iron mould. The shell was covered with a thin layer of latex foam and the upholstery material was cemented on top. The chair legs were to be of aluminium rod, welded to the chair by a new process which could bond wood to rubber, glass or metal, but this process was reserved for military purposes during the war. Wooden legs were substituted and a few models were made — at great expense and effort. But the chair was technically ahead of its time and was never mass-produced, although its influence can be seen in the later work of both architects (the closest descendant being a chair Saarinen designed for Knoll Associates in 1948), and in that of other architects and designers in the West.

During the war, Eames moved to California where he worked on moulded splints and

aircraft components in plywood. By the time he was able to concentrate on furniture again, he had learned a lot about plywood, and his first one-man exhibition, in 1946 and again at the Museum of Modern Art, owed the major part of its success to this research period. Bending plywood was no breakthrough in itself—the German firm of Thonet had pioneered it in the 1860s and the Finnish architect-designer Alvar Aalto (whose influence Eames freely acknowledged) was bending laminated sheet ply into two-way curves for chairs and stools in the 1930s. But Eames' achievement with his LCM chair was the 'compound' curve which moulded itself to the sitter in all directions. The chair attracted the attention of the Herman Miller Furniture Company of Michigan, which began making Eames' furniture the following year and has done so ever since, along with that of some of the most influential designers of our time.

Eames' next major breakthrough, in 1948, was again prompted by a Museum of Modern Art Competition, this time an international competition for 'Low Cost Furniture', and again technology developed initially during the war proved to have valuable peace-time applications. It had been discovered that glass-fibre could be used to make exceptionally strong and durable aircraft nose cones. Its

additional advantage was that it could be moulded in any direction. Eames' DAR chair in glass-fibre-reinforced plastic (GRP) was a shell of great strength and durability with complex curves and a soft sheen finish. It could be mounted on a variety of legs, bases or pedestals to serve a number of uses. It was the first commercial use of this material for furniture and the precursor to the spate of plastic furniture in the 1960s, although it took more than a decade for economic production methods to be worked out, and considerably longer for the average consumer to accept that plastic belonged anywhere else but in the kitchen. Eames' work with plywood was picked up much more quickly—the technique was less revolutionary—and led to other pieces that became classics of their type—from the low-cost, general-purpose stacking chair designed by Danish born Carl Jacobsen for the English firm of Kandya in 1950 to Joe Colombo's 4801 occasional chair for Kartell, Italy, in 1963.

The Museum of Modern Art competition in 1948 contained other pointers to the future, for among the prize-winners was David Pratt —whose early example of a pneumatic chair on legs preceded mass-production of 'blow-up' furniture by almost 20 years—and English designers Robin Day and Clive Latimer. Day

Right: Wire range by the sculptor, painter and architect Harry Bertoia for Knoll International, United States. Bertoia began working for Knoll in 1950, in a small workshop in Bally, Pennsylvania, where he produced variations on earlier sculptures which began to suggest new forms and materials for furniture manufacture. The wire chairs, now regarded as classics, were the result. The chromium-plated, steel-rod frame has a skid-type leg structure which has since been adopted by many other designers.

and Latimer's entry was a plywood storage system hung on tubular metal supports, but of the two designers it was Day who was, in 1963, eventually, to receive international recognition for his own moulded stacking chair in polypropylene for the British firm of Hille. This chair proved beyond doubt that, if every aspect of the design and manufacture was rationalized and if the manufacturer had sufficient faith in his product to cover the initial cost of the production system (over £95,000 in this case) by planning from the start for an international market, furniture in plastics made hard economic sense. The chair sold initially at around £3; by 1970, more than two million chairs had been sold and they were being imported, or made under licence, by about 23 different countries.

The 1950s

By the end of the 1940s, the major signposts pointing the way to the development of furniture design and technology over the next 20 years were already in place. But to leave the forties with one story untold, even though its most significant chapters belong in the next decade, would be misleading. In the late 1930s, Hans Knoll, a member of a noted German furniture-making factory which had produced early Mies van der Rohe

Left: The Swan chair by Arne Jacobsen for Fritz Hansen, Denmark, 1958. This chair was first designed for the SAS Royal Hotel in Copenhagen but, as with its companion the Egg chair, production quickly resulted in international acclaim and demand. It is both sculptural and comfortable, allowing a variety of seating positions.

designs, emigrated first to England and then to New York. He was in good company, as other prominent figures from the Bauhaus were already in the United States or finding their way there, among them Joseph Albers, Walter Gropius, Mies van der Rohe and Marcel Breuer. The buildings of the 'Bauhaus *émigrés*' were readily accepted, but furniture appropriate to them was non-existent.

Hans Knoll opened his first small woodworking shop in New York in 1938. In 1941, he met Florence Schust, an architect who had taught at the Cranbrook Academy of Art, Michigan, under Elial Saarinen and alongside his son, Eero Saarinen, Charles Eames and sculptor Harry Bertoia. The business association between Hans Knoll and Florence Schust began in 1943; they married in 1946 and by the end of the decade a team comprising some of the most avant-garde international designers was at work on projects for Knoll Associates. In 1951, Knoll International opened in France and Germany and by 1955 there were subsidiary companies in Belgium, Canada, Cuba, Sweden and Switzerland. The clearest indication of the Knolls' attitude to furniture design is given by the fact that, in the early 1950s, they put into production several pieces designed by Mies van der Rohe in the thirties. New pieces by other designers were quickly added to the collection (many of which have since been acclaimed as classics), including, in 1951, the wire range by Harry Bertoia and, between 1956 and 1957 (when Florence Knoll had taken over the company following her husband's death in an accident), Saarinen's pedestal range which included the celebrated 'Tulip' chair.

The wire range by Bertoia, who was originally engaged by the Knolls in 1950 as a sculptor with an entirely open brief to experiment inside or outside the furniture field, has the elegance, integrity and visual

economy which is typical of the Knoll stable. Bertoia's own comments about it include the explanation: 'In sculpture, I am concerned primarily with space, form and the characteristics of metal. In the chairs, many functional problems have to be satisfied first, but when you get right down to it, the chairs are studies in space, form and metal too. My sculpture is made up of a lot of little units, and these rectangles or hexagonals or triangles are added together and produce one large rectangular or hexagonal sculpture. The same with the chairs. The chair has a lot of little diamond shapes in its wire cage and they all add up to one very large diamond shape, and this is the shape of the whole chair. It is really an organic principle, like a cellular structure.' It is a lucid explanation and rare in that it is unpretentious, easily understood by the layman and to a certain extent sums up the preoccupations of many of the serious designers of that generation, who were concerned with organic forms and considerably influenced by contemporary abstract painting and sculpture.

The other major concern of serious designers during this period was the reduction of both form and material to their essentials; in other words, to reduce the number of parts so that each piece had a visual unity and so that the manufacturing process was minimized. The ideal was to make an item of furniture in one piece and, if possible, of one material only. Rietveld had hand-made a one-piece moulded chair in fibre-board in 1927 and Mies van der Rohe made drawings for a one-piece moulding in 1946, but neither of these was ever produced. Saarinen came near to it with his pedestal chair, but structural strength demanded that the base be made in aluminium, although painted white to match the plastic seat-shell. But it was not until Swiss designer Verner Panton's S-shaped stacking chair in moulded glass-fibre and polyester—designed in 1960 but only in production from 1967 (Herman Miller)—that it became possible to mass-produce a one-piece chair.

Harry Bertoia was not alone in his preoccupation with fine metal rod and organic form, either in America or overseas, but whereas Bertoia's furniture is as pleasing to the eye in the 1970s as when it was first designed, the bulk of fifties designs had dated within a decade. Notable exceptions are pieces such as those by the Danish architect, Arne Jacobsen. His teak-veneered, moulded plywood 'Ant' chair on slim tubular steel legs (1957) may echo Eames' work, and it could even be said that his famous moulded glass-fibre 'Swan' chair (1958) echoes that of Saarinen, but they are both still being made and sold today (by Fritz Hansen, Denmark), and they both have a quality that is timeless.

It is hard to find furniture designed in Britain in the 1950s of which one can say the same.

It may be unfair to suggest that the fifties in Britain was a period of 'dilettante design', but in retrospect the image is undoubtedly of preoccupations (knobs with everything) and prejudices (against American 'streamlining'), and of an attempt to marry a number of individual stylistic ingredients—most of which rapidly became *clichés*—into an acceptable package. The term 'Festival style' has

often been used as a convenient, comprehensive definition, but although existing trends were spotlighted by the Festival of Britain in 1951, they neither sprang into life overnight, nor might they have stayed on the scene for so long had not the euphoric, post-war Festival spirit lent them a certain false glamour.

The most recognizable of the fifties' furniture *clichés* were in splayed legs for chairs and tables (which gave them a stance somewhat like that of a sick horse), fine welded rod frames with knobs on (as 'feet' on chairs or tables) and 'quartics'—free-form shapes based on the ellipse, which replaced rectangles for table-tops, for example. There is always a danger in attributing influences, but the origins of some of these stylistic fancies seem quite clear. The influence of contemporary scientific research on painting and sculpture during the early part of the twentieth century has been well documented, but it was only in the 1950s that the decorative arts also found a three-dimensional expression of a scientific concept that could be applied to furniture. It was based on the models that scientists used to demonstrate molecular structure. It is hard to say who utilized the concept first—the fine artists or the designers. Certainly, the younger sculptors like Butler and Paolozzi were making fine wire constructions, but the Festival architects erected whole panels based on this structure, and the archetypal

Above: Lounge chair and ottoman by Charles Eames for Herman Miller, United States, 1956. Eames became increasingly preoccupied with function. Like other designers of his generation, he was attempting to translate the traditional concept of ultimate comfort, as represented by the massive well-padded armchair of an English club, into a form compatible with modern architecture and with his own inclination for lighter, more informal furniture. The frame is in rosewood-veneer, moulded plywood, mounted on a swivelling, cast-aluminium cruciform base and upholstered with leather over latex foam and down filling.

Right: The living-room from the Space and Form exhibition house, designed by Paul Gell and shown by Brown's of Chester in 1958, was one of the more elegant summaries of 1950s design in England. Primary colours are used with a lot of black. Texture is important, shown here in the natural wood, rush matting and Japanese-style paper lanterns, which were typical of the period. But unlike most of the spindle-shanked furniture, the classic Bertoia wire chair (centre) has not dated.

'Festival style' chair was made for it by Ernest Race. The chair had a fine wire frame and knob feet supporting a bent plywood seat; it was one of the earliest and best examples of the style, which subsequently spread and deteriorated until even lamp-standards and plant-holders balanced precariously on ungainly, ball-footed wire legs. The free-form shapes which crept onto table-tops were undoubtedly also influenced by the amoeboid shapes in contemporary abstract art, ranging from the Persian pear (most obviously recognizable in Paisley patterned fabrics) and the Magatama (a graphic Japanese symbol for the embryo) to the Chinese Yin and Yang motifs representing the female and male principles in creation and the Mandala, the Buddhist symbol of balance.

If neither the 'knobbed' nor the 'quartic' style had any fundamental justification such as function—being merely surface styling—the predilection for splaying the legs of chairs and tables can at least be seen to give these objects structural stability. But in the same way that the wire rod and ball style was used with conviction by American designer George Nelson for his 'Ball Clock' (1949) and his 'Marshmallow' sofa (1956), both for Herman Miller, and misused by less able designers, the Italian designers' use of splayed legs for organic, sculptural effect was lost in translation by designers in other countries who

either misunderstood or had no sympathy with the concept. One had only to compare Carlo de Carli's tables in the early fifties, in which the legs were carved or jointed to look as if they were growing out of the table-top, with the ugly, tapered wooden pegs stuck on the bases of the mass-produced tables and chairs in the northern European countries to appreciate the difference. But the comparison is slightly unfair, and it is in the intention to mass-produce that the unfairness lies. This is something which has often been forgotten when extolling the heights of excellence and originality to which the cream of post-war Italian furniture design climbed during the fifties and sixties.

Post-war Italy had the same material shortages and intensive reconstruction programmes that faced other European countries, but, just as in Renaissance Italy the painter was the jack-of-all-trades (Cellini ran a foundry, designed monuments, jewellery and candelabra, and painted society ladies as well), this century it has been the architect who has created whatever design was needed for any branch of industry. This situation has had both its strength and its weaknesses. In the immediate post-war period, it meant that the Italian architect, whose main task was to supervise the rebuilding of the thousands of working-class dwellings destroyed during the last years of the war, had little time to

devote to furniture, except for individual commissions, often of single pieces, for the clients with houses and incomes to accommodate them. But through these relatively few pieces, with the help of traditionally superb craftsmanship and despite the materials shortage, architects such as Mollino, Mangiarotti, Rosselli and Parisi managed to create an impressive new style in furniture construction out of virtually nothing. It was ingenious, simple, spare and sculptural and sometimes crossed the border from organic to surreal. A somewhat lyrical description of Mollino's work in the Italian magazine *Domus* in 1950 sets the mood of the time:

'Mollino's furniture shows the constant development of an idea, from solid, heavy wood to curved and hollowed triple-ply, from the purely optical effect of lightness to true elasticity, from single parts welded together to one-piece furniture in a single, uninterrupted piece of triple-ply. Thus one of his armchairs will have an arm that opens out like a leaf or a vegetable, one of his tables has a continuous hieroglyphic that is almost ghostlike in its quality. His forms record nature, not in a literal way like Art Nouveau, but by analogy. That is, after all, the fashion of the poet.'

To imagine giving that information as part of a working brief to a factory foreman is to realize how far the Italian architect-designers were from the concept of mass-production. With a few notable exceptions, the best of modern Italian furniture has always been made, by both its style and its price, for the few rather than for the many.

Yet, although individual designers and manufacturers in other countries made contributions that deserve recognition, it was Italy that provided the inspiration for a generation of designers in the late fifties and sixties. Design rapidly grew to become a national, almost obsessional pastime and, however élitist (the truly progressive furniture taking up only a tiny fraction of the country's furniture production), it had international repercussions on a scale which rarely occurs more than two or three times in a century.

The 1960s

It is as dangerous to attempt to be specific about the place, timing or individual responsible for the style which has become generally known as 'Italian modern' as it is to generalize

about its typical features. The movement was far more than an arbitrary change from wood to plastic and chrome tube, from the rectilinear to the curvilinear or from organic to geometric — although these elements were certainly present as was the much criticized tendency for revivalism.

Dino Gavina, not so much a designer as a man with an instinct for what is good and the courage of his considerable convictions, worked from a small shop in the late 1950s in Bologna. He began remaking and selling, under licence, items of furniture (including some in tubular chrome) which had originally been designed by Marcel Breuer more than 30 years earlier. In 1960, the Gavina Company was formed and, as with the Knolls in the United States (Knoll International subsequently took over Gavina in 1968), it rapidly acquired the kind of reputation which attracted some of the most progressive designers in Europe — including Vico Magistretti, Tobia Scarpa, Sebastian Matta, Kazuhide Takahama and Achille and Pier Castiglioni. By 1964, Scarpa and Magistretti,

among others, were designing complete interiors for Gavina which had an entirely new feeling about them — such as the living-room in a Sardinian house with low, square chairs in wood, upholstered with separate, leather-covered, rectangular, foam-slab cushions for seat, back and arms, low slab-topped rectangular tables on rectangular plinths against an overall colouring of restrained blues and terracottas on white. Imitations of the style were manifold, and the essential purity of Gavina's original concept became submerged in the kind of design free-for-all which took place over the next ten years. Styles were as many and varied as there were designers to create them and, by the second half of the decade, plastics had been thoroughly tamed and coloured black, white, emerald, scarlet, yellow and orange, op and pop art had added their graphic influence and the preoccupation had extended to the total interior environment. You could choose, if you could afford to, from Joe Colombo's padded living-blocks (central living-area plus night cell, kitchen box and bathroom box), Ettore Sotsass' shrine-like,

Right: Sacco chair by Piero Gatti/Cesare Paolini/Franco Teodoro for Zanotta, Italy, 1968. Made of synthetic leather, it was filled with expanded polystyrene granules, moulding itself comfortably to any seating position.

Far right: Ciprea chair by Afra and Tobia Scarpa for Cassina, Italy, 1967 — a moulded block of polyurethane foam with no internal frame, but mounted on a rigid plastic base to allow for castors.

Below right: T1 chair in chromed steel-tube and leather by OMK, England, 1966. This chair marked the first British appearance of the curved tubular frame.

Below far right: Toga chair by Sergio Mazza for Artemide, Italy, 1968 — a self-coloured glass-fibre shell, hot-pressed in one piece.

Above: Created as a publicity project by the British laminate manufacturer, Formica, this living-room for a young couple contains many typical ingredients of an early 1970s interior. The silver-crowned bulb in the table-lamp is significant, showing the public's new found interest in specialist effects.

free-standing wardrobes, linked to the walls of the room only by bands of brilliant colour (making it virtually impossible to put anything else in the room without destroying the effect), Rosselli's totally moulded plastic interiors for Saporitti (all plastic from bookshelves to fold-away bunk beds) — or settle for some of the comparatively few, good, reasonably-priced, mass-production pieces, like the plastics ranges by Artemide and Kartell.

The national tolerance shown in Italy to the fetishes and fantasies of the architect-

designer has not been repeated in other countries, where the second 'modern movement' in twentieth-century furniture was represented only in isolated pockets of progressive design. In America, Herman Miller and Knoll continued to thrive, the bulk of their market being architect-inspired 'contract' work for office interiors rather than for the domestic consumer, who preferred the New York 'decorator' style (which relied on co-ordinated fabrics and wallpapers for effect, rather than on simple furniture in a plain, uncluttered setting) or the rustic modernism of pine and gingham. The country feeling of pine furniture also became enormously popular in Britain in the mid to late sixties, but it took price-conscious retailing — in the form of Terence Conran's Habitat shops, the first in 1964 and 22 country-wide by 1974 — rather than a design cult to convert even a recognizable proportion of the British public to the idea of simple, functional furniture. It also took some years for small, avant-garde design-manufacturing companies such as OMK Design to interest retailers other than Conran in their chrome-tube furniture. When OMK's first low chair (a little reminiscent of Breuer's 'Wassily') appeared in 1966, it was considered to have cold, clinical overtones more suited to a hospital than a house. Britain came round to both chromed tube and plastics in the early seventies with some indigenous, if disappointing, designs. But the most outstanding pieces of modern furniture were, and still are, imported from abroad (and

from Italy in particular) by a few, mainly London-based stores such as Liberty's, Heal's and Harrods, and individual pioneers such as Walter Collins of Oscar Woollens and Zeev Aram, who, like Gavina in Italy, was responsible for re-introducing Breuer's furniture to Britain in 1964.

The French — designer, manufacturer and consumer alike — took just about as long as the British to come round to the new look of furniture. It was not until the early 1970s that the first coherent range of plastics furniture — by Marc Berthier for Ozoo — went into production, and French modern design from the mid-sixties onwards is substantially represented by relatively few names: by Olivier Morgue for his studies in open-plan living and furniture such as his Djinn chaise longue, acclaimed as a piece of applied sculpture; by the work of Kwok Hoi Chan for Steiner, whose production included tubular-framed chairs and low, ribbed seating units shaped to form circles or undulating, snake-like curves; and by Pierre Paulin's austere, angular, steel-framed pieces for Artifort.

The strength of Switzerland's reputation for furniture over the same period rests mainly on the work of two companies — De Sede, whose luxurious, leather-upholstered seating has sold internationally to those who can afford it, and Strässle & Sohne, an older firm whose main contribution to modern design has been in the massive, chromed-tube pieces by American-born sculptor Paul Tuttle.

The country which has shown least interest in really progressive design has been Germany, which has made its mark in the enormous variety of modular seating ranges and the similarly large range of wall-mounted or free-standing storage sytems. Outstanding in the latter field is the firm of Edwin Behr (the inventor of chipboard), which has also been largely responsible for the slow but sure awakening of German public taste to modern design with its chain of Good Furnishing showrooms. These showrooms display the firm's own products, alongside those by some

of the most eminent of the century's architect-designers such as Breuer, Le Corbusier, George Nelson and Hans Wegner.

In Scandinavia, the lightweight, craft-made wooden furniture which became popular in the 1950s remained in general favour during the sixties, and left room for only one or two pioneering manufacturers. Among Denmark's most progressive firms have been Fritz Hansen and Cado. Fritz Hansen, led by Peter Lassen, have made furniture in the modern idiom, alongside their traditional production, since the mid-sixties. Their very individual ranges include the 'Floating Dock' seating series—ultra-long, ultra-low units comprising flat, moulded foam cushions on a triangular-section aluminium frame—by Sydney Opera House architect Jorn Utzon, and a fine, chromed wire range by Verner Panton. Cado, led by Poul Cadovius, added glass-fibre to their range of wood, metal and upholstery production facilities in 1968 and have become the only big manufacturer of moulded, glass-fibre furniture in Denmark. In Sweden too, the pioneers stand out just because they are in the minority, and only in the early 1970s could this minority be said to have been activating the beginnings of a complete break from traditional methods and materials. This break has been most easily made by a large, well-established, influential manufacturer like Dux, who in the late 1960s appointed Bruno Mathsson as a design consultant. Mathsson's reputation was well established before the war with his furniture in bent, laminated ply, but he has remained Sweden's most outstanding furniture designer and has revitalized the mainstream modern Dux range with his two steel-framed seating series. Among the younger Swedish designers, the relatively new but highly successful Innovator company, run by Jan Dranger and Johann Huldt, has taken the ecology crisis and Mies van der Rohe's saying 'less is more' to heart.

In the early 1970s, these two designers produced an inexpensive, brightly-coloured, knock-down range of furniture in enamelled metal tube and canvas. In its unpretentious simplicity, backed by a philosophy which believes in selling good design at a good price, it indicates one direction in which mass-production furniture of the future could, and possibly should, go.

Changes in the type of furniture made and bought have been followed by changes in the way it reaches the purchaser. As furniture has become physically lighter in weight and increasingly multi-purpose, and as raw materials have become increasingly more expensive, various methods have been tried which cut cost-corners in production and make selling faster and easier—thus the arrival of knock-down furniture, assembled at home with relative ease by an amateur,

Left: One of the most ingenious exhibits at the 1972 Eurodomus exhibition at Turin, Italy, was this compact open-plan living unit by Luigi Massoni for Boffi. In graduated levels which allowed plenty of room for storage under each, it provided areas for relaxing, eating and sleeping. A small kitchen and neat bathroom were tucked at the back, under the top, sleeping level, access being along a tunnel on one side of the major structure.
A hatch under one seating level allowed food to be passed from kitchen to dining areas.

Below left: Stuns range by Jan Dranger and Johan Huldt for Innovator, Sweden, 1970—simple, strong, enamelled tubular steel frames with practical brightly-coloured canvas seats and backs and cushions.

Right: In 1970, Danish-born designer Verner Panton was commissioned to design a complete interior scheme for the German company, Bayer. The interior was constructed within a boat, moored next to and forming part of the International Furniture Fair at Cologne. Panton chose his colours from a superbly co-ordinated fabric range by Swiss manufacturers, Mira-X. With these he created fabric-covered, colour-graded tunnels and caves, a detail of which is shown here.

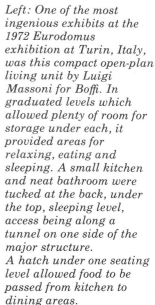

which is purchased either direct from a store or by mail order. In Britain, it has been the Habitat chain which has been most responsible for this retailing innovation in furniture, but Sweden has had out-of-town furniture supermarkets — now equipped with car parks, loading bays and restaurants — for more than 20 years. The French, too, have adopted this shopping method, and although it is less common to find furniture in the out-of-town supermarkets, major branches of the French version of Woolworth, Prisunic, stock simple, lightweight modern furniture to take away. In Britain, Woolworth itself has introduced a 'pedestal' range not completely dissimilar to the original Eero Saarinen series.

In their attempt to create furniture which is less obtrusive physically, designers have naturally also been concerned in making it less obtrusive visually, so that each piece or system of furniture operates efficiently within a simple, pleasing, unified form that is without unnecessary additions. This is no new problem, and despite technical advances and the availability of new furniture-making materials, there have been few improvements on the solutions provided by the Bauhaus designers — whose self-imposed task it was originally. But the various recent attempts at solving it have made a lot of difference to the appearance of furniture over the last two decades. At the most basic level of structural analysis, one of the best ways of observing the progress of furniture design, and of

categorizing a piece of furniture, is to look at the legs. One of the most fundamental preoccupations of designers during this period has been the attempt to integrate these awkward but necessary appendages so that they become an integral part of the overall form. Thus, over the period, rectangular tables lost their awkward, tapered splay legs and gained square-section, vertical legs, at first mounted slightly in from the corners of the table top, but later, and more successfully, mounted flush with the edges of the top, so that the side view of the table made three sides of a perfect rectangle; the origin of this last development is credited to Parson's School of Design in New York and one type of laminated, wood-frame table still bears the name of its birthplace. Round and elliptical tables became more common (partly as a practical and elegant way to seat more guests in a limited area), and have been supported by a variety of central pedestals, from sculpturally waisted stems which broadened at base and top for stability, to the cruder but more economical slim metal rod stem, with a cruci-form or disc base attached. Dining chairs have perhaps presented the hardest task of all, since their necessary dimensions demand that any support system takes up a substantial proportion of their overall form. But imagination coupled with technique has produced legs in the form of pedestals, sledge-like 'skids', inverted T-shapes and cantilevers, and with the development of one-piece moulded plastic

Above: The Hille Storage Wall system, England, 1964–65. Cupboards, shelves, work-surfaces and vanity basins are all based on a 4-inch (10-cm) module, hung from tall channels fixed horizontally to the wall.

Above right: Spray-enamelled Balmford metal library shelving in bright colours for inexpensive home storage by Habitat, 1972.

Above centre right: Elegant, free-standing storage unit of 1968 by Conran Associates, England, with cream drawers and doors.

Above far right: Storage system by Hille, England, 1962, in which shelves are supported by rods, spring-tensioned between floor and ceiling.

Right: The ultimate storage walls, by the German firm of Behr which has specialized in perfecting systems making the maximum use of vertical space.

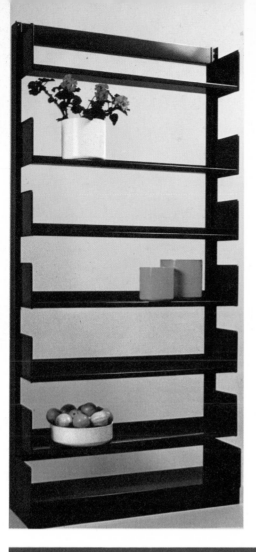

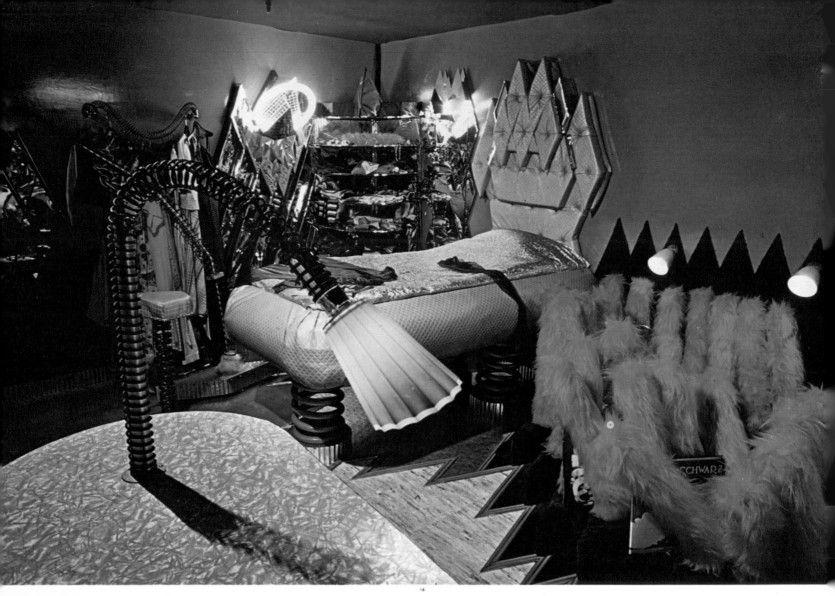

forms, or hot-pressing of plastic sheet, it has become possible to make the legs an extension of the seat and back. These chairs, where colour and material simply curve down to form the legs, are among the most successful solutions to the problem. Occasional and easy chairs underwent the most radical changes in form, and in many cases legs disappeared entirely as the seventies approached. In the more conventionally shaped armchairs — which have become lower and plumper, so that one lounges rather than sits — legs have been replaced with castors. But the concept of chairs made up of fat, upholstered cushions that are hinged together like the pages of a book (turn the pages to sit high or low), or of clear plastic bolsters filled with nothing but air, or of leather or plastic bags filled with polystyrene granules, defies conventional analysis.

By the early 1970s, plagiarism had diluted the stylistic strength of the Italian influence, leaving it weakened and cheapened. At the Turin 'Eurodomus' exhibition of 1972, there were brief signs of a revival, and of a return from metal and plastic to wood (cynics commented that this was simply so that even higher prices could be charged for a quality, natural material in shortening supply). But

the worsening world economic situation and the oil crisis affected prices of plastics and metals as well as wood, and took its toll on design, which is still generally regarded as a luxury and which is one of the first things to be discarded when there are budgets to be watched, by manufacturer and consumer alike. But some people never give up. In 1972, Dino Gavina, pioneer in the late 1950s of the modern Italian movement who had been bought out by Knoll International in the late 1960s, started all over again, very much as he had the first time, by opening a small showroom outside Bologna and naming the new firm, Simon International, after a long-standing business colleague Maria Simoncini. But this time the products were very different: individual or short-run pieces, by sculptors and artists as well as architects and designers, which ranged from starkly simple box shelves to the startling surrealism of a large, bright-green, felt apple in a black felt bowler hat (only sitting on it revealed it as a chair) and beaten, gilded metal thrones and side-tables straight out of ancient mythology. As furniture they were, and are, very near to art. But as the beginnings of a new movement they are probably, for reasons of economy as well as international mood, out of their time.

Above: By the end of the 1960s, the pop-art movement, pioneered by Andy Warhol and Klaus Oldenberg, was firmly ensconced in the rooms of the young. For a 1970 exhibition at the London Design Centre, the magazine Honey took pop-inspired interiors to an extreme which was seldom reached in actuality with this room for a career girl. A complexity of ingredients, such as diamanté, fake-fur, fabric flowers, combined to make an interior claustrophobic with colour and clutter in total reaction to the clean-lined, well-ordered statements of contemporary, architect-inspired furniture.

Glossary

Those words to be found under their own entry are shown in small capitals.

Acanthus The conventionalized leaf used in classical ornament and found particularly on the capitals of Corinthian and Composite COLUMNS and on furniture mounts.

Alabaster A pure granular rock of GYPSUM in white, pink, or yellowish colour used from the very earliest times for fashioning statues and urns.

Andirons Appliances for use in a hearth to support logs, which usually consist of a large decorated upright member (sometimes in pewter or brass) and a plain cast-iron bar projecting at right angles behind on which logs are intended to rest. (Also known as fire-dogs.)

A l'anglais In the English style, usually applied to French eighteenth-century pieces with characteristically English forms such as the CABRIOLE leg, or pierced SPLAT back.

Anthemion A stylized honeysuckle flower decoration. It was much used as a decorative motif in Greece and Rome, and throughout Europe and America during the neo-classical revival.

Apron The shaped piece of wood immediately below the seat-rail of a chair or settee, or below the frieze of a table, stand, or chest, stretching between the front legs and usually decorated in some way, either carved, pierced or shaped, or with the addition of a chased ORMOLU plate called the apron mount.

Arabesque A decoration of flowing lines, stylized foliage and scrolls, often intersecting and closely fitted into the outline of a panel or border. The word refers to its Arabian, Persian and Islamic origins.

Armoire A wardrobe, cupboard or clothes-press.

Armorials Heraldic arms, denoting the status and allegiances of a person or family.

Athénienne A form of tripod stand, which derives its name from the painting by J B Vien entitled *La Vertueuse Athénienne*, depicting a young priestess burning incense at an altar on a three-legged support.

Augsburg cabinet A general descriptive term for the large cabinets filled with small drawers, which were a distinctive product of Augsburg metal-workers and furniture-makers from the early sixteenth century, and were exported, and later imitated, all over Europe. The shape probably originated from the small jewel cabinets and reliquaries made by the goldsmiths and silversmiths in Augsburg and Nuremberg in the late Middle Ages.

Backstool The contemporary term for a single chair of the late seventeenth century, with a square upholstered back set at right angles to the seat, and with a considerable gap between them. Backstools placed close to each other, side by side round the walls, were a practically invariable concomitant of the Baroque state apartment.

Balloon-back chair An early nineteenth-century chair in which the traditional yoke rail of the back has been turned downwards at its ends to join the uprights in one continuous curve, and in which the intermediate back rail has been turned upwards so that the final form is a circular, open shape.

Banquette Form of long stool to seat two or three people, which has appeared in different forms from the time of the Renaissance.

Bas-relief A panel or frieze on which the ornamentation or portrait medallion is carved or moulded in low-relief

Basswood A generic name for the wood of various types of lime-tree, native to North America. The most common

Anthemion

Armoire

Bergère

Bonheur-du-jour

Bureau à cylindre

varieties are Silver basswood, White basswood and 'Michaux' basswood.

Batik Predominantly Dutch style of Art Nouveau decoration inspired by the Batik textiles produced in their old East Indian colony of Java. Materials of this kind are characterized by their colourful and schematic use of animals and plant forms.

Baywood Honduras mahogany, as opposed to the more widely used West Indian variety.

Beading Straight runs of ornament consisting of carving in the shape of a row of beads.

Bentwood A type of construction, perfected in the mid-nineteenth century, which allowed for the formation of furniture out of continuous members in strip form, instead of the traditional methods by which many different members were joined together.

Bergère A comfortable armchair, usually quite large, enclosed by an entirely upholstered, frequently curving, back, and with upholstered arms from the armrests down to the base of the seat: the seat itself was fitted with a thick down cushion. A bergère à oreilles (early eighteenth century) had a high back with wings at the level of the head, like the English wing chair. The word 'bergère' is used in England, and was corrupted in the eighteenth century into 'barjier', 'burjair' or 'barjair'.

Bevelled glass A glass or mirror with a narrow slope-edge border.

Blind arcading Series of pointed or trefoiled Gothic arches with their openings set against a solid panel of wood or stone.

Block front The cabinet-maker's term for a chest, cabinet or bookcase whose centre section either projects beyond, or is recessed behind, the side section.

Bobbin turning see Turning

Boiserie The French term for the panelling of walls in carved wood, generally painted or gilded, and for doors panelled *en suite*.

Bolt-head ornament Circular discs in imitation of the metal door decorations of Greece and Rome, adapted as furniture ornaments in the early nineteenth century.

Bombé A French word meaning literally 'blown out', applied to pieces of furniture of bulging or convex shape. Generally used for commodes and the lower parts of bureaux of the Louis Quinze period, made with convex curves on two axes at the same time. It is also used for the Dutch and American (Boston) chests and commodes, which have simpler swellings on the front and sides.

Bonheur-du-jour A small writing-table equipped with a superstructure of drawers or pigeon-holes at the back of the top. Made in both England and France in the late eighteenth century, its great popularity led to its name.

Bonnet top A term used in America for what would be called 'domed' or 'hooded' in England, referring to the projecting segmental or broken segmental pediment on a tallboy, cabinet or bookcase.

Bookrests Portable and adjustable reading-desks used for supporting manuscripts and large volumes on tables, commonly found in eighteenth- and nineteenth-century libraries.

Boulle work The technique of inlaying furniture with a decorative pattern, usually of brass or pewter against a background of ebony, but also on occasion using gold, silver or tortoiseshell. The technique is named after the great French cabinet-maker André-Charles Boulle (1642–1732), who is unlikely to have invented it, but who was certainly its leading exponent in the late seventeenth century. Boulle's own family, and many other cabinet-makers, continued to produce furniture of this type throughout the eighteenth century. Having been somewhat unfashionable in the mid-century, it regained its position in the Louis Seize period and remained in vogue throughout the nineteenth century. See also Partie

Boxwood The hard, light-coloured wood of the box-tree, which is capable of taking a fine polish. Used for INLAY and MARQUETRY and also for fine turned work.

Bracket foot A short foot that forms an extension of the PLINTH member on a chest of drawers, bureau or similar piece. It can be plain and rectangular, but in high quality furniture it may be carved and shaped in a number of ways.

Bronze-doré see Ormolu

Bronzeur Maker of bronze furnishings, such as lighting appliances, clock cases, door and fireplace furnishings, and furniture mounts in bronze or gilt-bronze. In France, they came under two guilds: the fondeurs, who were responsible for casting and finishing the articles, and the doreurs, sometimes known as CISELEURS-DOREURS, who were responsible for the chasing and gilding.

Buen Retiro Porcelain factory opened near Madrid in 1760 as an extension of the Neapolitan Capodimonte works, which continued in operation until 1808. Plaques for insetting into furniture were among its productions.

Buffet Originally a French word (sometimes 'buffet à deux corps') for a sideboard of the two-tier type known in Elizabethan England as a 'COURT CUPBOARD'. When used in conjunction with chairs, however, buffet means stuffed or padded.

Bureau à cylindre Large French desk, popular in the late Louis Quinze and Louis Seize periods, with a roll-top in the shape of a quarter-cylinder. This type was occasionally imitated in other countries besides France, particularly in Germany and Scandinavia in the last decades of the eighteenth century.

Bureau-cabinet A piece of furniture in two parts, with a bureau below. The cupboard section above may contain either plain shelves or drawers and other ornamental fittings. The cupboard doors are either glazed, panelled, or fitted with looking-glass.

Bureau de dame A small writing-desk, usually of the Louis Quinze period, suitable for a lady. Similar to the BONHEUR-DU-JOUR, though without the superstructure of drawers at the back of the top.

Bureau du roi The writing-table designed by J F Oeben in 1760 and completed by J H Riesener in 1769, for Louis XV. It may have been the first cylinder-top writing-table to have been made, and as such is occasionally used as a descriptive term for desks of this type, though these are more commonly called BUREAUX À CYLINDRE.

Bureau en pente The French version of the Anglo-Dutch type of bureau, with a sloping FALL-FRONT, generally raised on CABRIOLE legs. Occurs during the Louis Quinze period. Also known as a 'bureau à dos d'âne'.

Bureau Mazarin A type of kneehole writing-table, called after Cardinal Mazarin and made principally during the Louis Quatorze period, with a pedestal of three drawers either side, raised on curved legs. Often found executed in BOULLE marquetry.

Bureau-plat A large writing-table with a flat top of a rectangular or serpentine outline. It generally has three drawers on each side, and is supported on four sturdy legs.

Burr An abnormal knotted growth on the trunk or root of a tree that often results in a beautifully patterned or figured wood used for decorative veneers, for instance burr ash, elm, maple, oak, walnut and yew.

Butterfly table The name given to a type of table developed by joiners in New England, and particularly Connecticut, in the last quarter of the seventeenth and first quarter of the eighteenth century. The supports to the hinged flaps were shaped with bold curves like one-half of a CARTOUCHE, and are supposed to resemble butterflies' wings.

Cabriole A form of leg, which was popular in England from the Queen Anne period onwards, in the shape of a reversed 'S', curving outward at the knee, inward below it, and outward again at the foot.

Cadeira de sola Turned Portuguese chairs, developed in the last two decades of the seventeenth century. In form rather like the BACKSTOOLS and common slightly earlier in England, France and the Netherlands, all their structural members were turned—legs, arms, and stretchers—but they differed in almost always having an exaggerated type of bobbin, rather than spiral, TURNING, and in their very distinctive high backs with shaped tops.

Canapé A sofa or settee.

Canopy Covering held or suspended over a throne, bed or person.

Canted Cut on a slant, to avoid a sharp angle.

Cantilevers An architectural principle, best illustrated by the conventional shelf-bracket, in which a horizontal arm projects (usually at right angles) from a vertical support. This method was first used in furniture in 1926 by the Dutch architect Mart Stam for his S 33 chair, to reduce, for aesthetic reasons, the number of vertical elements in the chair's support system from four to two.

Carcase furniture Pieces whose outside shape encloses a volume, such as chests, wardrobes, cupboards, bookcases or commodes.

Cartonnier Form of filing-cabinet usually constructed to stand at the end of a BUREAU-PLAT and often containing small drawers in the upper part and a cupboard below.

Cartouche An ornament used from the sixteenth to the eighteenth century, consisting of a circular or shaped centre, often filled with some device such as a coat of arms or inscription, and surrounded by leaves, scrolls and STRAPWORK. It generally forms the centre of a piece of carving, such as an apron or tympanum, or may be found at salient points such as the knees of cabriole legs of chairs.

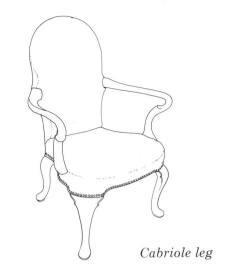

Cabriole leg

Cantilever (S33 chair)

Cartouche

315

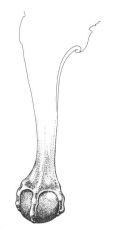

Claw-and-ball foot

Columns (left to right: Doric; Ionic; Corinthian; Composite)

Caryatid A female figure used as a column to support an entablature.

Case furniture see Carcase furniture

Cassapanca An Italian seat, whose form evolved during the Renaissance, used as a chest. The seat was lifted to reveal storage space below.

Cassoni The Italian marriage-chests used for storage since the Renaissance, which indicated by their rich and elaborate decoration the status of a family.

Centering A timber construction used as scaffolding in the construction of a dome.

Chaise longue A chair with an elongated seat to accommodate the legs in a horizontal position.

Chaise-percée There is no modern English word for this small, portable seat enclosing a chamber-pot. In the eighteenth century it was known as a 'close-stool' or 'night-stool'; in the twentieth century it has become a 'commode' (as used for invalids).

Chaise volante (Literally 'flying chair'.) A chair of the Louis Quinze period made of lightweight wood, which could easily be moved by the user.

Chanelling Incised grooving, resembling a furrow of semicircular or semi-oval section.

Chest-on-chest A large chest of drawers, supporting a slightly smaller one on top of it.

Cheval-glass A full-length looking-glass pivoted between upright supports, called a 'PSYCHÉ' in France, after the nymph whose beauty attracted the attention of Cupid.

Chiaroscuro (Literally 'light-dark'.) In painting or pictorial marquetry it implies exaggerated shading that produces an illusion of solid, three-dimensional objects.

Chinoiserie Any building, furniture or decoration carried out in the Chinese taste. The fashion grew during the seventeenth century, stimulated by the increasing trade with China, and was at its height during the Rococo period. It affected nearly all the decorative arts, including furniture, painting and engraving, wallpaper, textiles, ceramics and silver. Chinoiserie varies from the introduction of a few Chinese motifs to a deceptive imitation of an oriental work.

Chipboard An inexpensive boarding made by bonding wood waste material, in the form of chips, with resin, and compressing the mixture into sheets.

Chip-carving Chiselled geometric patterns designed with the aid of a compass.

Cipollino A marble, widely used in ancient Rome for monolith columns and surface treatment of walls. The pale ground is streaked with many different shades of green. The quarries, on the island of Euboea, Greece, were rediscovered in the late nineteenth century, and are worked today.

Ciseleur-doreur see Bronzeur

Citrus woods The generic term for the wood of fruit-trees including orange, lemon and lime.

Claw-and-ball foot Most typically found on the cabriole legs of chairs and tables made in Holland and England during the early eighteenth century, and slightly later, in America. The claw resembles that of an eagle, and the four talons clasp a slightly flattened ball. It is sometimes thought to have derived from the Chinese mythology of a dragon chasing a pearl in the clouds.

Clutha glass A type of streaked and bubbled glass named after the Gaelic word for 'cloudy', manufactured by James Couper & Sons of Glasgow between 1890 and 1920, and often used by Liberty's for the liners of pewter fruit stands.

Coffer A box, especially a strong-box for keeping valuables.

Coiffeuse A fitted dressing-table. The most typical eighteenth-century form had three rising flaps, the centre of which is fitted with a dressing-mirror. Such a piece is sometimes erroneously known as a poudreuse. 'Coiffeuse' can also mean a dressing chair, with a low back that allows the hair to be dressed.

Coil-spring A device, consisting of flexible metal wire spirals, incorporated into chair seats and, later on, mattresses, to give extra comfort to the user, and which returns the padding immediately to its original shape once the weight is removed. First patented in England about 1825.

Colonette A miniature form of the column.

Columns The five different orders of columns in Classical architecture, recognized by innumerable theorists from the time of Vitruvius onwards, and re-interpreted by the most famous architects of the Renaissance, such as Palladio and Scamozzi, are, in ascending order of elaboration: the Tuscan, Doric, Ionic, Corinthian and Composite. The different orders, when correctly used together, in buildings or in furniture, are ranged one above the other in this sequence, though the Tuscan and Composite are often omitted, and are anyway less frequently employed than the other three. The orders have always held roughly the same associations for architects and craftsmen. The Tuscan, being structurally the soundest, was used almost wholly for external work such as farm buildings; the Doric, considered simple yet noble, for public buildings, country houses, arcades or (in furniture) the bases of cabinets; the Ionic, with its more decorative capital of two curling volutes, where a lighter, yet still architectural, effect was desired; the Corinthian (the most ornate, and also perhaps the most often employed) to give an air of magnificence with its capital adorned with rows of acanthus leaves; and finally the Composite, often considered decadent, where the utmost richness was sought. The orders were often, too, given sexual connotations, from the severely masculine Tuscan to the frivolously feminine Composite. Variations can be given to columns by fluting, that is to say by carving small semicircular grooves out of them from top to bottom in parallel lines. The Doric and Corinthian orders are the most commonly fluted, and it is rare to find this technique used on any of the others.

Commode Invariably used in France and England in the eighteenth century to mean a chest of drawers, it began to be used (incorrectly) by the Victorians to describe a night-stool, or CHAISE-PERCÉE.

Commode à vantaux A commode which has two cupboard doors instead of the more usual drawer fronts. Inside, there may be drawers, or open shelves.

Commode en console A rather uncommon piece of eighteenth-century furniture, in the form of a narrow commode, usually with only one drawer supported on two legs and attached to the wall. Also known as a 'console d'applique'.

Composite see Columns

Confidante A sofa with attached chairs inset at either end, which could generally be removed to form separate BERGÈRES if necessary. Derived from France, it became fashionable in England in the late eighteenth century.

Console desserte Form of French sideboard usually with rounded ends and open shelves.

Console table An eighteenth-century table which is intended to be placed against a wall, with its top often supported on architectural brackets or 'consoles'.

Contre-partie see Partie

Conversation-seat A small sofa or settee of the early nineteenth century which provides seating for two or three people, disposed so that the occupants face one another.

Corinthian see Columns

Coromandel A variegated ebony, with grey or brown mottling. Also used in the late seventeenth and eighteenth centuries to describe the Chinese technique of deeply incised lacquer, in which this wood was employed, usually with the addition of vivid colouring. The name derived from the Coromandel coast of India, through whose trading stations practically all these panels of Chinese lacquer passed on their way to Europe.

Corona (Literally 'crown'.) A ring, sometimes elaborately ornamented, into which the upper part of a bed drapery could be gathered.

Court cupboard Sideboard with open shelves for the display of ceramics, silver or books. Sometimes with enclosed portions for security of valuable objects. See also Buffet.

Credenza Italian sideboard, sometimes covered with a DAMASK cloth.

Cresting The top moulding or finish to any piece of furniture, implying elaborate decoration.

Crocket Curled leaf or bud ornament usually associated with early Gothic capitals.

C-scroll A Rococo ornament: a scroll in the shape of a 'C' or 'Ɔ'.

Cushion mirror The standard form of mirror or pier-glass used in England from the Restoration to the end of the seventeenth century. The rectangular plate was surrounded by a wide, half-rounded (or slightly shallower) moulding, in walnut, ebony or other combinations of wood and metal variously decorated. The name may derive from the mirrors used in earlier, Elizabethan and Jacobean, toilet sets where the borders were literally stuffed like cushions and embroidered with STUMP-WORK.

Cusp (Cusping) The projecting point between the foils on a foiled Gothic arch or roundel. The foil is formed by the cusping of a circle: trefoil, quatrefoil, cinquefoil, multifoil, denoting the number of leaf shapes seen.

Cylinder bureau see Bureau à cylindre

Dado panelling The panelling between the skirting board or floor level and the dado railing, the moulding running roughly at waist height all round a room which has been correctly decorated in the classical style.

Commode

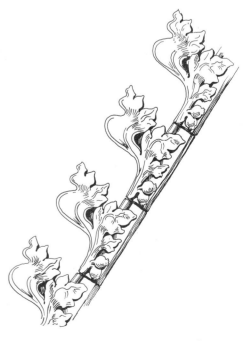

Crocket

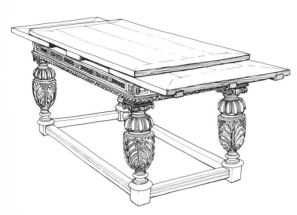

Draw-table

Encoignure

Damascene A watered or striped pattern on swords, armour, and metal furniture caused by hammering steel in which the carbon particles have separated on cooling. Also a gold or silver INLAY on a steel or iron surface.

Damask A reversible figured fabric for upholstery and wall-covering in which the design is worked in a different weave from the background in such a way that the two weaves appear on face and back in exchanged positions. Originally worked in silk and later in linen and cotton.

Dantesque Term used to describe a type of Italian neo-Renaissance furniture which attempted to imitate the styles of the time of Dante Alighieri (1265–1321).

Davenport A small slope-front desk on a solid base of drawers, which became popular in the early nineteenth century. The name may derive from a Colonel Davenport who ordered such a desk from Gillows of Lancaster in the late eighteenth century.

Deep-buttoned upholstery A method of restraining large quantities of filling by dividing it into small areas defined by buttons. The covering fabric is applied with diagonal folds to allow for movement.

Director style In the style of Thomas Chippendale (1718–79), the first edition of whose famous book of furniture designs, *The Gentleman and Cabinet-Maker's Director* appeared in 1754.

Draw-table One in which the length may be extended by drawing out extra leaves from beneath the main surface. Most commonly found in the fifteenth and sixteenth centuries.

Dressouer de parement Cited in early inventories and describing buffets surmounted by canopies, denoting status and importance.

Drop-front secrétaire see Secrétaire à abattant

Drop-front, drop-leaf front see Fall-front

Duchesse A BERGÈRE chair with an extended seat to accommodate the legs in a horizontal position; generally rather narrower, and more decorative than the CHAISE LONGUE. *Duchesse brisée:* made in two or three separate parts, resembling two bergère chairs with a stool in between. *Duchesse en bâteau:* a duchesse with a smaller chair-back at the foot.

Dumb-waiter A movable stand with two or more tiers of trays, usually circular, attached to a central column, often on a tripod base with castors on the feet. The term, and the form of furniture, originated in the 1720s, the contemporary name deriving from its function in the dining-room or tea-parlour.

Ebénisterie Furniture made by ébénistes (or cabinet-makers), whose art consisted in applying fine veneers to case furniture such as commodes, writing tables and cabinets. The word comes from ébène (ebony), which was the principal wood used for veneers in the sixteenth and early seventeenth centuries. In eighteenth-century Paris, ébénisterie was a craft quite distinct from menuiserie – which was the province of the joiner and carver.

Ebonized wood Wood veneered with ebony, a particularly hard, smooth black wood resistant to both warping and shrinkage. 'Ebonizing' can also be taken to mean a process by which wood could be stained black and polished to imitate ebony.

Egg-and-dart Ornament of Greek origin on mouldings in the form of eggs alternating with darts or anchors.

A l'égyptien In the Egyptian taste or style incorporating sphinxes, snakes and pyramidal forms, favoured especially in France after Napoleon's Egyptian campaign, but also to be found in the final phases of Neo-classicism elsewhere in Europe.

Elizabethan Dating from the reign of Queen Elizabeth I of England (1558–1603), or in the Renaissance style then prevalent.

Encaustic Tiles or bricks with a decorative pattern of different coloured clays or fusions of paint and clay burnt in and glazed. The practice, which originated in ancient Greece, was widely used in mediaeval churches and again revived in the nineteenth century.

Encoignure A small commode, of triangular section, made to fit into a corner, and normally having a cupboard door rather than drawers. They were usually made in pairs, often to match a commode.

Entablature The horizontal members above a column or solid structure, whose various parts are separately known as the architrave, FRIEZE and cornice.

Escabelle A low short bench, cited in sixteenth-century French inventories. Also a three-legged stool.

Etagère A set of open shelves placed vertically one above the other, for the display of ornaments, either as a free-standing piece of furniture, or built into the corner of a room.

Faience Glazed earthenware painted and decorated in a technique supposed to have originated in the Italian town of Faenza.

Fall-front The writing-flap of a desk which lowers to form a writing-surface. Also referred to as drop-front.

Fasces Bundle of rods and an axe carried by the lictor before a Roman magistrate, often used as a decorative motif in the neo-classical period.

Fauteuil An armchair, with a space between the arms and the seat. The back and seat were usually upholstered, but were sometimes caned. See Siège

Fauteuil à la reine An armchair of the Louis Quinze or Louis Seize periods, with a flat rectangular back. The name is said to have been a compliment to Queen Marie Lesczynska.

Fauteuil de bureau A desk chair, generally with a semicircular back and a projecting central, front leg. It may have either four or five legs. Also known as a 'fauteuil de cabinet'.

Fauteuil en cabriolet An armchair of the Louis Quinze or Louis Seize periods, with a slightly curved back. It was generally smaller and more easily moved than the fauteuil à la reine.

Fibre-board A building board made of compressed fibrous materials; in furniture, the main component is often paper.

Figure A technical term for the grain of a piece of wood, especially when used as a decorative feature. Walnut with its frequent knots and variations of colour is particularly suitable for this treatment, though mahogany, rosewood and different kinds of fruitwood can also have attractive markings, used by the cabinet-maker to give diversity to large areas, such as table-tops and the fall-fronts of secretaires.

Filigree Anything which is delicate: applied in furniture to ornamental work in which wood, or fine gold or silver wire is formed into delicate, pierced tracery.

Finial Decorative terminal, placed vertically to accentuate the ending of a structural feature such as an urn, pediment or post. In furniture, it is usually a small, turned, ornamental knob of some kind. A 'flame finial' is carved or moulded in the shape of a flame, or flaming urn.

Firedogs see Andirons

Fresco A wall painting on wet plaster: extensively found in Italy.

Fret (or Fretwork) Pierced decoration. It generally takes the form of a repeated motif on a gallery round a table-top, or on chair legs or stretchers. Thomas Chippendale published designs for frets in the Chinese and gothick styles.

Blindfret: a fret that is either carved in low relief on a solid rail or chair leg, or which is applied to a solid member to give the same appearance.

Frieze The middle division of a classical ENTABLATURE.

Fruitwood A convenient term to cover those woods which are less easily identifiable than, for instance, oak, mahogany or walnut. Fruitwood was used more in Europe especially when English blockades prevented the imports of rosewood and mahogany from the West Indies into France and recourse was made to native woods such as pearwood or cherrywood.

Fumed finish A process, carried out by subjecting wood to the action of chemical fumes, which results in a darkening of the surface to suggest age.

Galant scenes Pastoral scenes in the style of Watteau, Pater or Fragonard, often used as a decorative motif in the Rococo period, and so-called after the 'galants' or courtiers, dressed as shepherds and shepherdesses, who live out an idyllic and idealized existence within them.

Galerie des fêtes The state apartments, including Long Gallery, of a French palace, for example Fontainebleau.

Georgian Anything made in England during the reigns of the first four Georges, that is to say from 1714 to 1830. The word is usually associated with the Classical style in architecture and furniture.

Gesso Plaster of Paris (GYPSUM) prepared for use in modelling or as a ground for gilding and painting.

Gilt-bronze A term rather loosely used to denote gilded metal mounts on furniture (except those made of brass). The quality can vary from the finest Paris ormolu to mass-produced drawer handles of some inferior alloy. See also Ormolu

Gilt-wood Wood overlaid with a thin layer of gold leaf, usually on a base of GESSO. Oil-gilding and water-gilding refer to the different methods by which the gold leaf is attached: the former giving a thicker, duller finish particularly suitable for the exterior of houses, garden statues and sundials; the latter capable of more delicate ornamentation, and of burnishing (or highly polishing) certain areas so as to produce highlights.

Fret

Guilloche

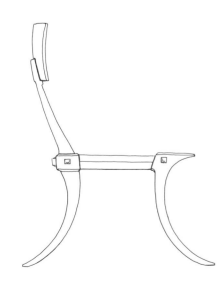

Klismos

Girandole Derived from the Italian, this word came into usage in the seventeenth century to describe a wall-light, though in France it grew to mean rather a chandelier or cluster of diamonds. By the mid-eighteenth century in England, however, it was generally thought of as the combination of carved wood and mirror plate, then fashionable for the Rococo wall-light. The word continued to be used in describing the more restrained mirrors with candle-branches of the neo-classical period in England.

Glass-fibre Glass which is melted and drawn into very fine, flexible fibres or threads which are then spun or woven, and, in furniture-manufacture, blended with resin or plastic to add strength.

Glazing bars The thin bars which divide the panes of glass in a glazed door or window.

A la grecque In the Greek taste or style, popular in the later stages of Neo-classicism.

Goût égyptien see À l'égyptienne

Goût grec see À la grecque

Goût pittoresque (or genre pittoresque) The name given to Rococo decoration of the type established by Pineau and Meissonnier around 1730, which incorporated vegetation, rocks, water, unreal fantasy buildings, and asymmetrical rocaille work.

Grotesques The Italian word, *grotteschi*, means 'belonging to grottoes'. A stylized type of decoration composed of leaves, honeysuckle, urns or fantastic creatures, painted on wall panelling, friezes, pilasters and ceilings. It imitates ancient Roman decoration that was found early in the sixteenth century in the Golden House of Nero and in tombs, that were often below ground level, and hence usually known as grottoes.

Guéridon A candlestand. From the time of Louis XIV they were made, as in England, in the form of small platforms supported on tall columns. By the mid-eighteenth century, a smaller type developed resembling a TABLE AMBULANTE with a rectangular or circular tray top, which could also be used as a worktable.

Guilloche A linear ornament, of Classical origin, composed of two continuous intersecting curves which form a succession of ovals or circles.

Gumwood A reddish-brown wood with streaks of darker brown, sometimes also known as satin walnut, which comes from the south-eastern states of North America. Although capable of an exceptionally close, smooth finish, it is very difficult to work and usually found only on New England joiners' pieces during the eighteenth century.

Gypsum A mineral from which plaster of Paris is made by driving off water by heating. Used in STUCCO.

Hammer-beam roof The beams which project at right angles from the top of a wall carrying arched braces to support the roof.

Hardwood The term applied to deciduous or leaf shedding trees such as maple, oak, birch, beech, ash, chestnut.

Harlequin A small rack of drawers contained in a box-like structure and concealed in the body of a small Pembroke or writing-table, so that it rises with the aid of springs and weights when the lid is opened. The name derives from a rare use of the word 'harlequin' (commoner, however, in the eighteenth century) meaning to 'conjure away'.

Highboy A modern name for the American high chest. This was developed from the English TALLBOY of the early eighteenth century.

Hoop-back A term for a chair-back whose uprights and top rail merge to form a continuous curve, as with many WINDSOR CHAIRS.

Horsebone decoration English seventeenth-century joiners' bills and inventories use this term to describe a type of carving commonly used for the aprons of chairs and daybeds and for the stands of lacquer chests and cabinets, made up of wide but shallow-relief scrolls, ultimately derived from the auricular style of the late Renaissance. Instead of the gristle of the human ear however (which gave the auricular style its name), these ancestors of C and S-scrolls were supposed to look like the bones of horses' hocks.

Inlay Ornamental patterns set flush into a (usually wooden) background panel, either in another type of wood of contrasting colour, or in materials such as ivory and mother-of-pearl. See also Boullework

Intarsia Inlay or marquetry. The technique, derived from Oriental ivory inlays, was much practised from the fourteenth century in northern Italy, where the Florentines became famous for their inlaid perspective views of buildings, musical instruments, or allegorical figures.

Ionic see Columns

Jacaranda The name often given to Brazilian ROSEWOOD, especially in Spain and Portugal, the countries which imported it in the largest quantities in the eighteenth and nineteenth centuries.

Jacobean Dating from the reign of James I of England (and VI of Scotland) 1603–1625.

Japan (or japanning) The European imitation of Chinese lacquer. Japanning has been practised since the early seventeenth century. It also stands for most painted decoration on eighteenth-century furniture, even when this is not in the oriental but in the European or classical style. (In French japan is known as vernis and, in Italian, as lacca.)

Japonisme A generic word for the influence of Japanese design on European art in the period from about 1865 to 1885. The word 'japonaiserie' is sometimes used but implies a higher degree of frivolity and a less precise imitation of oriental forms.

Jardinière A container for indoor plants, sometimes in the form of a silver cistern (and close to a wine-cooler in shape), more commonly of carved wood with a rectangular, circular or oval trough supported by a stand with four or more legs.

Joints *Mortised:* An abbreviation for 'tenon-and-mortise' joint, a tenon being a projection at the end of a piece of wood which is inserted into the socket, or mortise, of another to hold the two together.

Joints *Pegged:* Alternatively 'dowel-jointed', in which the ends of the two pieces of wood both have round sockets drilled in them and are connected by a separate wooden peg, or dowel, glued in place to hold them together.

Kas The Dutch word for the great cupboard, rather like the French armoire, to be found in every household and used for storing the valuable linen and plate by which a family's whole status was judged. The Kas, which can be seen in the background of so many Netherlandish genre pictures, was, apart from the four-post bedstead, the most important piece of furniture in most merchants' houses and was consequently the most elaborately decorated with increasingly complex arched crestings and panelled doors towards the end of the seventeenth century.

Kibotos The chest in which clothes and bedding were stored in ancient Greece.

Kingwood An 'exotic' wood, of a species allied to rosewood, imported from South America. It is of a golden-brown colour, with a fine grain. In the seventeenth century it was known as 'prince's wood', and used by the Dutch

for veneers and marquetry. More widely used on French commodes of the Louis Quinze period, and on Italian (especially Genoese) and other furniture. Not much used in eighteenth-century England, except for bordering in marquetry after 1770.

Kline The couch in ancient Greece, used for dining as well as for sleeping.

Klismos chair Classical chair with deeply-curved encompassing yoke back, and sabre legs, of Greek origin. Revived in the early nineteenth century by dedicated neo-classicists, such as Thomas Hope.

Knop A small decorative knob, used to accentuate the cresting or apron of a piece of furniture. See Finial

Kunstschrank Elaborate cabinets made especially at Augsburg and Nuremberg in the sixteenth century.

Lacca A word loosely used in Italy for painted decoration of all types of furniture or panelling, whether it be genuine oriental lacquer, its European imitation, or European landscapes, flowers or figurative scenes.

Lacquer An oriental decoration on furniture such as cabinets, screens or boxes, of which the most popular kind had gold figures, trees or landscapes against a black or red ground. The best Chinese or Japanese lacquer involved a long process using the gum of the lac-tree. It was imitated with other materials in Europe. Correctly, the word 'lacquer' should be used only for genuine oriental work. For European imitations, see japan, lacca, vernis.

Ladderback chair A chair whose back is made up of horizontal rails resembling the form of a ladder.

Lambrequin Originally a heraldic term, lambrequins were the pieces of material draped around the helmet and framing the shield, hanging at the bottom in a roughly semicircular shape. The shape became a favourite decorative motif in the Baroque period, becoming more stylized, usually with a tassel hanging from the bottom of each fold.

Lapis lazuli A natural silicate of bright blue colour, widely used from Egyptian times onwards for decoration of furniture.

Lattice Diagonally constructed cross-members common in chair-backs and table-supports; a variant of trellis-work.

Lectern A reading or singing desk in free-standing or table-top form, devised to hold books or music at a comfortable sloping angle to the reader.

Ladderback chair

Lambrequin

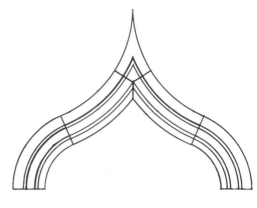

Ogee arch

Lectus The Roman couch, either of Greek shape like the KLINE or provided with a back like a sofa.

Linenfold A form of decoration of (usually) oak panelling in which there is a resemblance to linen laid in vertical folds.

Lit à colonne Bed whose tester is supported on columns.

Lit à la duchesse A bed which has no posts: the canopy is supported either by cantilevers to the wall, or suspended from the ceiling.

Lit à la française The traditional bed, generally with a head- and a footboard, and four posts which support the canopy or tester. Also sometimes used for the bed without the canopy and columns, for example, when made to fit into an alcove.

Lit à la polonaise A bed, with a small circular or oval canopy in the centre that covers about a third of the bed area. The posts, generally of iron, are curved, and are hidden by elaborately draped curtains.

Lit en housse A four-post bedstead whose curtains instead of running on rails, suspended from rings, are pulled up and tied by ropes. A form especially favoured in France and the Netherlands in the mid-seventeenth century.

Loggia A roofed recess or gallery which has one or more open sides.

Long-case clock Sometimes called a 'grandfather' clock. The pendulum and weights of this type of clock hang down, anything between three and five feet (one to one and a half metres) below the mechanism, thus accounting for their tall and narrow casing.

Louis styles Dating from the reigns of three successive French kings, Louis XIV (1638–1715), Louis XV (1710–1774) and Louis XVI (1754–1793). Sometimes more loosely used to denote the styles in art and architecture generally prevalent during these reigns: Baroque, Rococo and neo-classical.

Macassar ebony Also known as CORO-MANDEL ebony or Zebra wood, this type of ebony with its distinctive bold stripes was formerly imported from the East Indies but can now be obtained from most tropical countries.

Manx, or Manxman, piano The name given to a group of small upright pianos designed by Mackay Hugh Baillie Scott and made by John Broadwood & Sons in the last years of the nineteenth century. Baillie Scott was a native of the Isle of Man.

Marchand-mercier and **marchand-tapissier** Middle-man or dealer in furniture, decorative objects, tapestries, textiles and porcelain.

Marlborough leg On English and American chairs and tables: a straight leg, sometimes chamfered on the inner corner, and often with a projecting square plinth at the foot.

Marquetry A decorative VENEER of different coloured woods or other materials (mother-of-pearl, ivory) formed by interlocking patterns cut out of thin sheets and applied to the carcase.

Marquise A narrow sofa (or a wide BERGÈRE), to seat two persons.

Mechanical furniture Pieces with mechanically operated parts, drawers released by hidden springs, and rising compartments, made especially popular by Oeben in the Louis Seize period.

Menuiserie Furniture made by the joiner and carver (chairs, tables, looking glasses, beds) as opposed to cabinet-makers' pieces, (see ébénisterie).

Meuble à hauteur d'appui (or meuble d'appui) Resembling a commode à vantaux, but made slightly higher (hence the name 'of a height to lean upon'), this is no more than a sophisticated Parisian form of buffet. It was used principally for such things as papers, maps, books, clothes, or dining accessories.

Misericord seat Bracket on the underside of a hinged choir-stall seat. When turned up it provided the occupant with a support during long periods of standing. Usually decorated with amusing carvings of contemporary life.

Monopodium(ia) Generally topped by a lioness' head, and curving down to an accurately hocked foot and leg, this form appears in Classical sculpture and was adapted for chair legs, table legs and stands in the early nineteenth century.

Moulding A projecting band or edging, which may either have a repeated pattern in relief (often of Classical origin), or a curved section. *Scrolled moulding:* a moulding terminating in a scroll or volute. *Channelled moulding:* grooved moulding, not projecting but incised.

Nut A boss or clasp that joins structural members, such as converging table legs or crossed stretchers.

Ogee arch Arch of pointed Gothic form, but with a reverse curve near the crown, much used in the eighteenth-century fashion for the gothick style.

Opus anglicanum The name given to mediaeval embroideries for ecclesiastical use made in England, and famous all over Europe.

Organ-case The decorative casing that encloses the organ pipes in a church. In a chamber organ, the case encloses the keyboard and pedal board as well.

Organ-screen A decorated wood screen which houses the organ pipes, and sometimes the console, or keyboard.

Ormolu A method of fusing a layer of gold leaf onto brass or bronze, otherwise known as gilt-bronze, as made for wall-lights, candlesticks or mounts for furniture or porcelain, from the early eighteenth century onwards. Although the word derives from the French 'or-moulu' (ground gold), it is obsolete in France, where 'bronze-doré' is preferred. In England, the word was constantly used by Matthew Boulton for his products from 1762. 'Ormolu' now describes only work of the best quality, gilded by the expensive mercury process.

Ottomane A small sofa with an oval seat, the back sweeping down to the arms in a continuous curve. Made during the Louis Quinze period, and later.

Overmantel Any frame, mirror or carved panelling intended to be supported on the shelf of a fireplace.

Padouk wood A hard, heavy variety of rosewood imported from the Andaman Islands and Borneo; its colour when first cut ranges from golden brown to deep red. Used in England from about 1720.

Palladio Sixteenth-century Italian architect whose works in a revived classical style inspired what came to be known as the Palladian style in the eighteenth century.

Palmette Stylized spreading palm-leaf ornament, recurring frequently in treatises on classical architecture from Vitruvius onwards.

Papeleira A type of Spanish chest, like the VARGUEÑO, in that it was easily transportable and was usually placed on a simple folding stand. As its name implies the papeleira was intended specifically for the storage of papers and writing materials and, instead of having a fall-front like the vargueño, its top opened to reveal nests of drawers and boxes.

Papier-mâché furniture Pieces on which the basic wood structure was enriched by the addition of panels or parts which were formed out of decorated papier-mâché.

Parquetry The art of veneering with small pieces of wood in mosaic or abstract geometrical patterns. If the wood is uniform in texture, the pattern is given only by the directions of the grain. Alternatively, the pattern may be picked out by different species of woods.

Cube parquetry: a pattern resembling a honeycomb of cubes, generally made of contrasting woods to simulate the light and dark faces.

Partie, première and contre Terms used to describe different types of panel made in the BOULLE technique.

Première-partie is where the decorative pattern is cut in silver, brass or pewter and inlaid against a background of, for instance, ebony or tortoiseshell.

Contre-partie is where the first material becomes the background for the second —either by using the remaining metal from the initial cutting, or by cutting a fresh sheet from the same stencil.

Pastiche A loose term generally referring to an object designed in the style of an earlier period without necessarily being an exact copy, in which case the term 'reproduction' is more appropriate. A pastiche generally does not attempt to deceive or to disguise its modernity.

Pastiglia Paste or composition, which could be moulded and applied as a fine pattern on fronts of chests of drawers, stools or table legs to resemble carved wood.

Patera(ae) A small motif of Classical origin, carved in round or oval form, which was then applied to furniture. It was also occasionally depicted in paint, particularly on neo-classical furniture of the late eighteenth century.

Patina The word used to describe the surface appearance of materials such as bronze, silver and wood. Patina can either be artificially caused by polish, heat or chemicals or it can be the natural result of contact between the surface of the material and the elements over a long period of time.

Pearwood A European hardwood, sometimes used by carvers in the late seventeenth century, though harder to work than limewood. It was used less frequently by furniture-makers after American woods began to be imported in the early eighteenth century.

Pé de pincel (Literally 'paintbrush foot'.) Describes the feet of late seventeenth- and early eighteenth-century Portuguese chairs, where the legs end in a half-formed scroll resembling a paintbrush pressed gently down against the floor.

Pedestal Base or plinth on which something is set to show it off or raise it; form of cupboard, usually plain and rectangular in shape.

Palmette

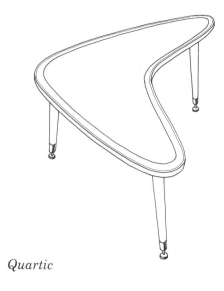

Quartic

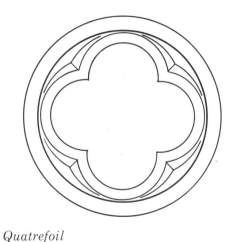

Quatrefoil

Rocaille

Pedestal clock Clock, usually for a table or overmantel, in a square or rectangular case roughly the shape of a pedestal.

Pembroke table Either oval or rectangular, this table has hinged side-flaps supported by brackets, which fold against the central drawer sides when not in use. Evolving from the single-drawered mid-eighteenth century breakfast table, it became very fashionable from about 1770 to 1800. The name appears to stem from the Countess of Pembroke (1737–1831), who, according to Sheraton, was the first person to order this design.

Piano-nobile The first floor of an Italian palace, containing the State apartments.

Pie de puente The stand on which the VARGUEÑO was placed.

Pier General architectural term for a solid support of masonry, used to describe the solid wall between windows in the interiors of houses. Furniture designed for this position is generally referred to by this term, hence pier-glass, pier-table.

Pietra dura A mosaic of semi-precious hard stones set into a marble ground. The 'Opificio delle Pietre Dure' was established in Florence in 1599 to supply the Medici family with vases, ornaments and mosaic panels for their own palaces and with gifts to send to foreign monarchs.

Pilaster A shallow pier, shaped like the face of a pillar, attached to a wall, or (in wood) to a cupboard or cabinet front.

Plafond à la française The beamed ceiling in a French château.

Plateresque Lively Renaissance ornament on Spanish furniture, but first applied to that on plate or silver vessels, hence the derivation of the name from the Spanish word for silver, *plata*.

Pliant A folding stool, with X-shaped legs (sometimes curved), hinged at the intersections.

Plinth The projecting base of a column, or piece of furniture.

Plywood A man-made board consisting of thin layers of veneer bonded together under pressure with waterproof cement. As the grain of the middle layer is at right angles to those on the outside, great tensile strength is obtained and far larger areas of wood can be produced than by using planks in their natural state. For heavy work five layers can be used and a variant—laminboard or ibus—has the central layer of heavier strips of wood glued together side by side.

Pneumatic In pneumatic furniture, flexible airtight sections, linked together or pre-shaped, are simply inflated to provide support which would in more conventional furniture be structured with frame, springs and stuffing.

Pole screen Firescreen of the standard type in the eighteenth century, consisting of a rectangular panel fixed (usually with adjustable rings) to a tall pole resting on tripod legs.

Polyptych A panel with several painted panels as opposed to a diptych, or TRIPTYCH which have only two, or three, panels.

Predella The altar-step or raised shelf at the back of an altar; the vertical face is frequently painted.

Prie-dieu A kneeling-desk for prayers, for use by one person. Made especially in Italy, Spain and south Germany. The French adapted special low-seated chairs for this purpose.

Prunkschrein In German, literally a 'show-shrine'—the term for those large cabinets made originally at Augsburg and Nuremberg whose purpose was generally ostentatious rather than practical, and whose form was based on reliquaries, ciboria and other ornaments of the altar. The large doors of these cabinets, painted on the inside and usually kept open, were also similar in effect to the religious TRIPTYCH.

Psyché see Cheval-glass

Purplewood An exotic wood, imported from British Guiana, used for veneers on French eighteenth-century furniture. When freshly cut it is of a rich purple colour, but when faded is liable to be confused with kingwood or rosewood. Also known as purpleheart.

Putti Cherubs, commonly used as a decorative motif since Classical times, for instance in flanking mirrors or as elements in a FRIEZE; later adapted by the Church as small angels or cherubim, but from the time of the Renaissance once again given secular connotations. Particularly popular after Raphael's 'playing boys', they became a favourite subject for carvers such as Grinling Gibbons in the seventeenth century, and continued to be used to decorate furniture by makers throughout the eighteenth century.

Quarter column The quarter-section of a column, used occasionally by furniture-makers in the angles of seventeenth-century cabinets of architectural form, or on eighteenth-century chests of drawers and tallboys.

Quartic A function, curve or surface of the fourth degree, the term being taken from co-ordinate geometry. Although the boomerang-like shape appears free-form, the regular curves of the quartic can be built up with elliptical compasses. This term was first applied to popular shapes in modern furniture of the 1950s by the mathematician and designer J A Wedd.

Quatrefoil A Gothic motif, derived from mediaeval window tracery or wood carving, in the form of a four-lobed medallion or flowerhead.

Queen Anne The term used to describe the type of English furniture made in the reign of Queen Anne, from 1702 to 1714. It implies the use of various features such as the CABRIOLE leg and SPLAT-BACK on chairs which were common at that time.

Redwood Wood from either of the two types of redwood trees native to California, the Coastal Redwood and the 'Big Tree' or *Wellingtonia*.

Rafraîchissoir Form of table with apertures for buckets of ice in which to stand bottles of wine.

Régence style The name given to the transitional period of design between the Baroque and the Rococo in France, roughly coinciding with the Regency of the duc d'Orléans, during Louis XV's minority (1715–1723).

Regency The style in architecture and furniture predominant during the reign of George IV (1820–1830) and his regency during the periods of his father's madness in the preceding years. The term implies a certain degree of elegance, and features such as the SABRE LEG made popular by the Prince's own decoration of Carlton House and the Pavilion at Brighton.

Reliquary Ornamented receptacles to house relics of saints, used from early Christian times.

Repoussé A process by which a design is beaten into silver, copper or brass (and occasionally lead in the Art Nouveau period) from the inside or underneath, and finished on the outer surface by chasing, that is by the use of chisels and engraving tools.

Rinceau A stylized ornament of scrolled stems with stiff acanthus leaves, taken from Classical Roman architecture. Most typically found on horizontal friezes or vertical pilasters; revived especially during the Renaissance and neo-classical periods.

Rocaille A specifically Rococo ornament, originating from shell forms which have become asymmetrical, in-dented and often pierced. Used as a decorative or border motif in engravings, ormolu, carved chair and table frames, and marquetry patterns, especially from about 1730 to 1755.

Romayne style Carved medallion heads on furniture, which show Renaissance influence in a pseudo-classical form.

Rood-screen The wooden screen across the west end of the chancel of a church. It divides the body or nave of the church from the chancel, at the east end of which the altar and cross are usually sited.

Rosewood A dark purplish-brown wood with a variegated FIGURE imported to Europe from Brazil and the East Indies from the seventeenth century onwards. Evelyn recommended it in 1664 for inlaying, but it was employed more often in the eighteenth century for veneer in bandings and small panels. Later in the century, and even more so in the first half of the nineteenth century, it was used in bulk for carcase pieces such as writing-tables and cabinets. The name was often also given to kingwood, which derives from the same genus, balbergia.

Roundel Any circular inset, low relief wreath or moulding of wood in circular form. In furniture, roundels were used for decorative purposes and were interpreted in a variety of materials—porcelain, pottery, metal, enamel, wood, and ivory being the most common.

Sabre leg Curved form used in classical furniture and widely revived in about 1800, especially in chair design. Also called 'Scimitar' leg.

Salon Reception-room in, especially, great French houses.

Sarcophagus A stone coffin, especially one adorned with inscriptions or sculptured reliefs.

Satinwood Many varieties of wood go by this name. The most common are pale yellow, highly figured woods from the West and East Indies. The West Indian wood was imported first, being used in European furniture from about 1765, while the East Indian variety is not found until about 1800.

Scagliola A composition of ground pieces of marble, plaster of Paris and glue used to imitate both plain marble and PIETRA DURA (inlaid marble). Made by the Romans, the art was revived in sixteenth-century Florence under Medici patronage. The material remained fashionable for interior decoration, especially table tops, in the eighteenth century.

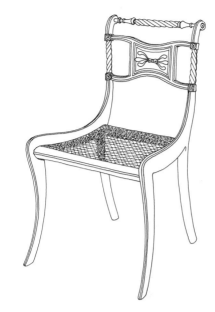

Sabre leg

Sarcophagus

Secrétaire à abattant

Schenkschieve A four-door cupboard, sometimes used for storage of plate and documents.

Sconce A general term for wall-light.

Scroll An ornamental design, usually in wood or metal, which in its spiral curving line imitates a roll of parchment or paper.

Seat-rail The horizontal members that support the caned or upholstered seat of a chair.

Seaweed marquetry A type of marquetry INLAY in intricate arabesque patterns, so called because of its convoluting scrolls and tendrils. The technique was originally popular in the Netherlands but spread to England towards the end of the seventeenth century.

Secretaire A writing-table or writing-cabinet, with a hinged drop-front that provides the writing surface. When closed, the panel is vertical. The secretaire occurs in many forms, from the sixteenth to the nineteenth century.

Secrétaire à abattant Form of desk with a fall-front enclosing drawers and pigeon-holes, usually with either drawers or a cupboard below.

Secretary desk (or secretary) The name given in eighteenth-century America to writing-tables of the English bureau or bureau-cabinet type.

Sedia curulis The name given to the type of stool used in Classical Rome.

Serpentine A graceful outline in the shape of an extended curve (as of a serpent in motion). Seen especially on the fronts of eighteenth-century chests of drawers. More loosely, the curvaceous nature of Rococo outlines, which Hogarth seized upon as his 'line of beauty'.

Settee The original word for a sofa, before the two words became interchangeable—a seat with back and arms made for two or more people. The word sofa is Arabic in origin, and the exotic Eastern connotations that this piece of furniture held for the eighteenth century is clear in the names given to slightly differing shapes of settee in France, such as 'Sultane', 'Turquoise', 'OTTOMANE' and 'Paphose'.

Sèvres porcelain plaque Plaque or panel of porcelain from the Sèvres factory, often used on furniture of the Louis Quinze and Seize periods to decorate table-tops and desks.

Sgabello The standard term for an Italian backstool of the Renaissance period, of a form which continued to be made until the end of the seventeenth century, the seat resting on two carved or shaped supports, canted inwards,

and the back carved like a CARTOUCHE. 'Sgabelloni' in Florence usually referred to the carved wooden stands for vases or busts, constructed in much the same way but with two more canted supports at each side.

Shagreen (or sharkskin) When properly treated sharkskin is stronger than leather with a rough surface; whether left in its natural creamy-beige colour or dyed in shades of green, it was extensively used in the eighteenth century for the exteriors of travelling-boxes, knife-boxes and small articles likely to experience much handling. Its use was revived in about 1920 by French designers such as Ruhlmann and Groult, with the natural surface smoothed and polished to reveal a pattern of circular spots.

Sheet ply Sheets of plywood-boarding made of thin layers of wood which are glued together, strength being achieved by placing the grain of one layer at right angles to that of the next.

Shield-back Chair-back of conventional shield outline which became popular in the 1780s and 1790s in England.

Siège A chair without arms. The seat may be either upholstered or caned.

Siège courant Chair designed to be moved around the room at will.

Siège meublant Chair designed to stand and remain *in situ* round the walls of a room.

Sillón de cadera Spanish for an X-frame folding-chair, usually with a stamped leather seat and back, the commonest type of seat furniture throughout the Iberian peninsula in the sixteenth and seventeenth centuries.

Sillón de fraileros A hinged Spanish chair frequently covered with leather or brocade.

Skid-legs Support system used for both chairs and tables in which each pair of legs is connected at floor level by a horizontal bar, either by jointing or by bending one continuous strip of material, to form two leg structures which resemble the 'skids' or runners of a sledge.

Sofa see Settee

Soft wood A loose term, generally the wood of coniferous trees such as pine, fir, deal. These fast-growing woods were cheaper than native hardwoods (oak, chestnut, walnut), besides being easier to work, and convenient for panelling or the case work of furniture, which would be either painted or veneered. Pine, however, could be of fine quality, and its soft texture made it very suitable for carving and gilding, especially for side-tables and looking-glasses.

Solium The Roman throne, of a shape usually following Greek models.

Spiral turning see Turning

Splat On a chair, the vertical member in the centre of the back, between the seat and the top-rail, hence 'splat-back chair'. On English 'Queen Anne' chairs, the splat is generally wide, flat and vase-shaped. On 'Chippendale' chairs, it is generally pierced and carved with delicate tracery.

Squab A very low, square or rect-angular carved stool frame, usually caned, on which were placed two large, squashy cushions. Squabs were an almost essential part of the furniture thought necessary for a state bed-room in the Baroque period, along with armchairs, chairs and stools.

S-scroll A Rococo ornament: a scroll shaped as an 'S' or 'Ƨ', generally elongated and asymmetrical.

Stanze The Italian word for 'rooms', usually describing those in the Vatican decorated by Raphael (1483–1520) and his assistants.

Steam-bending Method of manipu-lating flat surfaces of wood by heat.

Stick-back (As in traditional Swedish side-chairs), a descriptively accurate term for the back support which com-prises several slim, vertical bars (or 'sticks') within a rectangular frame.

Stippone The Italian term for a large cabinet on a stand, roughly equivalent to the German PRUNKSCHREIN. It par-ticularly applies to the cabinets made in seventeenth-century Florence, based initially on Augsburg models.

Strapwork Carved surface ornament or panels, taking interlacing straplike bands as the motif. Most used in Eliza-bethan and Jacobean work and fre-quently appearing in German engrav-ings of the sixteenth and seventeenth centuries.

Stretcher The wooden bar joining the legs of chairs or tables. It gives strength and is frequently decorated with inlays or, when in diagonal form, is sur-mounted at the crossing by urns, crowns or carved birds.

Strip ornament Any straight line of repeated decoration.

Stucco A mixture of sand and a bond-ing agent (lime or cement), applied to the outside of a building as a protective or decorative covering, either coloured, or deliberately treated to simulate the appearance of stonework. The idea

originated in the Mediterranean coun-tries, and was especially popular in Italy. Climatic conditions made it gen-erally unsuitable in northern European countries and here the word was gener-ally used to describe only internal ornamental plasterwork.

Stump-work Embroidery which has been padded to raise it from the ground to which it is sewn. Used on caskets and boxes and popular in late seventeenth-century England.

Sussex chair Traditional rural chairs from the south of England. There are two kinds, both with rush seats; a side-chair with cruciform back and an arm-chair with back-SPLATS curving in-wards.

Swag Draped decoration, often caught at either end into pendant festoon drops, of looped form.

Table à écrire A small eighteenth-century writing-table for a lady's use, generally with a flat surface and a fitted drawer below.

Table ambulante A small table that was easily moved for the convenience of the user. It generally implies such pieces as coffee-tables, writing, read-ing, work or dressing-tables of the eighteenth century, when these were light and portable. Such tables often had ormolu handles.

Table de chevet Bedside-table.

Table en commode Form of small table with two or more drawers.

Tabouret A stool with an upholstered seat, standing on four legs.

Tallboy A wide low chest carrying a slightly narrower, taller chest. The top chest has two or three drawers.

Tambour-fronted (desk or table) A roll-front of strips of wood glued on to a canvas backing. Used for desk-tops and cupboard-doors in late eighteenth-century England and France.

Tazza A shallow bowl or cup mounted on a base which is usually made of silver or mounted rock-crystal.

Tester A canopy, covering the whole area of a bed, sometimes supported on four corner posts, sometimes suspended from the ceiling. A 'half-tester' canopy was cantilevered from the headposts, and usually extended over approxi-mately one-third of the length of the bed.

Top-rail The highest horizontal mem-ber of a chair-back.

Torchère A general term for a candle-stand, often made in pairs or sets of four. Applied to the tall turned stands with tray tops of the seventeenth century, and the curved Italianate Palladian

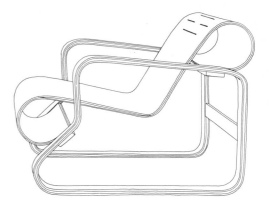

Skid-legs

Swag

327

Bobbin turning

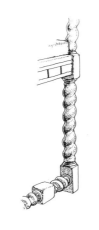

Spiral turning

versions, the Rococo fantasies and neo-classical tripods of the eighteenth century—all intended to support candelabra, or candlesticks.

Toupie feet Feet in the shape of spinning tops.

Tracery Intersecting ornamental patterns usually based on the segmentation of a circle, originally used in Gothic windows but also as a decorative form in Gothic furniture.

Transitional style The usual term to describe pieces of French furniture which combine Rococo and neo-classical motifs, and date from those years (the late 1750s and early 1760s) when the first style was being gradually superseded by the second. These years coincide with the end of Louis XV's reign and the beginning of Louis XVI's.

Trapeza The small, oblong or circular, three-legged portable table common in ancient Greece.

Trecento The fourteenth century in Italian art and literature. The Renaissance period also spanned the Quattrocento (the fifteenth century).

Trespolo A small, light table with a narrow top, on a column and tripod or other base, generally used as a candle- or mirror-stand. Made in north Italy, and especially Venice.

Triple-ply A term used to indicate thickness of plywood by the number of layers—just as with wool, for example, single-ply, two-ply.

Tripod stand Candlestand, or small table, on a three-legged support.

Tripod table A table on a column, raised on three curved (or CABRIOLE) feet. The top is usually circular, about two and a half to three feet (nearly one metre) in diameter, but the shape and decoration vary. Sometimes the top has a gallery. They were made in large numbers in England in the eighteenth century and later, usually for use as tea-tables.

Triptych Three painted panels hinged so that the two outer panels fold over the central one, as in an altarpiece.

Trompe l'oeil (Literally 'deceiving the eye'.) Painting or marquetry which is skilful enough in its resemblance, CHIAROSCURO and perspective to be mistaken for the objects themselves. Such decoration on furniture often represents a casual arrangement of books, papers or playing cards, for example.

Trumeau A pier-glass. The word implies the complete panel, made to fit between windows, including the painting or carving which was often placed above the mirror. In Italy, a trumeau or bureau-trumeau is the bureau-cabinet of the German type, made in Venice and elsewhere.

Tsuba The Japanese name for a sword-guard. Usually of iron and often inlaid with various metals, such as gold, silver and copper. This highly regarded form of metalwork produced many skilled craftsmen who, after the Imperial edict banning the wearing of swords in the early 1860s, turned to making vases and other items of decorative metalwork employing the same techniques.

Tulip wood A Brazilian hardwood, light brown in colour tinged with pink and with variegated stripes of yellow, brown or grey. Used for veneers and cross-banding in marquetry, especially by French cabinet-makers, in the eighteenth and early nineteenth centuries.

Turkey work The name generally given to cushions, carpets and upholstery knotted in the style of Near Eastern rugs. Often referred to in sixteenth- and seventeenth-century inventories.

Turning A method of carving legs, arms, or stretchers of chairs and tables by means of a revolving lathe, usually operated by a foot-pedal before machine lathes were developed in the nineteenth century. Various means of decoration were made possible by the revolving lathe. *Spiral turning*, the best known, where a continuous spiral groove was carved into the wood (sometimes known as 'barleytwist' or 'corkscrew'). *Bobbin turning*, where grooves were cut at intervals, and often at different depths, achieving an effect of a row of knobs, somewhat like a lace-maker's bobbins. Turned furniture, known to have existed in Greece as early as the sixth century BC, was especially popular in the seventeenth century, and reached heights of elaborate decoration in Spain and Portugal in the early eighteenth. Thereafter it was confined largely to provincial joiners' pieces such as WINDSOR CHAIRS, though in the Victorian era it was again revived for more ambitious work on aesthetic grounds.

Tuscan see Columns

Valance A length of material, often gathered or pleated, hung from the cornices of testers on four-post bedsteads to hide the attachment of the curtains to the rods. The similar strips covering the sides of the mattress and hanging down to the ground are also referred to on occasion as valances, though they also went under the name of 'souspentes' or 'sousbassements' when a more precise definition was required.

Vargueño Spanish term for a FALL-FRONT cabinet, supported on an open stand (called a 'PIE DE PUENTE') or a solid base of drawers.

Veilleuse A comfortable sofa for reclining, with a back, a high end and a low end. Often made in matching pairs to face each other.

Vellum The name given to the scraped and de-haired skin of a variety of animals such as sheep and goat, which is then dried under pressure. This process is crucial since it alters the fibrous structure of the skin, which is why vellum buckles so badly when wet—a process which partly restores the original structure.

Veneering The task of glueing thin sheets of wood (veneers) to the carcase of furniture for decorative effect.

Ventaglio ('A ventaglio' in Italian meaning literally 'fan-shaped'.) A type of eighteenth-century Italian sofa in which the arms incline outwards at an angle of approximately 45 degrees.

Verde antico A green brescia marble, occurring in many shades, embedded with black and greenish fragments. It was highly prized in the eighteenth century, when all examples were taken from ancient Roman ruins. The quarries in Thessaly were rediscovered in the nineteenth century, and this marble is not uncommon today.

Vernis A word to describe coloured varnishes and painted decoration on furniture and panelling of the eighteenth century. It includes lacquer, imitation of lacquer, and European-style decoration. In France, during the eighteenth century, its most famous exponents were the Martin brothers, after whom it is often called vernis-martin. See also Japan and Lacca.

Vitrine A bookcase or other type of display-case with a glass front. Primarily a nineteenth-century invention.

Volute Spiral scroll ornament, especially associated with architectural details; the Ionic capital consists of two volutes seen back to back in profile.

Voyeuse A chair made in the eighteenth century, with a flat padded rail across the back for a second person to lean over, in order to join in the conversation or watch a card game. Also a chair without arms, and with a narrow back with a padded rail at the top, so that a man could sit astride it.

Wainscot oak The word 'wainscot' was originally applied to wood suitable for the construction of wagons. Latterly, it came to mean heavy planks suitable for panelling or furniture-making. A smaller size of split oak was known as 'clapboard'.

Wall-sconce A wall light.

Wangentisch A solid table made in mediaeval Germany in the early sixteenth century. It has legs splayed at an angle joined by a STRETCHER.

Wave pattern A type of decoration on furniture achieved by carving a number of deep, parallel grooves in straight lines round panels along FRIEZES, or in more elaborate curving and pointed forms (the latter usually called 'flame' rather than 'wave' pattern). The practice originated in the Netherlands but received its most elaborate interpretation in Spain and Portugal, where it was called 'tremido'.

Wedgwood Term given to wares produced at the factory of Josiah Wedgwood (1730–95) which is still in operation today. Establishing his factory in 1759, Wedgwood did much to popularize creamware in England and went on to make basalts and jasperware which were both admired and copied in Europe and sometimes inset into furniture.

Whiplash style A decorative motif typical of Art Nouveau designs in France, Belgium and Spain, derived from floral patterns of flowing plant stems. It often relies on parallelism, that is to say several stems drawn or carved together, to give the impression of ceaseless nervous movement, in contrast to the angularity of most Art Nouveau design in Scotland, Germany and Austria.

Windsor chair A comfortable type of English country-made chair, usually executed in native woods such as oak and beech, generally with arms and an arched back with numerous spindles. The legs are dowelled into the seat and joined by STRETCHERS. The seat may be of elm, the legs of beech, while the hoops, rails and sometimes the spindles may be of yew, but there are many variations. First mentioned in the early eighteenth century, and manufactured on a large scale at High Wycombe from 1810. Windsor chairs were popular from the eighteenth century in America.

Wine-table A modern term, often used by dealers, for small, low tripod tables that were designed as kettlestands.

Writing-box Box fitted with writing surface and implements, divided into two sections opening on a hinge to produce the sloping effect of a desk.

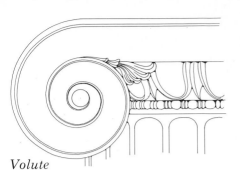

Volute

Windsor chair

Collections

Austria
Bundes Mobilien Verwaltung, VIENNA
Hofburg, Silberne Kapelle und Hofkirche,
 VIENNA
Kunstgewerbe Museum, VIENNA
Kunsthistorisches Museum, VIENNA
Osterreichisches Museum für Angewandte
 Kunst, VIENNA
Schönbrunn Palast und Park, VIENNA
Technisches Museum für Industrie und
 Gewerbe, VIENNA

Belgium
Hôtel Solvay, BRUSSELS
Hôtel van Eetevelde, BRUSSELS
Musée Horta, BRUSSELS
Musée Curtius, LIÈGE
Musée d'Ansembourg, LIÈGE
Musée de Mariemont, MARIEMONT

Czechoslovakia
Červeny Kamen, ČERVENY KAMEN
Hluboká Castle, ČESKÉ BUDĚJOVICE,
 South Bohemia
National Gallery, PRAGUE
Sychrov Castle, near PRAGUE

Denmark
Danske Kunstindustri Museet,
 COPENHAGEN
Nationalmuseet, COPENHAGEN
Rosenborg Castle, COPENHAGEN

Egypt
Cairo Museum, CAIRO

Federal Republic of Germany
Residenz, BAMBURG
Germanisches Nationalmuseum, BERLIN
Schloss Charlottenburg, BERLIN
Museum Folkwang, ESSEN
Museum für Kunsthandwerk, FRANKFURT-
 AM-MAIN
Museum für Kunst und Gewerbe,
 HAMBURG
Schloss Linderhof, LINDERHOF, Bavaria
Reiss-Museum, MANNHEIM
Bayerisches Nationalmuseum, MUNICH
Residenzmuseum, MUNICH
Landesmuseum für kunst und Kultur-
 geschichte, MUNSTER
Germanisches Nationalmuseum,
 NUREMBERG

Schloss Pommersfelden, POMMERSFELDEN
Residenz, WURZBURG

Finland
Finnish Society of Crafts and Design,
 HELSINKI

France
Château de Compiègne
Château de Ferrières
Château de Fontainebleau
Musée de Lyon, LYON
Musée de l'Ecole de Nancy, NANCY
Musée Thomas-Dobree et Musée archéo-
 logique, NANTES
Musée Condé, Château de Chantilly, OISE
Château de Malmaison, near PARIS
Collection Henriette Bouvier, Musée
 Carnavalet, PARIS
Musée de Cluny, PARIS
Musée des Arts Décoratifs, PARIS
Musée du Louvre, PARIS
Musée Jacquemart-Andre, PARIS
Musée Nissim-de-Camondo, PARIS
Château de Champs, Seine et Marne
Musée de Strasbourg, STRASBOURG
Musée de Versailles et de Trianons au
 Château de Versailles

German Democratic Republic
Historisches Museum, DRESDEN
Museum für Kunsthandwerke, DRESDEN
Schloss Pillnitz, near DRESDEN
Staatliche Schlösser und Gärten,
 POTSDAM-SANSOUCCI

Great Britain
The American Museum in Britain,
 Claverton Manor, near BATH, Avon
Waddesdon Manor, Buckinghamshire
Fitzwilliam Museum, CAMBRIDGE,
 Cambridgeshire
The Bowes Museum, Barnard Castle,
 County Durham
Hardwick Hall, Derbyshire
Glasgow University Collection, GLASGOW,
 Scotland
Dyrham Park, Gloucestershire
Osborne House, EAST COWES, Isle of Wight
The Newarke Houses, LEICESTER,
 Leicestershire
Bethnal Green Museum, LONDON
British Museum, LONDON

Geffreye Museum, Shoreditch, LONDON
Hampton Court Palace, Middlesex
Victoria & Albert Museum, LONDON
Wallace Collection, LONDON
William Morris Gallery, Walthamstow,
 LONDON
Ashmolean Museum, OXFORD, Oxfordshire
Clandon Park, Surrey
Ham House, PETERSHAM, Surrey
Brighton Art Gallery and Museums,
 BRIGHTON, Sussex
Corsham Court, Wiltshire
Nostell Priory, Yorkshire
Temple Newsam House, LEEDS, Yorkshire

Italy
Palazzo Rappini, ARPINO
Galleria degli Uffizi, FLORENCE
Museo Horne, FLORENCE
Palazzo Davanzati, FLORENCE
Palazzo Pitti, FLORENCE
Galleria di Palazzo Rosso, GENOA
Palazzo Balbi-Durazzo, GENOA
Galleria del Levante, MILAN
Museo d'Arte Antica: Castello Sforzesco,
 MILAN
Museo Poldi Pezzoli, MILAN
Palazzo Clerici, MILAN
Museo e Gallerie Nazionale di Capo-
 dimonte, NAPLES
Museo Nazionale, NAPLES
Galleria Nazionale d'Arte Moderna, ROME
Museo di Palazzo Venezia, ROME
Palazzo Barberini, ROME
Palazzo Colonna, ROME
Palazzo Doria, ROME
Vatican Museums, ROME
Pinacoteca Nazionale, SIENA
Villa La Rocca, SORAGNA
Museo 'Correale di Terranova', SORRENTO
Villa Pisani, Stra
Civico Museo Sartorio, TRIESTE
Museo dell'Arredamento, Stupinigi, TURIN
Palazzina di Caccia, Stupinigi, TURIN
Palazzo Madama, TURIN
Palazzo ex Reale, TURIN
Ca' Rezzonico, VENICE
Palazzo Querini-Stampalia, VENICE

The Netherlands
Rijksmuseum, AMSTERDAM
Stedelijk Museum, AMSTERDAM
Gemeentemuseum, THE HAGUE

Centraal Museum, UTRECHT
Kasteel Duivenoorde, VOORSCHOTEN

Norway
Kunstindustrimuseet i Oslo, OSLO
Nordenfjeldske Kundindustrimuseum,
 TRONDHEIM

Poland
National Museum, Warsaw

Portugal
Museu Nacional de Arte Antiga, LISBON
Museu-Escola de Artes Decorativas,
 LISBON
Museu Guerra Junqueira, OPORTO
Museu Nacional de Soares dos Reis,
 OPORTO
Palacio Nacional de Queluz, QUELUZ

Spain
Museo de Arte Moderno, BARCELONA
Museo Nacional de Artes Decorativas,
 BARCELONA
Museo Gaudí, BARCELONA
Museo Nacional de Artes Decorativas,
 MADRID
Palacio Nacional, MADRID

Sweden
Drottningholm Palace, near STOCKHOLM
Historiska Museum, STOCKHOLM
Nationalmuseum, STOCKHOLM
Nordiska Museet, STOCKHOLM
Skokloster Castle, SKOKLOSTER
Royal Palace, STOCKHOLM

Switzerland
Historisches Museum, BASLE
Musée de Valère, SION
Kunstgewerbemuseum und Museum
 Bellerive, ZURICH
Schweizerisches Landesmuseum
 Musée National Suisse, ZURICH

USA
Gamble House, Greene and Greene
 Library, PASADENA, California
Los Angeles County Museum of Art,
 California
Oakland Museum, OAKLAND, California
The Art Galleries, University of
 California, SANTA BARBARA, California

Art Institute of Chicago, CHICAGO
Chicago School of Architecture
 Foundation, CHICAGO
Wadsworth Atheneum, HARTFORD,
 Connecticut
Yale University Art Gallery, NEW HAVEN,
 Connecticut
Henry Francis du Pont Winterthur
 Museum, WINTERTHUR, Delaware
Victoria Mansion (Morse-Libby House),
 PORTLAND, Maine
Walters Art Gallery, BALTIMORE, Maryland
Boston Museum of Fine Arts, BOSTON,
 Massachusetts
Greenfield Village and Henry Ford
 Museum, DEARBORN, Michigan
Nelson-Atkins Gallery of Art, KANSAS
 CITY, Missouri
Albright-Knox Art Gallery, BUFFALO,
 New York State
Fine Arts Academy, BUFFALO, New York
 State
Brooklyn Museum, BROOKLYN, New York
 State
Cooper-Hewitt Museum of Decorative Arts
 and Design, NEW YORK
Frick Collection, NEW YORK
The Hispanic Society of America Museum,
 NEW YORK
Lyndhurst, TARRYTOWN, New York State
The Metropolitan Museum of Art,
 NEW YORK
The Museum of Modern Art, NEW YORK
Museum of the City of New York,
 NEW YORK
Philadelphia Museum of Art,
 PHILADELPHIA, Pennsylvania
Rhode Island School of Design, RHODE
 ISLAND
Colonial Williamsburg Foundation,
 WILLIAMSBURG, Virginia
The Virginia Museum of Fine Arts,
 RICHMOND, Virginia
Governor's House, Colonial Williamsburg,
 Virginia

USSR
Katalnaya Gorka, Oranienbaum, LENINGRAD
Museum Palaces and Parks in Pavlovsk,
 LENINGRAD
Palace of Peterhof, LENINGRAD
Palace of Tsarskoe Selo, LENINGRAD
State Hermitage Museum, LENINGRAD

Bibliography

General

Aprà, N *The Louis Styles* (Orbis Publishing, London 1972)

Ayres, J *American Antiques* (Orbis Publishing, London 1973)

Burr, G H *Hispanic Furniture from the 15th century through the 17th century* (Archive Press, New York 1964)

Copplestone, T (Ed) *World Architecture* (Paul Hamlyn, London 1963, 8th impression 1975)

Edwards, R (Ed) *The Dictionary of English furniture—from the Middle Ages to the late Georgian period*, 3 vols (Country Life, Feltham, 2nd revised edition 1954)

Edwards, R *The Shorter Dictionary of English Furniture* (Country Life, Feltham 1964)

Edwards, R & Jourdain, M *Georgian Cabinet-Makers* (Country Life, Feltham, 3rd edition 1955)

Fastnedge, R *English Furniture Styles 1500–1830* (Penguin Books, Harmondsworth 1955)

Fletcher, B *A History of Architecture* (The Athlone Press, University of London 1961)

Gloag, J (Ed) *A Short Dictionary of Furniture* (George Allen & Unwin, London, 2nd edition 1969)

Gonzales-Palacios, A *I mobili nei secoli*, 10 vols (Fabbri, Milan 1969)

Hayward, H (Ed) *World Furniture* (Paul Hamlyn, Feltham 1969)

Honour, H *Cabinet Makers and Furniture Designers* (Weidenfeld & Nicolson, London 1969)

Huth, H *Lacquer of the West: the History of a Craft and an Industry, 1600–1950* (University of Chicago Press, Chicago 1971)

Joy, E, *The Connoisseur Illustrated Guides: Furniture* (The Connoisseur, London 1975)

Kreisel, H (Ed) *Die Kunst des Deutsches Möbels*, 3 vols (C H Beck, Munich 1968–74)

Mercer, E *Furniture to 1700* (Weidenfeld & Nicolson, London 1969)

Philippe, J *Mobilier liègeois, moyen âge—XIXe siècle* (Liège 1962)

Salvy, C *Dictionnaire des meubles régionaux* (Hachette, Paris 1971)

Verlet, P (Ed) *Styles, meubles, décors du Moyen Age à nos jours*, 2 vols (Larousse, Paris 1972)

The Archaeological Record

Baker, H S *Furniture in the Ancient World* (The Connoisseur, London 1966)

Burford, A *Craftsmen in Greek and Roman Society* (Thames & Hudson, London 1972)

Carter, H *Tomb of Tutankhamen* (Barrie & Jenkins, London 1972; Sphere, London 1972)

Lasko, P *Ars Sacra 800–1200* (Penguin Books, Harmondsworth 1972)

Muller-Christensen, S *Alte Möbel vom Mittelalter bis zum Jugenstil* (F Bruckmann, Munich 1957)

Richter, G M A *The Furniture of the Greeks, Etruscans and Romans* (Phaidon Press, London 1966)

The Classical Revival

Bode, W *Die italienischen Hausmöbel der Renaissance* (H Seemann, Leipzig 1902; New York, trans M E Herrick 1921)

Boynton, L O J (Ed) *The Hardwick Hall Inventories of 1601* (Furniture History Society, London 1971)

Brunhammer, Y & de Fayet, M *Meubles et Ensembles, Epoque moyen âge et renaissance* (Larousse, Paris 1966)

Brunhammer, Y & de Fayet, M *Meubles et Ensembles, Louis XIII et Louis XIV* (Larousse, Paris 1966)

du Cerceau, J A *Oeuvres*, 2 vols (Guimard, Paris 1884–91)

Eberlein, H D *Interiors, fireplaces and furniture of the Italian renaissance* (The Architectural Book Publishing Co., New York 1916)

Enriquez, M D *El Mueble Español en los Siglos XV, XVI y XVII* (Panaceos, Madrid 1951)

von Falke, O (Ed) *Deutsche Möbel des Mittelalters und der Renaissance* (J Hoffmann, Stuttgart 1924)

Jervis, S (Ed) *Printed Furniture Designs 1650* (Furniture History Society, London 1974)

Lognon, H A & Huard, F W *French provincial furniture* (J B Lippincott Co., Philadelphia 1927)

Moller, L *Der Wrangelschrank und Die verwandten süddeutschen Intarsienmöbel des 16 Jahrhunderts* (R Linz, Berlin 1956)

Odom, W M *A history of Italian furniture from the 14th to the early 19th centuries*, 2 vols (Doubleday, Page & Co., New York 1918–19; 2nd ed. New York Archive Press 1966–67)

Pedrini, A *Il mobilio, gli ambienti e le decorazioni del Rinascimento in Italia, secoli XV e XVI* (Azienda libraria editoriale, Florence 1948)

Remnant, G L *A catalogue of Misericords in Great Britain* (Oxford University Press 1969)

Salvy, C *Les meubles régionaux en France* (Paris Libraire Gründ 1967)

Schubring, P *Cassoni* (K W Hersemann, Leipzig 1915 and supplement 1923)

Singleton, E *Dutch and Flemish Furniture* (London and New York 1907)

Vogelsang, W *Le meuble hollandais* (Amsterdam 1910)

Wills, G *English Furniture 1550–1760* (Guinness, London 1971)

Wills, G *English Furniture 1760–1900* (Guinness, London 1971)

Wolsey, S W & Luff, R W *Furniture in England: the age of the joiner* (Arthur Barker, London 1968)

Formal Splendour

Lizzani, G *Il Mobile Romano* (Görlich, Milan 1970)

Scarisbrick, D *Baroque—the age of exuberance* (Orbis Publishing, London 1973)

Smith, R C *The Art of Portugal 1500–1800* (Weidenfeld & Nicolson, London 1968)

Symonds, R W *Furniture making in Seventeenth and Eighteenth-century England* (Country Life, London 1955)

Verlet, P *French Royal Furniture* (Barrie & Jenkins, London 1963)

Ward-Jackson, P *English Furniture Designs of the Eighteenth Century* (Her Majesty's Stationery Office, London 1958)

The Line of Beauty

Baccheschi, E *Il mobile veneziano del settecento* (Görlich, Milan 1962)

Baccheschi, E *Mobili intarsiati del sei e settecento in Italia* (Görlich, Milan 1964)

Baccheschi, E *Mobili italiani del Meridione* (Görlich, Milan 1966)

Baccheschi, E *Mobili Tedeschi* (Görlich, Milan 1969)

Beck, D *Book of American Furniture* (Hamlyn, London & New York 1973)

Bjerkoe, E H *The cabinetmakers of America* (Doubleday, New York 1957)

Canonero, L *Barocchetto genovese* (Milan 1962)

Chippendale, T *The Gentleman and Cabinet-Maker's Director* (First edition 1754; third edition 1762; reduced facsimile of third edition, Dover Publications, New York 1966)

Coleridge, A *Chippendale Furniture* (Faber & Faber, London 1968)

Davis, T *Rococo—a style of fantasy* (Orbis Publishing, London 1973)

Downs, J *American Furniture of the Queen Anne and Chippendale periods in the Henry Francis Du Pont Winterthur Museum* (Macmillan, New York 1952)

Feduchi, L *El mueble español* (Ediciones Poligrafa, SA, Barcelona 1969)

Hayward, H *Thomas Johnson and English Rococo* (Tiranti, London 1964)

Kenworthy-Browne, J *Chippendale and his contemporaries* (Orbis Publishing, London 1973)

Mazzariol, G *Mobili italiani del seicento e del settecento* (Milan 1963)

Morazzoni, G *Il mobile veneziano del settecento* (Görlich, Milan 1958)

Verlet, P *French Furniture and Interior Decoration of the 18th Century* (Barrie & Rockliff, London 1967)

Verlet, P *Le style Louis XV* (Larousse, Paris 1942)

Ward-Jackson, P *English Furniture Designs of the Eighteenth Century* (Her Majesty's Stationery Office, London 1958)

Purity of Form

Aprà, N *Empire Style 1804–1815* (Orbis Publishing, London 1972)

Les Ebénistes du XVIIIᵉ Siècle Français (Connaissance des Arts, Hachette, Paris 1963)

Eriksen, S *Early Neo-Classicism in France* (Faber & Faber, London 1974)

Fastnedge, R *Sheraton Furniture* (Faber & Faber, London 1962)

Grandjean, S *Empire Furniture* (Faber & Faber, London 1966)

Harris, E *The Furniture of Robert Adam* (Alec Tiranti, London 1963)

Harris, J *Regency Furniture Designs from Contemporary Sourcebooks 1803–26* (Master Hand Series, 1961)

Jarry, M *Le Siège Français de Louis XIII à Napoleon III* (Office du Livre, Fribourg 1973)

Jourdain, M *Regency Furniture 1795–1820* (Country Life, Feltham 1934)

Ledoux-Lebard, D *Les Ebénistes Parisiens (1795–1830)—les oeuvres et leurs marques* (De Nobele, Paris 1965)

Montgomery, C *American Furniture of the Federal Period* (Winterthur Museum, Delaware 1967)

Musgrave, C *Adam and Hepplewhite and Other Neo-classical Furniture* (Faber & Faber, London 1966)

Praz, M *An Illustrated History of Interior Decoration from Pompeii to Art Nouveau* (Thames & Hudson, London 1964)

de Ricci, S *Louis XVI Furniture* (Heinemann, London 1913)

Salverte, Comte de *Les Ebénistes du XVIIIe Siècle* (De Nobele, Paris 1962)

Verlet, P *French Royal Furniture 1800–1825* (Barrie & Rockliff, London 1963)

Watkin, D *Thomas Hope and the Neo-classical Ideal* (John Murray, London 1968)

Watson, F J B *Louis XVI Furniture* (Alec Tiranti, London 1960)

CATALOGUES
de Bellaigue, G *Furniture, Clocks and Gilt Bronzes in the James A de Rothschild Collection at Waddesdon Manor* (Office du Livre, Fribourg 1974)

F J B Watson *Wallace Collection; Catalogue of Furniture* (William Clowes & Sons Ltd, 1956)

Wrightsman Collection Catalogue, 3 vols (The Metropolitan Museum of Art, New York 1966)

The Machine Age

American Antiques from the Revolution to the Civil War (The American Heritage Publishing Co., New York 1968)

Antiques from the Civil War to World War I (The American Heritage Publishing Co., New York 1969)

Aslin, E *19th Century English Furniture* (Faber & Faber, London 1962)

Brosio, V *Mobili Italiani dell'Ottocento* (Antonio Vallardi, Milan 1962)

The Connoisseur's Complete Period Guides: *The Early Victorian Period* (The Connoisseur, London 1958)

Faniel, S (Ed) *Le XIXe Siècle Français* (Hachette, Paris 1957)

Filomarino, A M C *L'Ottocento—i mobili del tempo dei nonni dal l'Impero al Liberty* (Görlich, Milan 1969)

Janneau, G *Le Mobilier Français* (series) (Vincent, Fréal et Cie, Paris 1967)

Nystrom, B G T *1800-tals Stolar* (Nordiska Museet, Stockholm 1967)

Otto, J C *American Furniture of the 19th Century* (Viking Press, New York 1965)

Stavenow, E *Siden, Sammet, Läder, Lärft* (ICA–Forlaget, Västerås 1961)

Symonds, R W & Whineray, B B *Victorian Furniture* (Country Life, London 1962)

CATALOGUES
19th Century America Exhibition *Furniture and other Decorative Arts* (Metropolitan Museum of Art, New York 1970)

The Rebirth of Design

Aslin, E *The Aesthetic Movement, Prelude to Art Nouveau* (Paul Elek, London 1969)

Bliss, D P *Charles Rennie Mackintosh and the Glasgow School of Art* (Glasgow School of Art 1961)

Bossaglia, R *Art Nouveau* (Orbis Publishing, London 1975)

Champney, F *Art and Glory: The Story of Elbert Hubbard* (New York 1968)

Howarth, T *Charles Rennie Mackintosh and the Modern Movement* (Routledge & Kegan Paul, London 1952)

MacCarthy, F *All things Bright and Beautiful. Design in Britain 1830 to today* (George Allen & Unwin, London 1972)

Macleod, R *Charles Rennie Mackintosh* (Country Life, London 1968)

Macleod, R *Charles Rennie Mackintosh* (Country Life, London 1968)

Naylor, G *Arts and Crafts Movement. A Study of its Sources, Ideals & Influence on Design Theory* (Studio Vista, London 1971)

Pevsner, N *Charles R Mackintosh*—Series: Architetti del movimento moderno (Milan 1950)

Pevsner, N *Pioneers of Modern Design from William Morris to Walter Gropius* (Penguin Books, Harmondsworth 1960)

Pevsner, N *The Sources of Modern Architecture and Design* (World of Art series, Thames & Hudson, London 1968)

Pevsner, N *Studies in Art, Architecture and Design: Vol II—Victorian and After* (Thames & Hudson, London 1968)

Pevsner, N & Richards, J M (Eds) *The Anti-Rationalists* (Architectural Press, London 1968)

Report by the Victoria & Albert Museum Concerning the Furniture in the House of Lords (Her Majesty's Stationery Office, London 1974)

Schmutzler, R *Art Nouveau* (Thames & Hudson, London 1964)

Some examples of Furniture by Charles Rennie Mackintosh in the Glasgow School of Art Collection (Glasgow School of Art, 1968)

Victorian and Edwardian Decorative Arts —*The Handley-Read Collection* (Royal Academy, London 1972)

Watkinson, R *Pre-Raphaelite Art and Design* (Studio Vista, London 1970)

CATALOGUES
The Aesthetic Movement and the Cult of Japan (Fine Art Society's exhibition catalogue, London 1972)

The Arts and Crafts Movement (Fine Art Society's exhibition catalogue, London 1973)

California Design 1910—exhibition catalogue (Pasadena Centre, 1974)

Clark, R J (Ed) *The Arts and Crafts Move-*

ment in America 1876–1916—exhibition catalogue (Princeton 1972)

Victorian and Edwardian Decorative Arts (Victoria & Albert Museum's exhibition catalogues, London 1972)

The Triumph of Style

Dowling, H *A survey of British industrial arts* (F Lewis, Benfleet 1935)

Frankl, P *New Dimensions. The Decorative Arts of Today in Words and Pictures* (Payson & Clarke, New York 1928)

Gloag, J (Ed) *Design in Modern Life* (George Allen & Unwin, London 1934)

Gloag, J *Industrial art explained* (George Allen & Unwin, London 1934)

Gloag, J *Simple schemes for decoration* (Duckworth & Co., London 1922)

Holme, G *Industrial design and the future* (The Studio, London 1934)

Ionides, B *Colour and Interior Decoration* (Country Life, London 1926)

Moreau, C *Intérieures au salon des artistes-décorateurs* (Charles Moreau, Paris 1929)

Les Anées 25 (Musée des Arts Décoratifs, Paris 1966)

L'Art Décoratif Français 1918–1925 (Editions Albert Levy, Paris 1925)

Battersby, M *Art Deco fashion—French designers 1908–25* (Academy Editions, London 1974)

Battersby, M *Art Nouveau* (Colour Library of Art, Hamlyn, London 1969)

Battersby, M *The Decorative Twenties* (Studio Vista, London 1969)

Battersby, M *The Decorative Thirties* (Studio Vista, London 1971)

Battersby, M *Trompe l'oeil: the eye deceived* (Academy Editions, London 1974)

Battersby, M *The World of Art Nouveau* (Arlington Books, New York 1968)

Brunhammer, Y *Lo Stile 1925* (Fratelli Fabri Editori, Milan 1966)

Design in modern industry (Ernest Benn, Kent 1922)

Joel, D *The adventure of British furniture* (Ernest Benn, Kent 1953)

Papini, R *Le arti d'oggi* (Casa Editrice d'Arte Bestetti e Tumminelli, Milan 1930)

Repertoire du gôut moderne (Editions Albert Levy, Paris 1929)

Report on the industrial arts in the international exhibition of Paris 1925 (HM Stationery Office, London 1925)

Shaw Sparrow, W (Ed) *The British home of today* (Hodder & Stoughton, London 1904)

Smithells & Woods *The Modern Home* (F Lewis, Benfleet 1936)

The Studio year book of Decorative Art (The Studio, London 1908–40)

Todd & Mortimer *The new interior decoration* (B T Batsford, London 1929)

de la Valette, J *The conquest of ugliness* (Methuen, London 1935)

Wainwright, S B *Modern Plywood* (Ernest Benn, Kent 1927)

Innovation

Bernard, J R *Le Système Utility* (Paris 1953)

Bonnett, D (Ed) *Contemporary Cabinet Design and Construction* (Batsford, London 1956)

Dexter, A *Charles Eames: Furniture from the Design Collection* (Museum of Modern Art, New York 1973)

Logie, G *Furniture from Machines* (George Allen & Unwin, London 1947)

Magnani, F *Room for the Seventies* (Studio Vista, London 1971)

Modern Interiors (Studio Vista, London 1969)

Møller S E (Ed) *Danish Design* (Danish Institute for Information, Copenhagen 1974)

Russell, G *Designer's Trade* (George Allen & Unwin, London 1968)

Wanscher, O *The Art of Furniture—five hundred years of Furniture and Interiors* (George Allen & Unwin, London 1966)

PERIODICALS
Architectural Review 9 Queen Anne's Gate, London SW1

Design The Design Council, 28 Haymarket, London SW1

Domus 20121 Milano, via Monte di Pieta 15

Industrial Design Whitney Publications, 1 Astor Plaza, New York 10036

Interiors Whitney Publications Inc., 1 Astor Plaza, New York 10036

Mobilia 3070 Snekkersten, Denmark

CATALOGUES
Britain Can Make It—exhibition catalogue (HM Stationery Office, London 1946)

Utility Furniture and Fashion 1941–1951—Catalogue to Geffrye Museum exhibition of 1974 (Inner London Education Authority 1974)

Modern Chairs 1918–1970—exhibition catalogue (Whitechapel Art Gallery, London 1970)

Index

Acknowledgements

We are grateful to the following for permission to reproduce the illustrations on pages:
endpapers Radio Times Hulton Picture Library; frontispiece by courtesy of the Victoria & Albert Museum, London. Angelo Hornak Library; 6 Victoria & Albert Museum, London. TOP—photo R Guillemot; 8–9 Louvre, Paris. Mercurio.

The Archaeological Record
10 © George Rainbird Ltd—photo F L Kenett; 12 © George Rainbird Ltd—photo F L Kenett; 12-13 Ronald Sheridan; 13 IGDA—photo R Pedicini; 14 (top) Scala; 14 (bottom) IGDA—Dagli Orti; 15 Scala; 16 (left) IGDA—photo Pineider; 16 (right) IGDA—photo Ciccione; 17 IGDA—Dagli Orti; 18 Universitete s Oldsaksamling, Oslo; 19 Courtesy of Viscount de L'Isle, Penshurst Place, Kent; 20 (left) Bulloz; 20 (right) National Gallery, Prague; 21 Bulloz; 22-23 IGDA—photo Ciccione; 23 IGDA.

The Classical Revival
24 IGDA; 26 (top) IGDA—Dagli Orti; 26 (bottom) Angelo Hornak Library; 27 IGDA—Dagli Orti; 28 IGDA—Dagli Orti; 29 IGDA; 30 (top) IGDA—Dagli Orti; 30 (bottom) IGDA; 31 Mauro Pucciarelli; 32 IGDA—Dagli Orti; 33 (left) IGDA—Dagli Orti; 33 (right) IGDA; 34 Bulloz; 35 (left) Teigens Fotoatelier; 35 (right) IGDA; 36-7 Ronald Sheridan; 38 (top) Giraudon; 38 (bottom) IGDA; 39 Angelo Hornak Library; 40 IGDA; 41 IGDA—Dagli Orti; 42 Hessisches Landesmuseum, Darmstadt; 43 Landesmuseum, Munster; 44 Uppsala University, Sweden; 45 photo Walter Steinkopf; 46 National Museum, Stockholm; 47 IGDA; 48 Scala; 49 Scala; 50 (top) IGDA—photo Freeman; 50 (bottom) Angelo Hornak Library; 51 Cooper-Bridgeman Library; 52 A F Kersting; 53 Angelo Hornak Library; 54 (top) Cooper-Bridgeman Library; 54 (bottom) Cooper-Bridgeman Library; 55 John Bethell.

Formal Splendour
56 Giraudon; 58 Weidenfeld & Nicolson Library & Archives; 59 (top) Giraudon; 59 (bottom) Europalia; 60-1 John Bethell; 62 J Whitaker; 63 John Bethell; 64 IGDA; 65 IGDA; 66 IGDA; 67 (top) IGDA; 67 (bottom) Angelo Hornak Library; 68 IGDA; 69 IGDA—Dagli Orti; 70-1 IGDA; 72 Wallace Collection; 73 IGDA; 74 IGDA; 75 IGDA; 76 IGDA—C Ciccione; 77 Musée de Versailles; 78 (top) Musée des Arts Décoratifs; 78 (bottom) IGDA; 79 IGDA; 80 Sothebys, London; 81 Rijksmuseum, Amsterdam; 82 Weidenfeld & Nicolson Library & Archives; 83 IGDA; 84 (left) IGDA; 84-5 Angelo Hornak Library; 86 IGDA; 87 IGDA; 88 Angelo Hornak Library; 89 Angelo Hornak Library; 90 Gemäldegalerie, Dresden—photo Gerhard Reinhold; 91 Country Life; 92 Sothebys, London; 93 IGDA; 94 Scala; 95 Rosenborg Castle, Copenhagen; 96 © The Counts Wrangel and Brake—Weidenfeld & Nicolson Library & Archives; 97 Cooper-Bridgeman Library; 98 C M Dixon; 99 IGDA.

The Line of Beauty
100 Edwin Smith; 102 IGDA; 103 The National Trust; 104 (top) IGDA; 104 (bottom) courtesy of F Partridge; 105 (top) IGDA; 105 (bottom) Christies, London; 106 (top) IGDA; 106 (bottom) IGDA; 107 Angelo Hornak Library; 108-9 IGDA; 110 (top) IGDA; 110 (bottom) Metropolitan Museum of Art, New York. Mr and Mrs Charles B Wrightsman Collection. IGDA; 111 IGDA; 112 Musée d'Ansembourg, Liège—photo R Roumat; 113 Musée de Mariemont; 114 IGDA; 115 (top) IGDA; 115 (bottom) IGDA; 116 IGDA; 117 IGDA; 118 MAS; 119 IGDA; 120 BPC Publishing Ltd, London; 121 (left) Schloss Charlottenburg, Berlin—photo Jorg P Anders; 121 (right) Sanssouci, Potsdam; 122 Christies; 123 (top) Kunstmuseum der Stadt Dusseldorf—photo Walter Klein; 123 (bottom) Angelo Hornak Library; 124 Rosenborg Castle, Copenhagen; 125 (top) Rosenborg Castle, Copenhagen: 125 (bottom)

Royal Palace, Stockholm—reproduced by gracious permission of HM the King of Sweden; 126 Rijksmuseum, Amsterdam; 127 IGDA; 128 IGDA; 129 (left) IGDA; 129 (right) courtesy of F Partridge; 130 Angelo Hornak Library; 131 Angelo Hornak Library; 132 (top) IGDA; 132 (bottom) Angelo Hornak Library; 133 National Gallery of Ireland; 134-5 Henry Francis Dupont Winterthur Museum, Delaware; 136 IGDA; 137 (left) Henry Francis Dupont Winterthur Museum, Delaware; 138 (right) Henry Francis Dupont Winterthur Museum, Delaware.

Purity of Form
138 Hermir Verlag; 140 IGDA; 141 IGDA; 142 TOP—photo R Guillemot; 143 Christies, London; 144 Sothebys, London; 145 IGDA—Dagli Orti; 146 (top) IGDA; 146 (bottom) Sothebys, London; 147 TOP—photo R Bonnefoy; 148 IGDA—photo Freeman; 149 (top) Sothebys, London; 149 (bottom) Sothebys; 150 (top) TOP—photo R Guillemot; 150 (bottom) Christies, London; 151 IGDA; 152 Giraudon; 153 (top) IGDA—photo Dagli Orti; 153 (bottom) IGDA—photo Dagli Orti; 154 (top) IGDA—photo Dagli Orti; 154 (bottom) IGDA; 155 IGDA; 156-7 A F Kersting; 158 IGDA; 159 IGDA—Dagli Orti; 160 A F Kersting; 161 IGDA; 162 Christies, London; 163 IGDA; 164 IGDA—photo Dagli Orti; 165 (top) IGDA; 165 (bottom) IGDA; 166 Mary Evans Picture Library; 167 (top) IGDA; 167 (bottom) IGDA; 168 National Trust; 169 Jonathan Bourne; 170 Angelo Hornak Library; 171 (top) IGDA; 171 (bottom) Malletts, London; 172 Sothebys, London; 173 Schloss Charlottenburg, Berlin—photo Jorg P Anders; 174 Schloss Charlottenburg, Berlin. Weidenfeld & Nicolson Library & Archives; 175 (top) Museum für Kunsthandwerk, Frankfurt; 175 (bottom) Residenzmuseum, Munich. Victoria & Albert Museum, London; 176 Weidenfeld & Nicolson Library & Archives—photo Edwin Smith; 177 (top) Swedish Royal Collection. Victoria & Albert Museum, London; 177 (bottom) Rijksmuseum, Amsterdam; 178 Royal Institute of British Architects. Weidenfeld & Nicolson Library & Archives; 179 (top) Biblioteca Vaticana; 179 (bottom) Sothebys, London; 180 Weidenfeld & Nicolson Library & Archives; 180-1 IGDA—photo Dagli Orti; 182 Soprintendenza ai Monumenti del Piemonte, Turin; 183 Scala; 184 (left) Metropolitan Museum of Art, New York—gift of Mrs J Insley Blair. IGDA; 184 (right) Jonathan Bourne; 185 The Henry Francis du Pont Winterthur Museum, Delaware; 186 (left) IGDA; 186 (right) IGDA; 187 Metropolitan Museum of Art, New York—gift of Mrs Russell Sage & others. IGDA.

The Machine Age
188 Baron Guy de Rothschild. TOP—photo R Guillemot; 190 IGDA; 191 Orbis—photo Angelo Hornak; 192 Country Life Publications, Derby; 193 Orbis—photo Angelo Hornak; 194 National Trust—photo Chris Newsholme; 196 A F Kersting; 197 Orbis—photo Angelo Hornak; 199 Giraudon; 200 Giraudon; 201 Oranje-Nassau Museum, Delft; 203 George Rainbird Ltd—photo Werner Neumeister; 204-5 Nordiska Museet, Stockholm; 205 Musei Civici di Brescia; 206 The American Museum in Britain, Bath; 207 IGDA; 208 Novosti; 209 Weidenfeld & Nicolson Library & Archives—photo Edwin Smith; 210 (top) Musée des Arts Décoratifs, Paris; 210 (bottom) Harriet Bridgeman Ltd; 211 Cooper-Bridgeman Library; 212 Mansell Collection; 213 (top) Private collection; 213 (bottom) Lyndhurst, Tarrytown, USA—photo Louis H Frohman; 214 National Trust; 215 IGDA; 216 (top) Metropolitan Museum of Art, New York—gift of Mr and Mrs James B Tracey. Harriet Bridgeman Ltd; 216 (bottom) Harriet Bridgeman Ltd; 217 Mary Evans Picture Library; 218 (left) Malletts, London; 218-9 Stadtische Museen Vienna; 219 (bottom) Mary Evans Picture Library; 220 Radio Times Hulton Picture Library; 221 Orbis—photo Angelo Hornak; 222-3 The Metropolitan Museum of Art, New York—gift of Frederic H Hatch; 224 The Metropolitan Museum of Art, New York. The Edgar J Kaufmann Charitable Foundation Fund 1968; 225 Harriet

Bridgeman Ltd; 226 Orbis—photo Angelo Hornak; 227 IGDA—photo Rizzi; 228-9 Brooklyn Museum, New York; 229 (right) Orbis—photo Angelo Hornak; 230 National Monuments Record; 231 IGDA; 232 Harriet Bridgeman Ltd; 233 (top), 233 (bottom), 234 (left) Orbis—photo Angelo Hornak; 234-5 Cooper-Bridgeman Library.

The Rebirth of Design
236 IGDA; 238 Perfecta Publications; 239 Angelo Hornak Library; 240 Victoria & Albert Museum, London; 241 Picturepoint; 242 Angelo Hornak Library; 243 Angelo Hornak Library; 244 Angelo Hornak Library; 245 A F Kersting; 246 (top) Angelo Hornak Library; 246 (bottom) Michael Holford—reproduced by courtesy of the William Morris Gallery, Walthamstow; 247 Mary Evans Picture Library; 248 (top) Octopus Ltd; 248 (bottom) Leicester City Museum & Art Gallery; 249 Angelo Hornak Library; 250 (left) Sothebys, London; 250-1 Annan, Glasgow; 251 (right) Sothebys, London; 252 (top) Heal & Son Ltd, London; 252 (bottom) Angelo Hornak Library; 253 Angelo Hornak Library; 254 Chicago School of Architecture Foundation. Gift of Mrs Charles F Batchelder. Picturepoint; 255 Chicago Institute of Art. Gift of Mr and Mrs John J Evans; 256 Chicago Institute of Art—gift of Mrs Theodore D Tieken; 257 Chicago Institute of Art—gift of Mr and Mrs F M Fahrenwald. IGDA; 258 IGDA; 259 IGDA; 260 Sothebys, London; 261 Cooper-Bridgeman Library; 262 Bulloz; 263 (top) Bibliothèque Doucet, Paris; 263 (bottom) IGDA; 264 (left) IGDA; 264 (right) IGDA; 265 IGDA; 266 Sothebys, London; 267 TOP—photo Guillemot.

The Triumph of Style
268 Robert Walker Collection. TOP—photo Guillemot; 270 Sunday Times; 271 Heal & Son Ltd; 272 (top) Cooper-Bridgeman Library; 272 (bottom) Martin Battersby; 273 Sunday Times; 274 (top) Musée des Arts Décoratifs, Paris; 274 (bottom) Musée des Arts Décoratifs, Paris; 275 Angelo Hornak Library; 276 Orbis—photo Angelo Hornak; 277 (top) Martin Battersby; 277 (bottom) Collection, Galerie Félix Marcilhac, Paris; 278 (top) Collection, Galerie Félix Marcilhac, Paris; 278 (bottom) TOP—photo Guillemot; 279 (left) Musée des Arts Décoratifs, Paris; 279 (right) Royal Pavilion, Art Gallery & Museums, Brighton; 280 Orbis—photo Angelo Hornak; 281 (top) Martin Battersby; 281 (bottom) Musée des Arts Décoratifs, Paris; 282-3 Victoria & Albert Museum, London; 284 (top) Royal Pavilion, Art Gallery & Museums, Brighton. Loaned by Martin Battersby. Orbis—photo Angelo Hornak; 284 (bottom) Design Council, London; 285 IGDA—photo Titti; 286-7 Angelo Hornak Library; 287 (right) Orbis—photo Angelo Hornak; 288 (top) Heal & Son Ltd; 288 (bottom) Orbis—photo Angelo Hornak; 289 Orbis—photo Angelo Hornak; 290 Angelo Hornak Library; 291 (top) Orbis—photo Angelo Hornak; 291 (bottom) Mary Evans Picture Library.

Innovation
292 Design Council; 294 Nordiske Press Foto, Copenhagen; 295 Design Council; 296 Architectural Press; 297 Design Council; 298 (top) Herman Miller; 298 (bottom) Herman Miller; 298-9 Knoll International; 299 Race Contracts Ltd; 300 Design Council; 300-1 Knoll International; 301 Design Council; 302 Herman Miller Ltd—photo Michael Nicholson; 303 Design Council; 304 (top) Design Council; 304 (bottom) Design Council; 305 (top left) Design Council; 305 (top right) © The Observer. Design Council; 305 (bottom left) Herman Miller; 305 (bottom right) © The Observer. Design Council; 306 (top) © Formica. Design Council; 306 (bottom) © The Observer. Design Council; 307 (top) David Hicks; 307 (bottom) © The Observer. Design Council; 308 (top) Professional Photo, Milan; 308 (bottom) © Innovator Design. Design Council; 309 Bayer Visiona, Germany; 310 Design Council; 311 (top left) © Conran. Design Council; 311 (centre top) Design Council; 311 (top right) Design Council; 311 (bottom) Ron Brown Interiors. Behr, Germany; 312 Design Council.

344